OXFORD WORLD'S CLASSICS

JOHN WEBSTER

The White Devil
The Duchess of Malfi
The Devil's Law-Case
A Cure for a Cuckold

Edited with an Introduction by
RENÉ WEIS

OXFORD
UNIVERSITY PRESS

OXFORD

UNIVERSITY PRESS

Great Clarendon Street, Oxford OX2 6DP

Oxford University Press is a department of the University of Oxford.
It furthers the University's objective of excellence in research, scholarship,
and education by publishing worldwide in

Oxford New York

Auckland Bangkok Buenos Aires Cape Town Chennai
Dar es Salaam Delhi Hong Kong Istanbul Karachi Kolkata
Kuala Lumpur Madrid Melbourne Mexico City Mumbai Nairobi
São Paulo Shanghai Taipei Tokyo Toronto

Oxford is a registered trade mark of Oxford University Press
in the UK and in certain other countries

Published in the United States
by Oxford University Press Inc., New York

British Library Cataloguing in Publication Data

Data available

Library of Congress Cataloging in Publication Data
Webster, John, 1580?—1625?
The Duchess of Malfi / John Webster; edited with an introduction
by René Weis; general editor, Michael Cordner; associate general
editors, Peter Holland, Martin Wiggins.
p. cm.
I. Weiss, René, 1953–   . II. Cordner, Michael. III. Title.
PR3184.D8 1996   822'.3—dc20   95–33715

ISBN 978–0–19–953928–4

5

Printed in Great Britain by
Clays Ltd, St Ives plc

OXFORD ENGLISH DRAMA

General Editor: MICHAEL CORDNER

Associate General Editors: PETER HOLLAND · MARTIN WIGGINS

THE DUCHESS OF MALFI

AND OTHER PLAYS

JOHN WEBSTER (*c*.1578–*c*.1634), poet and dramatist, was born in London, one of several children of a Merchant Taylor who was a wealthy coachmaker in Smithfield. He was probably educated at the Merchant Taylors' School in the City, and may have proceeded from there to the Middle Temple. In 1606 he married Sara Peniall. They had several children and seem to have lived near Snow Hill in Holborn. Webster started his career in drama as a collaborating and revising playwright. *The White Devil* (*c*.1612) may have been his first solo effort. The play failed during its first performance at the Red Bull in Clerkenwell, but *The Duchess of Malfi* (1614) attracted praise from his friends and contemporary dramatists. He followed it with a play (now lost) called *The Guise* (1614–15), and in 1615 he contributed several important sketches to Sir Thomas Overbury's *Characters*. That same year he became a Merchant Taylor, and in 1619 he wrote a tragicomedy, *The Devil's Law-Case*, which was his last non-collaborative dramatic work. In the years which followed he composed commendatory verses, wrote a pageant, *Monuments of Honour* (1624), and further collaborated on a number of plays. Among these his joint effort with William Rowley, *A Cure for a Cuckold* (1624–5), is a masterly comedy in need of reappraisal. Webster died (probably) in 1634.

RENÉ WEIS is Reader in English at University College, London, where he has taught since 1980. He has twice been a Visiting Professor at Dartmouth College, NH, and his publications include *Criminal Justice: The True Story of Edith Thompson* (Hamish Hamilton, 1988) and *King Lear: A Parallel Text Edition* (Longman, 1993). He has written extensively on Shakespeare and has completed an edition of *2 Henry IV* for Oxford University Press.

MICHAEL CORDNER is Reader in the Department of English and Related Literature at the University of York. He has edited George Farquhar's *The Beaux' Stratagem*, the *Complete Plays* of Sir George Etherege, and *Four Comedies* of Sir John Vanbrugh. His editions include *Four Restoration Marriage Comedies* and he is completing a book on *The Comedy of Marriage 1660–1737*.

PETER HOLLAND is McMeel Family Professor in Shakespeare Studies at the University of Notre Dame.

MARTIN WIGGINS is a Fellow of the Shakespeare Institute and Lecturer in English at the University of Birmingham.

OXFORD ENGLISH DRAMA

J. M. Barrie
Peter Pan and Other Plays

Aphra Behn
The Rover and Other Plays

George Farquhar
The Recruiting Officer and Other Plays

John Ford
'Tis Pity She's a Whore and Other Plays

Ben Jonson
The Alchemist and Other Plays

Ben Jonson
The Devil is an Ass and Other plays

D. H. Lawrence
The Widowing of Mrs Holroyd and Other Plays

Christopher Marlowe
Doctor Faustus and Other Plays

John Marston
The Malcontent and Other Plays

Thomas Middleton
Women Beware Women and Other Plays

Thomas Middleton
A Mad World, My Masters and Other Plays

Richard Brinsley Sheridan
The School for Scandal and Other Plays

J. M. Synge
The Playboy of the Western World and Other Plays

John Webster
The Duchess of Malfi and Other Plays

Oscar Wilde
The Importance of Being Earnest and Other Plays

William Wycherley
The Country Wife and Other Plays

Court Masques
ed. David Lindley

Eighteenth-Century Women Dramatists
ed. Melinda Finberg

Five Romantic Plays
ed. Paul Baines and Edward Burns

Four Jacobean Sex Tragedies
ed. Martin Wiggins

Four Restoration Marriage Plays
ed. Michael Cordner

Four Revenge Tragedies
ed. Katharine Maus

London Assurance and Other Victorian Comedies
ed. Klaus Stierstorfer

The New Woman and Other Emancipated Woman Plays
ed. Jean Chothia

The Roaring Girl and Other City Comedies
ed. James Knowles and Eugene Giddens

To David and Deborah Weis

CONTENTS

ACKNOWLEDGEMENTS

LIKE all editors I owe a huge debt to my predecessors in the field, particularly F. L. Lucas, John Russell Brown, Elizabeth Brennan, J. R. Mulryne, and David Gunby. Elizabeth Brennan generously shared her vast knowledge of Webster with me by commenting on the Introduction, as did Charles R. Forker, to whose ground-breaking work on Webster all scholars owe a major intellectual debt. I am deeply grateful to them both, and also to my colleagues Helen Hackett and Henry Woudhuysen in the English Department at University College London, who took time to read, and comment on, the Introduction. Other colleagues in the UCL Classics and Italian departments assisted me with several of the Notes to the plays. I must also thank the staff at the UCL Library, at Senate House, and at the British Library for all their help.

Michael Cordner as General Editor checked my texts of the plays with great thoroughness, and I owe much to his many suggestions. The Associate General Editor, Martin Wiggins, similarly provided long and detailed comments on my Annotations and Glossary, many of which have found their way into the edition, which has undoubtedly benefited from them. I am grateful to Patrick Kincaid for his careful checking of my texts against the original texts of Webster's plays. I wish to thank Susie Casement, Judith Luna, and Frances Whistler at Oxford University Press for their help, encouragement, and advice, and Mary Worthington for her expert copy-editing.

I want to thank my students at UCL for providing an invaluable and spirited sounding-board for ideas. I am grateful to Maryse Brochard for her good humour and generosity, and to my mother for all her support. My greatest debt, in this as in everything, is to Jean.

RENÉ WEIS

London,
May 1995

INTRODUCTION

JOHN WEBSTER was the author of *The White Devil* (*c.*1612), *The Duchess of Malfi* (*c.*1614), and *The Devil's Law-Case* (*c.*1619), and part-author of *A Cure for a Cuckold* (*c.*1624–5), the last two a tragicomedy and a comedy respectively. He collaborated, to a lesser extent, in a number of other plays, both before and after *The White Devil* and *The Duchess of Malfi*,[1] wrote elegiac poetry, a pageant, and some thirty-two sketches (including the famous 'An Excellent Actor' and 'A fair and happy Milkmaid') for the sixth edition of Sir Thomas Overbury's collection *Characters*, which was published in 1615 and probably edited by Webster himself. It is, however, for his two tragedies that Webster is best known, and by which his achievement ultimately needs to be measured. They were certainly foremost in the mind of the poet A. C. Swinburne, when he noted about John Webster in 1886 that 'The first quality which all readers recognize, and which may strike the superficial reader as the exclusive or excessive note of his genius and his work, is of course his command of terror'. Swinburne did not balk at Webster's 'tragic and noble horror'. Instead he thought that Webster's 'passionate and daring genius' made him round 'the final goal of tragedy' (Hunter 1969: 67–8). Swinburne's appraisal purported to reconcile the dramatist's use of horror with the higher poetic decorum of an Aristotelian tragic art, where we feel a purging of terror and pity. George Bernard Shaw, the most influential playwright-critic at the turn of the century, disagreed. In Shaw's judgement, it was only his intellectual and moral 'opacity that prevented Webster, the Tussaud laureate, from appreciating his own stupidity'. Webster was just another among 'the whole rabble of dehumanized specialists in elementary blank verse' who exploited sensational violence, and pandered to their audience's basest voyeuristic instincts (Hunter 1969: 306). A more balanced view was advanced by Rupert Brooke. While not denying that Webster's plays (which he described as 'full of the feverish and ghastly turmoil of a

---

[1] *The Famous History of Sir Thomas Wyatt* (1602), *The Malcontent* (1604; by Marston, but Webster revised it and wrote the Induction), *Westward Ho!* (1604–5), *Northward Ho!* (1604–5), *Anything for a Quiet Life* (1620–1), *The Late Murder of the Son upon the Mother, or Keep the Widow Waking* (1624), *The Fair Maid of the Inn* (1625–6), *Appius and Virginia* (*c.*1627), *Caesar's Fall* (lost), *Christmas Comes but Once a Year* (lost), *The Guise* (lost).

nest of maggots') raise acute moral questions, Brooke (1916: 158) above all admired their extraordinary vitality:

The world called Webster is a peculiar one. It is inhabited by people driven, like animals, and perhaps like men, only by their instincts . . . That is ultimately the most sickly, distressing feature of Webster's characters, their foul and indestructible vitality.

Brooke's acute observation, that Webster's characters are 'like animals, and perhaps like men', pin-points the precariousness of the divide in them between their humanity and their instinctive, animalistic natures. In Ferdinand, for example, the brother of the Duchess of Malfi, Webster allowed the barriers between human identity and animal passion finally to collapse when Ferdinand's wolfish instincts turn him into a *lycanthropos* (a 'wolfman'). The retributive treatment of Ferdinand by the dramatist, and other similar examples, may go some way towards mitigating the charges of moral opacity. The manifest demands and fulfilments of poetic justice in the plays need to be measured against the dramatist's alleged indulgence of his audience's taste for blood. The exposure to 'three hours of coarse and sanguinary melodrama' during a production in 1919 of *The Duchess of Malfi* was not, however, according to William Archer, redeemed by 'the privilege of listening to its occasional beauties of diction' (Hunter 1969: 94). Seeing the play on stage confirmed his earlier view (1893) of Webster's major tragedies as 'not constructed plays, but loose-strung, go-as-you-please romances in dialogue, full of vulgar lapses of taste and a love of horror' which are 'frigid, mechanical, brutal' (Hunter 1969: 83).[2]

---

[2] The comments by Archer in 1893, like G. B. Shaw's, came in response to an 1892 production of *The Duchess of Malfi* by William Poel with the Independent Theatre Society. The production 'pleased virtually no one' (McLuskie and Uglow 1989: 33). As Poel's own written defence of it (*Library Review*, 1893) indicates, he was drawn particularly to the figures of the Cardinal, Julia, and Bosola, whom he described as 'a masterly study of the Italian "familiar" who is at the same time a humanist . . . a criminal in action but not in constitution'. That Webster continues to disturb on some of the same lines even in the modern theatre is suggested by the reactions of two distinguished reviewers to different productions by the Royal Shakespeare Company of *The Duchess of Malfi* in 1971 and 1990. In 'Blood Soaked Circus' (*Observer* of 18 July 1971) Ronald Bryden noted that 'Perhaps the production comes closest to success when it abandons realism for waxwork dumbshows of heaped bodies . . . Webster's tragedy doesn't really attempt to understand evil. It only celebrates it, like the Chamber of Horrors at Tussaud's . . . Reviewing the Royal Shakespeare Company's 1990 transfer of *The Duchess of Malfi* to the Pit in the Barbican, Benedict Nightingale more subtly wrote that 'When Shaw dismissed Webster as "the Tussaud laureate", he was right and

The charges levelled against Webster by Shaw and Archer in particular were both moral and structural. They indicate the extent to which their critiques, and those of *aficionados* such as Symonds ('constructional weakness') and Gosse (who admired Webster's 'brilliant talents as a poet' while deploring his 'constructional inadequacies as a playwright'—Forker 1986: 485), came out of a turn-of-the-century Ibsenism and belated Victorian evangelism respectively (Forker 1986: 479). What their responses to Webster failed to appreciate was the extent to which his achievement might be seen more fruitfully as that of a 'literary and dramatic genius directed towards chaos' (Eliot 1924: 117), an art whose distinctly Elizabethan mingling of realism and unrealistic conventions renders it intriguingly 'impure', as Eliot put it in the same essay in a much debated phrase (see below, p. xxxix). Webster, no more than Shakespeare, never set out to write 'well-made' nineteenth-century plays in the Norwegian or Russian manners of Ibsen or Chekhov. Nevertheless the charge of structural weakness, if not of anarchy, has stuck. It is as if Eliot's brilliant perception about the imaginative thrust of Webster's *œuvre* towards chaos were thought by subsequent commentators to require a chaotic structural correlative. But it is precisely the dramatic construction of Webster's plays, and particularly of the two major tragedies, which has attracted much critical scrutiny, and increasingly vindication, during the second half of the twentieth century. This process has taken the direction of conceding that the elusive structures of the plays can be imaginatively enabling. Thus Inga-Stina Ewbank has argued that foremost among Jacobean dramatists Webster's art 'seems to build on a continual shifting of perspective—a method that makes both the moral attitude and the artistic unity of his plays difficult to define' (Ewbank 1970: 159); and J. R. Mulryne has suggested that the seeming formlessness of Webster's plays can be seen proleptically to anticipate an almost modernist agenda (Mulryne 1970). Most recently a distinguished formalist study has identified repetition and concentric circularities—rather than the traditional linear developments of 'causal narrative'—as the distinctive structural characteristics of Webster's dramaturgy (Luckyj 1989). The moral dilemmas which Webster's drama invites thus are not circumvented, nor is it the intention of the latest critics and editors of Webster to do so. Rather, a more complex

he was wrong, awfully wrong. Yes, those mad princelings, corrupt prelates and thoroughbred strumpets do belong in some Jacobean chamber of horrors. No, they are not made of anything remotely as bland and lifeless as wax.'

sense of Webster's disputed morality can be gathered from a study of his stagecraft and the way in which he presents his mostly, but not invariably, dark vision.

The White Devil and *The Duchess of Malfi*

That Webster's tragic vision is bleak even by the standards of the time, is indicated by the prominence in his two tragedies of Flamineo and Bosola. It is of considerable interest that, contrary to the requirements of rank and decorum, Bosola heads the 1623 cast list of *The Duchess of Malfi*; and at the end of *The White Devil*, Webster paid warm tribute to Richard Perkins who may have played the part of Flamineo. Between them Flamineo and Bosola epitomize the Websterian villain cast in the roles of disillusioned intelligencer, pimp, speaker of malicious asides, misogynist, and murderer. Webster furthermore invests both characters with semi-choric functions, in which they are made to voice legitimate grievances.[3] As former students at Galileo's university of Padua, Flamineo and Bosola could be seen to represent a version of Faustian or 'Galilean man, adrift from the old certainties' (Sturgess 1987: 97);[4] and, in spite of their degeneracy, the dramatist allows them to pose as 'frustrated moralists, desperately suppressing the "knowledge" that would stifle action' (Bliss 1983: 195).

That in these two plays Webster was 'using the framework and conventions of the Kydian revenge play' while also experimenting with new modes of dramatic presentation (Brennan 1970: 11), might be said to mitigate some of the use of violence in them: violent spectacle—in the form of dumb shows, cannibalistic banquets, and mutilations—traditionally constituted a formulaic part of the Elizabethan genre of blood drama, which included the ever-popular *Spanish Tragedy* (*c*.1587), *Titus Andronicus* (*c*.1594), and ultimately *Hamlet* (1600). The most frequently quoted line from Webster's work, 'I am

---

[3] It is worth stressing that Bosola's part is the largest speaking role in *The Duchess of Malfi*, followed by the Duchess in second, and Ferdinand in third place. Bosola is both part of the action, and outside it, simultaneously villain, avenger, and impresario, who opens four, and closes five, scenes in the play.

[4] Without wishing to mitigate the horrors perpetrated by Flamineo and Bosola, J. W. Lever notes in *The Tragedy of State* (1971: 85–6) that in Webster's plays 'Through a mass of fragmentary images and conceits the iniquities of the age fall into a kaleidoscopic pattern'. The world of Webster features 'the broken humanity of Renaissance Europe', and 'Webster's satirical tragedy looks beyond individuals to the society that has shaped them'.

Duchess of Malfi still', echoes and translates 'Medea superest' from Seneca's revenge play *Medea*. If Shakespeare and Marlowe could sometimes write in a Senecan mode, there is no reason why Webster should not have done so. He was, however, working at a late stage in the history of the genre. By the time *The Duchess of Malfi* appeared on stage, Ben Jonson, in the Induction to *Bartholomew Fair* (1614), was already deploring the continued popularity on the stage of old-fashioned plays such as *The Spanish Tragedy* and *Titus Andronicus*. Temporarily the steam had gone out of the tragedy of blood (though the audiences still enjoyed it), as Jonson's plays, Shakespeare's romances (the last of which, *The Tempest*, is contemporary with *The White Devil*), and the vogue of tragicomedies by Beaumont and Fletcher attest. Did Webster therefore deliberately set out, in his two tragedies, to relaunch a genre which had proved its longevity and commercial value in the theatre of the time, or was he trying to create a novel drama out of the ashes of the old, to produce in *The White Devil* a 'mixed tragedy of old conventions and new ideas' (Brennan 1970: 12), a tragedy about Galilean man, and particularly woman, steeped in 'a deeply concerned, even anguished agnosticism' (Mulryne 1970: 138)?

If Webster's intention had been primarily to please the masses with the kind of 'vulgar' entertainment that Shaw attributed to him, then *The White Devil* would probably have fared better during its first performance at a venue notorious for its robust populist stage shows. As it is, the famous failure of *The White Devil* at the Red Bull theatre in Clerkenwell was almost certainly owing to the fact that the play was too sophisticated for its audience, and left it 'directionless' (Leggatt 1992: 128).[5] In his revealing subsequent address 'To the Reader' in the first printed edition of the play, Webster sounded a defensively erudite note, protesting his integrity as a conscious, self-critical dramatist whose very highest standards caused him to write slowly, because he intended his verses to last. The court of literary appeal was not, he tells us, the undiscerning multitude always eager for novelty only, but a jury of his peers. This included Chapman, Jonson, Beaumont, and Fletcher, and 'lastly (without wrong last to be named) the right happy and copious industry of Master

[5] Sturgess (1987: 98–9) notes further that one of the surmised reasons why *The Duchess of Malfi* was so much more successful than the earlier play was because it was sold to the King's Men (not the Queen Anne's Men who performed at the Red Bull from 1609 to 1619: see Brennan 1970: 7–8) and was therefore put on at a more sophisticated venue, the Blackfriars theatre, in the winter of 1613–14.

Shakespeare, Master Dekker, and Master Heywood'. Webster's inclu-
sion of Shakespeare's name amongst his fellow dramatists (some of
whom were former collaborators and friends) may point towards an
awareness of his debt to Shakespeare. Francisco's hallucinatory vision
of Isabella (inspired by the dagger soliloquy in *Macbeth*), Cornelia's
dirge (which echoes Ophelia's mad speeches in *Hamlet*), the multiple
uses generally of *Hamlet*, *Measure for Measure*, *Othello*, and *The
Merchant of Venice* in *The Duchess of Malfi* and in *The Devil's
Law-Case*, demonstrate that Webster had been inspired by his famous
contemporary who, when *The White Devil* was first performed,
already had over thirty-six successful plays to his credit. Webster may
well have been 'the most persistent successor to the dark Shakespeare'
(Kott 1987: p. ix) among Jacobean dramatists, and Howard Felperin
has argued that, while the moral uncertainty in Webster's plays can
be traced to his 'deliberate deconstruction of the pious side of
Shakespeare's achievement', it may be the case that the 'theatrical
shiftiness also frequently pointed out is the result of an analogous
deconstruction of the romantic or subjective aspect of Shakespearian
drama as well' (Felperin 1977: 179).[6] But Webster does not shy away
from, or undervalue, 'romantic or subjective' values. Rather, in the
character of the Duchess of Malfi he may have created 'one of the
great romantic heroines of English drama, impulsive, impatient of
social proprieties, straightforward, warm, sensual, and elegantly
feminine' (Kernan 1975: 398). In *Love and Death in Renaissance
Tragedy*, Roger Stilling remarked that 'No dramatist of his time
(except . . . Shakespeare in *Antony and Cleopatra*) so persistently and
effectively made women the dominant figures in great tragedy'
(Stilling 1976: 225), while in *The Moral Vision of Jacobean Tragedy*
Robert Ornstein had compared the Duchess to a tender-loving,

---

[6] The wider question of Webster and Shakespeare is complicated by the weight of
recent evidence which suggests that Shakespeare and the Webster family may have been
acquainted in the London of the period. Webster's two tragedies, as well as his elegy
on the death of Prince Henry, *A Monumental Column* (1612), and his Lord Mayor's
pageant, *Monuments of Honour* (1624), were printed by Nicholas Okes, who had earlier
produced the first quarto ('Pied Bull') of *King Lear* (1608), and would later print the
first quarto of *Othello* (1622). The Okes family may have known the Websters, who
certainly knew William White, their next-door neighbour at the corner of Cow and
Hosier Lanes, and the printer of several Shakespearian texts. That Shakespeare might
have been acquainted with the Websters as early as 1594 has been surmised from 'the
joiner squirrel or old grub | Time out o' mind the fairies' coachmakers' (*Romeo and
Juliet*, 1.4.70–1), a glancing allusion perhaps to the Websters' thriving coachmaking
business in Smithfield; cf. Forker 1986: 3–61.

romantic Shakespearian heroine (Ornstein 1960: 147). Furthermore, rather than Felperin's 'theatrical shiftiness', Webster's 'perspective art' (as expounded by Ewbank 1970 and Luckyj 1989) should encourage us to see in a character such as Vittoria Corombona some of the complexity that informs Cleopatra's view of Antony, one way a Gorgon, the other a Mars.

The White Devil

From a multiplicity of sources about the life and death of Vittoria Accoramboni of Gubbio (1557–85) and her turbulent marriage (or repeated marriages) to the Duke of Bracciano, Webster fashioned a tragedy of sexual intrigue and murder. The play traces the couple's relationship, aided and abetted by Vittoria's brother Flamineo, from their first wooing to their separate deaths as husband and wife. Every other major feature of the plot and characters directly connects with this: the murders of the Duke's wife, Isabella, and Vittoria's husband, Camillo, in the two dumb shows in Act 2, the 'Arraignment of Vittoria' in Act 3, and the conspiracy headed by Francisco and Lodovico, brother and lover of Isabella respectively.

The play famously opens with 'Banished?', spoken by Lodovico who is exiled for 'certain murders . . . Bloody and full of horror'. Lodovico protests against the injustice of his treatment by the law, particularly its unfair discriminating between 'great men', like the Duke of Bracciano, and himself. That the world of Lodovico, and the Rome and Padua of the play, are morally skewed is clear from Lodovico's unchallenged assumption that his murders are mere 'flea-bitings', no worse, according to him, than the attempted prostituting of Vittoria by Bracciano. By allowing both Lodovico and Flamineo early in the play to articulate justified grievances about corruption and poverty, Webster shrewdly pre-empts conventional moral judgements (through attributing them to villains), while nevertheless drawing 'fine moral and dramatic distinctions' (Luckyj 1989: 39).

Although *The White Devil* reverts again and again to moral speeches and ethical positions, its power does not reside in its moral truths but 'in the force with which it presents the dark energies of the self uncoiling and striking whatever opposes them' (Kernan 1975: 396). Webster's portrayal of Vittoria during her trial illustrates this. From being a readily prostituted wife, who eggs her aristocratic lover on to murder both his wife and her husband, she achieves a measure of dignity and stature during her arraignment. It is her indomitable courage, that 'one redeeming feature in Webster's ugly world' (Boklund 1970: 126), which the English ambassador, strategically placed there by Webster as a choric voice, admires when he remarks that she 'hath a brave spirit'. As Lee Bliss points out, it is one of the triumphs of this scene that 'Vittoria must seem selfish . . . and yet totally unlike the conventional whore of Monticelso's "character" ' (Bliss 1983: 195); and in her subsequent encounter with Bracciano, when she is a prisoner in the house of the convertites, Vittoria successfully conveys a feeling of wounded womanhood when confronted by her lover's jealous mistrust. Nevertheless, her sexuality is viewed as reprehensible, and sterile. She bears no children to either her husband (Francisco tells Camillo that he is 'the happier' for having none of her offspring, and illustrates this by means of a parabolic tale of the projected marriage of Phoebus), or to Bracciano. Although at her trial Vittoria is found guilty of being a whore, her trial is hardly a fair one, for her accusers are also her judges. Furthermore the dramatist's notorious anticlericalism, particularly his casting of the Cardinal and future Pope as a scheming villain, enlists a measure of sympathy for Vittoria, whose morals are not the only ones that require scrutiny.

In *The White Devil* corruption and decay are all-pervasive, but so is a profoundly destabilizing sense of play and pretence. Isabella's use of 'mummia' is revealing in this respect. Telling Lodovico that he is justly doomed, Gasparo remarks that his followers have 'swallowed you like mummia, and being sick | With such unnatural and horrid physic | Vomit you up i'th'kennel' (*The White Devil* 1.1.16–18). Mummia, a substance prepared from corpses embalmed with bitumen, was taken medicinally in Jacobean England. The phrase occurs again in Act 2, when Isabella, the saintly and wronged wife of the Duke, launches into an invective against Vittoria Corombona. At this point in the play, Isabella, having failed to regain her husband's love, *pretends* to have turned fury. If only, she claims, she could dig out Vittoria's eyes, and let her lie

> Some twenty months a-dying, to cut off
> Her nose and lips, pull out her rotten teeth,
> Preserve her flesh like mummia, for trophies
> Of my just anger; hell to my affliction
> Is mere snow-water. (2.1.247–51)

This is how the saintly Isabella thinks she *ought* to sound in order to render her feigned jealousy believable.[7] It is this kind of dramatic strategy that partly contains our moral judgements. It may take the form of an extreme linguistic self-consciousness, as in Isabella's imagining a language of jealousy (which, unbeknown to her, echoes the language used by villains), or in the curious dialogue between Flamineo and Lodovico (3.3.66 ff.) after Vittoria's trial, where language is perceived as 'attitudinizing' (Ewbank 1970: 175); or it may assume the guise of Flamineo's gleeful pleasure which reflects 'just such an attitude as ours to the play-world: delighting in it but not of it, delight and mockery annealed in a flame of sheer zest' (Mulryne 1970: 144).

The sense of decay in the play extends to its odours. When Flamineo and Bracciano notice Marcello and Francisco whispering, Flamineo reassures the Duke that he will 'compound a medicine out of their two heads, stronger than garlic, deadlier than stibium' (2.1.282–3). At this point Doctor Julio enters. He is an accomplished poisoner, whose masterpiece it was 'to have prepared a deadly vapour in a Spaniard's fart that should have poisoned all Dublin' (2.1.299–300). Not surprisingly Webster's characters are worried about good and bad breath. Isabella is rebuffed by Bracciano because her breath smells sweet: 'O your breath! Out upon sweet meats and continued physic! | The plague is in them' (2.1.164–5). The contrary is true of course. Isabella's sweet breath, like the fragrance of the corpses of the saints, is a moral barometer, and Bracciano hates it for that reason. Similarly in *The Devil's Law-Case*, when Jolenta seemingly agrees to collude with her evil brother Romelio in a devious stratagem, she suddenly asks: 'But do you not think | I shall have a horrible strong breath now?' And then she explains why: 'O, with keeping your counsel, 'tis so terrible foul' (*The Devil's Law-Case* 3.3.161–3). When Bracciano lies dying, the conspirators tell him that his dead carcase will 'stink | Like a dead fly-blown dog', and Flamineo, pretending to be mortally wounded by Zanche and Vittoria, enacts an evil-smelling internal combustion parody of imminent death: 'O I smell soot, | Most stinking soot, the chimney is afire' (*The White Devil* 5.6.141–2).

[7] In *'The White Devil' and 'The Duchess of Malfi'* (1988) Richard Cave writes on the 'purposeful theatricality' of Webster, and notes that Isabella here speaks a script dictated by Bracciano, that Webster 'repeatedly places his characters in situations where they must act and the quality of their response to this necessity sharpens our perception . . . of the innermost reaches of their psyches' (1988: 34).

In *The White Devil* bodies rot even before they are dead, and the dead return to haunt the living. There are two ghosts in the play, and one hallucinatory vision of the devil. As if Bracciano's agony caused by the poisoned armour were not punishment enough, Webster extends it into the next world, when Bracciano sees that the devil who comes to claim him has a cod-piece 'stuck full of pins | With pearls o'th' head of them' (5.3.99–100). The fate that awaits the Duke in the next world, Webster intimates, is one of perpetual sexual torture. When Bracciano returns, silent, from the grave to visit Flamineo, he enters with '*a pot of lily-flowers with a skull in't*'. The skull is the most universal symbol of death, and its conjunction here with a pot of lilies emblematically suggests that under the surface of life there always lurks death.

Bracciano's dying illustrates powerfully what Mulryne has called a peculiarly modern 'crisis of feeling' in Webster's drama, analogous to the ambivalences in Kafka and Beckett. While the strangling of the already demented Bracciano repels us, it also appeals to our 'sense of the high comedy of the occasion and our relish of the witty deceits of Lodovico and the rest . . . jesting with death' (Mulryne 1970: 141). Hence Webster's use, as a means for expressing the irreconcilable perspectives of tragedy and comedy to the full, of a dramatic 'anti-construction', of 'a gothic [scenic] aggregation rather than a steady exposition and development towards a single consummation' (Brown 1960: p. xliv), which Charles Forker has further characterized as 'a plot structure commensurate to a world of labyrinthine deceit' (Forker 1986: 289). Act 4 of *The White Devil* best illustrates this, because, according to Luckyj (1989: 17), it is full of 'apparent irrelevancies', such as, for example, Francisco's adoption and rejection of revenge strategies (4.1), Flamineo's parable of the crocodile (4.2), and the papal election scene (4.3). In order for Webster's innovative dramatic rhythm to be understood, such episodicity as in Act 4 must be seen as 'instruments of the intensification of his tragic vision', where repetition is a way of 'de-emphasizing causation in drama' (Luckyj 1989: 17; 23).

At the same time, the satiric perspective on the play's tragic events supplied by Flamineo keeps the audience at arm's length by appealing to its intellectual judgements (Leech 1951: 47, 49–50; and Bogard 1955: 107–8). Like Shakespeare's Richard III, who comes out of the womb with his feet first and a full set of teeth, Flamineo is destined from the beginning to do evil. When he suckled at his mother's breast, he 'took the crucifix between his hands, | And broke a limb off'

(5.2.12–13). Flamineo's power within the play's action resides in his control over sex. When Bracciano fears that his affection for Vittoria may not be reciprocated, Flamineo points out that 'ladies . . . are politic; they know our desire is increased by the difficulty of enjoying' (1.2.19–21). He may be right about the particular lady in question, but he rarely stops at the particular. Mostly he applies his satiric wit to the general, not least because he is cast as a congenitally histrionic character who needs an audience with which to communicate, as in his frenzied shifting in and out of the dialogue with Camillo in 1.2 for the benefit of his audiences both on-stage (Bracciano and Vittoria) and off-stage (us). Everything female for Flamineo spells contempt: women's tears are meaningless, he notes, and a mother feeding her baby, in the world according to Flamineo, does not pass on life to it, but rather 'dissembling'. 'Trust a woman? Never, never' (5.6.165), Flamineo exclaims after foiling Zanche's and Vittoria's attempt to kill him. It is only in the extremity of dying that Flamineo shares an epiphanic moment of intimacy with the one woman he has shadowed throughout the play as a commodity: 'Thou'rt a noble sister: | I love thee now', he tells Vittoria.

The Duchess of Malfi

Another sibling relationship with 'all the possible variations of feeling within' it (Brennan 1963: 492) looms large in Webster's next play, which develops ethical, formal, and psychological complexities launched in *The White Devil*. What J. R. Brown called Webster's 'persistent and brooding mind' made him, like a painter, realign

the elements of one composition in his next to suggest less obvious inter-relations, new astringencies, or sudden simplifications of form. Within Webster's plays, scenes echo each other, and his two great tragedies, both set at court and with a central heroine, are in important ways two versions of a single subject. (Brown 1964: p. xxx)

At the core of *The Duchess of Malfi* is the triangular relationship between the Duchess—whose name we never learn—her steward-husband Antonio, and her twin brother Ferdinand, who nourishes an incestuous passion for her. The Duchess is a 'right noble' woman, whose 'discourse', Antonio claims, 'is so full of rapture | You only will begin then to be sorry | When she doth end her speech' (1.1.182–4); and her 'days are practised in such noble virtue | That sure her nights, nay more, her very sleeps, | Are more in heaven than

other ladies' shrifts' (1.1.193–5). Antonio's paean to the Duchess
contrasts sharply with her brothers' view of her a hundred lines later.
We already know by then, from the ubiquitous Bosola as well as from
Antonio's description of the brothers to Delio, that the Cardinal and
Ferdinand are 'twins' in their shared degeneracy. They do not want
their widowed sister to remarry because, it appears, they hope to
inherit her estates. Even Ferdinand, whose feelings towards his sister
are far more complex than his brother's, admits after the Duchess's
murder that he hoped 'Had she continued widow, to have gained |
An infinite mass of treasure by her death' (4.2.282–3).[8]

In defying the Aragonian brothers and their temporarily loyal
factotum Bosola, Antonio and the Duchess court destruction. Their
per verba de praesenti marriage, witnessed by Cariola, ends the first act
of the play on a note of 'happy confidence, wit, gaiety, and tenderness'
(Warren 1970: 51), in spite of the fact that death and danger lurk just
beneath the surface of this precarious happiness (Ekeblad/Ewbank
1958: 219). There is equally in the Duchess's resolution a tough-
minded defiance, not only of the brothers ('If all my royal kindred |
Lay in my way unto this marriage, | I'd make them my low footsteps'
1.1.334–6), but of spiritual orthodoxy. Secret marriages of this nature,
while legally binding, still needed the sanction of the church before
they could be consummated. The Duchess's twice-repeated claim for
the sanctity of this marriage, 'What can the church force more?' and
'How can the church build faster? | We now are man and wife, and
'tis the church | That must but echo this', indicates a potentially
self-destructive attitude of heart and mind. However, by the time we
reach Act 3, it appears from the Duchess's several statements to
Antonio ('In the eternal church, sir | I do hope we shall not part
thus': 3.5.71–2) and Ferdinand ('You violate a sacrament o'th' church
| Shall make you howl in hell for't': 4.1.39–40) that she and Antonio
may have since been lawfully, though secretly, married in church, and
that their children are legitimate.

The passage of time in the play is marked by the Duchess's
repeated pregnancies: at least nine months elapse between Acts 1 and
2, and some two years between Act 2 and 3 in which period the

[8] Webster's portrayal of the Aragonian family differs from the account in his sources,
William Painter's *The Palace of Pleasure* (1567) and Belleforest's *Histories Tragiques*
(1565), in that they repeatedly stress 'the dishonour of the Duchess in marrying beneath
her and thus staining the noble blood of Aragon. In *El Mayordomo de la Duquesa de
Amalfi* Lope de Vega grounded the brothers' motives explicitly on revenge for honour'
(Brennan 1963: 288).

Duchess bears two more children. This breach of the neo-classical unity of time is lightly acknowledged by Webster when, at the beginning of Act 3, Delio tells Antonio 'verily I should dream | It were within this half-hour' (3.1.10–11). They last met in Act 1, nearly three years before in the theatrical illusion, but indeed not much more than half an hour's playing time earlier. This collapsing of real and imagined time may be the dramatist's way of signalling the cyclical structural principles behind his tragedy (Luckyj 1989: 19 ff.), a dramaturgical disjunction (as opposed to linearity) which produces complex scenic movements such as the sudden crowding of the stage in 3.3 (so that the episode cannot be played realistically: Sturgess 1987: 105 ff.), or the Duchess's sudden turn in 3.2 when she expects to see Antonio, but instead sees Ferdinand. Both men, in very different ways, love her, and Webster's use here of a lightning shift of focus ensures that his audience is forcefully alerted to Ferdinand's role as incestuous lover-substitute. This is a striking instance of what Peter Thomson has described as Webster's ingenious and economical use in the theatre of spatial 'distance and proximity, stillness and movement, as a visible reinforcement of the action' (Thomson 1970: 35).

In 3.2 Webster grants us a unique view of the private, domestic lives of the Duchess and Antonio, with the Duchess getting ready for bed and combing out her hair in front of a mirror.[9] The banter between the Duchess, Antonio, and Cariola conveys a rare sense of tenderness and intimacy, and the moment Antonio and Cariola silently leave is the closest the Duchess comes to soliloquy. She is at her most private, when Ferdinand, holding a dagger, enters her sanctuary. The scene is almost violatory. He is indeed an 'apparition', a 'terrible thing'. What began as a scene of lovers enjoying their mutuality ends in separation, with Antonio being enjoined by his wife

[9] For an opposite reading, see Sturgess (1987: 114), who argues that the Duchess in front of the mirror is 'a Renaissance moral emblem of shattering power . . . the vain woman, her vanity symbolised by the mirror, visited by Death as a retribution for a moral laxity of which the play never acquits her'. This reading follows on partly from the author's contention that the play exhibits the characteristics of stylized private drama, and that it constitutes 'the highest reach of mannerist tragedy . . . a species of melodrama which mixes farce and sentiment in a challenging way' (Sturgess 1987: 7). Leech similarly compared the Duchess and Antonio to Vittoria and Bracciano, and noted that 'the more we consider the Duchess, the more hints of guilt seem to appear' (Leech 1951: 75). William Empson replied to this that 'The moral of this play, driven home as with the sledge-hammer of Dickens I should have thought, is not that the duchess was wanton but that her brothers were sinfully proud' (Empson 1994: 111).

to seek refuge in Ancona. In the death scene in 4.2, the Duchess and Cariola are alone with her tormentors. This scene follows her cruel exposure to Ferdinand's fake corpses. With its anti-masque of dancing madmen, the perverse epithalamic echoes in Bosola's song, and the murder of the Duchess, her children, and Cariola, 4.2 constitutes the grim climax of the tragedy. In the hands of a lesser dramatist, the fifth act might therefore have become almost an irrelevance. But, as Mulryne points out, to 'present the play as though it were her [the Duchess's] personal tragedy' is to underestimate the scope of the play and commit a romantic fallacy; rather, 'this last act is brilliant in its "expressionistic" statement of the tragicomic world to which the Duchess has contributed so important, but also so integral, a part' (Mulryne 1970: 153). Luckyj develops this further by noting that the play's 'split structure' is required if the death of the Duchess is to be tragic. Only after the focus shifts from the victim to the destroyers do we recognize, through the 'humanization' of Bosola, the Cardinal, and Ferdinand, that the Duchess has become a victim not of abstract Satanic forces, but of evil created by 'simply frail humanity' (Luckyj 1989: 101).

It is Bosola particularly who epitomizes 'frail humanity' in collusion with evil. From being the brothers' hired spy and executioner during most of the play, he becomes in its final stages the avenger of their sister's wrongs. As a student at Padua he studied hard 'to gain the name of a speculative man' (3.3.46), but became subsequently disenchanted because service performed by him for the Cardinal went unrewarded. His use of the pitiful image of a disabled soldier, who takes swings on 'crutches, from hospital to hospital' (1.1.61–2), to express his sense of wrong, indicates that Bosola's moral being has not entirely been twisted by circumstances. But his malice can be savage, as in his gruesome exposition to the midwife of her 'closet' (2.1.32–40), and his Hamlet-like 'meditation' about what it is 'in this outward form of man | To be beloved?' (2.1.41–2) is acerbically dismissive of any form of idealistic aspiration. But when Ferdinand asks how his sister bears up in prison, Bosola describes her behaviour as 'so noble | As gives a majesty to adversity' (4.1.5–6). He repeatedly urges Ferdinand to show some pity ('Faith, end here, | And go no farther in your cruelty': 4.1.117–8), and professes regret and sorrow about the strangled children, but these sentiments do not sway his better self enough to refrain from overseeing the torture of the Duchess in 4.1 and 4.2, and from crudely dismissing Cariola's desperate pleas to be spared. His moral nature surfaces *in extremis* (and too late), when the dying Duchess briefly recovers consciousness: 'her eye opes, | And heaven in it seems to ope, that late was shut, | To take me up to mercy' (4.2.345–7). A similarly tragic irony operates in Ferdinand's lupine metamorphosis. At the sight of his dead sister, he says: 'Cover her face: mine eyes dazzle: she died young', and then, wishing the deed undone, tells Bosola: 'She and I were twins; | And should I die this instant, I had lived | Her time to a minute' (4.2.265–7). Only a few lines earlier he had refused to be moved by the sight of the dead children, because the 'death | Of young wolves is never to be pitied'. When we next hear of him (5.2), he has gone mad.

Webster pities the bad as well as the good (Boklund 1970: 126), and allows for a resurgence of a moral identity even in his villains. *The Duchess of Malfi* is a tragedy about the failure of love, innocence, and family in a world of sexual perversion and uncurbed material ambitions. In spite of its pain, the play has a seemingly inexhaustible ability to surprise us, as when the Duchess tells Cariola in front of her killers 'look thou giv'st my little boy | Some syrup for his cold, and let the girl | Say her prayers, ere she sleep' (4.2.197–9). It is indeed the case that if the Duchess is 'defeated by a confused and demonic world . . . as a wife and mother she gains a kind of victory' (Ewbank 1970: 174).

The Devil's Law-Case

Like *The White Devil*, *The Devil's Law-Case, or When Women go to Law, the Devil is full of Business* (its complete title) features a devil-woman, and reflects some of Webster's other favourite themes, such as potentially unnatural sibling and family relations, the law, and an acute awareness of 'the skull beneath the skin' (T. S. Eliot, Whispers of Immortality', 1920). The play contains no fewer than three striking meditations on death and human nature (2.3.93–130; 3.3.232–76; 5.4.110–32), two of them by its villain, Romelio, and the other by the matronly Leonora, his mother and the 'devil-woman' of the title. The continuity of this 'new tragi-comedy' (according to the title-page) with the preceding works was stressed by Gunnar Boklund, who attributed the play's structural blemishes to the fact that Webster 'was trying to adapt himself and his motley material to the technique of Fletcherian tragicomedy, with its extreme emotional conflicts, unexpected reversals of fortune, and arbitrary final settlements' (Boklund 1970: 129). Certainly the play is more obviously stylized than the great tragedies, both as regards its axiomatic deference to the 'laws' of the tragicomic genre (it eschews death itself, though not the threat of it),[10] and its use of language and spectacle. The work plays the two off against each other to the point where ultimately 'spectacle replaces the ambiguities of language with its mute solidity' (Pearson 1980: 113–14).

Although there are unmistakable flashes of Webster's characteristic rhetoric in the play, in general the tone is more relaxed. The poetry to some extent lacks the earlier 'tragic intensity'. It has become a 'poetry of everyday, domestic utterance' (Brennan 1975: p. xxiii), as in Leonora's wistful, almost Chekhovian, recalling of the past spent with her waiting-woman: 'we have grown old together, | As many ladies and their women do, | With talking nothing, and with doing less' (3.3.373–5). The dramatist's characteristic theatrical iconography surfaces intermittently, and particularly in 3.3. The scene opens with an elaborate stage-direction: '*A table [is] set forth with two tapers, a death's head, a book. [Enter] Jolenta in mourning, Romelio sits by her*'. Romelio has newly returned from stabbing Contarino (ironically the fresh wound cures him instead), and invites his sister to join him in a conspiracy to inherit the estates of both her lovers by means of a faked pregnancy. The ramifications of this involve a young nun whom Romelio has impregnated, his mother's misplaced love for Contarino, and some shrewd legal and materialistic speculations about precontracts in marriage, inheritance, and paternity. Romelio, not unlike Flamineo, completely disregards his sister's honour, but contemplates making her 'enter into religion', while he enjoys the spoils of her shame and his treachery. When Leonora realizes that her love is thwarted by her own son, she brings a suit of bastardy against Romelio, intent on disinheriting him, even if it means indicting herself as a formerly unfaithful wife.

The ricocheting of the plot at times verges on the farcical (Brennan 1975: pp. xx–xxi; Bradbrook 1980: 173–4), which we enjoy because the genre itself provides reassurance. Thus, while the vitality and dramatic skill of the long trial scene (4.2) recall 'The Arraignment of Vittoria', here we are never in doubt that the outcome will be happy. Not only is Contarino alive, but one of the parties falsely accused of past adultery is sitting in judgement on the case, and it will be the revelation of his identity which is to resolve the suit in the time-honoured mode of comedy. Whereas the law in *The White Devil* was corrupt, in this play the law is as fair as its practitioners, notably

[10] John Fletcher's 'Preface' to *The Faithful Shepherdess* (1608) stipulates that 'A tragi-comedy is not so called in respect of mirth and killing but in respect it wants deaths, which is enough to make it no tragedy, yet brings some near it, which is enough to make it no comedy'.

Crispiano and Ariosto. The health and safety of the social framework is therefore guaranteed, and not without a measure of good humour, for Crispiano, the great corregidor from Seville, is portrayed as tolerant, even indulgent of youth and its foibles, while Ariosto is a just man, who takes no fee from his clients, and believes that legal right is founded on moral right.

Equally true to the spirit of comedy is the nobility of Jolenta's two lovers, Ercole and Contarino. Although they fight and wound each other in a duel over her, their friendship and generosity extends beyond death. When Ercole learns that Jolenta is 'pregnant' by the now 'dead' Contarino, he exclaims:

> Here begin all my compassion. O poor soul,
> She is with child by Contarino; and he dead,
> By whom should she preserve her fame to th'world,
> But by myself that loved her 'bove the world?

> (3.3.310–13)

The key words here are 'compassion' and 'loved'. There is room in this play even for Romelio to be redeemed (Gunby 1968: 550). The concepts of love, forgiveness and redemption feature importantly in the two plots of the next play.

A Cure for a Cuckold

Commenting on the 'redemption . . . by a passage through some sort of "death" ' in both *The Devil's Law-Case* and *A Cure for A Cuckold*, Peter Murray attributed the basic differences between the two plays to the influence of Webster's collaborator William Rowley, an accomplished writer of low comedy and farce. In *A Cure for Cuckold* the actuality of death loses its sting, and 'death is never more than an equivocation, and an illegitimate child born of a barren couple is the central symbol of the recovery from death' (Murray 1969: 235). It is indeed 'a lively, vivid, compassionate play' (Pearson 1980: 134), and the interaction of its 'high' and 'low' contrasting plots gently rebukes the excesses of tragedy and particularly of tragicomedy. Rowley was (almost certainly) responsible for 2.1; 2.2; 2.3; 3.2; 4.3, while Webster wrote 3.1; 3.3; 4.2.[11] The remaining sections are harder to attribute,

---

[11] In a seminal article on Webster's dramaturgy and rhetoric, 'Webster's Constructional Rhythm' (1957), Ewbank supports the attributions to Webster and Rowley on the lines set out by Lucas (1927–8: iii. 11), which differ somewhat from the ones credited to Rowley and Webster here, mostly because Lucas shares out Rowley's part

but such a division gives Rowley most of the low-life scenes in the play with the irrepressible Compass, while Webster would be largely in charge of the 'aristocratic' romance plot, involving Clare, Annabel, Lessingham, and Bonvile.[12]

The Fletcherian plot pits friendship against romantic love, while the robust city-comedy plot turns the more customary treatments of cuckoldry inside out, when its benevolent sailor hero insists on claiming as his own his wife's son by another man. Whereas romantic comedy usually works towards a marriage, here it is the marriage at the beginning between Annabel and Bonvile which generates the discord in the play; and the marriage between Compass and his wife which concludes it is a re-marriage by the same parties in order to legitimize the illegitimate issue of the first. Webster and Rowley are playing with form, to indicate that this is a madcap comedy in which an ordinary world temporarily out of joint is re-established by extraordinary plot devices. Parts of the main plot (mostly Webster's) show the influence of *The Devil's Law-Case*, and Lessingham and Bonvile at times echo Contarino and Ercole. But whereas the duel in the earlier work produced two near-deaths, the issue is here settled philosophically, through forensic equivocation: to kill a friend, Bonvile explains to Lessingham, does not necessarily mean physically to destroy him. Losing a friend through abusing his trust amounts to the same thing, and they are therefore now sworn enemies.

Compass is one of the great comic characters in the Jacobean theatre: generous, full of mother wit and sailor's grit, he has been described as a Dickensian figure who refuses to be daunted by the law of the land, opposing against it his own 'natural' logic, and forgiveness for his wife's trespass.[13] He wins the day by sheer force of personality and, notwithstanding his exclusion from verse in the play, easily becomes its protagonist, as the play's title further indicates. When

between him and Heywood. Lagarde (1968: i. 245) notes that Francis Kirkman's information can be trusted to the extent that he is 'un libraire doué de bonnes intentions plutôt que de dons pour les recherches en paternité littéraire'. Greg (1951) also leans towards believing Kirkman's attributions: see below, *A Cure for a Cuckold*, 420.

[12] Edmund Gosse's suggestion that the aristocratic plot should be treated separately was carried into effect by S. E. Spring-Rice in 1885 under the title *Love's Graduate* (see Forker 1986: 551; Ranald 1989: 128).

[13] Fernand Lagarde suggests that Compass recalls Simon Eyre from Thomas Dekker's *The Shoemaker's Holiday* and that Compass appears Dickensian 'pour la sympathie avec laquelle son créateur l'a traité, et pour la fougue dont il témoigne; Compass est dessiné avec verve et vraisemblance lorsqu'il défend son bonheur d'homme simple (et aussi son honneur) contre ces riches marchands . . .' (Lagarde 1968: i. 251).

compared to the actions of this figure who anticipates Joyce's Bloom by three centuries, the irrational passions of the tragicomic plot seem to be lacking in sanity (Pearson 1980: 119).

A Cure for a Cuckold is less experimental than the earlier plays, but its mixed style, pressed into the service of complex ideas, is well honed and metaphysically 'witty' in the high plot, dense and robust in the 'low' plot. The collaborating dramatists may have found the Fletcherian framework, with its 'tendency to satire and self-parody', too limiting, as C. R. Forker argued, when he also suggested that the 'concern with love's confusions and perversities yields little in the way of moral insight' (Forker 1986: 187). But Webster's achievement in this collaborative play cannot be measured solely, or even primarily, against the two solo tragedies. That he was moving away from extreme tragic situations and rhetoric was evident in *The Devil's Law-Case*. It would be a pity to lose sight of the delights of *A Cure for a Cuckold* by reading or seeing it in terms of something other than what it intended to be: a riveting piece of theatre which still addresses the human condition.

LIST OF SOURCES

Bliss, Lee (1983), *The World's Perspective: John Webster and the Jacobean Drama*.

Bogard, Travis (1955), *The Tragic Satire of John Webster*.

Boklund, Gunnar (1970), 'The Devil's Law-Case—an End or a Beginning?', in Brian Morris (ed.), *John Webster* (Mermaid Critical Commentaries).

Bradbrook, M. C. (1980), *John Webster: Citizen and Dramatist*.

Brennan, E. M. (1963), 'The Relationship between Brother and Sister in the Plays of John Webster', *Modern Language Review*, 58: 488–94.

—— (1964) (ed.), *John Webster: The Duchess of Malfi*.

—— (1970), 'An Understanding Auditory: An Audience for John Webster', in Brian Morris (ed.), *John Webster* (Mermaid Critical Commentaries).

—— (1975) (ed.), *John Webster: The Devil's Law-Case*.

Brooke, Rupert (1916), *John Webster and the Elizabethan Drama*.

Brown, John Russell (1960) (ed.), *John Webster: The White Devil*.

—— (1964) (ed.), *John Webster: The Duchess of Malfi*.

Cave, Richard (1988), *'The White Devil' and 'The Duchess of Malfi'*.

Ekeblad (Ewbank), Inga-Stina (1958), 'The "Impure Art" of John Webster', *Review of English Studies*, 9: repr. in Hunter 1969.

Eliot, T. S. (1924), 'Four Elizabethan Dramatists', in *Selected Essays* (1932).

Empson, William (1994), *William Empson: Essays on Renaissance Literature*, ed. John Haffenden.

Ewbank, Inga-Stina (1957), 'Webster's Constructional Rhythm', *English Literary History*, 24/3.

—— (1970), 'Webster's Realism, or, "A Cunning Piece Wrought Perspective" ', in Brian Morris (ed.), *John Webster* (Mermaid Critical Commentaries).

Felperin, Howard (1977), *Shakespearean Representation: Mimesis and Modernity in Elizabethan Tragedy*.

Forker, C. R. (1986), *Skull Beneath the Skin: The Achievement of John Webster*.

Greg, W. W. (1951), *A Bibliography of the English Printed Drama to the Restoration*.

Gunby, D. C. (1968), '*The Devil's Law-Case*: An Interpretation', *Modern Language Review*, 63.

Hunter, G. K. and S. K. (1969) (eds.), *John Webster: A Critical Anthology*.

Kernan, Alvin (1975), ' "Banisht!": The Dark World of Jacobean Tragedy', in *The Revels History of Drama in English*, vol. iii: 1576–1613.

Kott, Jan (1987), 'The Cruel Webster', in John and Claire Saunders (eds.), *The Duchess of Malfi* (Longman Study Texts).

Lagarde, Fernand (1968), *John Webster*, 2 vols.

Leech, Clifford (1951), *John Webster: A Critical Study*.

Leggatt, Alexander (1992), *Jacobean Public Theatre*.

Lever, J. W. (1971), *The Tragedy of State*.

Lucas, F. L. (1927–8), *The Complete Works of John Webster*, 4 vols.

Luckyj, Christina (1989), *A Winter's Snake: Dramatic Form in the Tragedies of John Webster*.

McLuskie, Kathleen, and Uglow, Jennifer (1989), *Plays in Performance: 'The Duchess of Malfi'*.

Mulryne, J. R. (1970), 'Webster and the Uses of Tragicomedy', in Brian Morris (ed.), *John Webster* (Mermaid Critical Commentaries).

Murray, P. B. (1969), *A Study of John Webster*.

Ornstein, Robert (1960), *The Moral Vision of Jacobean Tragedy*.

Pearson, Jacqueline (1980), *Tragedy and Tragicomedy in the Plays of John Webster*.

Ranald, M. L. (1989), *John Webster*.

Stilling, Roger (1976), *Love and Death in Renaissance Tragedy*.

Sturgess, Keith (1987), *Jacobean Private Theatre*.

Thomson, Peter (1970), 'Webster and the Actor', in Brian Morris (ed.), *John Webster*.

Warren, Roger (1970). '*The Duchess of Malfi* on the Stage', in Brian Morris (ed.), *John Webster* (Mermaid Critical Commentaries).

NOTE ON THE TEXTS

In accordance with the general practice of the series, the spelling and punctuation have been modernized throughout. I have used participle '-ed' even where Q has '-d', but have marked with a grave participles which the verse requires to be syllabic and scanned.

I have departed from editorial precedent by standardizing the type throughout, notably in Webster's frequent use of sententiae and apophthegms, which Q marks by italics and inverted commas. Q's typographical highlighting interferes unduly with the natural flow of a character's speech on the page, and confers a misleading emphasis on what are often commonplace pronouncements.

I have moved all the material in the quartos which is foreign to the play texts themselves into appendices. Wherever I differ from Q in significant ways, this is indicated in the notes.

Like all editors I am greatly indebted to my predecessors, for textual guidance and for help with the notes. The particular editions which I have used are, in chronological order:

The White Devil: F. L. Lucas, *The Works of John Webster*, i (1927); J. R. Brown, *The White Devil* (The Revels Plays, 1960); E. M. Brennan, *The White Devil* (The New Mermaids, 1966), J. R. Mulryne, *The White Devil* (Regents Renaissance Drama Series, 1970); D. C. Gunby, *John Webster: Three Plays* (1972).

The Duchess of Malfi: F. L. Lucas, *The Works of John Webster*, ii (1927); Elizabeth Brennan, *The Duchess of Malfi* (The New Mermaids, 1964); J. R. Brown, *The Duchess of Malfi* (The Revels Plays, 1964); D. C. Gunby, *John Webster: Three Plays* (1972).

The Devil's Law-Case: F. L. Lucas, *The Works of John Webster*, ii (1927); F. A. Shirley, *The Devil's Law-Case* (Regents Renaissance Drama, 1971); D. C. Gunby, *John Webster: Three Plays* (1972); Elizabeth Brennan, *The Devil's Law-Case* (The New Mermaids, 1975).

Cure for a Cuckold: William Hazlitt, *The Dramatic Works of John Webster*, iv (1857), and F. L. Lucas, *The Works of John Webster*, iii (1927).

The White Devil

This edition is based on the first quarto (1612) of *The White Devil*, which was printed by Nicholas Okes shortly after its first performance (probably from Webster's manuscript), and is the only authoritative text for the play. Q2 (1631) derives from Q1, Q3 (1665) from Q2 (with some reference to Q1), and Q4 (1672) from Q3. Q1 was corrected twice while in the press, probably by Webster himself (cf. J. R. Brown, 'The Printing of John Webster's Plays', *Studies in Bibliography*, 8 (1956); The Revels edition of *The White Devil*, 1960, pp. lxii–lxix).

Q's title-page gives the play's title as 'THE WHITE DIVEL, OR, The Tragedy of *Paulo Giordano* | *Ursini*, Duke of *Brachiano*, | with | The Life and Death of Vittoria | Corombona the famous | Venetian Curtizan. | *Acted by the Queenes Maiesties Servants*. | Written by IOHN WEBSTER. | *Non inferiora secutus*. [Virgil, *Aeneid*, vi. 170, where it means (lit.) 'engaged in a no less worthy service' (i.e. following [Aeneas] is as worthy as following [Hector]); (here) 'addressing a theme no less noble than my predecessors have done.']'. The title printed at the head of the Q text is 'THE TRAGEDY | OF PAULO GIORDANO | Ursini Duke of Brachiano, and Vittoria | Corombona'. But the play's proper title is *The White Devil*, the title used in the Stationers' Register and by Webster himself when he refers to it in the epistle to *The Devil's Law-Case*.

The text of Q does not mark act or scene divisions, except in setting off 'The Arraignment of Vittoria'. The breaks in this edition were first introduced by W. W. Greg ('Webster's *White Devil*: An Essay in Formal Criticism', *MLQ* 3 (1900), 112–26) and are retained by most modern editors of the play. The punctuation in Q is very light, and where the compositors used commas extensively, I have often had to use a more graded punctuation to mark pauses and breaks in sentences to conform to modern usage. Where Q loosely exchanges speech prefixes (*Zanche* and *Moor*; or *Francisco* and *Florence*), I have silently regularized the usage, i.e. ZANCHE and FRANCISCO are here used throughout.

The Duchess of Malfi

This edition is based on the first quarto of *The Duchess of Malfi*, published in 1623, some nine or ten years after the play was first performed. The title-page calls it 'THE | TRAGEDY | OF THE DUTCHESSE | OF MALFY. | *As it was Presented priuatly, at the Black- | Friers; and publiquely at the Globe, By the* | Kings Maiesties Seruants. | The perfect and exact Coppy, with diuerse | *things Printed, that the length of the Play would* | not beare in the Presentment. | WRITTEN by *John Webster*. Hora.—*Si quid—*|—

Candidus Imperti si non his vtere mecum [from Horace, *Epistles*, 1. vi. 67–8 which, in Webster's truncated version, translates: '. . . if anything . . . be kind and tell me; if not, practise these with me'; the meaning appears to be (Lucas, *Works of John Webster*, ii, 126) 'If you know a better play, let's hear it; if not, hear mine']'.

The fact that the Blackfriars theatre is mentioned prominently before the Globe may suggest that the play was intended primarily for a 'private' rather than a 'public' performance. The title-page also indicates that the play contains material that was not performed in the theatre. Conversely, the version seen by Orazio Busino in 1618 contains a scene which is not in Q (Forker 1986: 114), and Webster dissociates himself from the 'ditty' in 3.4. The Q text therefore shows signs of being simultaneously pre-performance, with additional material that was not performed, and post-performance, i.e. contaminated by material that was performed, but was not written by the author (cf. also below, 'The Actors' Names' n.)

Q1 was printed by Nicholas Okes and corrected twice by (probably) Webster himself, and is the only authoritative source text. Of the other seventeenth-century reprints of the play, Q2 (1640) is based on Q1 and, while it corrects some errors, introduces others; Q3 (1678) is derived from Q2, while Q4, an altered version of the play, did not appear till 1708.

The manuscript for Q1 was probably a professional transcript prepared by Ralph Crane (cf. J. R. Brown, 'The Printing of John Webster's Plays', *Studies in Bibliography*, 8 (1965); The Revels edition of *The Duchess of Malfi*, 1964, pp. lix–lxix) whose predilections for commas and colons are reflected in the usage of one (A) of the two compositors of the play.

I have departed from Q act and scene division in Act 1 scene 2, where Q's 'Scena II' seemed to me an unwarranted interruption of the ongoing dialogue between Antonio and Delio. Accordingly, following Lucas (1927) and Brown (1964) but not Brennan (1964), I have elided the scenic break in this edition.

Q has block entries of characters for each scene, which, following previous editors, I have split up to have the characters enter at the appropriate dramatic moments in the play.

The Devil's Law-Case

This edition is based on the quarto of 1623, the only seventeenth-century edition of the play, which was first published some four years after its first performance in *c*.1619. The title-page reads 'The **Deuils Law-case**. | OR, | When Women goe to Law, the | Deuill is full of Businesse. | *A new Tragecomedy.* | *The true and perfect Copie from the Originall.* | As it was approouedly well Acted | by her Maiesties Seruants. | *Written by* IOHN WEBSTER. | *Non quam diu, sed quam bene*' [Seneca, *Epistles*, 77: 'not a matter of how long, but how good'; the full quotation from Seneca reads 'It is with life as it is with a play,—it matters not how long the action is spun out, but how good the acting is']'.

The text contains only act divisions, but no scenic breaks. Scene divisions were first established by Dyce (1830; rev. 1857) and have been followed by subsequent editors. At 5.5 I have accepted Dyce's introduction of a scenic break not in Q.

Q was corrected while in the press, and the nature of the corrections (4.1.15: Qa = 'ith Margent sheet'; Qb = 'i'th Margent'; 5.1.35: Qa = 'salt water'; Qb = 'rough water') suggests that Webster may himself have been responsible for them.

The line divisions in Q are extremely irregular and may result from Webster's use of an increasingly freer versification which can stretch to fourteen syllables and almost merges into the rhythms of prose speech. Editorial practice with regard to Q here varies greatly. If my text errs, it is on the side of verse, especially in arranging as verse part-lines of dialogue shared by different speakers. I have not, however, deemed it right to carry lines longer than fifteen syllables as verse, as even a speech-based and accentual prosody could not easily make such lines scan as pentameters. The fact that no '-ed' participles require stresses for the lines to scan further indicates that the verse/prose divisions in the play are generally looser than in the earlier texts.

Quarto's Latin act divisions have been modernized throughout.

A Cure for a Cuckold

There is only one seventeenth-century text of *A Cure for a Cuckold*, which was printed by Francis Kirkman in 1661. Its title-page reads 'A | CURE | FOR A | CUCKOLD. | A PLEASANT | COMEDY, | As it hath been several times Acted | with great Applause. | *Written by* JOHN WEBSTER *and* WILLIAM ROWLEY. | *Placere Cupio*'.

Internal evidence (Compass's reference to the general pardon of May 1624 at 4.3.122, and the reference to letters of mart at 2.4.137 which were issued in February 1625, but anticipated before that) provides a *terminus a quo* in probably late 1624 or early 1625 when hostilities with Spain were well under way and could be represented on the stage; while the plague which closed the theatres from 27 March 1625 to December of that year, and certainly the death of Rowley (Webster's collaborator) in early 1626, provide a *terminus ad quem*. On balance, it may be safest to date the play to sometime late in 1624.

The title-page attributes it to Webster and Rowley, and although at times Heywood's hand has been suspected of revising the play (cf. Lucas, *Works of John Webster*, iii, 12 ff.) it is generally agreed that Webster and Rowley wrote the bulk of the text, with Rowley contributing most of the sub-plot (see Introduction, p. xxv). Dyce (1830; rev. 1857) and Hazlitt (1857) edited the text of the play, and Lucas did in 1927.

Although the text of Q is mostly sound, it generally prints as prose what is clearly verse. This is the case particularly in the first four acts. I have followed editorial precedent in setting out as verse most of the speeches of the main plot characters, and occasionally that of characters in the sub-plot. Where characters from the two plots interact, as e.g. in 4.1 (where Compass unusually speaks verse), editors are bound to disagree from time to time on prosody, and exercise discretion, as also in the case of part-lines. Since in *The Devil's Law-Case* Webster already opted for a rather free verse, decisions on verse and prose in the few contested instances in the later play necessarily remain conjectural.

This edition is based on the 1661 Q of the play.

SELECT BIBLIOGRAPHY

(a) Editions

The student of John Webster is well served by a number of excellent editions, of which the single most comprehensive for the plays and other works remains *The Complete Works of John Webster* in 4 vols. (1927–8) by F. L. Lucas. Among Webster's plays, Lucas includes some of his collaborative ventures, notably *Appius and Virginia*, *Anything for a Quiet Life*, and *The Fair Maid of the Inn*. In the appendices to volume iv Lucas discusses 'The Spurious Plays' (i.e. works wrongly attributed to Webster), *The Weakest Goeth to the Wall* and *The Thracian Wonder*, his alleged 'additions' to *The Spanish Tragedy*, and his early collaborations with Dekker, *Sir Thomas Wyatt*, *Northward Ho!*, *Westward Ho!*. These three are well edited by Fredson Bowers in *The Dramatic Works of Thomas Dekker* (4 vols.: 1953–61). Other more readily accessible selected collections of the plays are *John Webster: Three Plays*, introduced by D. C. Gunby (1972) and *The Selected Plays of John Webster*, ed. Jonathan Dollimore and Alan Sinfield (1983). Elizabeth M. Brennan's three volumes in the New Mermaid Series include *The Duchess of Malfi* (1964), *The White Devil* (1966), and *The Devil's Law-Case* (1975). Brennan's New Mermaids offer scrupulously edited texts, notes, and introductory essays. Also valuable are the two wide-ranging Revels editions of *The White Devil* (1960) and *The Duchess of Malfi* (1964) by John Russell Brown; and the Regents Renaissance Drama editions of *The White Devil* by J. R. Mulryne (1969) and *The Devil's Law-Case* by Frances A. Shirley (1971) are illuminating.

(b) Critical Studies

(i) Guidance to the critical literature on Webster is provided by William E. Mahaney, *John Webster: A Classified Bibliography* (Salzburg 1973), by Don D. Moore in 'Recent Studies in Webster (1972–1980)', *English Literary Renaissance*, 12 (1982), and by Samuel Schuman's *John Webster: A Reference Guide* (1985), an annotated bibliography of 'Writings about John Webster, 1602–1981', which is structured year by year and usefully cross-referenced where relevant. This should be supplemented by the same author's annotated lists of productions of Webster's plays in 'John Webster on Stage: A Selected Annotated Bibliography' (*Jacobean Miscellany* no. 4: Salzburg 1985). A useful checklist of productions of Webster's three solo plays is offered by David Carnegie's 'A Preliminary Checklist of Professional Productions of the Plays of John Webster' (*Research Opportunities in Renaissance Drama*, 26 (1983)), and also by Michael Shapiro's list of early productions in 'Annotated Bibliography on Original Staging in Elizabethan Plays' (*Research Opportunities in Renaissance Drama*, 23 (1981)). Louis Charles Stagg's *An Index to the*

Figurative Language of John Webster's Tragedies (1967) lists key terms in Webster's images, and thus provides an indispensable research tool, as does the more com- prehensive *A Concordance to the Works of John Webster*, compiled by R. Corballis and J. M. Harding (4 vols. in 12 parts: Salzburg 1978–81).

(ii) Of use to the beginning student of Webster is the essay on 'Webster, Tourneur, and Ford' by Inga-Stina Ewbank in *English Drama (Excluding Shakespeare): Select Bibliographical Guides* (ed. Stanley Wells, 1975), and particularly Antony Hammond's comprehensive entry on John Webster in the *Dictionary of Literary Biography*, 58 (ed. Fredson Bowers, 1987) which offers one of the most penetrating discussions of Webster's achievements and of his failures. In a survey study, *John Webster and His Critics* 1617–1964 (1966), Don D. Moore assesses the evolution of Webster studies historically. In *Webster: The Critical Heritage* (1981), Don D. Moore (as editor) surveys the fate of Webster's reputation in a lengthy introductory essay, and offers a judicious selection of important writing on the playwright, from Webster's own comments early in the seventeenth century to his appearance in the *Dictionary of National Biography* in 1899. On the way he includes Lewis Theobald's rewriting of *The Duchess of Malfi* (in 1733), as well as Lamb's, Hazlitt's, Swinburne's, Symonds's, and Archer's critical reflections.

(iii) There are several collections of essays, critical comments, and theatre reviews on Webster. *Twentieth Century Interpretations of 'The Duchess of Malfi'*, ed. Norman Rabkin (1968), divides its material into Part I, 'Interpretations', and Part II, 'View Points'. Part I reproduces a number of excerpts and essays (which appear elsewhere) by Rupert Brooke, Una Ellis-Fermor, M. C. Bradbrook, *et al.*, whereas Part II offers a series of shorter pieces on Webster, including T. S. Eliot's important note from the *Listener* (18 Dec. 1941) on Webster's 'gift of style' and the way his style is harnessed to a tragic drama about 'the soul and its destiny'. Among the collections, *John Webster: A Critical Anthology* (Penguin), ed. G. K. and S. K. Hunter (1969), is particularly generous in its selection of material. Under the heading of 'Part One: Contemporaneous Criticism', the volume covers some of the same ground as Moore's, ranging from Webster's own comments on his plays to Theobald's Preface to *The Fatal Secret* (1735). 'Part Two: The Developing Debate' anthologizes some of the major critical essays and responses to Webster, from 1805 (Charles Lamb writing to Hazlitt) to 1964 (John Russell Brown on Webster). Hunter includes such important pieces as Inga-Stina Ekeblad's (Ewbank) essay 'The "Impure Art" of John Webster' (*Review of English Studies* 9: 1958), H. T. Price's 'The Function of Imagery in Webster' (*PMLA* 70, 1955), and William Empson's review essay 'Mine Eyes Dazzle'. Empson's essay is also included in *William Empson: Essays on Renaissance Literature*, ed. John Haffenden (1994), where it precedes an extended draft essay (ch. 8) on *The Duchess of Malfi* in which Empson enlarges on his spirited defence of the Duchess against the critics. *John Webster*, ed. Brian Morris in the Mermaid Critical Commentaries (1970), is an indispensable companion to Webster studies. It prints a number of important essays that were delivered for, or contributed to, a symposium on Webster by several distinguished scholars. The collection includes such important essays as Elizabeth Brennan's study of the reception and genre of Webster's plays, 'An Understanding Auditory: An Audience for John Webster', Roger Warren's perceptive piece '*The Duchess of Malfi* on the Stage', which stresses the importance of rhythm and style in the play, Inga-Stina Ewbank's essay on realism and perspective in Webster's plays, and J. R. Mulryne's study of Webster's uses of tragicomedy and the extent to which Webster's dramatic idiom anticipates some of the ambivalences found in modern drama and fiction. '*The White Devil*' and '*The Duchess of Malfi*': *A Casebook*, ed. R. V. Holdsworth (1975), reproduces 'Comments' from 1617 to 1957, and follows this with a series of well-known essays from 1949 to 1972, including J. W. Lever's seminal study of Webster's 'satirical tragedy' from *The Tragedy of State* (1971). Part Three consists of reviews of productions from 1919 to 1971. Also worth mentioning is a collection of essays edited and introduced by Harold Bloom, *John Webster's 'Duchess of Malfi'* (1987). Among others, it anthologizes two interesting contributions by Catherine Belsey ('Emblems and Antithesis in *The Duchess of Malfi*') and Lisa Jardine ('*The Duchess of Malfi*: A Case Study in the Literary Representation of Women'), which anticipate some of the feminist issues raised also by Dympna Callaghan's comments on Webster in *Woman and Gender in Renaissance Tragedy* (see below).

(iv) Webster's sources are thoroughly charted by R. W. Dent in *John Webster's Borrowings* (1960), and by Gunnar Boklund in *The Sources of 'The White Devil'* (1957) and '*The Duchess of Malfi*': *Sources, Themes, Characters* (1962). There are a number of full-length critical and biographical studies of Webster. E. E. Stoll's *John Webster: The Periods of his Work as Determined by his Relations to the Drama of his day* (1905) remains valuable for its insights into doubtful attributions and its readings of the two major tragedies in the context of 'Revenge Plays'. Similarly, Rupert Brooke's *John Webster and the Elizabethan Drama* (1916) has stood the tests of time and scholarship, partly because it formulates anxieties about Webster more felicitously than has ever been done before, or since. In *John Webster: A Critical Study* (1951) Clifford Leech concludes that the Duchess of Malfi is tainted by guilt, a reading partly espoused by, among others, J. L. Calderwood in '*The Duchess of Malfi*: Styles of Ceremony' (*Essays in Criticism*, 12, 1962), Robert F. Whitman in 'The Moral Paradox of Webster's Tragedy' (*PMLA* 90, 1962), and by Joyce E. Peterson in *Curs'd Example: 'The Duchess of Malfi' and Commonweal Tragedy* (1978). Leech elaborated some of his views on *The Duchess of Malfi* in *John Webster: The Duchess of Malfi* (1963), which elicited an incisive review essay from William Empson, 'Mine Eyes Dazzle' (*Essays in Criticism*, 14, 1964), in which he praised the Duchess for her courage and sense of duty. In *The Tragic Satire of John Webster* (1955) Travis Bogard argues that Webster's tragedies portray mankind struggling against a world in the grip of evil, and in his comprehensive two-volume study, *John Webster* (1968), Fernand

Lagarde offers an ambitious survey of Webster's entire work. Vol. I covers the canon, and then launches into an in-depth discussion of the plays' exploration of Machiavellianism. This continues into the second volume, most of which deals with Webster's dramatic technique. Lagarde's study contains an excellent discussion of *A Cure for a Cuckold*, and in several ways anticipates C. R. Forker's masterly account of Webster. In *A Study of John Webster* (1969) Peter B. Murray similarly explores the question posed, according to him, by Webster of 'What is humanity to do in a world governed by evil?' Murray concludes that Webster's moral 'vision might be described as a Christian compromise between Stoicism and the ideas of Montaigne'. This book remains one of the most useful on Webster, with separate chapters on the major plays as well as good discussions of *A Cure for a Cuckold* and *Appius and Virginia*. In *The Art of John Webster* (1972) Ralph Berry argues that the 'relationship between evil and the Law is the intellectual tension that grips' the plays, and he draws on analogies with baroque art to study Webster's presentation of this and his relationship with his audience. In *Tragedy and Tragicomedy in the Plays of John Webster* (1980) Jacqueline Pearson studies the development of tragicomedy in the period, its submerged presence (through 'extreme contrasts within a single dramatic structure') in Webster's tragedies, and its full flowering in the later plays, particularly *The Devil's Law-Case* and *A Cure for a Cuckold*. M. C. Bradbrook's *John Webster: Citizen and Dramatist* (1980) provides an illuminating introduction to the life and work of the poet-playwright in two parts. Part I, 'The London of John Webster', avails itself of the knowledge we now possess about the Webster family through the research of Mary Edmond ('In Search of John Webster', *TLS* 24 Dec. 1976) and Mark Eccles (*TLS* 21 Jan. 1977), while Part II, 'John Webster the Dramatist', focuses on the two great tragedies. In *The World's Perspective: John Webster and the Jacobean Drama* (1983) Lee Bliss argues that the action in Webster's plays stretches between 'the poles of pragmatic materialism and romantic idealism', and that he employs 'character types and preoccupations more readily associated with satiric city comedy and tragicomedy'. In his valuable London University M.Phil. thesis 'The Role of Death and Dying in Webster's "The Duchess of Malfi" and "The White Devil" ' (1984) Nicholas de Jongh argues that Webster was a 'man bemused and appalled by the inevitable cruelties of his time', a staunch anti-Catholic whose two masterpieces are permeated by female erotic passion. The single most important study of Webster's life and writing is *Skull Beneath the Skin: The Achievement of John Webster* (1986) by Charles R. Forker. The book is divided into four parts: Part I deals with Webster's life, Part II covers the entire canon of Webster's works, from his early attempts at collaborative writing to 'The Final Phase' which includes *A Cure for a Cuckold*, *The Fair Maid of the Inn*, and *Appius and Virginia*. Part III studies the 'chaos', 'indeterminacy', and 'affirmation' in the major tragedies and *The Devil's Law-Case* with an interesting focus on the 'love–death nexus' (which is explored by other Jacobean dramatists as well), while Part IV concentrates on

Webster's posthumous reputation. With extraordinary thoroughness and tact, Forker analyses the moral, formal, and theatrical issues raised by Webster's plays. It is an additional merit of this distinguished study that it is delightful to read. In *Between Worlds: A Study of the Plays of John Webster* (1987), Dena Goldberg examines Webster's treatment of individuality and social order, against the background of Renaissance philosophy and law. Margaret Loftus Ranald's *John Webster* (1989) is a comprehensive and judicious introduction to the entire canon, dramatic and non-dramatic, and she includes *A Cure for a Cuckold*, *The Fair Maid of the Inn*, and *Appius and Virginia* in her discussion. For every major play Ranald gives its textual history, date, stage history, sources, synopsis, and 'critical comments'. As well as offering full notes, Ranald also has a useful 'Selected Bibliography'. Of great interest is Christina Luckyj's more formalist and intellectually challenging study, *A Winter's Snake: Dramatic Form in the Tragedies of John Webster* (1989). Luckyj approaches her subject through a series of thematic chapter headings, each of which divides into a *White Devil* and a *Duchess of Malfi* subsection. The main thrust of Luckyj's argument is to shift the critical ground away from conventional moral perspectives which, she argues, Webster's drama eschews by 'de-emphasizing causation' through 'repetitive form'. Webster's is a drama of 'gothic aggregation' in which 'multiplicity' produces vastly variant perspectives, moral and visual. She acclaims the careful construction of *The Duchess of Malfi*, and views it as Webster's most accomplished artistic achievement.

(v) Among single contributions on Webster published in wider collections, T. S. Eliot's essay 'Four Elizabethan Dramatists' (1924) in *Selected Essays* (1932, etc.) should be mentioned, not least because it contains the famous characterization of Webster as a great 'literary and dramatic genius directed towards chaos'. Inga-Stina Ekeblad's (Ewbank) distinguished essay 'Webster's Constructional Rhythm' (*English Literary History*, 24/3, 1957) examines the rhetorical structure of key scenes in the Webster *œuvre*, notably the trial scene in *The White Devil* and the prison scene in *The Duchess of Malfi*, and uses these to analyse the attributions of authorship in *A Cure for a Cuckold*. In chapter 5 of *The Moral Vision of Jacobean Tragedy* (1960) Robert Ornstein examines the imaginative teleology of Webster's universe, and offers one of the outstanding discussions of the relationship between *The White Devil* and *The Duchess of Malfi*. In '*The Devil's Law-Case*: An Interpretation' (*Modern Language Review*, 63, 1968), David Gunby argues that the play has a didactic purpose and that its villain, Romelio, ultimately functions as an instrument of divine will. Alvin Kernan's essay ' "Banisht!": The Dark World of Jacobean Tragedy', in *The Revels History of Drama in English*, vol. iii: 1576–1613 (1975), is a lucid and useful introduction to the playwright. In 'The Tragedies of Webster, Tourneur and Middleton: Symbols, Imagery and Conventions' (*Sphere History of Literature in the English Language*, vol. iii, 1971), Christopher Ricks argues for the importance of Shakespeare when dealing with Webster and his contemporaries, as does Howard Felperin in an important study, *Shakespearean Representation: Mimesis and Modernity in*

Elizabethan Tragedy (1977). In chapter 9 of *English Drama: Shakespeare to the Restoration: 1590–1660* (1988) Alexander Leggatt reappraises Webster's drama as a 'heroic tragedy' which absorbs and uses the satiric vision, and in chapter 5 of *English Renaissance Tragedy* (1986; rev. 1988) T. McAlindon analyses Webster's structuring uses of symbol and myth, and admires the complexity of Webster's portrayal of 'moral honesty' in a character such as Flamineo. In chapter 9 of *Journeymen in Murder* (1991), Martin Wiggins offers close critical readings of 'Webster's killers', particularly Flamineo and Bosola, against the wider context of the assassin in English Renaissance drama. Of importance particularly for the more specialized student of Webster are John Russell Brown's 'The Printing of John Webster's Plays', *Studies in Bibliography* (6: 1954; 8: 1956; 15: 1962), and Antony Hammond's '*The White Devil* in Nicholas Okes's Shop', *Studies in Bibliography* (39: 1986).

(vi) Dramatic aspects of Webster's writing are covered in most major studies of his *œuvre*, but the following particularly address his theatre. In *Jacobean Private Theatre* (1987), Keith Sturgess has an excellent, detailed chapter on *The Duchess of Malfi* in the theatre, and in '*The White Devil' and 'The Duchess of Malfi'* (1988) Richard Allen Cave (in the Macmillan Text and Performance series) offers useful insights into the theatrical aspects of the plays and several particularly striking performances. *Plays in Performance: 'The Duchess of Malfi'* (1989) by Kathleen McLuskie and Jennifer Uglow charts the theatrical fortunes of *The Duchess of Malfi* since the early seventeenth century, and 'edits' the play itself with a series of notes referring to famous and infamous productions such as William Poel's of 1892; and in *Jacobean Public Theatre* (1992), Alexander Leggatt re-examines the causes for the original failure of *The White Devil* at the Red Bull theatre.

(vii) Actors, critics, and audiences of Webster alike will welcome Betty Jane Schlerman's *The Meters of John Webster* (1989). Her model use of theoretical linguistics to understand the registers of literary language allows Schlerman to make sense of Webster's complex and seemingly loose metrics, with lines which, syllabically, almost become heptameters. She concludes that Webster's reliance on 'the temporal norm implicit in the isochronous stress pulses of the metrical template' ensures that his 'verse is a principled instantiation of the iambic pentameter', and that hypermetricity (through 'syllabic exfoliation') produces a cumulative effect which sharply lowers the dramatic register.

A CHRONOLOGY OF JOHN WEBSTER

*c.*1550   John Webster senior born; apprenticed to Anne Sylver (widow of Anthony Sylver, Merchant Taylor) and later becomes a wealthy coachmaker.

1571   (10 Dec.) John Webster senior made free of the Merchant Taylors' Company.

1577   (4 Nov.) John Webster senior marries Elizabeth Coates at St Giles without Cripplegate. They have several children, including John Webster the future dramatist, Edward, and probably three daughters, of whom one was called Margery.

*c.*1578–9   Birth of John Webster the dramatist and poet, hereafter 'Webster'.

*c.*1587   Webster probably enters the Merchant Taylors' School in London.

1589   (20 Apr.) Sara Peniall, the dramatist's future wife, baptized at St Bride's, Fleet Street.

*c.*1590–1   Birth of Edward Webster, the poet's younger brother

1598   (1 Aug.) Records of the Middle Temple show a 'Master John Webster, lately of the New Inn, gentleman, son and heir apparent of John Webster of London, gentleman'. This could be the dramatist.

1602   (May) Philip Henslowe pays an advance to a group of playwrights including Webster for *Caesar's Fall* (lost; otherwise known as *Two Shapes*); (Oct.) Webster paid by Henslowe for a part in a play named *Lady Jane*, a version of which survives as (probably) *The Famous History of Sir Thomas Wyatt*, published in a bad quarto in 1607 and carrying the names of Dekker and Webster on the title-page; (Nov.) Webster and Heywood are paid an advance by Henslowe for *Christmas Comes But Once a Year* (lost). Webster contributes a commendatory poem to Part III of Anthony Munday's translation of *Palmerin of England*.

1604   Webster revises Marston's *The Malcontent* for the King's Men, and adds the Induction. Webster also contributes a commendatory ode to Stephen Harrison's *Arches of Triumph*.

1604–5   Webster collaborates with Thomas Dekker on *Westward Ho!* and *Northward Ho!*, written for the Children of Paul's.

1605   Robert Dowe, Merchant Taylor, endows the parish of St Sepulchre with £50 for ministering to the spiritual needs of the condemned prisoners at Newgate. John Webster senior was one of the twenty-four signatories of the benevolence.

1606   (18 Mar.) Webster marries Sara Peniall, aged 17, and seven months' pregnant, at St Mary's, Islington; (8 May) John

Webster junior baptized at St Dunstan-in-the-West. Several other children are later born to the couple, including two daughters, Elizabeth and Sara. Webster and his wife probably move to Nag's Head Alley off Snow Hill.

1607   *Northward Ho!*, *Westward Ho!*, and *Sir Thomas Wyatt* published.

1612   *The White Devil* is performed unsuccessfully at the Red Bull in Clerkenwell by Queen Anne's Men. It is published in Quarto the same year. Webster contributes prefatory poems to Thomas Heywood's *An Apology for Actors*; (Dec.) Webster writes an elegy, *A Monumental Column*, on the death in Nov. 1612 of Henry, Prince of Wales.

1613   Thomas Dekker, in debt to John Webster senior for £40.

1614   *The Duchess of Malfi* is acted at the Blackfriars and Globe theatres by the King's Men; (Apr.) John Webster senior makes his will and (probably) dies in the course of that year.

1614–15 Webster writes *The Guise* (lost).

1615   John Stephens of Lincoln's Inn offends Webster with the portrait of 'A Common Player' in *Satirical Essays, Characters, and Others*. Webster contributes the essays 'An Excellent Actor' and 'A fair and happy Milkmaid' to the 6th edn. of Sir Thomas Overbury's *Characters*, and may be the author of a further group of thirty 'characters' in the volume, which he himself may have edited; (Feb.) Edward Webster renews the lease on the property at the juncture of Cow and Hosier Lanes in Smithfield, next door to William White, Master Warden of the Stationers' Company; (June) Webster claims membership of the Merchant Taylors' Company by right of birth.

1617   Webster is caricatured by Henry Fitzjeffrey of Lincoln's Inn in his poem *Notes from Blackfriars*.

1618   (7 Feb.) Orazio Busino, the Venetian envoy, describes a performance of *The Duchess of Malfi* and remarks on its hostility to 'the grandeur of the Church'.

c.1619 Webster writes *The Devil's Law-Case* which is performed by Queen Anne's Men at (probably) the Cockpit.

c.1620–1 Webster collaborates (probably) with Thomas Middleton on *Anything for a Quiet Life*.

1623   *The Duchess of Malfi* and *The Devil's Law-Case* published in Quarto; Webster contributes verses of commendation to Henry Cockeram's *English Dictionary*.

1624   Webster collaborates with Dekker, Rowley, and Ford on *The Late Murder of the Son upon the Mother, or Keep the Widow Waking* (otherwise known as *The Late Murder in Whitechapel*), a play (lost) based on two contemporary scandals. He writes his pageant *Monuments of Honour* to celebrate the inauguration of

Sir John Gore of the Merchant Taylors' Company as Lord Mayor of London on 29 October.

*c.*1624   Webster and William Rowley collaborate on *A Cure for a Cuckold* (published in 1661).

early 1625   Webster translates and, probably, composes brief complimentary verses as captions for figures in a portrait of the royal family.

1625–6   Webster contributes to the writing of *The Fair Maid of the Inn*, which also involved John Fletcher, John Ford, and Philip Massinger. The play was licensed on 22 January 1626.

*c.*1627?   Webster collaborates (probably) with Thomas Heywood on *Appius and Virginia* (published in 1654).

*c.*1634   Webster dies, aged 56.

THE WHITE DEVIL

THE PERSONS OF THE PLAY

Vittoria Corombona, *a Venetian lady, married to Camillo and sister of
    Flamineo; later marries Bracciano*
Bracciano, *Duke of Bracciano, otherwise Paulo Giordano Orsini;
    married to Isabella de Medici, and later Vittoria*
Flamineo, *secretary to Bracciano and brother of Vittoria*
Cornelia, *mother to Vittoria, Flamineo and Marcello*
Zanche, *a Moor and servant to Vittoria*
Camillo, *husband of Vittoria and related to Monticelso*
Hortensio, *of Bracciano's household*
Francisco de Medici, *the Great Duke of Florence; later disguised as the
    Moor Mulinassar*
Isabella, *first wife of Bracciano and sister of Francisco*
Giovanni, *Bracciano's son by Isabella*
Jaques,° *a Moor and servant to Giovanni*
Marcello, *elder brother of Flamineo, and of Francisco's household*
Lodovico, *an Italian count in love with Isabella; later conspires against
    Bracciano*
Gasparo, *friend of Lodovico; later conspires with Francisco*
Antonelli, *friend of Lodovico*
Carlo ⎫
       ⎬ *of Bracciano's household, secretly in league with Francisco*
Pedro ⎭
Monticelso, *a cardinal; later Pope Paul IV*
Aragon, *a cardinal*
Doctor Julio, *a quack and conjuror*

Ambassadors	Armourer
Attendants	Cardinals
Chancellor	Conclavist
Conjurer	Courtiers
Lawyer	Matron of the House of Convertites
Officers and Guards	Physicians
Page	Register
Servants	
Christophero°	Ferneze°
Guid-Antonio°	

2

To the Reader

In publishing this tragedy, I do but challenge° to myself that liberty which other men have ta'en before me; not that I affect praise by it, for *nos haec novimus esse nihil*,° only since it was acted in so dull a time of winter, presented in so open and black a theatre,° that it wanted (that which is the only grace and setting out of a tragedy) a full and understanding auditory; and that since that time I have noted, most of the people that come to that playhouse resemble those ignorant asses (who visiting stationers' shops, their use is not to inquire for good books, but new books) I present it° to the general view with this confidence:

> *Nec rhonchos metues, maligniorum,*
> *Nec scombris tunicas, dabis, molestas.*°

If it be objected this is no true dramatic poem, I shall easily confess it; *non potes in nugas dicere plura meas: ipse ego quam dixi.*° Willingly, and not ignorantly, in this kind have I faulted; for should a man present to such an auditory the most sententious tragedy that ever was written, observing all the critical laws, as height of style, and gravity of person, enrich it with the sententious *Chorus*, and as it were lifen death,° in the passionate and weighty *Nuntius*;° yet after all this divine rapture, *O dura messorum ilia*,° the breath that comes from the uncapable multitude is able to poison it, and ere it be acted, let the author resolve to fix to every scene this of Horace:

> *Haec hodie porcis comedenda relinques.*°

To those who report I was a long time in finishing this tragedy, I confess I do not write with a goose-quill, winged with two feathers; and if they will needs make it my fault, I must answer them with that of Euripides to Alcestides,° a tragic writer: Alcestides objecting that Euripides had only in three days composed three verses, whereas himself had written three hundred, 'Thou tell'st truth,' quoth he, 'but here's the difference: thine shall only be read for three days, whereas mine shall continue three ages.'

Detraction is the sworn friend to ignorance. For mine own part I have ever truly cherished my good opinion of other men's worthy labours, especially of that full and heightened style of Master Chapman,° the laboured and understanding works of Master Jonson;°

3

the no less worthy composures of the both worthily excellent Master Beaumont,° and Master Fletcher;° and lastly (without wrong last to be named) the right happy and copious industry of Master Shakespeare, Master Dekker,° and Master Heywood,° wishing what I write may be read by their light: protesting that, in the strength of   40
mine own judgement, I know them so worthy, that though I rest silent in my own work, yet to most of theirs I dare (without flattery) fix that of Martial:°

   non norunt, haec monumenta mori.°

The White Devil

[1.1]

Enter Count Lodovico, Antonelli and Gasparo

LODOVICO Banished?

ANTONELLI   It grieved me much to hear the sentence.

LODOVICO Ha, ha, O Democritus thy gods°
That govern the whole world! Courtly reward,
And punishment! Fortune's a right whore.
If she give aught, she deals it in small parcels,   5
That she may take away all at one swoop.
This 'tis to have great enemies, God quite them:
Your wolf no longer seems to be a wolf
Than when she's hungry.

GASPARO   You term those enemies°
Are men of princely rank.

LODOVICO   O I pray for them.   10
The violent thunder is adored by those
Are pashed in pieces by it.

ANTONELLI   Come, my lord,
You are justly doomed; look but a little back
Into your former life: you have in three years
Ruined the noblest earldom.

GASPARO   Your followers   15
Have swallowed you like mummia, and being sick
With such unnatural and horrid physic
Vomit you up i'th' kennel.°

ANTONELLI   All the damnable degrees
Of drinkings have you staggered through; one citizen°
Is lord of two fair manors, called you master   20
Only for caviare.°

GASPARO   Those noblemen°
Which were invited to your prodigal feasts,
Wherein the phoenix scarce could scape your throats,°
Laugh at your misery, as foredeeming you
An idle meteor which drawn forth the earth   25
Would be soon lost i'th' air.

ANTONELLI   Jest upon you,°
  And say you were begotten in an earthquake,
  You have ruined such fair lordships.

LODOVICO   Very good;
  This well goes with two buckets, I must tend
  The pouring out of either.

GASPARO   Worse than these,   30
  You have acted certain murders here in Rome,
  Bloody and full of horror.

LODOVICO   'Las they were flea-bitings:
  Why took they not my head then?

GASPARO   O my lord,
  The law doth sometimes mediate, thinks it good
  Not ever to steep violent sins in blood;   35
  This gentle penance may both end your crimes,
  And in th'example better these bad times.°

LODOVICO So; but I wonder then some great men scape
  This banishment; there's Paulo Giordano Orsini,
  The Duke of Bracciano, now lives in Rome,   40
  And by close panderism seeks to prostitute°
  The honour of Vittoria Corombona,
  Vittoria, she that might have got my pardon
  For one kiss to the duke.

ANTONELLI   Have a full man within you.°
  We see that trees bear no such pleasant fruit   45
  There where they grew first, as where they are new set.
  Perfumes the more they are chafed the more they render°
  Their pleasing scents, and so affliction
  Expresseth virtue, fully, whether true,
  Or else adulterate.

LODOVICO   Leave your painted comforts.   50
  I'll make Italian cut-works in their guts
  If ever I return.

GASPARO   O sir.

LODOVICO   I am patient.
  I have seen some ready to be executed
  Give pleasant looks, and money, and grown familiar
  With the knave hangman; so do I—I thank them,   55
  And would account them nobly merciful
  Would they dispatch me quickly.

ANTONELLI   Fare you well,
We shall find time, I doubt not, to repeal
Your banishment.
   A sennet sounds°
LODOVICO   I am ever bound to you.
This is the world's alms (pray make use of it):°   60
Great men sell sheep, thus to be cut in pieces,
When first they have shorn them bare and sold their fleeces.
   Exeunt

[1.2]

  Enter Bracciano, Camillo, Flamineo, Vittoria Corombona,
  [and Attendants carrying torches]
BRACCIANO *[to Vittoria]* Your best of rest.
VITTORIA   Unto my lord the Duke,°
The best of welcome. *[To Attendants]* More lights, attend the duke.
   [Exeunt Camillo and Vittoria]
BRACCIANO Flamineo.
FLAMINEO   My lord.
BRACCIANO   Quite lost, Flamineo.
FLAMINEO Pursue your noble wishes; I am prompt
As lightning to your service. O my lord!   5
(*Whispers*) The fair Vittoria, my happy sister,
Shall give you present audience.—Gentlemen,
Let the caroche go on, and 'tis his pleasure
You put out all your torches and depart.
   [Exeunt Attendants]
BRACCIANO Are we so happy?
FLAMINEO   Can't be otherwise?°   10
Observed you not tonight, my honoured lord
Which way soe'er you went she threw her eyes?
I have dealt already with her chambermaid
Zanche the Moor, and she is wondrous proud
To be the agent for so high a spirit.   15
BRACCIANO We are happy above thought, because 'bove merit.
FLAMINEO 'Bove merit! We may now talk freely! 'Bove merit! What
is't you doubt? Her coyness? That's but the superficies of lust most

women have. Yet why should ladies blush to hear that named, which they do not fear to handle? O they are politic; they know our desire is increased by the difficulty of enjoying, where a satiety is a blunt, weary and drowsy passion. If the buttery-hatch at court stood continually open there would be nothing so passionate crowding, nor hot suit after the beverage.

BRACCIANO O but her jealous husband.

FLAMINEO Hang him, a gilder° that hath his brains perished with quicksilver is not more cold in the liver. The great barriers moulted not more feathers° than he hath shed hairs,° by the confession of his doctor. An Irish gamester that will play himself naked, and then wage all downward° at hazard, is not more venturous. So unable to please a woman that like a Dutch doublet° all his back° is shrunk into his breeches.
Shroud you within this closet, good my lord;
Some trick now must be thought on to divide
My brother-in-law from his fair bedfellow.

BRACCIANO O should she fail to come—

FLAMINEO I must not have your lordship thus unwisely amorous:
I myself have loved a lady and pursued her with a great deal of under-age protestation,° whom some three or four gallants that have enjoyed would with all their hearts have been glad to have been rid of. 'Tis just like a summer bird-cage in a garden: the birds that are without despair to get in, and the birds that are within despair and are in a consumption for fear they shall never get out. Away, away, my lord.
    [Enter Camillo. Exit Bracciano]
[Aside] See here he comes; this fellow by his apparel
Some men would judge a politician;
But call his wit in question, you shall find it
Merely an ass in's foot-cloth. [To Camillo] How now, brother,
What, travelling to bed to your kind wife?°

CAMILLO I assure you, brother, no. My voyage lies
More northerly, in a far colder clime;
I do not well remember, I protest,
When I last lay with her.

FLAMINEO   Strange you should lose your count.°

CAMILLO We never lay together but ere morning
There grew a flaw between us.

FLAMINEO   'Thad been your part
To have made up that flaw.

CAMILLO   True, but she loathes°
  I should be seen in't.
FLAMINEO   Why sir, what's the matter?
CAMILLO The Duke your master visits me; I thank him,
  And I perceive how like an earnest bowler
  He very passionately leans that way   60
  He should have his bowl run.
FLAMINEO   I hope you do not think—
CAMILLO That noblemen bowl booty? 'Faith, his cheek°
  Hath a most excellent bias; it would fain
  Jump with my mistress.
FLAMINEO   Will you be an ass
  Despite your Aristotle, or a cuckold°   65
  Contrary to your ephemerides
  Which shows you under what a smiling planet
  You were first swaddled?
CAMILLO   Pew wew, sir, tell not me
  Of planets nor of ephemerides;
  A man may be made cuckold in the daytime   70
  When the stars' eyes are out.
FLAMINEO   Sir, God boy you,°
  I do commit you to your pitiful pillow
  Stuffed with horn-shavings.
CAMILLO   Brother.
FLAMINEO   God refuse me,°
  Might I advise you now your only course
  Were to lock up your wife.
CAMILLO   'Twere very good.   75
FLAMINEO Bar her the sight of revels.
CAMILLO   Excellent.
FLAMINEO Let her not go to church, but like a hound
  In lyam at your heels.
CAMILLO   'Twere for her honour.
FLAMINEO And so you should be certain in one fortnight,
  Despite her chastity or innocence,   80
  To be cuckolded, which yet is in suspense:
  This is my counsel and I ask no fee for't.
CAMILLO Come, you know not where my nightcap wrings me.
FLAMINEO Wear it i'th' old fashion, let your large ears° come
  through, it will be more easy. Nay, I will be bitter. Bar your wife   85
  of her entertainment! women are more willingly and more

gloriously chaste, when they are least restrained of their liberty. It
seems you would be a fine capricious mathematically jealous
coxcomb, take the height of your own horns with a Jacob's staff°
afore they are up. These politic enclosures for paltry mutton°   90
makes more rebellion in the flesh than all the provocative elec-
tuaries° doctors have uttered since last Jubilee.°

CAMILLO This doth not physic me.

FLAMINEO It seems you are jealous. I'll show you the error of it by
a familiar example. I have seen a pair of spectacles fashioned with   95
such perspective art° that, lay down but one twelvepence o'th'
board, 'twill appear as if there were twenty; now should you wear
a pair of these spectacles, and see your wife tying her shoe, you
would imagine twenty hands were taking up of your wife's clothes,
and this would put you into a horrible causeless fury.   100

CAMILLO The fault there, sir, is not in the eye-sight.

FLAMINEO True, but they that have the yellow jaundice think all
objects they look on to be yellow. Jealousy is worser: her fits
present to a man, like so many bubbles in a basin of water, twenty
several crabbed faces; many times makes his own shadow his   105
cuckold-maker.

　　　Enter [Vittoria] Corombona

See she comes; what reason have you to be jealous of this
creature? What an ignorant ass or flattering knave might he be
counted, that should write sonnets to her eyes, or call her brow the
snow of Ida,° or ivory of Corinth,° or compare her hair to the   110
blackbird's bill, when 'tis liker the blackbird's feather.° This is
all: be wise, I will make you friends and you shall go to bed
together. Marry, look you, it shall not be your seeking, do you
stand upon that by any means; walk you aloof, I would not have
you seen in't. Sister, [*whispers to Vittoria*] my lord attends you in   115
the banqueting-house—[*aloud*] your husband is wondrous discon-
tented.

VITTORIA I did nothing to displease him; I carved° to him at
supper-time.

FLAMINEO [*whispers to Vittoria*] You need not have carved him in   120
faith, they say he is a capon already. I must now seemingly fall
out with you. [*Aloud*] Shall a gentleman so well descended as
Camillo—[*aside*] a lousy slave that within this twenty years rode
with the blackguard° in the Duke's carriage 'mongst spits and
dripping-pans—   125

CAMILLO [*aside*] Now he begins to tickle her.

FLAMINEO [*aloud*] An excellent scholar, [*aside*] one that hath a head
filled with calf's brains° without any sage° in them, [*aloud*] come
crouching in the hams to you for a night's lodging? [*aside*] that
hath an itch in's hams, which like the fire at the glass-house° hath   130
not gone out this seven years. [*Aloud*] Is he not a courtly
gentleman? [*Aside*] When he wears white satin one would take him
by his black muzzle to be no other creature than a maggot. [*Aloud*]
You are a goodly foil,° I confess, well set out, [*aside*] but covered
with a false stone,° yon counterfeit diamond.   135

CAMILLO [*aside*] He will make her know what is in me.

FLAMINEO Come, my lord attends you; thou shalt go to bed to my
lord—

CAMILLO [*aside*] Now he comes to't.

FLAMINEO With a relish as curious as a vintner going to taste new   140
wine. [*To Camillo*] I am opening your case hard.

CAMILLO [*aside*] A virtuous brother, o'my credit.

FLAMINEO He will give thee a ring with a philosopher's stone in it.

CAMILLO [*aside*] Indeed I am studying alchemy.

FLAMINEO Thou shalt lie in a bed stuffed with turtles'° feathers,   145
swoon in perfumed linen like the fellow was smothered in roses;
so perfect shall be thy happiness, that as men at sea think land and
trees and ships go that way they go, so both heaven and earth shall
seem to go your voyage. Shalt meet him, 'tis fix'd, with nails of
diamonds to inevitable necessity.   150

VITTORIA [*aside to Flamineo*] How shall's rid him hence?

FLAMINEO [*aside to Vittoria*] I will put breeze° in's tail, set him
gadding presently. [*To Camillo*] I have almost wrought her to it, I
find her coming; but, might I advise you now, for this night I would
not lie with her: I would cross her humour to make her more humble.   155

CAMILLO Shall I, shall I?

FLAMINEO It will show in you a supremacy of judgement.

CAMILLO True, and a mind differing from the tumultuary opinion,
for *quae negata grata*.°

FLAMINEO Right: you are the adamant shall draw her to you, though   160
you keep distance off.

CAMILLO A philosophical reason.

FLAMINEO Walk by her i'the nobleman's fashion, and tell her you
will lie with her at the end of the progress.°

CAMILLO Vittoria, I cannot be induced, or as a man would say   165
incited—

VITTORIA To do what, sir?

CAMILLO To lie with you tonight; your silkworm useth to fast every
third day, and the next following spins the better. Tomorrow at
night I am for you.   170

VITTORIA You'll spin a fair thread, trust to't.

FLAMINEO [*aside to Camillo*] But do you hear, I shall have you steal
to her chamber about midnight.

CAMILLO Do you think so? Why, look you, brother, because you
shall not think I'll gull you, take the key, lock me into the chamber,   175
and say you shall be sure of me.

FLAMINEO In troth I will, I'll be your gaoler once.
But have you ne'er a false door?

CAMILLO A pox on't, as I am a Christian. Tell me tomorrow how
scurvily she takes my unkind parting.   180

FLAMINEO I will.

CAMILLO Didst thou not mark the jest of the silkworm? Good-night.
In faith, I will use this trick often.

FLAMINEO Do, do, do.
          Exit Camillo
So now you are safe. Ha, ha, ha, thou entanglest thyself in thine   185
own work like a silkworm. Come, sister, darkness hides your blush.
Women are like cursed dogs: civility keeps them tied all daytime,
but they are let loose at midnight; then they do most good or most
mischief.
          Enter Bracciano
My lord, my lord.   190

BRACCIANO Give credit: I could wish time would stand still°
And never end this interview, this hour,
But all delight doth itself soon'st devour.
          *Zanche brings out a carpet, spreads it and lays on it two fair
          cushions. Enter Cornelia [behind listening]*
Let me into your bosom, happy lady,
Pour out instead of eloquence my vows;   195
Loose me not, madam, for if you forgo me°
I am lost eternally.

VITTORIA   Sir, in the way of pity
I wish you heart-whole.

BRACCIANO   You are a sweet physician.

VITTORIA Sure, sir, a loathèd cruelty in ladies
Is as to doctors many funerals: 200
It takes away their credit.

BRACCIANO   Excellent creature.

We call the cruel fair, what name for you
That are so merciful?

ZANCHE   See now they close.

FLAMINEO Most happy union.

CORNELIA [aside] My fears are fall'n upon me. O my heart!   205
My son the pander! Now I find our house°
Sinking to ruin. Earthquakes leave behind,
Where they have tyrannized, iron, or lead, or stone,
But, woe to ruin, violent lust leaves none.

BRACCIANO What value is this jewel?

VITTORIA   'Tis the ornament   210
Of a weak fortune.

BRACCIANO In sooth I'll have it; nay, I will but change
My jewel for your jewel.

FLAMINEO [aside]   Excellent,
His jewel for her jewel; well put in, Duke.

BRACCIANO Nay, let me see you wear it.

VITTORIA   Here, sir?   215

BRACCIANO Nay lower, you shall wear my jewel lower.

FLAMINEO [aside] That's better; she must wear his jewel lower.°

VITTORIA To pass away the time, I'll tell your grace
A dream I had last night.

BRACCIANO   Most wishedly.

VITTORIA A foolish idle dream: 220
Methought I walked about the mid of night
Into a churchyard, where a goodly yew-tree
Spread her large root in ground; under that yew,
As I sat sadly leaning on a grave,°
Chequered with cross-sticks, there came stealing in°   225
Your duchess and my husband; one of them
A pickaxe bore, th'other a rusty spade,
And in rough terms they gan to challenge me
About this yew.

BRACCIANO   That tree.

VITTORIA   This harmless yew.°
They told me my intent was to root up   230
That well-grown yew, and plant i'th' stead of it
A withered blackthorn, and for that they vowed
To bury me alive; my husband straight
With pickaxe gan to dig, and your fell duchess
With shovel, like a Fury, voided out   235

The earth and scattered bones. Lord, how methought
I trembled, and yet for all this terror
I could not pray.

FLAMINEO [*aside*] No, the devil was in your dream.

VITTORIA When to my rescue there arose methought   240
A whirlwind, which let fall a massy arm
From that strong plant,
And both were struck dead by that sacred yew
In that base shallow grave that was their due.

FLAMINEO [*aside*] Excellent devil.   245
She hath taught him in a dream
To make away his duchess and her husband.

BRACCIANO Sweetly shall I interpret this your dream:
You are lodged within his arms who shall protect you
From all the fevers of a jealous husband,
From the poor envy of our phlegmatic duchess.   250
I'll seat you above law and above scandal,
Give to your thoughts the invention of delight
And the fruition; nor shall government
Divide me from you longer than a care   255
To keep you great: you shall to me at once
Be dukedom, health, wife, children, friends and all.

CORNELIA [*coming forward*] Woe to light hearts: they still forerun
    our fall.

FLAMINEO What Fury raised thee up? Away, away!   260
        Exit Zanche

CORNELIA What make you here, my lord, this dead of night?
Never dropped mildew on a flower here
Till now.

FLAMINEO I pray will you go to bed then,
Lest you be blasted?

CORNELIA   O that this fair garden   265
Had with all poisoned herbs of Thessaly°
At first been planted, made a nursery
For witchcraft; rather than a burial plot
For both your honours.

VITTORIA   Dearest mother, hear me.

CORNELIA O thou dost make my brow bend to the earth   270
Sooner than nature. See the curse of children!
In life they keep us frequently in tears,
And in the cold grave leave us in pale fears.

BRACCIANO Come, come, I will not hear you.

VITTORIA Dear my lord.   275

CORNELIA Where is thy Duchess now, adulterous Duke?
  Thou little dreamed'st this night she is come to Rome.

FLAMINEO How? come to Rome?

VITTORIA   The Duchess—

BRACCIANO   She had been better—

CORNELIA The lives of princes should like dials move,
  Whose regular example is so strong,   280
  They make the times by them go right or wrong.

FLAMINEO So, have you done?

CORNELIA   Unfortunate Camillo.

VITTORIA [kneels] I do protest if any chaste denial,
  If anything but blood could have allayed°
  His long suit to me—

CORNELIA [kneels]   I will join with thee,   285
  To the most woeful end e'er mother kneeled:
  If thou dishonour thus thy husband's bed,
  Be thy life short as are the funeral tears
  In great men's.

BRACCIANO   Fie, fie, the woman's mad.°

CORNELIA Be thy act Judas-like: betray in kissing.   290
  May'st thou be envied during his short breath,
  And pitied like a wretch after his death.

VITTORIA O me accursed!
        Exit Vittoria

FLAMINEO [to Cornelia]   Are you out of your wits? [To Bracciano]
    My lord,
  I'll fetch her back again.

BRACCIANO   No, I'll to bed.   295
  Send Doctor Julio to me presently.
  Uncharitable woman, thy rash tongue
  Hath raised a fearful and prodigious storm;
  Be thou the cause of all ensuing harm.
        Exit Bracciano

FLAMINEO Now, you that stand so much upon your honour,   300
  Is this a fitting time o'night, think you,
  To send a duke home without e'er a man?
  I would fain know where lies the mass of wealth
  Which you have hoarded for my maintenance,
  That I may bear my beard out of the level   305

    Of my lord's stirrup.

CORNELIA   What? Because we are poor,°
    Shall we be vicious?

FLAMINEO   Pray what means have you
    To keep me from the galleys, or the gallows?
    My father proved himself a gentleman,
    Sold all's land, and like a fortunate fellow,   310
    Died ere the money was spent. You brought me up,°
    At Padua, I confess, where I protest
    For want of means—the university judge me—
    I have been fain to heel my tutor's stockings
    At least seven years. Conspiring with a beard°   315
    Made me a graduate; then to this Duke's service;
    I visited the court, whence I returned,
    More courteous, more lecherous by far,
    But not a suit the richer; and shall I,
    Having a path so open and so free   320
    To my preferment, still retain your milk
    In my pale forehead? No, this face of mine
    I'll arm and fortify with lusty wine
    'Gainst shame and blushing.

CORNELIA O that I ne'er had borne thee.

FLAMINEO   So would I.   325
    I would the common'st courtezan in Rome
    Had been my mother rather than thyself.
    Nature is very pitiful to whores
    To give them but few children, yet those children
    Plurality of fathers; they are sure   330
    They shall not want. Go, go,
    Complain unto my great lord Cardinal;
    Yet maybe he will justify the act.
    Lycurgus wondered much men would provide°
    Good stallions for their mares, and yet would suffer   335
    Their fair wives to be barren.

CORNELIA Misery of miseries.

      Exit Cornelia

FLAMINEO The Duchess come to court! I like not that.
    We are engaged to mischief and must on:
    As rivers to find out the ocean   340
    Flow with crook bendings beneath forcèd banks,
    Or as we see, to aspire some mountain's top,

The way ascends not straight, but imitates
The subtle foldings of a winter's snake,°
So who knows policy and her true aspect,   345
Shall find her ways winding and indirect.
    Exit

[2.1]

*Enter Francisco de Medici, Cardinal Monticelso, Marcello,
Isabella, young Giovanni, with little Jaques the Moor°*

FRANCISCO Have you not seen your husband since you arrived?
ISABELLA Not yet, sir.
FRANCISCO   Surely he is wondrous kind.
  If I had such a dove-house as Camillo's,
  I would set fire on't, were't but to destroy
  The polecats that haunt to't. [*To Giovanni*] My sweet cousin.°   5
GIOVANNI Lord uncle, you did promise me a horse
  And armour.
FRANCISCO   That I did, my pretty cousin;
  Marcello, see it fitted.
MARCELLO [*looking off-stage*] My lord, the Duke is here.
FRANCISCO   Sister, away,
  You must not yet be seen.
ISABELLA   I do beseech you
  Entreat him mildly; let not your rough tongue   10
  Set us at louder variance; all my wrongs
  Are freely pardoned, and I do not doubt,
  As men to try the precious unicorn's horn
  Make of the powder a preservative circle
  And in it put a spider, so these arms   15
  Shall charm his poison, force it to obeying°
  And keep him chaste from an infected straying.
FRANCISCO I wish it may. Be gone.
        Exit [Isabella]. Enter Bracciano and Flamineo
                        Void the chamber.
      [*Exeunt Flamineo, Marcello, Giovanni, and little Jaques*]
  You are welcome; will you sit? I pray, my lord,
  Be you my orator, my heart's too full;   20
  I'll second you anon.
MONTICELSO   Ere I begin
  Let me entreat your grace forgo all passion
  Which may be raisèd by my free discourse.
BRACCIANO As silent as i'th' church; you may proceed.
MONTICELSO It is a wonder to your noble friends,   25
  That you that have as 'twere entered the world

With a free sceptre in your able hand,
And have to th' use of nature well applied
High gifts of learning, should in your prime age°
Neglect your awful throne for the soft down   30
Of an insatiate bed. O my lord,
The drunkard after all his lavish cups
Is dry, and then is sober; so at length,
When you awake from this lascivious dream,
Repentance then will follow, like the sting   .   35
Placed in the adder's tail. Wretched are princes
When fortune blasteth but a petty flower
Of their unwieldy crowns, or ravisheth
But one pearl from their sceptre. But alas!
When they to wilful shipwreck loose good fame,   40
All princely titles perish with their name.°
BRACCIANO You have said, my lord.
MONTICELSO   Enough to give you taste
How far I am from flattering your greatness?
BRACCIANO Now you that are his second, what say you?
Do not like young hawks fetch a course about;°   45
Your game flies fair and for you.
FRANCISCO   Do not fear it.
I'll answer you in your own hawking phrase:
Some eagles that should gaze upon the sun°
Seldom soar high, but take their lustful ease,
Since they from dunghill birds their prey can seize.°   50
You know Vittoria.
BRACCIANO   Yes.
FRANCISCO   You shift your shirt there
When you retire from tennis.
BRACCIANO   Happily.°
FRANCISCO Her husband is lord of a poor fortune,
Yet she wears cloth of tissue.
BRACCIANO   What of this?
Will you urge that, my good lord Cardinal,   55
As part of her confession at next shrift,
And know from whence it sails.
FRANCISCO   She is your strumpet.
BRACCIANO Uncivil sir, there's hemlock in thy breath
And that black slander; were she a whore of mine
All thy loud cannons, and thy borrowed Switzers,°   60

Thy galleys, nor thy sworn confederates,
Durst not supplant her.
FRANCISCO   Let's not talk on thunder.
Thou hast a wife, our sister; would I had given
Both her white hands to death, bound and locked fast
In her last winding-sheet, when I gave thee   65
But one.
BRACCIANO Thou hadst given a soul to God then.
FRANCISCO   True.
Thy ghostly father with all's absolution,
Shall ne'er do so by thee.
BRACCIANO   Spit thy poison.
FRANCISCO I shall not need, lust carries her sharp whip
At her own girdle; look to't, for our anger   70
Is making thunder-bolts.
BRACCIANO   Thunder? in faith,
They are but crackers.
FRANCISCO   We'll end this with the cannon.
BRACCIANO Thou'lt get nought by it but iron in thy wounds,
And gunpowder in thy nostrils.
FRANCISCO   Better that
Than change perfumes for plasters.
BRACCIANO   Pity on thee;°   75
'Twere good you'd show your slaves or men condemned
Your new-ploughed forehead. Defiance! and I'll meet thee,
Even in a thicket of thy ablest men.
MONTICELSO My lords, you shall not word it any further
Without a milder limit.
FRANCISCO   Willingly.   80
BRACCIANO Have you proclaimed a triumph that you bait
A lion thus?
MONTICELSO My lord.
BRACCIANO   I am tame, I am tame, sir.°
FRANCISCO We send unto the Duke for conference
'Bout levies 'gainst the pirates; my lord Duke
Is not at home. We come ourself in person,   85
Still my lord Duke is busied; but we fear
When Tiber to each prowling passenger
Discovers flocks of wild ducks, then, my lord—°
'Bout moulting time I mean—we shall be certain°
To find you sure enough and speak with you.

BRACCIANO   Ha?   90
FRANCISCO A mere tale of a tub, my words are idle;°
    But to express the sonnet by natural reason,°
    When stags grow melancholic you'll find the season.°
       Enter Giovanni, [wearing armour, and little Jaques with a
       weapon]
MONTICELSO No more, my lord, here comes a champion
    Shall end the difference between you both,   95
    Your son, the prince Giovanni. See, my lords,
    What hopes you store in him; this is a casket
    For both your crowns, and should be held like dear.
    Now is he apt for knowledge; therefore know
    It is a more direct and even way   100
    To train to virtue those of princely blood
    By examples than by precepts. If by examples,
    Whom should he rather strive to imitate
    Than his own father? Be his pattern then,
    Leave him a stock of virtue that may last   105
    Should fortune rend his sails and split his mast.
BRACCIANO Your hand, boy: growing to a soldier?
GIOVANNI Give me a pike.
       [*Little Jaques passes Giovanni his weapon*]
FRANCISCO What, practising your pike so young, fair coz?°
GIOVANNI Suppose me one of Homer's frogs, my lord,°   110
    Tossing my bulrush thus; pray, sir, tell me,
    Might not a child of good discretion°
    Be leader to an army?
FRANCISCO   Yes, cousin, a young prince
    Of good discretion might.
GIOVANNI   Say you so?
    Indeed I have heard 'tis fit a general   115
    Should not endanger his own person oft,
    So that he make a noise, when he's o'horseback,°
    Like a Dansk drummer. O 'tis excellent!
    He need not fight; methinks his horse as well
    Might lead an army for him. If I live   120
    I'll charge the French foe, in the very front
    Of all my troops, the foremost man.
FRANCISCO   What, what—
GIOUANNI And will not bid my soldiers up and follow
    But bid them follow me.

BRACCIANO   Forward lapwing!
  He flies with the shell on's head.
FRANCISCO   Pretty cousin.°   125
GIOVANNI The first year, uncle, that I go to war,
  All prisoners that I take I will set free
  Without their ransom.
FRANCISCO   Ha, without their ransom?
  How then will you reward your soldiers
  That took those prisoners for you?
GIOVANNI   Thus, my lord: 130
  I'll marry them to all the wealthy widows
  That falls that year.
FRANCISCO   Why then, the next year following
  You'll have no men to go with you to war.
GIOVANNI Why then, I'll press the women to the war,
  And then the men will follow.
MONTICELSO   Witty prince.   135
FRANCISCO See: a good habit makes a child a man,°
  Whereas a bad one makes a man a beast;
  Come, you and I are friends.
BRACCIANO   Most wishedly;
  Like bones which broke in sunder and well set
  Knit the more strongly.   140
FRANCISCO [to Attendant off-stage] Call Camillo hither.
  You have received the rumour, how Count Lodovic
  Is turned a pirate?
BRACCIANO   Yes.
FRANCISCO   We are now preparing
  Some ships to fetch him in.
     [Enter Isabella]
                  Behold your Duchess;
  We now will leave you and expect from you   145
  Nothing but kind entreaty.
BRACCIANO   You have charmed me.
     Exeunt Francisco, Monticelso, Giovanni
  You are in health we see.
ISABELLA   And above health
  To see my lord well.
BRACCIANO   So; I wonder much
  What amorous whirlwind hurried you to Rome.
ISABELLA Devotion, my lord.

BRACCIANO   Devotion?° 150
  Is your soul charged with any grievous sin?
ISABELLA 'Tis burdened with too many, and I think
  The oftener that we cast our reckonings up,°
  Our sleeps will be the sounder.
BRACCIANO   Take your chamber!°
ISABELLA Nay, my dear lord, I will not have you angry; 155
  Doth not my absence from you two months
  Merit one kiss?
BRACCIANO   I do not use to kiss;°
  If that will dispossess your jealousy,
  I'll swear it to you.
ISABELLA   O my lovèd lord,
  I do not come to chide. My jealousy? 160
  I am to learn what that Italian means;°
  You are as welcome to these longing arms
  As I to you a virgin.
    [*She tries to embrace him; he turns away.*]
BRACCIANO   O your breath!
  Out upon sweet meats and continued physic!
  The plague is in them.
ISABELLA   You have oft for these two lips 165
  Neglected cassia or the natural sweets
  Of the spring violet; they are not yet much withered.
  My lord, I should be merry; these your frowns
  Show in a helmet lovely, but on me,
  In such a peaceful interview methinks 170
  They are too too roughly knit.
BRACCIANO   O dissemblance!
  Do you bandy factions 'gainst me? Have you learnt°
  The trick of impudent baseness to complain
  Unto your kindred?
ISABELLA   Never, my dear lord.
BRACCIANO Must I be haunted out, or was't your trick 175
  To meet some amorous gallant here in Rome
  That must supply our discontinuance?
ISABELLA I pray, sir, burst my heart, and in my death
  Turn to your ancient pity, though not love.°
BRACCIANO Because your brother is the corpulent Duke,° 180
  That is the Great Duke,—'s death, I shall not shortly
  Racket away five hundred crowns at tennis,

But it shall rest upon recòrd! I scorn him
Like a shaved Polack; all his reverend wit°
Lies in his wardrobe; he's a discreet fellow   185
When he's made up in his robes of state,
Your brother the Great Duke, because he's galleys,
And now and then ransacks a Turkish fly-boat—
Now all the hellish Furies take his soul!—
First made this match. Accursèd be the priest   190
That sang the wedding mass, and even my issue!
ISABELLA   O too too far you have cursed.
BRACCIANO   Your hand I'll kiss,
This is the latest ceremony of my love;°
Henceforth I'll never lie with thee, by this,
This wedding-ring; I'll ne'er more lie with thee.°   195
And this divorce shall be as truly kept,
As if the judge had doomed it; fare you well,
Our sleeps are severed.
ISABELLA   Forbid it, the sweet union
Of all things blessèd; why, the saints in heaven
Will knit their brows at that.
BRACCIANO   Let not thy love   200
Make thee an unbeliever; this my vow
Shall never, on my soul, be satisfied
With my repentance; let thy brother rage°
Beyond a horrid tempest or sea-fight,°
My vow is fixèd.
ISABELLA   O my winding-sheet,   205
Now shall I need thee shortly! Dear my lord,
Let me hear once more what I would not hear:
Never?
BRACCIANO   Never.
ISABELLA   O my unkind lord, may your sins find mercy,
As I upon a woeful widowed bed   210
Shall pray for you, if not to turn your eyes
Upon your wretchèd wife, and hopeful son,
Yet that in time you'll fix them upon heaven.
BRACCIANO   No more! Go, go, complain to the Great Duke.
ISABELLA   [weeping] No, my dear lord, you shall have present witness   215
How I'll work peace between you: I will make
Myself the author of your cursèd vow;
I have some cause to do it, you have none.

Conceal it, I beseech you, for the weal
Of both your dukedoms, that you wrought the means   220
Of such a separation; let the fault
Remain with my supposèd jealousy,
And think with what a piteous and rent heart
I shall perform this sad ensuing part.

   Enter Francisco, Flamineo, Monticelso, Marcello

BRACCIANO Well, take your course. My honourable brother!   225
FRANCISCO Sister—this is not well, my lord—why, sister!—
  She merits not this welcome.
BRACCIANO   Welcome, say?
  She hath given a sharp welcome.
FRANCISCO [*to Isabella*]   Are you foolish?
  Come, dry your tears; is this a modest course°
  To better what is naught, to rail and weep?°   230
  Grow to a reconcilement, or by heaven,
  I'll ne'er more deal between you.
ISABELLA   Sir, you shall not;
  No, though Vittoria upon that condition
  Would become honest.
FRANCISCO   Was your husband loud
  Since we departed?
ISABELLA   By my life, sir, no;   235
  I swear by that I do not care to lose.
  Are all these ruins of my former beauty
  Laid out for a whore's triumph?
FRANCISCO   Do you hear?
  Look upon other women, with what patience
  They suffer these slight wrongs, with what justice   240
  They study to requite them; take that course.
ISABELLA O that I were a man, or that I had power
  To execute my apprehended wishes,°
  I would whip some with scorpions.
FRANCISCO   What? Turned Fury?°
ISABELLA To dig the strumpet's eyes out, let her lie   245
  Some twenty months a-dying, to cut off
  Her nose and lips, pull out her rotten teeth,
  Preserve her flesh like mummia, for trophies
  Of my just anger; hell to my affliction°
  Is mere snow-water. [*To Bracciano*] By your favour, sir—   250
  Brother, draw near, and my lord Cardinal—

25

[*To Bracciano*] Sir, let me borrow of you but one kiss;
Henceforth I'll never lie with you, by this,
This wedding-ring.

FRANCISCO   How? Ne'er more lie with him?

ISABELLA And this divorce shall be as truly kept,   255
As if in throngèd court a thousand ears
Had heard it, and a thousand lawyers' hands
Sealed to the separation.

BRACCIANO Ne'er lie with me?

ISABELLA   Let not my former dotage
Make thee an unbeliever; this my vow   260
Shall never, on my soul, be satisfied
With my repentance: *manet alta mente repostum.*°

FRANCISCO Now by my birth you are a foolish, mad,
And jealous woman.

BRACCIANO   You see 'tis not my seeking.

FRANCISCO Was this your circle of pure unicorn's horn   265
You said should charm your lord? Now horns upon thee,
For jealousy deserves them; keep your vow,
And take your chamber.

ISABELLA No, sir, I'll presently to Padua;
I will not stay a minute.

MONTICELSO   O good madam.   270

BRACCIANO 'Twere best to let her have her humour;
Some half day's journey will bring down her stomach,°
And then she'll turn in post.

FRANCISCO   To see her come°
To my lord Cardinal for a dispensation
Of her rash vow will beget excellent laughter.   275

ISABELLA [*aside*] Unkindness do thy office, poor heart break;°
Those are the killing griefs which dare not speak.°
        Exit [Isabella]. Enter Camillo

MARCELLO Camillo's come, my lord.

FRANCISCO   Where's the commission?

MARCELLO 'Tis here.

FRANCISCO   Give me the signet.
        [*Monticelso, Francisco, Camillo, and Marcello walk apart,
        and confer in low voices*]

FLAMINEO [*to Bracciano*] My lord, do you mark their whispering? I   280
will compound a medicine out of their two heads, stronger than
garlic, deadlier than stibium;° the cantharides° which are scarce

seen to stick upon the flesh when they work to the heart, shall not
do it with more silence or invisible cunning.
    Enter Doctor [Julio]

BRACCIANO About the murder.   285

FLAMINEO They are sending him to Naples, but I'll send him to
Candy;° here's another property too.

BRACCIANO O the doctor.

FLAMINEO A poor quack-salving knave, my lord, one that should
have been lashed for's lechery, but that he confessed a judge-   290
ment, had an execution° laid upon him, and so put the whip to a
non plus.

JULIO And was cozened, my lord, by an arranter knave than myself,
and made pay all the colourable execution.

FLAMINEO He will shoot pills into a man's guts, shall make them   295
have more ventages than a cornet° or a lamprey;° he will poison a
kiss, and was once minded, for his masterpiece, because Ireland
breeds no poison, to have prepared a deadly vapour in a Spaniard's
fart that should have poisoned all Dublin.

BRACCIANO O Saint Anthony's fire!°   300

JULIO Your secretary is merry, my lord.

FLAMINEO O thou cursed antipathy to nature! Look his eye's
bloodshed° like a needle a chirurgeon stitcheth a wound with.
Let me embrace thee, toad, and love thee. O thou abominable
loathsome gargarism, that will fetch up lungs, lights, heart, and   305
liver by scruples.°

BRACCIANO No more. I must employ thee, honest doctor;
    You must to Padua and by the way
    Use some of your skill for us.

JULIO   Sir, I shall.

BRACCIANO But for Camillo?   310

FLAMINEO He dies this night by such a politic strain,°
    Men shall suppose him by's own engine slain.
    But for your Duchess' death?

JULIO   I'll make her sure.

BRACCIANO Small mischiefs are by greater made secure.°

FLAMINEO Remember this, you slave: when knaves come to prefer-   315
ment they rise [*aside*] as gallowses° are raised i'th' Low Countries,°
[*aloud*] one upon another's shoulders.
    Exeunt [Bracciano, Flamineo, and Doctor Julio]

MONTICELSO Here is an emblem, nephew, pray peruse it.
    'Twas thrown in at your window.

CAMILLO   At my window?
  Here is a stag, my lord, hath shed his horns,   320
  And for the loss of them the poor beast weeps—
  The word 'Inopem me copia fecit'.°
MONTICELSO   That is,
  Plenty of horns hath made him poor of horns.°
CAMILLO What should this mean?
MONTICELSO   I'll tell you: 'tis given out
  You are a cuckold.
CAMILLO   Is it given out so?   325
  I had rather such report as that, my lord,
  Should keep within doors.
FRANCISCO   Have you any children?
CAMILLO None, my lord.
FRANCISCO   You are the happier.
  I'll tell you a tale.
CAMILLO   Pray, my lord.
FRANCISCO   An old tale.
  Upon a time Phoebus, the god of light,   330
  Or him we call the sun, would need be married.
  The gods gave their consent, and Mercury
  Was sent to voice it to the general world.°
  But what a piteous cry there straight arose
  Amongst smiths, and felt-makers, brewers and cooks,   335
  Reapers and butter-women, amongst fishmongers
  And thousand other trades, which are annoyed
  By his excessive heat; 'twas lamentable.
  They came to Jupiter all in a sweat
  And do forbid the bans. A great fat cook   340
  Was made their speaker, who entreats of Jove
  That Phoebus might be gelded, for if now
  When there was but one sun, so many men
  Were like to perish by his violent heat,
  What should they do if he were married   345
  And should beget more, and those children
  Make fireworks like their father? So say I,°
  Only I will apply it to your wife:
  Her issue, should not providence prevent it,
  Would make both nature, time, and man repent it.   350
MONTICELSO Look you, cousin,
  Go change the air for shame, see if your absence°

Will blast your cornucopia: Marcello°
Is chosen with you joint commissioner
For the relieving our Italian coast   355
From pirates.

MARCELLO   I am much honoured in't.

CAMILLO   But, sir,
Ere I return the stag's horns may be sprouted
Greater than these are shed.

MONTICELSO   Do not fear it,
I'll be your ranger.

CAMILLO   You must watch i'th' nights,
Then's the most danger.

FRANCISCO   Farewell, good Marcello.   360
All the best fortunes of a soldier's wish
Bring you o'ship-board.°

CAMILLO Were I not best, now I am turned soldier,
Ere that I leave my wife, sell all she hath
And then take leave of her?

MONTICELSO   I expect good from you,   365
Your parting is so merry.

CAMILLO Merry, my lord, o'th' captain's humour right;
I am resolvèd to be drunk this night.
        Exit [Camillo with Marcello]

FRANCISCO So, 'twas well fitted; now shall we discern,
How his wished absence will give violent way   370
To Duke Bracciano's lust.

MONTICELSO   Why, that was it;
To what scorned purpose else should we make choice
Of him for a sea-captain? and besides,
Count Lodovic which was rumoured for a pirate
Is now in Padua.

FRANCISCO   Is't true?

MONTICELSO   Most certain.   375
I have letters from him, which are suppliant
To work his quick repeal from banishment;
He means to address himself for pension
Unto our sister Duchess.

FRANCISCO   O 'twas well.°
We shall not want his absence past six days;°   380
I fain would have the Duke Bracciano run
Into notorious scandal, for there's nought

In such cursed dotage to repair his name,
Only the deep sense of some deathless shame.°
MONTICELSO It may be objected I am dishonourable,   385
To play thus with my kinsman; but I answer,
For my revenge I'd stake a brother's life,
That being wronged durst not avenge himself.
FRANCISCO Come to observe this strumpet.
MONTICELSO   Curse of greatness!
Sure he'll not leave her.
FRANCISCO   There's small pity in't;°   390
Like mistletoe on sere elms spent by weather,
Let him cleave to her and both rot together.
        Exeunt

[2.2]

Enter Bracciano with one in the habit of a Conjurer
BRACCIANO Now, sir, I claim your promise. 'Tis dead midnight,
The time prefixed to show me by your art
How the intended murder of Camillo
And our loathèd Duchess grow to action.
CONJURER You have won me by your bounty to a deed   5
I do not often practise; some there are,
Which by sophistic tricks aspire that name
Which I would gladly lose, of nigromancer;°
As some that use to juggle upon cards,
Seeming to conjure, when indeed they cheat;   10
Others that raise up their confederate spirits°
'Bout windmills, and endanger their own necks°
For making of a squib; and some there are°
Will keep a curtal to show juggling tricks°
And give out 'tis a spirit; besides these   15
Such a whole ream of almanac-makers, figure-flingers,°
Fellows indeed that only live by stealth,
Since they do merely lie about stol'n goods,°
They'd make men think the devil were fast and loose,°
With speaking fustian Latin. Pray sit down,   20
Put on this night cap, sir, 'tis charmed;
    [*Bracciano puts on a night cap*]
                              and now

I'll show you by my strong-commanding art
The circumstance that breaks your Duchess' heart.

A dumb show

[*Music sounds softly.*°] *Enter suspiciously Julio and
[Christophero]. They draw a curtain where Bracciano's
picture is. They put on spectacles of glass, which cover their
eyes and noses, and then burn perfumes afore the picture, and
wash the lips of the picture. That done, quenching the fire and
putting off their spectacles, they depart laughing.
Enter Isabella in her nightgown as to bedward, with lights;
after her, Count Lodovico, Giovanni, Guid-Antonio, and
others waiting on her. She kneels down as to prayers, then
draws the curtain of the picture, does three reverences to it,
and kisses it thrice. She faints and will not suffer them to
come near it; dies. Sorrow expressed in Giovanni and in
Count Lodovico. She's conveyed out solemnly.*

BRACCIANO Excellent, then she's dead.

CONJURER   She's poisonèd
By the fumèd picture. 'Twas her custom nightly,   25
Before she went to bed, to go and visit
Your picture and to feed her eyes and lips
On the dead shadow. Doctor Julio°
Observing this, infects it with an oil
And other poisoned stuff, which presently   30
Did suffocate her spirits.

BRACCIANO   Methought I saw
Count Lodovic there.

CONJURER   He was, and by my art
I find he did most passionately dote
Upon your Duchess. Now turn another way,
And view Camillo's far more politic fate;   35
Strike louder music from this charmèd ground
To yield, as fits the act, a tragic sound.

The second dumb show.

[*Music sounds, with tragic jarring notes.*] *Enter Flamineo,
Marcello, Camillo, with four more as Captains. They drink
healths and dance. A vaulting-horse is brought into the room.
Marcello and two more whispered out of the room, while
Flamineo and Camillo strip themselves into their shirts, as to
vault; compliment who shall begin. As Camillo is about to
vault, Flamineo pitcheth him upon his neck, and with the*

help of the rest writhes his neck about; seems to see if it be
broke, and lays him folded double as 'twere under the horse;°
makes shows to call for help. Marcello comes in, laments,
sends for the Cardinal [Monticelso] and Duke [Francisco],
who comes forth with armed men; wonder at the act.
[Francisco] commands the body to be carried home,
apprehends Flamineo, Marcello, and the rest, and go as 'twere
to apprehend Vittoria.

BRACCIANO 'Twas quaintly done, but yet each circumstance
  I taste not fully.

CONJURER   O 'twas most apparent,°
  You saw them enter charged with their deep healths°   40
  To their boon voyage, and to second that,
  Flamineo calls to have a vaulting-horse
  Maintain their sport. The virtuous Marcello
  Is innocently plotted forth the room,
  Whilst your eye saw the rest and can inform you   45
  The engine of all.

BRACCIANO It seems Marcello and Flamineo
  Are both committed.

CONJURER   Yes, you saw them guarded,
  And now they are come with purpose to apprehend
  Your mistress, fair Vittoria; we are now   50
  Beneath her roof; 'twere fit we instantly
  Make out by some back postern.

BRACCIANO   Noble friend,
  You bind me ever to you. This shall stand
  As the firm seal annexèd to my hand.°
  It shall enforce a payment.

CONJURER   Sir, I thank you.   55
    Exit Bracciano
  Both flowers and weeds spring when the sun is warm,
  And great men do great good, or else great harm.
    Exit

[3.1]

Enter Francisco, and Monticelso, their Chancellor and Register.

FRANCISCO You have dealt discreetly to obtain the presence
  Of all the grave lieger ambassadors
  To hear Vittoria's trial.

MONTICELSO　　　　　　'Twas not ill,
  For, sir, you know we have nought but circumstances
  To charge her with, about her husband's death.　　　　　　5
  Their approbation therefore to the proofs
  Of her black lust shall make her infamous
  To all our neighbouring kingdoms; I wonder
  If Bracciano will be here.

FRANCISCO　　　　　　　O fie,
  'Twere impudence too palpable.　　　　　　10

  *[Exeunt Francisco and Monticelso, and their Chancellor and
  Register. Enter Flamineo and Marcello guarded, and a
  Lawyer]*

LAWYER What, are you in by the week?° So, I will try now whether
thy wit be close prisoner. Methinks none should sit upon° thy
sister but old whoremasters.

FLAMINEO Or cuckolds, for your cuckold is your most terrible tickler°
of lechery. Whoremasters would serve, for none are judges at　　15
tilting,° but those that have been old tilters.

LAWYER My lord Duke and she have been very private.

FLAMINEO You are a dull ass; 'tis threatened they have been very
public.°

LAWYER If it can be proved they have but kissed one another—　　20

FLAMINEO What then?

LAWYER My lord Cardinal will ferret them.

FLAMINEO A cardinal, I hope, will not catch conies.°

LAWYER For to sow kisses—mark what I say—to sow kisses is to reap
lechery, and I am sure a woman that will endure kissing is half won.　　25

FLAMINEO True, her upper part by that rule; if you will win her
nether part too, you know what follows.

LAWYER Hark, the ambassadors are lighted.°

FLAMINEO *[aside]* I do put on this feignèd garb of mirth

    To gull suspicion.

MARCELLO   O my unfortunate sister!   30
    I would my dagger's point had cleft her heart
    When she first saw Bracciano. You, 'tis said,
    Were made his engine and his stalking-horse
    To undo my sister.

FLAMINEO   I made a kind of path
    To her and mine own preferment.

MARCELLO   Your ruin.   35

FLAMINEO Hum! Thou art a soldier,
    Followest the Great Duke, feedest his victories,
    As witches do their serviceable spirits,°
    Even with thy prodigal blood. What hast got?
    But like the wealth of captains, a poor handful,   40
    Which in thy palm thou bear'st, as men hold water:
    Seeking to grip it fast, the frail reward
    Steals through thy fingers.

MARCELLO   Sir—

FLAMINEO   Thou hast scarce maintenance
    To keep thee in fresh chamois.

MARCELLO   Brother.

FLAMINEO   Hear me:°
    And thus when we have even poured ourselves   45
    Into great fights, for their ambition
    Or idle spleen, how shall we find reward?
    But as we seldom find the mistletoe
    Sacred to physic on the builder oak°
    Without a mandrake by it, so in our quest of gain.°   50
    Alas the poorest of their forced dislikes
    At a limb proffers, but at heart it strikes:°
    This is lamented doctrine.

MARCELLO   Come, come.

FLAMINEO When age shall turn thee
    White as a blooming hawthorn—

MARCELLO   I'll interrupt you.   55
    For love of virtue bear an honest heart,
    And stride over every politic respect,
    Which where they most advance they most infect.°
    Were I your father, as I am your brother,
    I should not be ambitious to leave you   60
    A better patrimony.

Enter Savoy [Ambassador]. Here there is a passage of the
lieger Ambassadors over the stage severally. Enter French
Ambassador.

FLAMINEO I'll think on't.

The lord ambassadors.

LAWYER O my sprightly Frenchman: do you know him? He's an
admirable tilter.

FLAMINEO I saw him at last tilting; he showed like a pewter candle- 65
stick fashioned like a man in armour, holding a tilting-staff in his
hand little bigger than a candle of twelve i'th' pound.

LAWYER O but he's an excellent horseman.

FLAMINEO A lame one in his lofty tricks;° he sleeps o'horseback like
a poulter.° 70

Enter English and Spanish [Ambassadors]

LAWYER Lo you, my Spaniard.

FLAMINEO He carries his face in's ruff, as I have seen a serving-man
carry glasses in a cypress hat-band, monstrous steady for fear of
breaking; he looks like the claw of a blackbird, first salted and then
broiled in a candle. 75

Exeunt.

[3.2]

Enter Francisco, Monticelso, the six lieger Ambassadors,
Bracciano,° Vittoria, [Flamineo, Marcello], Lawyer, and a
guard [and Servant]

MONTICELSO [*to Bracciano*] Forbear, my lord, here is no place as-
signed you.

This business by his holiness is left

To our examination.

BRACCIANO   May it thrive with you.

Lays a rich gown under him

FRANCISCO A chair there for his lordship.

BRACCIANO Forbear your kindness; an unbidden guest 5

Should travel as Dutchwomen go to church:

Bear their stools with them.

MONTICELSO   At your pleasure, sir.

Stand to the table, gentlewoman. Now, signor,

Fall to your plea.

LAWYER *Domine judex converte oculos in hanc pestem mulierum cor-*
ruptissimam.°   10
VITTORIA What's he?
FRANCISCO   A lawyer that pleads against you.
VITTORIA Pray, my lord, let him speak his usual tongue;
 I'll make no answer else.
FRANCISCO Why, you understand Latin.
VITTORIA I do, sir, but amongst this auditory   15
 Which come to hear my cause, the half or more
 May be ignorant in't.
MONTICELSO   Go on, sir.
VITTORIA   By your favour,
 I will not have my accusation clouded
 In a strange tongue. All this assembly
 Shall hear what you can charge me with.
FRANCISCO   Signor,   20
 You need not stand on't much; pray change your language.
MONTICELSO O for God sake! Gentlewoman, your credit
 Shall be more famous by it.
LAWYER   Well then, have at you.°
VITTORIA I am at the mark, sir, I'll give aim to you,°
 And tell you how near you shoot.   25
LAWYER Most literated judges, please your lordships
 So to connive your judgements to the view°
 Of this debauched and diversivolent woman,
 Who such a black concatenation
 Of mischief hath effected, that to extirp   30
 The memory of't must be the consummation
 Of her and her projections.
VITTORIA   What's all this?
LAWYER Hold your peace.
 Exorbitant sins must have exulceration.
VITTORIA Surely, my lords, this lawyer here hath swallowed   35
 Some pothecary's bills, or proclamations.°
 And now the hard and undigestible words
 Come up like stones we use give hawks for physic.
 Why, this is Welsh to Latin.
LAWYER   My lords, the woman
 Knows not her tropes nor figures, nor is perfect°   40
 In the academic derivation
 Of grammatical elocution.

FRANCISCO   Sir, your pains
  Shall be well spared, and your deep eloquence
  Be worthily applauded amongst those
  Which understand you.
LAWYER   My good lord.
FRANCISCO (*speaks this as in scorn*)   Sir,   45
  Put up your papers in your fustian bag—°
  Cry mercy, sir, 'tis buckram—and accept,
  My notion of your learn'd verbosity.
LAWYER I most graduatically thank your lordship.
  I shall have use for them elsewhere.   50
      [*Exit Lawyer*]
MONTICELSO I shall be plainer with you, and paint out
  Your follies in more natural red and white
  Than that upon your cheek.
VITTORIA   O you mistake.
  You raise a blood as noble in this cheek
  As ever was your mother's.   55
MONTICELSO I must spare you till proof cry whore to that.
  Observe this creature here, my honoured lords,
  A woman of a most prodigious spirit
  In her effected.
VITTORIA   Honourable my lord,°
  It doth not suit a reverend Cardinal   60
  To play the lawyer thus.
MONTICELSO O your trade instructs your language!
  You see, my lords, what goodly fruit she seems;
  Yet like those apples travellers report
  To grow where Sodom and Gomorrah stood,   65
  I will but touch her and you straight shall see
  She'll fall to soot and ashes.
VITTORIA   Your envenomed°
  Pothecary should do't.
MONTICELSO   I am resolved°
  Were there a second paradise to lose°
  This devil would betray it.
VITTORIA   O poor charity,   70
  Thou art seldom found in scarlet.°
MONTICELSO Who knows not how, when several night by night
  Her gates were choked with coaches, and her rooms
  Outbraved the stars with several kind of lights,

When she did counterfeit a prince's court?   75
In music, banquets and most riotous surfeits
This whore, forsooth, was holy.
VITTORIA   Ha? Whore? What's that?
MONTICELSO Shall I expound whore to you? Sure I shall,
  I'll give their perfect character. They are first,°
  Sweet-meats which rot the eater; in man's nostril   80
  Poisoned perfumes. They are cozening alchemy,
  Shipwrecks in calmest weather! What are whores?
  Cold Russian winters, that appear so barren,
  As if that nature had forgot the spring.
  They are the true material fire of hell,°   85
  Worse than those tributes i'th' Low Countries paid,°
  Exactions upon meat, drink, garments, sleep;
  Ay, even on man's perdition, his sin.°
  They are those brittle evidences of law
  Which forfeit all a wretched man's estate   90
  For leaving out one syllable. What are whores?
  They are those flattering bells have all one tune,
  At weddings, and at funerals; your rich whores
  Are only treasuries by extortion filled,
  And emptied by cursed riot. They are worse,   95
  Worse than dead bodies, which are begged at gallows
  And wrought upon by surgeons to teach man
  Wherein he is imperfect. What's a whore?°
  She's like the guilty counterfeited coin
  Which, whosoe'er first stamps it, brings in trouble   100
  All that receive it.
VITTORIA   This character scapes me.
MONTICELSO You, gentlewoman?
  Take from all beasts, and from all minerals,
  Their deadly poison.
VITTORIA   Well, what then?
MONTICELSO   I'll tell thee;
  I'll find in thee a pothecary's shop   105
  To sample them all.
FRENCH AMBASSADOR [aside] She hath lived ill.
ENGLISH AMBASSADOR [aside] True, but the Cardinal's too bitter.
MONTICELSO You know what whore is: next the devil, Adult'ry,
  Enters the devil, Murder.
FRANCISCO   Your unhappy

Husband is dead.

VITTORIA　　　　　　O he's a happy husband　　110
Now he owes nature nothing.°

FRANCISCO And by a vaulting engine.

MONTICELSO　　　　　　　　An active plot:
He jumped into his grave.

FRANCISCO　　　　　　What a prodigy was't
That from some two yards' height a slender man
Should break his neck!

MONTICELSO　　　　　I'th'rushes.

FRANCISCO　　　　　　　And what's more,°　　115
Upon the instant lose all use of speech,
All vital motion, like a man had lain
Wound up three days. Now mark each circumstance.°

MONTICELSO And look upon this creature was his wife.
She comes not like a widow; she comes arm'd　　120
With scorn and impudence: is this a mourning habit?

VITTORIA Had I foreknown his death as you suggest,
I would have bespoke my mourning.

MONTICELSO O you are cunning.

VITTORIA You shame your wit and judgement　　125
To call it so, What, is my just defence
By him that is my judge called impudence?
Let me appeal then from this Christian court°
To the uncivil Tartar.

MONTICELSO　　　　　See, my lords,
She scandals our proceedings.

VITTORIA [bowing]　　　　　Humbly thus,　　130
Thus low, to the most worthy and respected
Lieger ambassadors, my modesty
And womanhood I tender; but withal
So entangled in a cursèd accusation
That my defence of force, like Perseus,　　135
Must personate masculine virtue. To the point!°
Find me but guilty, sever head from body—
We'll part good friends. I scorn to hold my life
At yours or any man's entreaty, sir.

ENGLISH AMBASSADOR She hath a brave spirit.　　140

MONTICELSO Well, well, such counterfeit jewels
Make true ones oft suspected.

VITTORIA　　　　　　You are deceived;

For know that all your strict-combinèd heads,
Which strike against this mine of diamonds,
Shall prove but glassen hammers: they shall break.   145
These are but feignèd shadows of my evils.
Terrify babes, my lord, with painted devils;
I am past such needless palsy. For your names
Of whore and murd'ress, they proceed from you,
As if a man should spit against the wind,   150
The filth returns in's face.
MONTICELSO Pray you, mistress, satisfy me one question:
Who lodged beneath your roof that fatal night
Your husband brake his neck?
BRACCIANO   That question
Enforceth me break silence: I was there.   155
MONTICELSO Your business?
BRACCIANO   Why, I came to comfort her,
And take some course for settling her estate,
Because I heard her husband was in debt
To you, my lord.
MONTICELSO   He was.
BRACCIANO   And 'twas strangely feared
That you would cozen her.
MONTICELSO   Who made you overseer?   160
BRACCIANO Why, my charity, my charity, which should flow
From every generous and noble spirit
To orphans and to widows.
MONTICELSO   Your lust.
BRACCIANO Cowardly dogs bark loudest. Sirrah priest,
I'll talk with you hereafter. Do you hear?   165
The sword you frame of such an excellent temper,°
I'll sheathe in your own bowels.
There are a number of thy coat resemble
Your common post-boys.
MONTICELSO   Ha?
BRACCIANO [preparing to leave] Your mercenary post-boys.
Your letters carry truth, but 'tis your guise   170
To fill your mouths with gross and impudent lies.
SERVANT My lord, your gown.
BRACCIANO   Thou liest, 'twas my stool.
Bestow't upon thy master that will challenge
The rest o'th' household stuff, for Bracciano

Was ne'er so beggarly to take a stool   175
Out of another's lodging. Let him make
Valance for his bed on't, or a demi-footcloth
For his most reverend mule. Monticelso,
Nemo me impune lacessit.°
    Exit Bracciano

MONTICELSO Your champion's gone.

VITTORIA   The wolf may prey the better. 180

FRANCISCO My lord, there's great suspicion of the murder,
  But no sound proof who did it. For my part
  I do not think she hath a soul so black
  To act a deed so bloody. If she have,
  As in cold countries husbandmen plant vines,   185
  And with warm blood manure them, even so
  One summer she will bear unsavoury fruit,
  And ere next spring wither both branch and root.
  The act of blood let pass, only descend
  To matter of incontinence.

VITTORIA   I discern poison   190
  Under your gilded pills.

MONTICELSO Now the Duke's gone, I will produce a letter,
  Wherein 'twas plotted he and you should meet,
  At an apothecary's summer-house,
  Down by the river Tiber (view't, my lords),   195
  Where after wanton bathing and the heat
  Of a lascivious banquet—I pray read it,
  I shame to speak the rest.

VITTORIA [*passes the letter round*] Grant I was tempted,
  Temptation to lust proves not the act;
  Casta est quam nemo rogavit.°   200
  You read his hot love to me, but you want
  My frosty answer.

MONTICELSO   Frost i'th'dog-days! Strange!

VITTORIA Condemn you me for that the Duke did love me?
  So may you blame some fair and crystal river
  For that some melancholic distracted man   205
  Hath drown'd himself in't.

MONTICELSO   Truly drowned indeed.

VITTORIA Sum up my faults I pray, and you shall find
  That beauty and gay clothes, a merry heart,
  And a good stomach to a feast, are all,

All the poor crimes that you can charge me with.   210
In faith, my lord, you might go pistol flies,°
The sport would be more noble.
MONTICELSO   Very good.
VITTORIA But take you your course, it seems you have beggared
    me first
And now would fain undo me. I have houses,
Jewels, and a poor remnant of crusadoes;   215
Would those would make you charitable.
MONTICELSO   If the devil
Did ever take good shape, behold his picture.°
VITTORIA You have one virtue left:
You will not flatter me.
FRANCISCO   Who brought this letter?
VITTORIA I am not compelled to tell you.   220
MONTICELSO My lord Duke sent to you a thousand ducats,°
The twelfth of August.
VITTORIA   'Twas to keep your cousin
From prison; I paid use for't.
MONTICELSO   I rather think
'Twas interest for his lust.
VITTORIA Who says so but yourself? If you be my accuser   225
Pray cease to be my judge; come from the bench,
Give in your evidence 'gainst me, and let these
Be moderators. My lord Cardinal,
Were your intelligencing ears as long
As to my thoughts, had you an honest tongue°   230
I would not care though you proclaimed them all.
MONTICELSO Go to, go to.
After your goodly and vainglorious banquet,
I'll give you a choke-pear.
VITTORIA   O' your own grafting?
MONTICELSO You were born in Venice, honourably descended   235
From the Vitelli. 'Twas my cousin's fate—°
Ill may I name the hour—to marry you;
He bought you of your father.
VITTORIA   Ha?
MONTICELSO He spent there in six months
Twelve thousand ducats, and to my acquaintance   240
Received in dowry with you not one julio.
'Twas a hard pennyworth, the ware being so light.

I yet but draw the curtain.° Now to your picture:
You came from thence a most notorious strumpet,
And so you have continued.
VITTORIA   My lord.
MONTICELSO   Nay, hear me,   245
You shall have time to prate. My Lord Bracciano—
Alas I make but repetition
Of what is ordinary and Rialto talk,°
And balladed, and would be played o'th'stage,
But that vice many times finds such loud friends   250
That preachers are charmed silent.
You gentlemen, Flamineo and Marcello,
The court hath nothing now to charge you with;
Only you must remain upon your sureties°
For your appearance.
FRANCISCO   I stand for Marcello.   255
FLAMINEO And my lord Duke for me.
MONTICELSO For you, Vittoria, your public fault,
Joined to th'condition of the present time,
Takes from you all the fruits of noble pity.
Such a corrupted trial have you made   260
Both of your life and beauty, and been styled
No less in ominous fate than blazing stars
To princes. Here's your sentence: you are confin'd°
Unto a house of convertites, and your bawd—
FLAMINEO [aside] Who, I?
MONTICELSO   The Moor.
FLAMINEO [aside]   O, I am a sound man again. 265
VITTORIA A house of convertites, what's that?
MONTICELSO   A house
Of penitent whores.
VITTORIA   Do the noblemen in Rome
Erect it for their wives, that I am sent
To lodge there?
FRANCISCO You must have patience.
VITTORIA   I must first have vengeance. 270
I fain would know if you have your salvation
By patent, that you proceed thus.
MONTICELSO   Away with her.°
Take her hence.
VITTORIA A rape, a rape!

MONTICELSO   How?

VITTORIA   Yes, you have ravished justice,
   Forced her to do your pleasure.

MONTICELSO   Fie, she's mad.   275

VITTORIA Die with those pills in your most cursèd maw,
   Should bring you health, or while you sit o'th' bench,
   Let your own spittle choke you.

MONTICELSO   She's turned fury.

VITTORIA That the last day of judgement may so find you,
   And leave you the same devil you were before.   280
   Instruct me some good horse-leech to speak treason,
   For since you cannot take my life for deeds,
   Take it for words. O woman's poor revenge
   Which dwells but in the tongue. I will not weep.°
   No, I do scorn to call up one poor tear   285
   To fawn on your injustice. Bear me hence,
   Unto this house of—what's your mitigating title?

MONTICELSO Of convertites.

VITTORIA It shall not be a house of convertites.
   My mind shall make it honester to me   290
   Than the Pope's palace, and more peaceable
   Than thy soul, though thou art a cardinal.
   Know this, and let it somewhat raise your spite:
   Through darkness diamonds spread their richest light.
        Exit Vittoria [guarded]. Enter Bracciano

BRACCIANO Now you and I are friends, sir, we'll shake hands,   295
   In a friend's grave together, a fit place,
   Being the emblem of soft peace t'atone our hatred.

FRANCISCO Sir, what's the matter?

BRACCIANO I will not chase more blood from that loved cheek;
   You have lost too much already. Fare you well.   300
        [*Exit Bracciano.*]

FRANCISCO How strange these words sound. What's the interpreta-
      tion?

FLAMINEO [*aside*] Good, this is a preface to the discovery of the
   Duchess' death; he carries it well. Because now I cannot counterfeit a whining passion for the death of my lady, I will feign a mad
   humour for the disgrace of my sister, and that will keep off idle   305
   questions. Treason's tongue hath a villainous palsy in't;° I will
   talk to any man, hear no man, and for a time appear a politic
   madman.

[Exit Flamineo]. Enter Giovanni, Count Lodovico

FRANCISCO How now, my noble cousin? What, in black?

GIOVANNI Yes, uncle, I was taught to imitate you   310
    In virtue, and you must imitate me
    In colours for your garments. My sweet mother
    Is—

FRANCISCO How? Where?

GIOVANNI Is there, no yonder; indeed, sir, I'll not tell you,   315
    For I shall make you weep.

FRANCISCO Is dead.

GIOVANNI   Do not blame me now,
    I did not tell you so.

LODOVICO   She's dead, my lord.

FRANCISCO Dead?

MONTICELSO Blessèd lady, thou art now above thy woes.   320
    Wilt please your lordships to withdraw a little?
        [Exeunt Ambassadors]

GIOVANNI What do the dead do, uncle? Do they eat,
    Hear music, go a-hunting, and be merry,
    As we that live?

FRANCISCO No, coz, they sleep.

GIOVANNI   Lord, Lord, that I were dead;   325
    I have not slept these six nights. When do they wake?

FRANCISCO When God shall please.

GIOVANNI   Good God let her sleep ever,
    For I have known her wake an hundred nights,
    When all the pillow, where she laid her head,
    Was brine-wet with her tears.   330
    I am to complain to you, sir.
    I'll tell you how they have used her now she's dead:
    They wrapped her in a cruel fold of lead,
    And would not let me kiss her.

FRANCISCO   Thou didst love her.

GIOVANNI I have often heard her say she gave me suck,   335
    And it should seem by that she dearly loved me,
    Since princes seldom do it.

FRANCISCO O, all of my poor sister that remains!
    Take him away for God's sake.
        [Exit Giovanni with Lodovico]

MONTICELSO How now, my lord?   340

FRANCISCO Believe me, I am nothing but her grave,

And I shall keep her blessèd memory
Longer than thousand epitaphs.
      [*Exeunt*]

[3.3]

Enter Flamineo as distracted, [Marcello, and Lodovico,
unobserved by either]

FLAMINEO We endure the strokes like anvils or hard steel,
Till pain itself make us no pain to feel.
Who shall do me right now? Is this the end of service?
I'd rather go weed garlic; travel through France, and be mine own
ostler; wear sheepskin linings, or shoes that stink of blacking; be   5
entered into the list of the forty thousand pedlars in Poland.°
      Enter Savoy [Ambassador]
Would I had rotted in some surgeon's house at Venice, built upon
the pox as well as on piles,° ere I had served Bracciano.

SAVOY AMBASSADOR You must have comfort.

FLAMINEO Your comfortable words are like honey. They relish well   10
in your mouth that's whole; but in mine that's wounded they go
down as if the sting of the bee were in them. O they have wrought
their purpose cunningly, as if they would not seem to do it of
malice. In this a politician imitates the devil, as the devil imitates
a cannon. Wheresoever he comes to do mischief, he comes with   15
his backside towards you.
      Enter the French [Ambassador]

FRENCH AMBASSADOR The proofs are evident.

FLAMINEO Proof! 'Twas corruption. O gold, what a god art thou!
And O man, what a devil art thou to be tempted by that cursed
mineral! Yon diversivolent lawyer, mark him; knaves turn in-   20
formers, as maggots turn to flies: you may catch gudgeons with
either. A Cardinal! I would he would hear me: there's nothing
so holy but money will corrupt and putrify it, like victual under
the line.°
      Enter English Ambassador
You are happy in England, my lord; here they sell justice with   25
those weights they press men to death with.° O horrible salary!

ENGLISH AMBASSADOR Fie, fie, Flamineo.

FLAMINEO Bells ne'er ring well, till they are at their full pitch, and
I hope yon Cardinal shall never have the grace to pray well, till he
come to the scaffold.   30
        [*Exeunt Ambassadors*]
If they were racked now to know the confederacy! But your
noblemen are privileged from the rack; and well may.° For a little
thing would pull some of them i'pieces afore they came to their
arraignment. Religion! O how it is commeddled with policy. The
first bloodshed in the world happened about religion.° Would I   35
were a Jew.
MARCELLO O, there are too many.
FLAMINEO You are deceived. There are not Jews enough, priests
enough, nor gentlemen enough.
MARCELLO How?   40
FLAMINEO I'll prove it. For if there were Jews enough, so many
Christians would not turn usurers; if priests enough, one should
not have six benefices; and if gentlemen enough, so many early
mushrooms, whose best growth sprang from a dunghill, should
not aspire to gentility. Farewell. Let others live by begging. Be   45
thou one of them. Practise the art of Wolner° in England to
swallow all's given thee; and yet let one purgation make thee as
hungry again as fellows that work in a sawpit. I'll go hear the
screech-owl.°
        Exit [*Flamineo*]
LODOVICO [*aside*] This was Bracciano's pander, and 'tis strange   50
That in such open and apparent guilt
Of his adulterous sister, he dare utter
So scandalous a passion. I must wind him.
        Enter Flamineo,
FLAMINEO [*aside*] How dares this banished count return to Rome,
His pardon not yet purchased? I have heard   55
The deceasèd Duchess gave him pension,
And that he came along from Padua
I'th'train of the young prince. There's somewhat in't.
Physicians that cure poisons still do work
With counterpoisons.
MARCELLO [*aside*]   Mark this strange encounter.   60
FLAMINEO The god of melancholy turn thy gall to poison,
And let the stigmatic wrinkles in thy face,
Like to the boisterous waves in a rough tide,
One still overtake another.

LODOVICO   I do thank thee,
And I do wish ingeniously for thy sake   65
The dog-days all year long.
FLAMINEO   How croaks the raven?
Is our good Duchess dead?
LODOVICO   Dead.
FLAMINEO   O fate!
Misfortune comes like the coroner's business,
Huddle upon huddle.
LODOVICO Shalt thou and I join housekeeping?
FLAMINEO   Yes, content.   70
Let's be unsociably sociable.
LODOVICO Sit some three days together, and discourse.
FLAMINEO Only with making faces;
Lie in our clothes.
LODOVICO With faggots for our pillows.
FLAMINEO   And be lousy.   75
LODOVICO In taffeta linings: that's gentle melancholy;
Sleep all day.
FLAMINEO   Yes, and like your melancholic hare°
Feed after midnight.
          *Enter Antonelli [with Lodovico's pardon, and Gasparo, both
          laughing]*
We are observed: see how yon couple grieve.°
LODOVICO What a strange creature is a laughing fool,   80
As if man were created to no use
But only to show his teeth.
FLAMINEO   I'll tell thee what:
It would do well instead of looking-glasses,
To set one's face each morning by a saucer
Of a witch's congealèd blood.
LODOVICO   Precious girn, rogue.°   85
We'll never part.
FLAMINEO Never: till the beggary of courtiers,
The discontent of churchmen, want of soldiers,
And all the creatures that hang manacled,
Worse than strappadoed, on the lowest felly°   90
Of fortune's wheel be taught in our two lives
To scorn that world which life of means deprives.
ANTONELLI My lord, I bring good news. The Pope on's death-bed,
At the earnest suit of the Great Duke of Florence,

Hath signed your pardon, and restored unto you—   95
LODOVICO I thank you for your news. Look up again,
 Flamineo, see my pardon.
FLAMINEO   Why do you laugh?
 There was no such condition in our covenant.
LODOVICO   Why?
FLAMINEO You shall not seem a happier man than I.
 You know our vow, sir: if you will be merry,   100
 Do it i'th' like posture, as if some great man
 Sat while his enemy were executed:
 Though it be very lechery unto thee,
 Do't with a crabbèd politician's face.
LODOVICO Your sister is a damnable whore.
FLAMINEO   Ha?   105
LODOVICO Look you, I spake that laughing.
FLAMINEO Dost ever think to speak again?
LODOVICO   Do you hear?
 Wilt sell me forty ounces of her blood
 To water a mandrake?
FLAMINEO   Poor lord, you did vow
 To live a lousy creature.
LODOVICO   Yes.
FLAMINEO   Like one   110
 That had for ever forfeited the daylight,
 By being in debt.
LODOVICO   Ha, ha!
FLAMINEO I do not greatly wonder you do break:
 Your lordship learnt long since. But I'll tell you—
LODOVICO What?
FLAMINEO   And't shall stick by you.
LODOVICO   I long for it.   115
FLAMINEO This laughter scurvily becomes your face.
 If you will not be melancholy, be angry.
   Strikes him
 See, now I laugh too.
MARCELLO [*to Flamineo*] You are to blame; I'll force you hence.
   [*Marcello hustles Flamineo out, while Antonelli and Gasparo*
   restrain Lodovico]
LODOVICO   Unhand me!
   Exeunt Marcello and Flamineo
 That e'er I should be forced to right myself   120

Upon a pander.

ANTONELLI   My lord.

LODOVICO He'd been as good met with his fist a thunderbolt.

GASPARO How this shows!

LODOVICO   Ud's death, how did my sword miss him?
These rogues that are most weary of their lives
Still scape the greatest dangers.   125
A pox upon him. All his reputation,
Nay all the goodness of his family,
Is not worth half his earthquake.
I learnt it of no fencer to shake thus.°
Come, I'll forget him, and go drink some wine.   130

    [Exeunt]

[4.1]

Enter Francisco and Monticelso

MONTICELSO Come, come, my lord, untie your folded thoughts,
And let them dangle loose as a bride's hair.°
Your sister's poisoned.

FRANCISCO   Far be it from my thoughts
To seek revenge.

MONTICELSO   What, are you turned all marble?

FRANCISCO Shall I defy him, and impose a war   5
Most burdensome on my poor subjects' necks,
Which at my will I have not power to end?
You know, for all the murders, rapes, and thefts,
Committed in the horrid lust of war,
He that unjustly caused it first proceed.   10
Shall find it in his grave and in his seed.

MONTICELSO That's not the course I'd wish you. Pray, observe
   me.
We see that undermining more prevails
Than doth the cannon. Bear your wrongs concealed,°
And, patient as the tortoise, let this camel   15
Stalk o'er your back unbruised; sleep with the lion,°
And let this brood of secure foolish mice
Play with your nostrils, till the time be ripe
For th'bloody audit, and the fatal gripe.
Aim like a cunning fowler, close one eye,   20
That you the better may your game espy.

FRANCISCO Free me, my innocence, from treacherous acts.
I know there's thunder yonder; and I'll stand
Like a safe valley, which low bends the knee
To some aspiring mountain, since I know   25
Treason, like spiders weaving nets for flies,
By her foul work is found, and in it dies.
To pass away these thoughts, my honoured lord,
It is reported you possess a book
Wherein you have quoted, by intelligence,   30
The names of all notorious offenders
Lurking about the city.

MONTICELSO   Sir, I do;

And some there are which call it my black book.°
Well may the title hold, for though it teach not
The art of conjuring, yet in it lurk   35
The names of many devils.
FRANCISCO   Pray let's see it.
MONTICELSO I'll fetch it to your lordship.
        Exit Monticelso
FRANCISCO   Monticelso,
I will not trust thee, but in all my plots
I'll rest as jealous as a town besieged.
Thou canst not reach what I intend to act.°   40
Your flax soon kindles, soon is out again,
But gold slow heats, and long will hot remain.
        Enter Monticelso, [who] presents Francisco with a book
MONTICELSO 'Tis here, my lord.
FRANCISCO First, your intelligencers; pray let's see.
MONTICELSO Their number rises strangely, and some of them   45
    You'd take for honest men.
                        [*Turning the pages*] Next are panders.
These are your pirates; and these following leaves
For base rogues that undo young gentlemen
By taking up commodities; for politic bankrupts;°
For fellows that are bawds to their own wives,   50
Only to put off horses and slight jewels,
Clocks, defaced plate, and such commodities,
At birth of their first children.
FRANCISCO   Are there such?°
MONTICELSO These are for impudent bawds
That go in men's apparel; for usurers   55
That share with scriveners for their good reportage;°
For lawyers that will antedate their writs;°
And some divines you might find folded there
But that I slip them o'er for conscience' sake.
Here is a general catalogue of knaves.   60
A man might study all the prisons o'er,
Yet never attain this knowledge.
FRANCISCO   Murderers.
Fold down the leaf, I pray.
Good my lord, let me borrow this strange doctrine.
MONTICELSO Pray use't, my lord.
FRANCISCO   I do assure your lordship,   65

You are a worthy member of the state,
And have done infinite good in your discovery
Of these offenders.
MONTICELSO   Somewhat, sir.
FRANCISCO   O God!
Better than tribute of wolves paid in England;°
'Twill hang their skins o'th' hedge.
MONTICELSO   I must make bold°   70
To leave your lordship.
FRANCISCO   Dearly, sir, I thank you.
If any ask for me at court, report
You have left me in the company of knaves.
          Exit Monticelso
I gather now by this, some cunning fellow
That's my lord's officer, one that lately skipped   75
From a clerk's desk up to a justice' chair,
Hath made this knavish summons, and intends,
As the Irish rebels wont were to sell heads,
So to make prize of these. And thus it happens°
Your poor rogues pay for't, which have not the means   80
To present bribe in fist; the rest o'th' band
Are razed out of the knaves' record, or else
My lord he winks at them with easy will,
His man grows rich, the knaves are the knaves still.
But to the use I'll make of it: it shall serve   85
To point me out a list of murderers,
Agents for any villainy. Did I want
Ten leash of courtezans, it would furnish me,
Nay, laundress three armies. That in so little paper,°
Should lie the undoing of so many men!   90
'Tis not so big as twenty declarations.
See the corrupted use some make of books:
Divinity, wrested by some factious blood,
Draws swords, swells battles, and o'erthrows all good.
To fashion my revenge more seriously,   95
Let me remember my dead sister's face.
Call for her picture? No, I'll close mine eyes,
And in a melancholic thought I'll frame
Her figure 'fore me.
          Enter Isabella's Ghost
                    Now I ha't. How strong

Imagination works! How she can frame   100
Things which are not! Methinks she stands afore me,
And by the quick idea of my mind,
Were my skill pregnant, I could draw her picture.
Thought, as a subtle juggler, makes us deem
Things supernatural which have cause   105
Common as sickness. 'Tis my melancholy.°
How cam'st thou by thy death? How idle am I
To question mine own idleness. Did ever
Man dream awake till now? Remove this object,
Out of my brain with't. What have I to do   110
With tombs, or death-beds, funerals, or tears,
That have to meditate upon revenge?
        [*Exit Ghost*]
So now 'tis ended, like an old wives' story.
Statesmen think often they see stranger sights
Than madmen. Come, to this weighty business.   115
My tragedy must have some idle mirth in't,
Else it will never pass. I am in love,
In love with Corombona; and my suit
Thus halts to her in verse.
        He writes
I have done it rarely. O the fate of princes!   120
I am so used to frequent flattery
That, being alone, I now flatter myself;
But it will serve, 'tis sealed.
        Enter Servant
                    Bear this
To the house of convertites; and watch your leisure
To give it to the hands of Corombona,   125
Or to the matron, when some followers
Of Bracciano may be by. Away.
        Exit Servant
He that deals all by strength, his wit is shallow:
When a man's head goes through, each limb will follow.°
The engine for my business, bold Count Lodovic.   130
'Tis gold must such an instrument procure,
With empty fist no man doth falcons lure.
Bracciano, I am now fit for thy encounter.
Like the wild Irish I'll ne'er think thee dead,
Till I can play at football with thy head.   135

Flectere si nequeo superos, Acheronta movebo.°
     Exit

[4.2]

     Enter the Matron, and Flamineo
MATRON Should it be known the Duke hath such recourse°
     To your imprisoned sister, I were like
     T'incur much damage by it.
FLAMINEO   Not a scruple.
     The Pope lies on his death-bed, and their heads°
     Are troubled now with other business   5
     Than guarding of a lady.
          Enter [Francisco's] Servant
SERVANT [*aside*] Yonder's Flamineo in conference
     With the matrona. [*To the Matron*] Let me speak with you.
     I would entreat you to deliver for me
     This letter to the fair Vittoria.   10
MATRON I shall, sir.
          Enter Bracciano
SERVANT   With all care and secrecy.
     Hereafter you shall know me, and receive
     Thanks for this courtesy.
          [*Exit Servant*]
FLAMINEO   How now? What's that?
MATRON A letter.
FLAMINEO   To my sister. I'll see't delivered.
          [*Exit Matron*]
BRACCIANO What's that you read, Flamineo?
FLAMINEO   Look.   15
BRACCIANO Ha? [*Reads*] 'To the most unfortunate his best respected
     Vittoria'
     Who was the messenger?
FLAMINEO   I know not.
BRACCIANO No! Who sent it?
FLAMINEO   Ud's foot, you speak as if a man
     Should know what fowl is coffined in a baked meat°   20
     Afore you cut it up.
BRACCIANO I'll open't, were't her heart. What's here subscribed?

55

'Florence'? This juggling is gross and palpable.
I have found out the conveyance. Read it, read it.
FLAMINEO 'Your tears I'll turn to triumphs, be but mine.   25
 Your prop is fall'n. I pity that a vine
 Which princess heretofore have longed to gather,
 Wanting supporters, now should fade and wither.'
 Wine i'faith, my lord, with lees would serve his turn.
 'Your sad imprisonment I'll soon uncharm,   30
 And with a princely uncontrollèd arm
 Lead you to Florence, where my love and care
 Shall hang your wishes in my silver hair.'
 A halter on his strange equivocation!°
 'Nor for my years return me the sad willow,°   35
 Who prefer blossoms before fruit that's mellow?'
 Rotten, on my knowledge, with lying too long i'th' bed-straw.°
 'And all the lines of age this line convinces:°
 The gods never wax old, no more do princes.'
 A pox on't! Tear it, let's have no more atheists for God's° sake.   40
BRACCIANO Ud's death, I'll cut her into atomies
 And let th'irregular north-wind sweep her up
 And blow her int' his nostrils. Where's this whore?
FLAMINEO That——! what do you call her?
BRACCIANO   O, I could be mad,
 Prevent the cursed disease she'll bring me to,   45
 And tear my hair off. Where's this changeable stuff?°
FLAMINEO O'er head and ears in water, I assure you.
 She is not for your wearing.
BRACCIANO   In, you pander!°
FLAMINEO What, me, my lord, am I your dog?
BRACCIANO A bloodhound. Do you brave? Do you stand me?   50
FLAMINEO Stand you? Let those that have diseases run;
 I need no plasters.
BRACCIANO Would you be kicked?
FLAMINEO   Would you have your neck broke?
 I tell you, Duke, I am not in Russia;°
 My shins must be kept whole.
BRACCIANO   Do you know me?   55
FLAMINEO O, my lord, methodically.
 As in this world there are degrees of evils,
 So in this world there are degrees of devils.
 You're a great duke, I your poor secretary.

I do look now for a Spanish fig, or an Italian salad daily.°   60

BRACCIANO Pander, ply your convoy,° and leave your prating.

FLAMINEO All your kindness to me is like that miserable courtesy of
    Polyphemus to Ulysses:° you reserve me to be devoured last. You
    would dig turves out of my grave to feed your larks: that would
    be music to you. Come, I'll lead you to her.   65

BRACCIANO Do you face me?°

FLAMINEO O, sir, I would not go before a politic enemy with my
    back towards him, though there were behind me a whirlpool.
       Enter Vittoria to Bracciano and Flamineo
       [*Bracciano hands her the letter*]

BRACCIANO Can you read, mistress? Look upon that letter;
    There are no characters nor hieroglyphics.°   70
    You need no comment; I am grown your receiver.°
    God's precious, you shall be a brave great lady,
    A stately and advancèd whore.

VITTORIA   Say, sir?

BRACCIANO Come, come, let's see your cabinet, discover
    Your treasury of love-letters. Death and furies,   75
    I'll see them all.

VITTORIA   Sir, upon my soul,
    I have not any. Whence was this directed?

BRACCIANO Confusion on your politic ignorance!
    [*Gives her the letter*]
    You are reclaimèd, are you? I'll give you the bells°
    And let you fly to the devil.

FLAMINEO   Ware hawk, my lord.°   80

VITTORIA [*reads*] 'Florence'! This is some treacherous plot, my
    lord.
    To me he ne'er was lovely, I protest,
    So much as in my sleep.

BRACCIANO   Right: they are plots.
    Your beauty! O, ten thousand curses on't.
    How long have I beheld the devil in crystal?°   85
    Thou hast led me, like an heathen sacrifice,
    With music, and with fatal yokes of flowers
    To my eternal ruin. Woman to man
    Is either a god or a wolf.

VITTORIA   My lord—

BRACCIANO   Away.
    We'll be as differing as two adamants: 90

The one shall shun the other. What? dost weep?
Procure but ten of thy dissembling trade,
Ye'ld furnish all the Irish funerals
With howling, past wild Irish.
FLAMINEO   Fie, my lord.°
BRACCIANO That hand, that cursèd hand, which I have wearied   95
With doting kisses! O my sweetest Duchess,
How lovely art thou now! [*To Vittoria*] Thy loose thoughts
Scatter like quicksilver. I was bewitched,°
For all the world speaks ill of thee.
VITTORIA   No matter.
I'll live so now I'll make that world recant   100
And change her speeches. You did name your Duchess.
BRACCIANO Whose death God pardon.
VITTORIA   Whose death God revenge
On thee, most godless Duke.
FLAMINEO [*aside*] Now for two whirlwinds.
VITTORIA What have I gained by thee but infamy?   105
Thou hast stained the spotless honour of my house,
And frighted thence noble society;
Like those which, sick o'th' palsy and retain
Ill-scenting foxes 'bout them, are still shunned°
By those of choicer nostrils. What do you call this house?   110
Is this your palace? Did not the judge style it
A house of penitent whores? Who sent me to it?
Who hath the honour to advance Vittoria
To this incontinent college? Is't not you?
Is't not your high preferment? Go, go brag   115
How many ladies you have undone, like me.
Fare you well, sir; let me hear no more of you.
I had a limb corrupted to an ulcer,°
But I have cut it off; and now I'll go
Weeping to heaven on crutches. For your gifts,   120
I will return them all; and I do wish
That I could make you full executor
To all my sins. O that I could toss myself
Into a grave as quickly. For all thou art worth,
I'll not shed one tear more; I'll burst first.   125
          She throws herself upon a bed
BRACCIANO I have drunk Lethe. Vittoria?
My dearest happiness? Vittoria?

What do you ail, my love? Why do you weep?
VITTORIA Yes, I now weep poniards, do you see?°
BRACCIANO Are not those matchless eyes mine?
VITTORIA   I had rather   130
  They were not matches.
BRACCIANO   Is not this lip mine?°
VITTORIA Yes: thus to bite it off, rather than give it thee.
FLAMINEO Turn to my lord, good sister.
VITTORIA   Hence, you pander.
FLAMINEO Pander! Am I the author of your sin?
VITTORIA Yes: he's a base thief that a thief lets in.   135
FLAMINEO We're blown up, my lord.
BRACCIANO   Wilt thou hear me?°
  Once to be jealous of thee is t'express
  That I will love thee everlastingly,
  And never more be jealous.
VITTORIA   O thou fool,
  Whose greatness hath by much o'ergrown thy wit!   140
  What dar'st thou do that I not dare to suffer,
  Excepting to be still thy whore? For that,
  In the sea's bottom sooner thou shalt make
  A bonfire.
FLAMINEO   O, no oaths for God's sake.
BRACCIANO Will you hear me?
VITTORIA   Never.   145
FLAMINEO What a damned imposthume is a woman's will?
  Can nothing break it? Fie, fie, my lord.
  [Whispers to Bracciano] Women are caught as you take tortoises,
  She must be turned on her back. [Aloud] Sister, by this hand
  I am on your side. Come, come, you have wronged her.   150
  What a strange credulous man were you, my lord,
  To think the Duke of Florence would love her?
  [Aside] Will any mercer take another's ware°
  When once 'tis toused and sullied? [Aloud] And yet, sister,
  How scurvily this frowardness becomes you!   155
  [To Bracciano] Young leverets stand not long; and women's anger°
  Should, like their flight, procure a little sport:°
  A full cry for a quarter of an hour,°
  And then be put to th'dead quat.
BRACCIANO   Shall these eyes,
  Which have so long time dwelt upon your face,   160

Be now put out?

FLAMINEO   No cruel landlady i'th' world,
Which lends forth groats to broom-men, and takes use for them,
Would do't.
[*Whispers to Bracciano*] Hand her, my lord, and kiss her. Be not
like°
A ferret to let go your hold with blowing.°   165

BRACCIANO Let us renew right hands.

VITTORIA   Hence.

BRACCIANO Never shall rage, or the forgetful wine,°
Make me commit like fault.

FLAMINEO [*whispers to Bracciano*] Now you are i'th' way on't,
follow't hard.

BRACCIANO Be thou at peace with me, let all the world   170
Threaten the cannon.

FLAMINEO   Mark his penitence.°
Best natures do commit the grossest faults,
When they're given o'er to jealousy, as best wine
Dying makes strongest vinegar. I'll tell you:
The sea's more rough and raging than calm rivers,   175
But nor so sweet nor wholesome. A quiet woman
Is a still water under a great bridge.
A man may shoot her safely.

VITTORIA O ye dissembling men!

FLAMINEO   We sucked that, sister,
From women's breasts, in our first infancy.   180

VITTORIA To add misery to misery.

BRACCIANO   Sweetest.

VITTORIA Am I not low enough?
Ay, ay, your good heart gathers like a snowball
Now your affection's cold.

FLAMINEO   Ud's foot, it shall melt
To a heart again, or all the wine in Rome   185
Shall run o'th' lees for't.

VITTORIA Your dog or hawk should be rewarded better
Than I have been. I'll speak not one word more.

FLAMINEO Stop her mouth with a sweet kiss, my lord.
    [*Bracciano and Vittoria kiss*]
[*aside*] So now the tide's turned, the vessel's come about.   190
He's a sweet armful. O we curled-haired men
Are still most kind to women. This is well.

BRACCIANO That you should chide thus!

FLAMINEO   O, sir, your little chimneys
Do ever cast most smoke. I sweat for you.
Couple together with as deep a silence   195
As did the Grecians in their wooden horse.
My lord, supply your promises with deeds;
You know that painted meat no hunger feeds.

BRACCIANO Stay—ingrateful Rome!°

FLAMINEO Rome! It deserves to be called Barbary, for our villainous   200
usage.

BRACCIANO Soft; the same project which the Duke of Florence
(Whether in love or gullery I know not)
Laid down for her escape, will I pursue.

FLAMINEO And no time fitter than this night, my lord: 205
The Pope being dead, and all the cardinals entered
The conclave for th'electing a new Pope,
The city in a great confusion,
We may attire her in a page's suit,
Lay her post-horse, take shipping, and amain°   210
For Padua.

BRACCIANO I'll instantly steal forth the Prince Giovanni,
And make for Padua. You two with your old mother
And young Marcello that attends on Florence,
If you can work him to it, follow me.°   215
I will advance you all. For you, Vittoria,
Think of a duchess' title.

FLAMINEO   Lo you, sister.
Stay, my lord, I'll tell you a tale. The crocodile, which lives in the
river Nilus, hath a worm breeds i'th' teeth of't, which puts it to
extreme anguish. A little bird, no bigger than a wren, is barber-   220
surgeon to this crocodile, flies into the jaws of't, picks out the
worm, and brings present remedy. The fish, glad of ease but
ingrateful to her that did it, that the bird may not talk largely of
her abroad for non-payment, closeth her chaps intending to
swallow her, and so put her to perpetual silence. But nature,   225
loathing such ingratitude, hath armed this bird with a quill or prick
on the head, top o'th' which wounds the crocodile i'th' mouth;
forceth her open her bloody prison; and away flies the pretty
tooth-picker from her cruel patient.

BRACCIANO Your application is, I have not rewarded°   230
The service you have done me.

FLAMINEO   No, my lord.
  You, sister, are the crocodile: you are blemished in your fame, my
  lord cures it. And though the comparison hold not in every
  particle, yet observe, remember, what good the bird with the prick
  i'th' head hath done you, and scorn ingratitude.   235
  [*Aside*] It may appear to some ridiculous
  Thus to talk knave and madman, and sometimes
  Come in with a dried sentence, stuffed with sage.
  But this allows my varying of shapes.
  Knaves do grow great by being great men's apes.   240
      Exeunt

[4.3]

      Enter Lodovico, Gasparo, and six Ambassadors. At another
      door [Francisco] the Duke of Florence
FRANCISCO So, my lord, I commend your diligence.
  Guard well the conclave, and, as the order is,
  Let none have conference with the cardinals.
LODOVICO I shall, my lord. Room for the ambassadors.
GASPARO They're wondrous brave today. Why do they wear   5
  These several habits?
LODOVICO   O sir, they're knights
  Of several orders.
  That lord i'th' black cloak with the silver cross
  Is Knight of Rhodes; the next Knight of St Michael;
  That of the Golden Fleece; the Frenchman there   10
  Knight of the Holy Ghost; my lord of Savoy
  Knight of th'Annunciation; the Englishman
  Is Knight of th'honoured Garter, dedicated°
  Unto their saint, St George. I could describe to you
  Their several institutions, with the laws   15
  Annexèd to their orders, but that time
  Permits not such discovery.
FRANCISCO   Where's Count Lodovic?
LODOVICO Here, my lord.
FRANCISCO   'Tis o'th' point of dinner time,
  Marshall the cardinals' service.
LODOVICO   Sir, I shall.

Enter Servants with several dishes covered

Stand, let me search your dish. Who's this for?   20

[FIRST] SERVANT For my Lord Cardinal Monticelso.

LODOVICO Who's this?

[SECOND] SERVANT   For my Lord Cardinal of Bourbon.

FRENCH AMBASSADOR Why doth he search the dishes? To observe
What meat is dressed?

ENGLISH AMBASSADOR No, sir, but to prevent,   25
Lest any letters should be conveyed in
To bribe or to solicit the advancement
Of any cardinal. When first they enter
'Tis lawful for the ambassadors of princes
To enter with them, and to make their suit   30
For any man their prince affecteth best;
But after, till a general election,
No man may speak with them.

LODOVICO You that attend on the lord cardinals
Open the window, and receive their viands.   35

    [*A Conclavist° appears at the window*]

CONCLAVIST You must return the service. The lord cardinals
Are busied 'bout electing of the Pope.
They have given o'er scrutiny, and are fallen°
To admiration.

    [*Conclavist exits*]

LODOVICO   Away, away.°

    [*Exeunt Servants*]

FRANCISCO I'll lay a thousand ducats you hear news   40
Of a Pope presently. Hark, sure he's elected.

    [*The*] Cardinal [*of Aragon appears*] *on the terrace.*

Behold! my lord of Aragon appears
On the church battlements.

ARAGON *Denuntio vobis gaudium magnum. Reverendissimus Cardinalis
Lorenzo de Monticelso electus est in sedem apostolicam, et elegit sibi*   45
nomen Paulum Quartum.

ALL *Vivat Sanctus Pater Paulus Quartus.°*

    [*Enter Servant*]

SERVANT Vittoria, my lord—

FRANCISCO   Well, what of her?

SERVANT Is fled the city.

FRANCISCO   Ha!

SERVANT   With Duke Bracciano.

FRANCISCO Fled? Where's the prince Giovanni?
SERVANT   Gone with his father.   50
FRANCISCO Let the matrona of the convertites
   Be apprehended. Fled? O damnable!
      [*Exit Servant*]
      [*Aside*] How fortunate are my wishes. Why, 'twas this
   I only laboured. I did send the letter
   T''instruct him what to do. Thy fame, fond duke,   55
   I first have poison'd; directed thee the way
   To marry a whore. What can be worse? This follows:
   The hand must act to drown the passionate tongue,
   I scorn to wear a sword and prate of wrong.
      Enter Monticelso in state [*as Pope Paul IV*]
MONTICELSO *Concedimus vobis apostolicam benedictionem et remissio-*   60
   nem peccatorum.°
      [*Francisco whispers to him*]
   My lord reports Vittoria Corombona
   Is stol'n from forth the house of convertites
   By Bracciano, and they're fled the city.
   Now, though this be the first day of our seat,°   65
   We cannot better please the divine power
   Than to sequester from the holy church
   These cursèd persons. Make it therefore known
   We do denounce excommunication
   Against them both. All that are theirs in Rome   70
   We likewise banish. Set on.
      Exeunt [*all except Francisco and Lodovico*]
FRANCISCO Come, dear Lodovico,
   You have ta'en the sacrament to prosecute
   Th'intended murder.
LODOVICO   With all constancy.
   But, sir, I wonder you'll engage yourself,   75
   In person, being a great prince.
FRANCISCO   Divert me not.
   Most of his court are of my faction,
   And some are of my counsel. Noble friend,
   Our danger shall be 'like in this design;°
   Give leave, part of the glory may be mine.   80
      Exit Francisco. Enter Monticelso
MONTICELSO Why did the Duke of Florence with such care
   Labour your pardon? Say.

LODOVICO Italian beggars will resolve you that,°
  Who, begging of an alms, bid those they beg of
  Do good for their own sakes. Or't may be   85
  He spreads his bounty with a sowing hand,
  Like kings, who many times give out of measure;°
  Not for desert so much as for their pleasure.
MONTICELSO I know you're cunning. Come, what devil was that
  That you were raising?
LODOVICO   Devil, my lord?
MONTICELSO   I ask you   90
  How doth the Duke employ you, that his bonnet
  Fell with such compliment unto his knee,
  When he departed from you?
LODOVICO   Why, my lord,
  He told me of a resty Barbary horse
  Which he would fain have brought to the career,   95
  The sault, and the ring-galliard. Now, my lord,°
  I have a rare French rider.
MONTICELSO   Take you heed,°
  Lest the jade break your neck. Do you put me off
  With your wild horse-tricks? Sirrah, you do lie.
  O, thou'rt a foul black cloud, and thou dost threat   100
  A violent storm.
LODOVICO   Storms are i'th' air, my lord;
  I am too low to storm.
MONTICELSO   Wretched creature!
  I know that thou art fashioned for all ill,
  Like dogs, that once get blood, they'll ever kill.
  About some murder? Was't not?
LODOVICO   I'll not tell you;   105
  And yet I care not greatly if I do.
  Marry, with this preparation. Holy father,
  I come not to you as an intelligencer,
  But as a penitent sinner. What I utter
  Is in confession merely, which you know   110
  Must never be revealed.
MONTICELSO   You have o'erta'en me.
LODOVICO Sir, I did love Bracciano's duchess dearly;
  Or rather I pursued her with hot lust,
  Though she ne'er knew on't. She was poison'd,
  Upon my soul she was, for which I have sworn   115

T'avenge her murder.
MONTICELSO   To the Duke of Florence?
LODOVICO To him I have.
MONTICELSO   Miserable creature!
  If thou persist in this, 'tis damnable.
  Dost thou imagine thou canst slide on blood
  And not be tainted with a shameful fall?   120
  Or like the black and melancholic yew tree,
  Dost think to root thyself in dead men's graves,
  And yet to prosper? Instruction to thee
  Comes like sweet showers to over-hardened ground:
  They wet, but pierce not deep. And so I leave thee   125
  With all the Furies hanging 'bout thy neck,
  Till by thy penitence thou remove this evil,
  In conjuring from thy breast that cruel devil.
     Exit Monticelso
LODOVICO I'll give it o'er. He says 'tis damnable.
  Besides, I did expect his suffrage,   130
  By reason of Camillo's death.
     Enter Servant and Francisco [apart]
FRANCISCO Do you know that count?
SERVANT   Yes, my lord.
FRANCISCO Bear him these thousand ducats to his lodging;
  Tell him the Pope hath sent them. Happily
  That will confirm more than all the rest.
     [Exit Francisco]
SERVANT   Sir.   135
LODOVICO To me, sir?
     [Servant hands over money]
SERVANT His Holiness hath sent you a thousand crowns,
  And wills you, if you travel, to make him
  Your patron for intelligence.
LODOVICO   His creature°
  Ever to be commanded.   140
     [Exit Servant]
  Why, now 'tis come about. He railed upon me,
  And yet these crowns were told out and laid ready,°
  Before he knew my voyage. O the art,
  The modest form of greatness! that do sit
  Like brides at wedding dinners, with their looks turned   145
  From the least wanton jests, their puling stomach°

Sick of the modesty, when their thoughts are loose,
Even acting of those hot and lustful sports
Are to ensue about midnight: such his cunning!
He sounds my depth thus with a golden plummet.   150
I am doubly armed now. Now to th'act of blood.
There's but three Furies found in spacious hell,
But in a great man's breast three thousand dwell.
    [*Exit*]

[5.1]

*A passage over the stage of Bracciano, Flamineo, Marcello,
Hortensio, [Vittoria] Corombona, Cornelia, Zanche and
others. [Enter Flamineo and Hortensio]*

FLAMINEO In all the weary minutes of my life,
Day ne'er broke up till now. This marriage
Confirms me happy.

MORTENSIO   'Tis a good assurance.
Saw you not yet the Moor that's come to court?

FLAMINEO Yes, and conferred with him i'th' Duke's closet.   5
I have not seen a goodlier personage,
Nor ever talked with man better experienced
In state affairs or rudiments of war.
He hath, by report, served the Venetian
In Candy these twice seven years, and been chief   10
In many a bold design.

HORTENSIO   What are those two
That bear him company?

FLAMINEO Two noblemen of Hungary, that living in the emperor's
service as commanders, eight years since, contrary to the expectation of all the court entered into religion, into the strict order of   15
Capuchins;° but being not well settled in their undertaking, they
left their order and returned to court: for which, being after
troubled in conscience, they vowed their service against the
enemies of Christ; went to Malta; were there knighted;° and in
their return back, at this great solemnity, they are resolved for ever   20
to forsake the world, and settle themselves here in a house of
Capuchins in Padua.

HORTENSIO 'Tis strange.

FLAMINEO One thing makes it so. They have vowed for ever to wear
next their bare bodies those coats of mail they served in.   25

HORTENSIO Hard penance. Is the Moor a Christian?

FLAMINEO He is.

HORTENSIO Why proffers he his service to our duke?

FLAMINEO Because he understands there's like to grow
Some wars between us and the Duke of Florence,   30
In which he hopes employment.
I never saw one in a stern bold look

Wear more command, nor in a lofty phrase
Express more knowing, or more deep contempt
Of our slight airy courtiers. He talks°   35
As if he had travelled all the princes' courts
Of Christendom; in all things strives t'express
That all that should dispute with him may know
Glories, like glow-worms, afar off shine bright
But, looked to near, have neither heat nor light.   40
The Duke!
　　　　Enter Bracciano, [Francisco Duke of] Florence disguised
　　　　like Mulinassar; Lodovico, Antonelli, Gasparo [disguised],
　　　　Farnese bearing their swords and helmets, [Carlo and Pedro]
BRACCIANO You're nobly welcome. We have heard at full
Your honourable service 'gainst the Turk.
To you, brave Mulinassar, we assign
A competent pension, and are inly sorrow   45
The vows of these two worthy gentlemen
Make them incapable of our proffered bounty.°
Your wish is you may leave your warlike swords
For monuments in our chapel. I accept it°
As a great honour done me, and must crave   50
Your leave to furnish out our Duchess' revels.
Only one thing, as the last vanity
You e'er shall view, deny me not to stay
To see a Barriers prepared tonight.
You shall have private standings. It hath pleased   55
The great ambassadors of several princes,
In their return from Rome to their own countries,
To grace our marriage, and to honour me
With such a kind of sport.
FRANCISCO　　　　　　　I shall persuade them
To stay, my lord.
BRACCIANO　　　　Set on there to the presence.   60
　　　　Exeunt Bracciano, Flamineo, and [Hortensio]
CARLO Noble my lord, most fortunately welcome.
　　　　The conspirators here embrace
You have our vows sealed with the sacrament
To second your attempts.
PEDRO　　　　　　　And all things ready.
He could not have invented his own ruin,
Had he despaired, with more propriety.°   65

LODOVICO You would not take my way.
FRANCISCO   'Tis better ordered.
LODOVICO T'have poisoned his prayer book, or a pair of beads,°
    The pommel of his saddle, his looking-glass,°
    Or th'handle of his racket. O that, that!
    That while he had been bandying at tennis,   70
    He might have sworn himself to hell, and struck
    His soul into the hazard! O my lord!°
    I would have our plot be ingenious,
    And have it hereafter recorded for example
    Rather than borrow example.
FRANCISCO   There's no way   75
    More speeding than this thought on.
LODOVICO   On then.
FRANCISCO And yet methinks that this revenge is poor,
    Because it steals upon him like a thief,
    To have ta'en him by the casque in a pitched field,
    Led him to Florence!
LODOVICO   It had been rare. And there   80
    Have crowned him with a wreath of stinking garlic,
    T'have shown the sharpness of his government
    And rankness of his lust. Flamineo comes.
       Exeunt [all except Francisco]. Enter Flamineo, Marcello, and
       Zanche
MARCELLO Why doth this devil haunt you? say.
FLAMINEO   I know not.
    For by this light I do not conjure for her.   85
    'Tis not so great a cunning as men think
    To raise the devil, for here's one up already;
    The greatest cunning were to lay him down.
MARCELLO She is your shame.
FLAMINEO   I prithee pardon her.
    In faith, you see women are like to burs;   90
    Where their affection throws them, there they'll stick.°
ZANCHE That is my countryman, a goodly person,
    When he's at leisure I'll discourse with him
    In our own language.
FLAMINEO   I beseech you do.
       Exit Zanche
    [*To Francisco*] How is't, brave soldier? O that I had seen   95
    Some of your iron days! I pray relate

Some of your service to us.

FRANCISCO 'Tis a ridiculous thing for a man to be his own chronicle;
I did never wash my mouth with mine own praise for fear of
getting a stinking breath.   100

MARCELLO You're too stoical. The Duke will expect other discourse
from you.

FRANCISCO I shall never flatter him. I have studied man too much
to do that. What difference is between the Duke and I? No
more than between two bricks, all made of one clay. Only't may   105
be one is placed on the top of a turret, the other in the bottom of
a well by mere chance. If I were placed as high as the Duke, I
should stick as fast, make as fair a show, and bear out weather
equally.

FLAMINEO [aside] If this soldier had a patent to beg in churches, then   110
he would tell them stories.

MARCELLO I have been a soldier too.

FRANCISCO How have you thrived?

MARCELLO Faith, poorly.

FRANCISCO That's the misery of peace. Only outsides are then   115
respected. As ships seem very great upon the river, which show
very little upon the seas, so some men i'th' court seem Colossuses°
in a chamber who, if they came into the field, would appear pitiful
pigmies.

FLAMINEO Give me a fair room yet hung with arras, and some great   120
cardinal to lug me by th'ears as his endeared minion.

FRANCISCO And thou may'st do the devil knows what villainy.

FLAMINEO And safely.

FRANCISCO Right: you shall see in the country in harvest time,
pigeons, though they destroy never so much corn, the farmer dare   125
not present the fowling-piece to them! Why? Because they belong
to the lord of the manor; whilst your poor sparrows that belong to
the Lord of heaven, they go to the pot for't.

FLAMINEO I will now give you some politic instruction. The Duke
says he will give you pension: that's but bare promise; get it under   130
his hand.° For I have known men that have come from serving
against the Turk; for three or four months they have had pension
to buy them new wooden legs and fresh plasters; but after 'twas
not to be had. And this miserable° courtesy shows, as if a
tormenter should give hot cordial drinks to one three-quarters   135
dead o'th' rack, only to fetch the miserable soul again to endure
more dog-days.

Enter Hortensio, a young Lord, Zanche, and two more
How now, gallants; what, are they ready for the Barriers?
[*Exit Francisco*]

YOUNG LORD Yes: the lords are putting on their armour.   140

HORTENSIO [*aside to Flamineo*] What's he?

FLAMINEO A new upstart: one that swears like a faloner, and will lie
in the Duke's ear day by day like a maker of almanacs; and yet I
knew him since he came to th'court smell worse of sweat than an
under-tennis-court-keeper.

HORTENSIO Look you, yonder's your sweet mistress.   145

FLAMINEO Thou art my sworn brother; I'll tell thee, I do love that
Moor, that witch, very constrainedly;° she knows some of my
villainy. I do love her, just as a man holds a wolf by the ears.° But
for fear of turning upon me, and pulling out my throat, I would
let her go to the devil.   150

HORTENSIO I hear she claims marriage of thee.

FLAMINEO 'Faith, I made to her some such dark promise, and in
seeking to fly from't I run on, like a frighted dog with a bottle at's
tail, that fain would bite it off and yet dares not look behind him.
[*To Zanche*] Now, my precious gipsy!°   155

ZANCHE Ay, your love to me rather cools than heats.

FLAMINEO Marry, I am the sounder lover.° We have many wenches
about the town heat too fast.

HORTENSIO What do you think of these perfumed gallants then?

FLAMINEO Their satin cannot save them. I am confident   160
They have a certain spice of the disease,
For they that sleep with dogs shall rise with fleas.

ZANCHE Believe it! A little painting° and gay clothes make you loathe
me.

FLAMINEO How? Love a lady for painting or gay apparel? I'll unken-   165
nel one example more for thee. Æsop had a foolish dog that let go
the flesh to catch the shadow. I would have courtiers be better diners.

ZANCHE You remember your oaths.

FLAMINEO Lovers' oaths are like mariners' prayers, uttered in
extremity; but when the tempest is o'er, and that the vessel leaves   170
tumbling,° they fall from protesting to drinking. And yet amongst
gentlemen protesting and drinking go together, and agree as well
as shoemakers and Westphalia bacon. They are both drawers-
on,° for drink draws on protestation, and protestation draws on
more drink. Is not this discourse better now than the morality of   175
your sunburnt° gentleman?

Enter Cornelia

CORNELIA Is this your perch, you haggard? Fly to th'stews.
    [*Strikes Zanche*]

FLAMINEO You should be clapped by th'heels now: strike i'th'
  court!°
    [*Exit Cornelia*]

ZANCHE She's good for nothing but to make her maids   180
  Catch cold o' nights. They dare not use a bedstaff,°
  For fear of her light fingers.

MARCELLO   You're a strumpet.
  An impudent one.
    [*Kicks Zanche*]

FLAMINEO   Why do you kick her? Say,
  Do you think that she's like a walnut tree?
  Must she be cudgelled ere she bear good fruit?°   185

MARCELLO She brags that you shall marry her.

FLAMINEO   What then?

MARCELLO I had rather she were pitched upon a stake
  In some new-seeded garden, to affright
  Her fellow crows thence.

FLAMINEO   You're a boy, a fool.
  Be guardian to your hound, I am of age.   190

MARCELLO If I take her near you, I'll cut her throat.

FLAMINEO With a fan of feathers?

MARCELLO   And for you, I'll whip°
  This folly from you.

FLAMINEO   Are you choleric?
  I'll purge't with rhubarb.

HORTENSIO   O your brother!

FLAMINEO   Hang him.°
  He wrongs me most that ought t'offend me least.   195
  I do suspect my mother played foul play
  When she conceived thee.

MARCELLO   Now by all my hopes,
  Like the two slaughtered sons of Œdipus,°
  The very flames of our affection
  Shall turn two ways. Those words I'll make thee answer   200
  With thy heart blood.

FLAMINEO   Do; like the gests in the progress,°
  You know where you shall find me.

MARCELLO   Very good.

[*Exit Flamineo*]
And thou beest a noble friend, bear him my sword,
And bid him fit the length on't.

YOUNG LORD   Sir, I shall.°
[*Exeunt all but Zanche.*] *Enter Francisco the Duke of Florence* [*disguised as Mulinassar*]

ZANCHE [*aside*] He comes. Hence petty thought of my disgrace.   205
[*To him*] I ne'er loved my complexion till now,
'Cause I may boldly say without a blush,
I love you.

FRANCISCO Your love is untimely sown:
There's a spring at Michaelmas, but 'tis but a faint one;°   210
I am sunk in years, and I have vowed never to marry.

ZANCHE Alas, poor maids get more lovers than husbands; yet you may
mistake my wealth. For, as when ambassadors are sent to congratulate
princes, there's commonly sent along with them a rich present, so
that, though the prince like not the ambassador's person nor words,   215
yet he likes well of the presentment; so I may come to you in the same
manner, and be better loved for my dowry than my virtue.

FRANCISCO I'll think on the motion.

ZANCHE Do; I'll now detain you no longer. At your better leisure I'll
tell you things shall startle your blood.   220
Nor blame me that this passion I reveal:
Lovers die inward that their flames conceal.

FRANCISCO [*aside*] Of all intelligence this may prove the best.
Sure I shall draw strange fowl, from this foul nest.
[*Exeunt*]

[5.2]

Enter Marcello and Cornelia

CORNELIA I hear a whispering all about the court,
You are to fight. Who is your opposite?
What is the quarrel?

MARCELLO   'Tis an idle rumour.

CORNELIA Will you dissemble? Sure you do not well
To fright me thus. You never look thus pale   5
But when you are most angry. I do charge you
Upon my blessing. Nay, I'll call the Duke,

And he shall school you.
MARCELLO   Publish not a fear
Which would convert to laughter. 'Tis not so.
Was not this crucifix my father's?
CORNELIA   Yes.°   10
MARCELLO I have heard you say, giving my brother suck,
He took the crucifix between his hands,
          Enter Flamineo
And broke a limb off.
CORNELIA   Yes: but 'tis mended.
FLAMINEO I have brought your weapon back.
          Flamineo runs Marcello through
CORNELIA   Ha, O my horror!
MARCELLO You have brought it home indeed.
CORNELIA   Help, O he's murdered.   15
FLAMINEO Do you turn your gall up? I'll to sanctuary,°
And send a surgeon to you.
          [Exit Flamineo]. Enter [Lodovico disguised] Carlo, Hortensio,
          [Gasparo disguised], Pedro
MORTENSIO   How? O'th'ground?
MARCELLO O mother, now remember what I told
Of breaking off the crucifix. Farewell,
There are some sins which heaven doth duly punish   20
In a whole family. This it is to rise
By all dishonest means. Let all men know
That tree shall long time keep a steady foot
Whose branches spread no wider than the root.
          [Marcello dies]
CORNELIA O my perpetual sorrow!
MORTENSIO   Virtuous Marcello.   25
He's dead. Pray leave him, lady; come, you shall.
CORNELIA Alas, he is not dead: he's in a trance.
Why, here's nobody shall get any thing by his death. Let me call
him again for God's sake.
CARLO I would you were deceived.   30
CORNELIA O you abuse me, you abuse me, you abuse me. How many
have gone away thus for lack of tendance. Rear up's head, rear up's
head; his bleeding inward will kill him.
HORTENSIO You see he is departed.
CORNELIA Let me come to him. Give me him as he is, if he be   35
turned to earth. Let me but give him one hearty kiss, and you shall

put us both into one coffin. Fetch a looking-glass, see if his breath
will not stain it; or pull out some feathers from my pillow, and lay
them to his lips. Will you lose him for a little pains-taking?

HORTENSIO Your kindest office is to pray for him.   40

CORNELIA Alas! I would not pray for him yet. He may live to lay me
i'th' ground, and pray for me, if you'll let me come to him.

> *Enter Bracciano all armed, save the beaver, with Flamineo,*
> *[Francisco disguised as Mulinassar, a Page, and Lodovico*
> *disguised]*

BRACCIANO Was this your handiwork?

FLAMINEO It was my misfortune.

CORNELIA He lies, he lies, he did not kill him: these have killed him,   45
that would not let him be better looked to.

BRACCIANO Have comfort my grieved mother.

CORNELIA O you screech-owl!

HORTENSIO Forbear, good madam.

CORNELIA Let me go, let me go.   50

> *She runs to Flamineo with her knife drawn and, coming to*
> *him, lets it fall*

The God of heaven forgive thee. Dost not wonder
I pray for thee? I'll tell thee what's the reason:
I have scarce breath to number twenty minutes,
I'd not spend that in cursing. Fare thee well.
Half of thyself lies there; and may'st thou live   55
To fill an hour-glass with his mouldered ashes,
To tell how thou shouldst spend the time to come
In blessed repentance.

BRACCIANO   Mother, pray tell me,
How came he by his death? What was the quarrel?

CORNELIA Indeed my younger boy presumed too much   60
Upon his manhood; gave him bitter words;
Drew his sword first; and so I know not how,
For I was out of my wits, he fell with's head
Just in my bosom.

PAGE This is not true, madam.

CORNELIA   I pray thee peace.   65
One arrow's grazed already; it were vain°
T'lose this, for that will ne'er be found again.

BRACCIANO Go, bear the body to Cornelia's lodging;

> *[Carlo, Pedro, and Hortensio carry off the body]*

And we command that none acquaint our Duchess

With this sad accident. For you, Flamineo, 70
Hark you, I will not grant your pardon.
FLAMINEO No?
BRACCIANO Only a lease of your life. And that shall last
But for one day. Thou shalt be forced each evening
To renew it, or be hanged.
FLAMINEO At your pleasure.
Lodovico sprinkles Bracciano's beaver with a poison
Your will is law now, I'll not meddle with it. 75
BRACCIANO You once did brave me in your sister's lodging;
I'll now keep you in awe for't. Where's our beaver?
FRANCISCO [*aside*] He calls for his destruction. Noble youth,
I pity thy sad fate. Now to the Barriers.
This shall his passage to the black lake further: 80
The last good deed he did, he pardon'd murder.'
Exeunt

[5.3]

Charges and shouts. They fight at Barriers; first single pairs,
then three to three. Enter Bracciano [in full armour] and
Flamineo with others [following, including Vittoria,
Giovanni, and Francisco disguised as Mulinassar]
BRACCIANO An armourer! Ud's death, an armourer!
FLAMINEO Armourer! Where's the armourer?
BRACCIANO Tear off my beaver.
FLAMINEO Are you hurt, my lord?
BRACCIANO O my brain's on fire,
Enter Armourer
the helmet is poisoned.
ARMOURER My lord, upon my soul.
BRACCIANO Away with him to torture. 5
[*Exit Armourer, guarded*]
There are some great ones that have hand in this,
And near about me.
VITTORIA O my loved lord: poisoned?
FLAMINEO Remove the bar. Here's unfortunate revels.°
Call the physicians.

Enter two Physicians
                        A plague upon you!
We have too much of your cunning here already.   10
I fear the ambassadors are likewise poisoned.
BRACCIANO O I am gone already: the infection
Flies to the brain and heart. O thou strong heart!
There's such a covenant 'tween the world and it,
They're loth to break.
GIOVANNI   O my most loved father!   15
BRACCIANO Remove the boy away.
        [*Exit Giovanni, attended*]
Where's this good woman? Had I infinite worlds,
They were too little for thee. Must I leave thee?
What say yon screech-owls, is the venom mortal?
PHYSICIAN Most deadly.
BRACCIANO   Most corrupted politic hangman!   20
You kill without book, but your art to save°
Fails you as oft as great men's needy friends.
I that have given life to offending slaves
And wretched murderers, have I not power
To lengthen mine own a twelvemonth?   25
[*To Vittoria*] Do not kiss me, for I shall poison thee.
This unction is sent from the Great Duke of Florence.
FRANCISCO Sir, be of comfort.
BRACCIANO O thou soft natural death, that art joint-twin
To sweetest slumber, no rough-bearded comet°   30
Stares on thy mild departure; the dull owl
Beats not against thy casement; the hoarse wolf
Scents not thy carrion. Pity winds thy corpse
Whilst horror waits on princes.
VITTORIA   I am lost for ever.
BRACCIANO How miserable a thing it is to die   35
'Mongst women howling!
        [*Enter Lodovico and Gasparo, disguised as Capuchins*]
                        What are those?
FLAMINEO   Franciscans.°
They have brought the extreme unction.
BRACCIANO On pain of death, let no man name death to me.
It is a word infinitely terrible.
Withdraw into our cabinet.   40

Exeunt but Francisco and Flamineo

FLAMINEO To see what solitariness is about dying princes. As heretofore they have unpeopled towns, divorced friends, and made great houses unhospitable, so now, O justice! where are their flatterers now? Flatterers are but the shadows of princes' bodies; the least thick cloud makes them invisible.   45

FRANCISCO There's great moan made for him.

FLAMINEO 'Faith, for some few hours salt water will run most plentifully in every office o'th' court. But believe it: most of them do but weep over their stepmothers' graves.

FRANCISCO How mean you?   50

FLAMINEO Why! they dissemble, as some men do that live within compass o'th' verge.°

FRANCISCO Come, you have thrived well under him.

FLAMINEO 'Faith, like a wolf in a woman's breast, I have been fed with poultry.° But for money, understand me, I had as good a will   55
to cozen him, as e'er an officer of them all. But I had not cunning enough to do it.

FRANCISCO What didst thou think of him? Faith, speak freely.

FLAMINEO He was a kind of statesman, that would sooner have reckoned how many cannon-bullets he had discharged against a   60
town, to count his expense that way, than how many of his valiant and deserving subjects he lost before it.

FRANCISCO O, speak well of the Duke.

FLAMINEO I have done. Wilt hear some of my court wisdom?

Enter Lodovico [disguised]

To reprehend princes is dangerous, and to over-commend some   65
of them is palpable lying.

FRANCISCO How is it with the Duke?

LODOVICO   Most deadly ill.
He's fallen into a strange distraction.
He talks of battles and monopolies,
Levying of taxes, and from that descends   70
To the most brainsick language. His mind fastens
On twenty several objects, which confound
Deep sense with folly. Such a fearful end
May teach some men that bear too lofty crest,
Though they live happiest, yet they die not best.   75
He hath conferred the whole state of the dukedom
Upon your sister, till the Prince arrive

At mature age.

FLAMINEO   There's some good luck in that yet.

FRANCISCO See here he comes.

> *Enter Bracciano, presented in a bed, Vittoria and others,*
> *[including Gasparo, disguised]*

There's death in's face already.

VITTORIA O my good lord!

BRACCIANO [*speaks distractedly*] Away, you have abused me.°   80
You have conveyed coin forth our territories,°
Bought and sold offices, oppressed the poor,
And I ne'er dreamt on't. Make up your accounts;
I'll now be mine own steward.

FLAMINEO   Sir, have patience.

BRACCIANO Indeed I am to blame.°   85
For did you ever hear the dusky raven
Chide blackness? Or was't ever known the devil
Railed against cloven creatures?

VITTORIA   O my lord!

BRACCIANO Let me have some quails to supper.

FLAMINEO   Sir, you shall.°

BRACCIANO No: some fried dog-fish. Your quails feed on poison.   90
That old dog-fox, that politician Florence—
I'll forswear hunting and turn dog-killer.
Rare! I'll be friends with him; for mark you, sir, one dog
Still sets another a-barking. Peace, peace,
Yonder's a fine slave come in now.

FLAMINEO   Where?

BRACCIANO   Why, there.   95
In a blue bonnet, and a pair of breeches
With a great cod-piece. Ha, ha, ha,
Look you, his cod-piece is stuck full of pins
With pearls o'th' head of them. Do not you know him?

FLAMINEO No, my lord.

BRACCIANO   Why, tis the devil.   100
I know him by a great rose he wears on's shoe°
To hide his cloven foot. I'll dispute with him.
He's a rare linguist.

VITTORIA   My lord, here's nothing.°

BRACCIANO Nothing? Rare! Nothing! When I want money,
Our treasury is empty. There is nothing.   105
I'll not be used thus.

VITTORIA   O! lie still, my lord.

BRACCIANO See, see, Flamineo that killed his brother
Is dancing on the ropes there; and he carries
A money-bag in each hand, to keep him even,
For fear of breaking's neck. And there's a lawyer   110
In a gown whipped with velvet, stares and gapes
When the money will fall. How the rogue cuts capers!°
It should have been in a halter.
'Tis there. What's she?

FLAMINEO   Vittoria, my lord.

BRACCIANO Ha, ha, ha. Her hair is sprinkled with orris powder,° 115
that makes her look as if she had sinned in the pastry.

> *Bracciano seems here near his end. Lodovico and Gasparo in*
> *the habit of Capuchins present him in his bed with a crucifix*
> *and hallowed candle*

What's he?

FLAMINEO A divine, my lord.

BRACCIANO He will be drunk; avoid him. Th'argument is fearful
when churchmen stagger in't.   120
Look you, six grey rats that have lost their tails
Crawl up the pillow; send for a rat-catcher.
I'll do a miracle: I'll free the court
From all foul vermin. Where's Flamineo?

FLAMINEO [aside] I do not like that he names me so often,   125
Especially on's death-bed. 'Tis a sign
I shall not live long. See, he's near his end.

LODOVICO Pray give us leave. *Attende Domine Brachiane,*°

FLAMINEO See, see, how firmly he doth fix his eye
Upon the crucifix.

VITTORIA   O hold it constant.   130
It settles his wild spirits; and so his eyes
Melt into tears.

LODOVICO (*by the crucifix*) *Domine Brachiane, solebas in bello tutus esse*
tuo clipeo, nunc hunc clipeum hosti tuo opponas infernali.

GASPARO (*by the hallowed taper*) *Olim hasta valuisti in bello; nunc hanc* 135
sacram hastam vibrabis contra hostem animarum.

LODOVICO *Attende Domine Brachiane si nunc quoque probas ea quae*
acta sunt inter nos, flecte caput in dextrum.

GASPARO *Esto securus Domine Brachiane: cogita quantum habeas meri-*
torum—denique memineris meam animam pro tua oppignoratam si quid 140
esset periculi.

LODOVICO *Si nunc quoque probas ea quae acta sunt inter nos, flecte*
  caput in laevum.°
  He is departing. Pray stand all apart,
  And let us only whisper in his ears   145
  Some private meditations, which our order
  Permits you not to hear.
  > *Here the rest being departed, Lodovico and Gasparo discover*
  > *themselves.*

GASPARO   Bracciano.

LODOVICO Devil Bracciano. Thou art damned.

GASPARO   .   Perpetually.

LODOVICO A slave condemned, and given up to the gallows
  Is thy great lord and master.

GASPARO   True: for thou   150
  Art given up to the devil.

LODOVICO   O you slave!
  You that were held the famous politician,
  Whose art was poison.

GASPARO   And whose conscience murder.°

LODOVICO That would have broke your wife's neck down the
      stairs
  Ere she was poisoned.

GASPARO   That had your villainous salads—   155

LODOVICO And fine embroidered bottles, and perfumes°
  Equally mortal with a winter plague—

GASPARO Now there's mercury—

LODOVICO   And copperas—

GASPARO   And quicksilver—

LODOVICO With other devilish pothecary stuff
  A-melting in your politic brains. Dost hear?   160

GASPARO This is Count Lodovico.

LODOVICO   This Gasparo.
  And thou shalt die like a poor rogue.

GASPARO   And stink
  Like a dead fly-blown dog.

LODOVICO   And be forgotten
  Before thy funeral sermon.

BRACCIANO   Vittoria?
  Vittoria!   165

LODOVICO O the cursèd devil,
  Come to himself again! We are undone.

Enter Vittoria and the Attendants.

GASPARO [*aside to Lodovico*] Strangle him in private.
  [*Aloud*] What? Will you call him again
  To live in treble torments? For charity,   170
  For Christian charity, avoid the chamber.°
    [*Exeunt Vittoria and Attendants*]
LODOVICO You would prate, sir. This is a true-love knot
  Sent from the Duke of Florence.
    Bracciano is strangled.
GASPARO What, is it done?
LODOVICO The snuff is out. No woman-keeper i'th' world,   175
  Though she had practised seven year at the pesthouse,
  Could have done't quaintlier. My lords, he's dead.°
    [*Enter Vittoria, Francisco, and Flamineo, with Attendants*]
ALL Rest to his soul.
VITTORIA   O me! this place is hell.
    *Exit Vittoria [followed by all except Lodovico, Francisco, and
      Flamineo]*
FRANCISCO How heavily she takes it.
FLAMINEO   O yes, yes;
  Had women navigable rivers in their eyes   180
  They would dispend them all. Surely I wonder
  Why we should wish more rivers to the city,°
  When they sell water so good cheap. I'll tell thee,
  These are but moonish shades of griefs or fears;°
  There's nothing sooner dry than women's tears.   185
  Why, here's an end of all my harvest; he has given me nothing.
  Court promises! Let wise men count them cursed,
  For while you live he that scores best pays worst.°
FRANCISCO Sure this was Florence' doing.
FLAMINEO   Very likely.
  Those are found weighty strokes which come from th'hand,   190
  But those are killing strokes which come from th'head.
  O the rare tricks of a Machiavellian!
  He doth not come like a gross plodding slave
  And buffet you to death: no, my quaint knave,
  He tickles you to death, makes you die laughing,   195
  As if you had swallowed down a pound of saffron.°
  You see the feat: 'tis practised in a trice,
  To teach court-honesty it jumps on ice.°
FRANCISCO Now have the people liberty to talk

And descant on his vices.

FLAMINEO   Misery of princes,   200
  That must of force be censured by their slaves!
  Not only blamed for doing things are ill,
  But for not doing all that all men will.
  One were better be a thresher.
  Ud's death, I would fain speak with this Duke yet.   205

FRANCISCO Now he's dead?

FLAMINEO I cannot conjure, but if prayers or oaths
  Will get to th'speech of him, though forty devils
  Wait on him in his livery of flames,
  I'll speak to him, and shake him by the hand,   210
  Though I be blasted.
        Exit Flamineo.

FRANCISCO   Excellent Lodovico!
  What? Did you terrify him at the last gasp?

LODOVICO Yes; and so idly that the Duke had like
  T'have terrified us.

FRANCISCO   How?
        Enter [Zanche] the Moor

LODOVICO   You shall hear that hereafter.
  See, yon's the infernal that would make up sport.°   215
  Now to the revelation of that secret
  She promised when she fell in love with you.

FRANCISCO *[to Zanche]* You're passionately met in this sad world.°

ZANCHE I would have you look up, sir. These court tears
  Claim not your tribute to them. Let those weep   220
  That guiltily partake in the sad cause.
  I knew last night by a sad dream I had
  Some mischief would ensue; yet to say truth.
  My dream most concerned you.

LODOVICO   Shall's fall a-dreaming?

FRANCISCO Yes, and for fashion sake I'll dream with her.   225

ZANCHE Methought, sir, you came stealing to my bed.

FRANCISCO Wilt thou believe me, sweeting? By this light
  I was a-dreamt on thee too, for methought
  I saw thee naked.

ZANCHE   Fie, sir! As I told you,
  Methought you lay down by me.

FRANCISCO   So dreamt I;   230
  And lest thou shouldst take cold, I covered thee

With this Irish mantle.
ZANCHE   Verily, I did dream°
  You were somewhat bold with me; but to come to't.
LODOVICO How? How? I hope you will not go to't here—
FRANCISCO Nay, you must hear my dream out.
ZANCHE   Well, sir, forth.   235
FRANCISCO When I threw the mantle o'er thee, thou didst laugh
  Exceedingly methought.
ZANCHE   Laugh?
FRANCISCO   And cried'st out.
  The hair did tickle thee.
ZANCHE   There was a dream indeed.
LODOVICO Mark her, I prithee: she simpers like the suds
  A collier hath been washed in.   240
ZANCHE Come, sir, good fortune tends you. I did tell you
  I would reveal a secret: Isabella,
  The Duke of Florence' sister, was empoisoned,
  By a fumed picture, and Camillo's neck
  Was broke by damned Flamineo, the mischance   245
  Laid on a vaulting-horse.
FRANCISCO   Most strange!
ZANCHE   Most true.
LODOVICO [aside] The bed of snakes is broke.
ZANCHE I sadly do confess I had a hand
  In the black deed.
FRANCISCO   Thou kept'st their counsel.
ZANCHE   Right,
  For which, urged with contrition, I intend   250
  This night to rob Vittoria.
LODOVICO   Excellent penitence!
  Usurers dream on't while they sleep out sermons.
ZANCHE To further our escape, I have entreated
  Leave to retire me, till the funeral,
  Unto a friend i'th' country. That excuse   255
  Will further our escape. In coin and jewels
  I shall, at least, make good unto your use
  An hundred thousand crowns.
FRANCISCO   O noble wench!
LODOVICO Those crowns we'll share.
ZANCHE   It is a dowry,
  Methinks, should make that sunburnt proverb false,   260

And wash the Ethiop white.
FRANCISCO   It shall. Away!°
ZANCHE Be ready for our flight.
FRANCISCO   An hour 'fore day.
   Exit [Zanche]
O strange discovery! Why, till now we knew not
The circumstance of either of their deaths.
   [Enter Zanche]
ZANCHE You'll wait about midnight in the chapel.
FRANCISCO   There.   265
   [Exit Zanche]
LODOVICO Why, now our action's justified.
FRANCISCO   Tush for justice.
What harms it justice? We now like the partridge°
Purge the disease with laurel: for the fame
Shall crown the enterprise and quit the shame.
   Exeunt.

[5.4]

Enter Flamineo and Gasparo [disguised as a Knight of St
John] at one door, another way Giovanni attended

GASPARO *[to Flamineo]* The young Duke. Did you e'er see a sweeter
 prince?
FLAMINEO I have known a poor woman's bastard better favoured.
 This is behind him. Now, to his face all comparisons were hateful.
 Wise was the courtly peacock, that being a great minion, and being   5
 compared for beauty, by some dottrels that stood by, to the kingly
 eagle, said the eagle was a far fairer bird than herself, not in respect
 of her feathers, but in respect of her long talons. His will grow out
 in time. *[To Giovanni]* My gracious lord.
GIOVANNI I pray leave me, sir.   10
FLAMINEO Your grace must be merry. 'Tis I have cause to mourn,
 for wot you what said the little boy that rode behind his father on
 horseback?
GIOVANNI Why, what said he?
FLAMINEO 'When you are dead, father', said he, 'I hope then I shall   15
 ride in the saddle'. O, 'tis a brave thing for a man to sit by himself:
 he may stretch himself in the stirrups, look about, and see the

whole compass of the hemisphere; you're now, my lord, i'th'
saddle.

GIOVANNI Study your prayers, sir, and be penitent.   20
'Twere fit you'd think on what hath former been;
I have heard grief named the eldest child of sin.
    [*Exeunt Giovanni and Attendants, with Gasparo*]

FLAMINEO Study my prayers? He threatens me divinely. I am falling
to pieces already. I care not, though like Anacharsis° I were
pounded to death in a mortar. And yet that death were fitter for   25
usurers' gold and themselves to be beaten together, to make a most
cordial cullis for the devil.
He hath his uncle's villainous look already,
    Enter Courtier
In *decimo-sexto*. Now, sir, what are you?°

COURTIER It is the pleasure, sir, of the young Duke   30
That you forbear the presence, and all rooms
That owe him reverence.

FLAMINEO   So, the wolf and the raven
Are very pretty fools when they are young.
Is it your office, sir, to keep me out?

COURTIER So the duke wills.   35

FLAMINEO Verily, master courtier, extremity is not to be used in all
offices. Say that a gentlewoman were taken out of her bed about
midnight, and committed to Castle Angelo,° to the tower yonder,
with nothing about her,° but her smock: would it not show a cruel
part in the gentleman porter to lay claim to her upper garment,   40
pull it o'er her head and ears, and put her in naked?

COURTIER Very good: you are merry.
    [*Exit Courtier*]

FLAMINEO Doth he make a court ejectment of me? A flaming
firebrand° casts more smoke without a chimney, than within't. I'll
smoor some of them.   45
    Enter [Francisco Duke of] Florence, [disguised as Mulinassar]
How now? Thou art sad.

FRANCISCO I met even now with the most piteous sight.

FLAMINEO Thou met'st another here: a pitiful
Degraded courtier.

FRANCISCO   Your reverend mother
Is grown a very old woman in two hours.   50
I found them winding of Marcello's corpse,°
And there is such a solemn melody

'Tween doleful songs, tears, and sad elegies
(Such as old grandames, watching by the dead,
Were wont t'outwear the nights with), that, believe me,   55
I had no eyes to guide me forth the room,
They were so o'ercharged with water.
FLAMINEO   I will see them.
FRANCISCO 'Twere much uncharity in you, for your sight
Will add unto their tears.
FLAMINEO   I will see them.
They are behind the traverse. I'll discover   60
Their superstitious howling.
        [*Draws the traverse*]. *Cornelia, [Zanche] the Moor and three
        other Ladies [are] discovered, winding Marcello's corpse. A
        song*
CORNELIA This rosemary is withered, pray get fresh;°
I would have these herbs grow up in his grave
When I am dead and rotten. Reach the bays,
I'll tie a garland here about his head: 65
'Twill keep my boy from lightning. This sheet°
I have kept this twenty year, and every day
Hallowed it with my prayers; I did not think
He should have wore it.
ZANCHE   Look you: who are yonder?
CORNELIA O reach me the flowers.   70
ZANCHE Her ladyship's foolish.
LADY   Alas, her grief
Hath turned her child again.
CORNELIA (*to Flamineo*)   You're very welcome.
There's rosemary for you, and rue for you,°
Heart's-ease for you. I pray make much of it.°
I have left more for myself.
FRANCISCO   Lady, who's this?   75
CORNELIA You are, I take it, the grave-maker.
FLAMINEO   So.
ZANCHE 'Tis Flamineo.
CORNELIA Will you make me such a fool? Here's a white hand:
Can blood so soon be washed out? Let me see:
When screech-owls croak upon the chimney-tops,   80
And the strange cricket i'th' oven sings and hops,°
When yellow spots do on your hands appear,
Be certain then you of a corpse shall hear.

Out upon't, how'tis speckled! H'as handled a toad sure.°
Cowslip-water is good for the memory:°   85
Pray buy me three ounces of't.

FLAMINEO I would I were from hence.

CORNELIA   Do you hear, sir?
I'll give you a saying which my grandmother
Was wont, when she heard the bell toll, to sing o'er
Unto her lute.

FLAMINEO   Do an you will, do.   90

    Cornelia [sings] this in several forms of distraction

CORNELIA *Call for the robin red breast and the wren,*
  Since o'er shady groves they hover,
  And with leaves and flowers do cover
  The friendless bodies of unburied men.°
Call unto his funeral dole°   95
  The ant, the field-mouse, and the mole
To rear him hillocks, that shall keep him warm,
And, when gay tombs are robb'd, sustain no harm;
But keep the wolf far thence, that's foe to men,
For with his nails he'll dig them up again.°   100
[*Speaks*] They would not bury him 'cause he died in a quarrel,
But I have an answer for them.
[*Sings*] *Let holy church receive him duly,*
Since he paid the church tithes truly.
[*Speaks*] His wealth is summed, and this is all his store:°   105
This poor men get; and great men get no more.
Now the wares are gone, we may shut up shop.
Bless you all, good people.

    Exeunt Cornelia, [Zanche], and Ladies

FLAMINEO I have a strange thing in me, to th'which
I cannot give a name, without it be°   110
Compassion. I pray leave me.

    Exit Francisco

This night I'll know the utmost of my fate,
I'll be resolv'd what my rich sister means
T'assign me for my service. I have lived
Riotously ill, like some that live in court;   115
And sometimes, when my face was full of smiles
Have felt the maze of conscience in my breast.
Oft gay and honoured robes those tortures try;
We think caged birds sing, when indeed they cry.

Enter Braccciano's Ghost, in his leather cassock° and breeches,
boots, [and] a cowl, [in his hand] a pot of lily-flowers° with
a skull in't

Ha! I can stand thee. Nearer, nearer yet.   120
What a mockery hath death made of thee?°
Thou look'st sad.
In what place art thou? In yon starry gallery,
Or in the cursèd dungeon? No? Not speak?
Pray, sir, resolve me, what religion's best   125
For a man to die in? Or is it in your knowledge
To answer me how long I have to live?
That's the most necessary question.
Not answer? Are you still like some great men
That only walk like shadows up and down,   130
And to no purpose? say.
        The Ghost throws earth upon him and shows him the skull
What's that? O fatal! He throws earth upon me.
A dead man's skull beneath the roots of flowers.
I pray, speak, sir. Our Italian churchmen
Make us believe dead men hold conference   135
With their familiars, and many times
Will come to bed to them, and eat with them.
        Exit Ghost
He's gone; and see, the skull and earth are vanished.
This is beyond melancholy. I do dare my fate°
To do its worst. Now to my sister's lodging,   140
And sum up all these horrors: the disgrace
The prince threw on me; next the piteous sight
Of my dead brother, and my mother's dotage;
And last this terrible vision. All these
Shall with Vittoria's bounty turn to good,   145
Or I will drown this weapon in her blood.
        Exit

[5.5]

Enter Francisco, Lodovico, and Hortensio [overhearing them]

LODOVICO My lord, upon my soul you shall no further:
　You have most ridiculously engaged yourself
　Too far already. For my part, I have paid
　All my debts, so if I should chance to fall
　My creditors fall not with me; and I vow　　　　　　　5
　To quit all in this bold assembly
　To the meanest follower. My lord, leave the city,°
　Or I'll forswear the murder.
FRANCISCO　　　　　　　　　Farewell, Lodovico.
　If thou dost perish in this glorious act,
　I'll rear unto thy memory that fame　　　　　　　　10
　Shall in the ashes keep alive thy name.
　　　　[Exeunt Francisco and Lodovico severally]
HORTENSIO There's some black deed on foot. I'll presently
　Down to the citadel, and raise some force.
　These strong court factions that do brook no checks,
　In the career oft break the riders' necks.　　　　　　15
　　　　[Exit]

[5.6]

*Enter Vittoria with a [prayer-] book° in her hand, Zanche;
[and] Flamineo, following them*

FLAMINEO What, are you at your prayers? Give o'er.
VITTORIA　　　　　　　　　　　　　　　How, ruffin?
FLAMINEO I come to you 'bout worldly business.
　Sit down, sit down *[Zanche begins to leave]*—Nay, stay, blowze,
　　you may hear it,
　The doors are fast enough.
VITTORIA　　　　　　　　Ha, are you drunk?
FLAMINEO Yes, yes, with wormwood water; you shall taste　　5
　Some of it presently.
VITTORIA　　　　　　　What intends the fury?
FLAMINEO You are my lord's executrix, and I claim
　Reward for my long service.

VITTORIA   For your service?

FLAMINEO Come therefore, here is pen and ink, set down
  What you will give me.   10
    She writes

VITTORIA There.

FLAMINEO   Ha, have you done already?
  'Tis a most short conveyance.

VITTORIA   I will read it.
  [*Reads*] 'I give that portion to thee, and no other,
  Which Cain groaned under, having slain his brother.'°

FLAMINEO A most courtly patent to beg by.   15

VITTORIA You are a villain.

FLAMINEO Is't come to this? They say affrights cure agues.
  Thou hast a devil in thee; I will try
  If I can scare him from thee. Nay, sit still:
  My lord hath left me yet two case of jewels   20
  Shall make me scorn your bounty; you shall see them.
    [*Exit Flamineo*]

VITTORIA Sure he's distracted.

ZANCHE   O, he's desperate.
  For your own safety give him gentle language.
    Enter [Flamineo] with two case of pistols

FLAMINEO Look, these are better far at a dead lift°
  Than all your jewel house.

VITTORIA   And yet methinks   25
  These stones have no fair lustre, they are ill set.

FLAMINEO I'll turn the right side towards you; you shall see
  How they will sparkle.

VITTORIA   Turn this horror from me.
  What do you want? What would you have me do?
  Is not all mine, yours? Have I any children?   30

FLAMINEO Pray thee, good woman, do not trouble me
  With this vain worldly business. Say your prayers.
  I made a vow to my deceasèd lord,
  Neither yourself, nor I should outlive him
  The numbering of four hours.

VITTORIA   Did he enjoin it?   35

FLAMINEO He did, and 'twas a deadly jealousy,
  Lest any should enjoy thee after him,
  That urged him vow me to it. For my death,
  I did propound it voluntarily, knowing

If he could not be safe in his own court   40
Being a great Duke, what hope then for us?
VITTORIA This is your melancholy and despair.
FLAMINEO   Away,
Fool thou art to think that politicians
Do use to kill the effects of injuries
And let the cause live. Shall we groan in irons,   45
Or be a shameful and a weighty burden
To a public scaffold? This is my resolve:
I would not live at any man's entreaty
Nor die at any's bidding.
VITTORIA   Will you hear me?
FLAMINEO My life hath done service to other men,   50
My death shall serve mine own turn. Make you ready.
VITTORIA Do you mean to die indeed?
FLAMINEO   With as much pleasure
As e'er my father gat me.
VITTORIA [whispers to Zanche] Are the doors locked?
ZANCHE [whispers to Vittoria] Yes, madam.   55
VITTORIA Are you grown an atheist? Will you turn your body,
Which is the goodly palace of the soul,
To the soul's slaughter house? O the cursed devil°
Which doth present us with all other sins
Thrice candied o'er; despair with gall and stibium,   60
Yet we carouse it off;—[whispers to Zanche] cry out for help—°
Makes us forsake that which was made for man,
The world, to sink to that was made for devils,
Eternal darkness.
ZANCHE   Help, help!
FLAMINEO   I'll stop your throat
With winter plums.
VITTORIA   I prithee yet remember°   65
Millions are now in graves, which at last day
Like mandrakes shall rise shrieking.
FLAMINEO   Leave your prating,
For these are but grammatical laments,
Feminine arguments, and they move me
As some in pulpits move their auditory   70
More with their exclamation than sense°
Of reason, or sound doctrine.
ZANCHE [whispers to Vittoria]   Gentle madam,

Seem to consent, only persuade him teach
The way to death: let him die first.

VITTORIA [*whispers to Zanche*] 'Tis good, I apprehend it.   75
[*Aloud*] To kill one's self is meat that we must take
Like pills, not chew't, but quickly swallow it;
The smart o'th' wound, or weakness of the hand
May else bring treble torments.

FLAMINEO   I have held it
A wretched and most miserable life,   80
Which is not able to die.

VITTORIA   O but frailty!
Yet I am now resolved. Farewell, affliction.
Behold Bracciano, I that while you lived
Did make a flaming altar of my heart
To sacrifice unto you, now am ready   85
To sacrifice heart and all. Farewell, Zanche.

ZANCHE How, madam! Do you think that I'll outlive you?
Especially when my best self Flamineo
Goes the same voyage.

FLAMINEO   O most lovèd Moor!

ZANCHE Only by all my love let me entreat you: 90
Since it is most necessary none of us
Do violence on ourselves, let you or I
Be her sad taster, teach her how to die.°

FLAMINEO Thou dost instruct me nobly. Take these pistols:
Because my hand is stained with blood already,   95
Two of these you shall level at my breast,
Th'other 'gainst your own, and so we'll die,
Most equally contented. But first swear
Not to outlive me.

VITTORIA *and* ZANCHE Most religiously.   100

FLAMINEO Then here's an end of me. Farewell, daylight,
And O contemptible physic! that dost take
So long a study, only to preserve
So short a life: I take my leave of thee.
            Showing the pistols
These are two cupping-glasses, that shall draw°   105
All my infected blood out. Are you ready?

VITTORIA *and* ZANCHE Ready.

FLAMINEO Whither shall I go now? O Lucian°, thy ridiculous

purgatory! To find Alexander the Great cobbling shoes, Pompey
tagging points,° and Julius Caesar making hair buttons, Hannibal   110
selling blacking, and Augustus crying 'garlic',° Charlemagne sell-
ing lists by the dozen, and King Pepin° crying 'apples' in a cart
drawn with one horse.
Whether I resolve to fire, earth, water, air,
Or all the elements by scruples, I know not   115
Nor greatly care. Shoot, shoot,
Of all deaths the violent death is best,
For from ourselves it steals ourselves so fast
The pain once apprehended is quite past.

They shoot and run to him and tread upon him

VITTORIA What, are you dropped?   120
FLAMINEO I am mixed with earth already. As you are noble,
    Perform your vows, and bravely follow me.
VITTORIA Whither, to hell?
ZANCHE   To most assurèd damnation.
VITTORIA O thou most cursed devil.
ZANCHE   Thou art caught.
VITTORIA In thine own engine. I tread the fire out   125
    That would have been my ruin.
FLAMINEO Will you be perjured? What a religious oath was Styx that
    the gods never durst swear by and violate? O that we had such an
    oath to minister, and to be so well kept in our courts of justice.
VITTORIA Think whither thou art going.
ZANCHE   And remember   130
    What villanies thou hast acted.
VITTORIA   This thy death
    Shall make me like a blazing ominous star,
    Look up and tremble.
FLAMINEO   O I am caught with a springe!
VITTORIA You see the fox comes many times short home;
    'Tis here proved true.
FLAMINEO   Killed with a couple of braches.°   135
VITTORIA No fitter offering for the infernal Furies
    Than one in whom they reigned while he was living.
FLAMINEO O the way's dark and horrid! I cannot see.
    Shall I have no company?
VITTORIA   O yes, thy sins
    Do run before thee to fetch fire from hell,   140

To light thee thither.
FLAMINEO   O I smell soot,
　Most stinking soot, the chimney is afire,
　My liver's parboiled like Scotch holy bread;°
　There's a plumber, laying pipes in my guts, it scalds.
　Wilt thou outlive me?
ZANCHE   Yes, and drive a stake   145
　Through thy body; for we'll give it out°
　Thou didst this violence upon thyself.
FLAMINEO O cunning devils! now I have tried your love,
　And doubled all your reaches.
　　　　　Flamineo riseth
　　　　　　　　　　　　I am not wounded;°
　The pistols held no bullets: 'twas a plot   150
　To prove your kindness to me, and I live
　To punish your ingratitude. I knew
　One time or other you would find a way
　To give me a strong potion. O men
　That lie upon your death-beds, and are haunted   155
　With howling wives, ne'er trust them: they'll re-marry
　Ere the worm pierce your winding-sheet, ere the spider
　Make a thin curtain for your epitaphs.
　How cunning you were to discharge! Do you practise at the
　Artillery Yard?° Trust a woman? Never, never. Bracciano be my   160
　precedent: we lay our souls to pawn to the devil for a little
　pleasure, and a woman makes the bill of sale. That ever man
　should marry! For one Hypermnestra° that saved her lord and
　husband, forty-nine of her sisters cut their husbands' throats all in
　one night. There was a shoal of virtuous horse-leeches.   165
　Here are two other instruments.
　　　　　Enter Lodovico, Gasparo, [disguised as Capuchins,] Pedro
　　　　　[and] Carlo
VITTORIA   Help, help!°
FLAMINEO What noise is that? Ha, false keys i'th' court!
LODOVICO We have brought you a masque.
FLAMINEO   A matachin, it seems,
　By your drawn swords. Churchmen turned revellers!
CARLO Isabella, Isabella!   170
LODOVICO Do you know us now?
　　　　　[They throw off their disguises]
FLAMINEO   Lodovico and Gasparo.

LODOVICO Yes, and that Moor the Duke gave pension to,
  Was the Great Duke of Florence.

VITTORIA   O we are lost.

FLAMINEO You shall not take justice from forth my hands;
  O let me kill her. I'll cut my safety   175
  Through your coats of steel. Fate's a spaniel,
  We cannot beat it from us. What remains now?
  Let all that do ill take this precedent:
  Man may his fate foresee, but not prevent.
  And of all axioms this shall win the prize: 180
  'Tis better to be fortunate than wise.

GASPARO Bind him to the pillar.

        [*Pedro and Carlo tie up Flamineo*]

VITTORIA   O your gentle pity.
  I have seen a blackbird that would sooner fly
  To a man's bosom, than to stay the grip
  Of the fierce sparrow-hawk.

GASPARO   Your hope deceives you.°   185

VITTORIA If Florence be i'th' court, would he would kill me.

GASPARO Fool! Princes give rewards with their own hands,
  But death or punishment by the hands of others.

LODOVICO Sirrah, you once did strike me; I'll strike you
  Into the centre.°   190

FLAMINEO Thou'lt do it like a hangman; a base hangman;
  Not like a noble fellow, for thou seest
  I cannot strike again.

LODOVICO   Dost laugh?

FLAMINEO Wouldst have me die, as I was born, in whining?

GASPARO Recommend yourself to heaven.   195

FLAMINEO No, I will carry mine own commendations thither.

LODOVICO O could I kill you forty times a day,
  And use't four year together, 'twere too little.
  Nought grieves but that you are too few to feed
  The famine of our vengeance. What dost think on?   200

FLAMINEO Nothing; of nothing. Leave thy idle questions,
  I am i'th' way to study a long silence,
  To prate were idle; I remember nothing.
  There's nothing of so infinite vexation
  As man's own thoughts.

LODOVICO [*to Vittoria*]   O thou glorious strumpet,°   205
  Could I divide thy breath from this pure air

When't leaves thy body, I would suck it up
And breathe't upon some dunghill.

VITTORIA   You, my death's-man;
Methinks thou dost not look horrid enough,
Thou hast too good a face to be a hangman;   210
If thou be, do thy office in right form:
Fall down upon thy knees, and ask forgiveness.

LODOVICO O thou hast been a most prodigious comet,
But I'll cut off your train. Kill the Moor first.°

VITTORIA You shall not kill her first. Behold my breast: 215
I will be waited on in death; my servant
Shall never go before me.

GASPARO Are you so brave?

VITTORIA   Yes, I shall welcome death,
As princes do some great ambassadors;
I'll meet thy weapon half way.

LODOVICO   Thou dost tremble.   220
Methinks fear should dissolve thee into air.

VITTORIA O thou art deceived, I am too true a woman:
Conceit can never kill me. I'll tell thee what:°
I will not in my death shed one base tear,
Or if look pale, for want of blood, not fear.   225

CARLO Thou art my task, black Fury.

ZANCHE   I have blood
As red as either of theirs: wilt drink some?°
'Tis good for the falling sickness; I am proud
Death cannot alter my complexion,
For I shall ne'er look pale.

LODOVICO   Strike, strike,   230
With a joint motion.
                    [*They strike*]

VITTORIA   'Twas a manly blow.
The next thou giv'st, murder some sucking infant,
And then thou wilt be famous.

FLAMINEO   O what blade is't?
A Toledo, or an English fox?°
I ever thought a cutler should distinguish   235
The cause of my death, rather than a doctor.
Search my wound deeper, tent it with the steel
That made it.

VITTORIA O my greatest sin lay in my blood;

Now my blood pays for't.

FLAMINEO   Thou'rt a noble sister: 240
I love thee now. If woman do breed man,
She ought to teach him manhood. Fare thee well.
Know many glorious women that are famed
For masculine virtue, have been vicious:
Only a happier silence did betide them.°   245
She hath no faults, who hath the art to hide them.

VITTORIA My soul, like to a ship in a black storm,
Is driven I know not whither.

FLAMINEO   Then cast anchor.
Prosperity doth bewitch men seeming clear,
But seas do laugh, show white, when rocks are near.   250
We cease to grieve, cease to be fortune's slaves,
     [Zanche dies]
Nay cease to die by dying. [To Zanche] Art thou gone,
[to Vittoria] And thou so near the bottom? False report°
Which says that women vie with the nine Muses
For nine tough durable lives. I do not look   255
Who went before, nor who shall follow me;
No, at myself I will begin and end:
While we look up to heaven we confound
Knowledge with knowledge. O I am in a mist.°

VITTORIA O happy they that never saw the court,   260
Nor ever knew great man but by report.
     Vittoria dies

FLAMINEO I recover like a spent taper, for a flash,
And instantly go out.
Let all that belong to great men remember th'old wives' tradition,
to be like the lions° i'th' Tower on Candlemas° day, to mourn   265
if the sun shine, for fear of the pitiful remainder of winter to
come.
'Tis well yet there's some goodness in my death,
My life was a black charnel: I have caught
An everlasting cold. I have lost my voice   270
Most irrecoverably. Farewell, glorious villains.
This busy trade of life appears most vain,
Since rest breeds rest, where all seek pain by pain.°
Let no harsh flattering bells resound my knell
Strike, thunder, and strike loud to my farewell.   275
     [Flamineo] dies

ENGLISH AMBASSADOR [*within*] This way, this way, break ope the
    doors, this way.

LODOVICO Ha, are we betrayed?
    Why then, let's constantly die all together,
    And having finished this most noble deed,
    Defy the worst of fate, not fear to bleed.   280
       Enter [Ambassador] and Giovanni [with Guards]

ENGLISH AMBASSADOR Keep back the Prince! Shoot, shoot!
       [*They shoot, and wound Lodovico*]

LODOVICO O I am wounded.
    I fear I shall be ta'en.

GIOVANNI   You bloody villains,
    By what authority have you committed
    This massacre?

LODOVICO   By thine.

GIOVANNI   Mine?

LODOVICO   Yes, thy uncle,   285
    Which is a part of thee, enjoined us to't.
    Thou know'st me, I am sure: I am Count Lodovic,
    And thy most noble uncle in disguise
    Was last night in thy court.

GIOVANNI   Ha!

CARLO   Yes, that Moor
    Thy father chose his pensioner.

GIOVANNI   He turned murderer?   290
    Away with them to prison, and to torture;
    All that have hands in this shall taste our justice,
    As I hope heaven.

LODOVICO   I do glory yet,
    That I can call this act mine own. For my part,
    The rack, the gallows, and the torturing wheel   295
    Shall be but sound sleeps to me. Here's my rest:
    I limned this night-piece, and it was my best.°

GIOVANNI Remove the bodies.
       [*The Guards begin to remove the bodies*]
                     See, my honoured lord,
    What use you ought make of their punishment.
    Let guilty men remember their black deeds
    Do lean on crutches, made of slender reeds.   300
       [*Exeunt*]

[Epilogue]

Instead of an epilogue only this of Martial supplies me:
Haec fuerint nobis praemia si placui.°

For the action° of the play, 'twas generally well, and I dare affirm,
with the joint testimony of some of their own quality, for the true
imitation of life, without striving to make nature a monster,° the
best that ever became them; whereof as I make a general acknowledgement, so in particular I must remember the well approved   5
industry of my friend Master Perkins,° and confess the worth of
his action did crown both the beginning and end.

THE DUCHESS OF MALFI

THE PERSONS OF THE PLAY°

The Duchess of Malfi	*R. Sharpe*
Cariola, *her waiting-woman*	*R. Pallant*
Ferdinand, Duke of Calabria, *her twin brother*	1. *R. Burbage*
	2. *J. Taylor*
The Cardinal of Aragon, *their elder brother*	1. *H. Condell*
	2. *R. Robinson*
Daniel de Bosola, *provisor of horse to the*	*J. Lowin*
Duchess and retained as a spy by Ferdinand	
Antonio Bologna, *steward of the household to*	1. *W. Ostler*
the Duchess, later her husband	2. *R. Benfield*
Delio, *his friend*	*J. Underwood*
Julia, *the Cardinal's mistress*	*J. Tomson*
Castruccio, *her aged husband*	
Old Lady, *a midwife*	
Marquis of Pescara, *a soldier*	*J. Rice*
Malateste, *a count*	
Silvio ⎤	*T. Pollard*
Roderigo ⎬ Lords	
Grisolan ⎦	
A Doctor	*R. Pallant*
Two Pilgrims	
Three Young Children	
Eight Madmen, an astrologer, a broker, a	*N. Towley,*
doctor, a farmer, a gentleman usher, a	*J. Underwood*, etc.
lawyer, a priest, a tailor	
Court Officers	
Executioners	
Ladies-in-waiting	
Attendants	
Servants	
Forobosco°	*N. Towley*

[Dedication]

To the Right Honourable George Harding,° Baron Berkeley of Berkeley Castle, and Knight of the Order of the Bath to the Illustrious Prince Charles.

My Noble Lord,

That I may present my excuse why, being a stranger to your 5
lordship, I offer this poem to your patronage, I plead this warrant: men who never saw the sea, yet desire to behold that regiment of waters, choose some eminent river to guide them thither, and make that, as it were, their conduct° or postilion. By the like ingenious means has your fame arrived at my knowledge, receiving it from 10
some of worth who both in contemplation and practice owe to your honour their clearest service. I do not altogether look up at your title, the ancientest nobility being but a relic of time past, and the truest honour indeed being for a man to confer honour on himself, which your learning strives to propagate and shall make you arrive 15
at the dignity of a great example. I am confident this work is not unworthy your honour's perusal, for by such poems as this, poets have kissed the hands of great princes and drawn their gentle eyes to look down upon their sheets of paper when the poets themselves were bound up in their winding sheets. The like courtesy from 20
your lordship shall make you live in your grave and laurel spring out of it, when the ignorant scorners of the Muses (that like worms in libraries seem to live only to destroy learning) shall wither, neglected and forgotten. This work and myself I humbly present to your approved censure, it being the utmost of my wishes to have 25
your honourable self my weighty and perspicuous comment: which grace so done me, shall ever be acknowledged

By your Lordship's
in all duty and observance,
John Webster

[Commendatory Verses]

In the just worth of that well-deserver, Mr John Webster, and
upon this masterpiece of tragedy.

In this thou imitat'st one rich, and wise,
That sees his good deeds done before he dies;
As he by works, thou by this work of fame,   5
Hast well provided for thy living name.
To trust to others' honourings is worth's crime—
Thy monument is raised in thy life-time;
And 'tis most just; for every worthy man
Is his own marble, and his merit can   10
Cut him to any figure and express
More art than Death's cathedral palaces,
Where royal ashes keep their court. Thy note
Be ever plainness, 'tis the richest coat,
Thy epitaph only the title be—   15
Write, 'Duchess', that will fetch a tear for thee,
For who e'er saw this duchess live, and die,
That could get off under a bleeding eye?

> *In Tragediam.*
> *Ut lux ex tenebris ictu percussa Tonantis,*   20
> *Illa, ruina malis, claris fit vita poetis.*
> > Thomas Middletonus,°
> > *Poeta & Chron. Londinensis*°

To his friend, Mr John Webster, upon his *Duchess of Malfi.*

I never saw thy duchess till the day   25
That she was lively bodied in thy play;°
Howe'er she answered her low-rated love,°
Her brothers' anger did so fatal prove,
Yet my opinion is, she might speak more,
But never, in her life, so well before.   30
> > *Wil. Rowley*°

To the reader of the author, and his *Duchess of Malfi.*

Crown him a poet, whom nor Rome, nor Greece,
Transcend in all theirs, for a masterpiece:

In which, whiles words and matter change, and men   35
Act one another, he, from whose clear pen
They all took life, to memory hath lent
A lasting fame, to raise his monument.

       John Ford°

The Duchess of Malfi

1.1

[*Enter Antonio and Delio*]

DELIO You are welcome to your country, dear Antonio.
    You have been long in France, and you return
    A very formal Frenchman in your habit.
    How do you like the French court?

ANTONIO   I admire it;
    In seeking to reduce both state and people   5
    To a fixed order, their judicious king
    Begins at home: quits first his royal palace
    Of flattering sycophants, of dissolute
    And infamous persons, which he sweetly terms
    His Master's masterpiece, the work of heaven,   10
    Considering duly that a prince's court
    Is like a common fountain, whence should flow
    Pure silver drops in general; but if't chance
    Some cursed example poison 't near the head,
    Death, and diseases through the whole land spread.   15
    And what is't makes this blessèd government,
    But a most provident Council, who dare freely
    Inform him the corruption of the times?
    Though some o'th' court hold it presumption
    To instruct princes what they ought to do,   20
    It is a noble duty to inform them
    What they ought to foresee.
        [*Enter Bosola*]
                      Here comes Bosola,
    The only court-gall; yet I observe his railing
    Is not for simple love of piety;
    Indeed he rails at those things which he wants,   25
    Would be as lecherous, covetous, or proud,
    Bloody, or envious, as any man,
    If he had means to be so.
        [*Enter Cardinal*]
                     Here's the Cardinal.

BOSOLA I do haunt you still.

CARDINAL   So.

BOSOLA   I have done you
Better service than to be slighted thus.   30
Miserable age, where only the reward°
Of doing well, is the doing of it.

CARDINAL You enforce your merit too much.°

BOSOLA I fell into the galleys in your service, where, for two years
together, I wore two towels instead of a shirt, with a knot on the   35
shoulder, after the fashion of a Roman mantle. Slighted thus? I will
thrive some way: blackbirds fatten best in hard weather;° why not
I, in these dog-days?

CARDINAL Would you could become honest.

BOSOLA With all your divinity, do but direct me the way to it.   40
[Exit Cardinal]
I have known many travel far for it, and yet return as arrant knaves
as they went forth, because they carried themselves always along
with them. Are you gone? [To Antonio and Delio] Some fellows,
they say, are possessed with the devil, but this great fellow were
able to possess the greatest devil, and make him worse.   45

ANTONIO He hath denied thee some suit?

BOSOLA He and his brother are like plum-trees that grow crooked
over standing pools; they are rich, and o'erladen with fruit, but
none but crows, pies, and caterpillars° feed on them. Could I be
one of their flattering panders, I would hang on their ears like a   50
horse-leech till I were full, and then drop off. I pray leave me. Who
would rely upon these miserable dependences, in expectation to be
advanced tomorrow? What creature ever fed worse than hoping
Tantalus?° Nor ever died any man more fearfully than he that
hoped for a pardon. There are rewards for hawks,° and dogs, and   55
(. . .), when they have done us service; but for a soldier, that
hazards his limbs in a battle, nothing but a kind of geometry° is
his last supportation.

DELIO Geometry?

BOSOLA Ay, to hang in a fair pair of slings, take his latter swing in   60
the world upon an honourable pair of crutches, from hospital to
hospital; fare ye well, sir. And yet do not you scorn us, for places
in the court are but like beds in the hospital, where this man's head
lies at that man's foot, and so lower, and lower.
[Exit Bosola]

DELIO I knew this fellow seven years in the galleys   65

For a notorious murder, and 'twas thought
The Cardinal suborned it; he was released
By the French general, Gaston de Foix,°
When he recovered Naples.

ANTONIO   'Tis great pity
He should be thus neglected. I have heard   70
He's very valiant. This foul melancholy
Will poison all his goodness, for, I'll tell you,
If too immoderate sleep be truly said
To be an inward rust unto the soul,
It then doth follow want of action   75
Breeds all black malcontents, and their close rearing,
Like moths in cloth, do hurt for want of wearing.
    [*Enter Silvio, Castruccio, Roderigo, and Grisolan*]°

DELIO The presence 'gins to fill. You promised me
To make me the partaker of the natures
Of some of your great courtiers.

ANTONIO   The Lord Cardinal's   80
And other strangers', that are now in court?
I shall.
    [*Enter Ferdinand*]
        Here comes the great Calabrian Duke.

FERDINAND Who took the ring oftenest?°

SILVIO Antonio Bologna, my lord.

FERDINAND Our sister Duchess' great master of her household? 85
Give him the jewel.
    [*Antonio receives the jewel*]
    When shall we leave this sportive action, and fall to action
    indeed?

CASTRUCCIO Methinks, my lord, you should not desire to go to war
in person.   90

FERDINAND Now for some gravity. Why, my lord?

CASTRUCCIO It is fitting a soldier arise to be a prince, but not
necessary a prince descend to be a captain.

FERDINAND No?

CASTRUCCIO No, my lord, he were far better do it by a deputy.   95

FERDINAND Why should he not as well sleep, or eat, by a deputy?
This might take idle, offensive, and base office from him,
whereas the other deprives him of honour.

CASTRUCCIO Believe my experience: that realm is never long in
quiet, where the ruler is a soldier.   100

FERDINAND Thou told'st me thy wife could not endure fighting.

CASTRUCCIO True, my lord.

FERDINAND And of a jest she broke of a captain she met full of wounds: I have forgot it.

CASTRUCCIO She told him, my lord, he was a pitiful fellow, to lie, like the children of Israel°, all in tents.°

FERDINAND Why, there's a wit were able to undo all the chirurgeons o' the city, for although gallants should quarrel, and had drawn their weapons, and were ready to go to it, yet her persuasions would make them put up.°

CASTRUCCIO That she would, my lord.

FERDINAND How do you like my Spanish jennet?

RODERIGO He is all fire.

FERDINAND I am of Pliny's° opinion, I think he was begot by the wind; he runs as if he were ballasted with quicksilver.°

SILVIO True, my lord, he reels from the tilt often.°

RODERIGO and GRISOLAN Ha, ha, ha!

FERDINAND Why do you laugh? Methinks you that are courtiers should be my touchwood, take fire, when I give fire; that is, laugh when I laugh, were the subject never so witty.

CASTRUCCIO True, my lord, I myself have heard a very good jest, and have scorned to seem to have so silly a wit as to understand it.

FERDINAND But I can laugh at your fool, my lord.

CASTRUCCIO He cannot speak, you know, but he makes faces: my lady cannot abide him.

FERDINAND No?

CASTRUCCIO Nor endure to be in merry company, for she says too much laughing, and too much company, fills her too full of the wrinkle.

FERDINAND I would then have a mathematical instrument made for her face, that she might not laugh out of compass°. I shall shortly visit you at Milan, Lord Silvio.

SILVIO Your grace shall arrive most welcome.

FERDINAND You are a good horseman, Antonio; you have excellent riders in France; what do you think of good horsemanship?

ANTONIO Nobly, my lord. As out of the Grecian horse° issued many famous princes, so out of brave horsemanship arise the first sparks of growing resolution, that raise the mind to noble action.

FERDINAND You have bespoke it worthily.

[*Enter Cardinal, Julia, Duchess, Cariola, with Attendants*]

SILVIO Your brother, the Lord Cardinal, and sister Duchess.

CARDINAL Are the galleys come about?°

GRISOLAN They are, my lord.

FERDINAND Here's the Lord Silvio, is come to take his leave.

DELIO (*to Antonio*) Now, sir, your promise: what's that cardinal?   145
    I mean his temper? They say he's a brave fellow,
    Will play his five thousand crowns at tennis, dance,
    Court ladies, and one that hath fought single combats.

ANTONIO Some such flashes superficially hang on him, for form; but
    observe his inward character: he is a melancholy churchman. The   150
    spring° in his face is nothing but the engendering of toads; where
    he is jealous of any man, he lays worse plots for them than ever
    was imposed on Hercules,° for he strews in his way flatterers,
    panders, intelligencers, atheists, and a thousand such political
    monsters. He should have been Pope; but instead of coming to it   155
    by the primitive decency° of the church, he did bestow bribes so
    largely, and so impudently, as if he would have carried it away
    without heaven's knowledge. Some good he hath done.

DELIO You have given too much of him. What's his brother?

ANTONIO The Duke there? A most perverse, and turbulent nature: 160
    What appears in him mirth, is merely outside—
    If he laugh heartily, it is to laugh
    All honesty out of fashion.

DELIO   Twins?

ANTONIO   In quality:
    He speaks with others' tongues, and hears men's suits
    With others' ears; will seem to sleep o'th' bench   165
    Only to entrap offenders in their answers;
    Dooms men to death by information,
    Rewards by hearsay.

DELIO   Then the law to him
    Is like a foul black cobweb to a spider:
    He makes it his dwelling, and a prison   170
    To entangle those shall feed him.

ANTONIO   Most true.
    He ne'er pays debts, unless they be shrewd turns,°
    And those he will confess that he doth owe.
    Last: for his brother, there, the Cardinal,
    They that do flatter him most say oracles   175
    Hang at his lips; and verily I believe them,
    For the devil speaks in them.

But for their sister, the right noble Duchess,
You never fixed your eye on three fair medals,
Cast in one figure, of so different temper.°   180
For her discourse, it is so full of rapture,
You only will begin then to be sorry
When she doth end her speech; and wish, in wonder,
She held it less vainglory to talk much,
Than your penance to hear her. Whilst she speaks,°   185
She throws upon a man so sweet a look,
That it were able raise one to a galliard
That lay in a dead palsy, and to dote
On that sweet countenance; but in that look
There speaketh so divine a continence°   190
As cuts off all lascivious and vain hope.
Her days are practised in such noble virtue
That sure her nights, nay more, her very sleeps,
Are more in heaven than other ladies' shrifts.
Let all sweet ladies break their flatt'ring glasses,   195
And dress themselves in her.
DELIO   Fie, Antonio,
You play the wire-drawer with her commendations.°
ANTONIO I'll case the picture up: only thus much—°
All her particular worth grows to this sum:
She stains the time past, lights the time to come.   200
        [*Cariola joins Antonio and Delio*]
CARIOLA You must attend my lady, in the gallery,
Some half an hour hence.
ANTONIO I shall.
FERDINAND Sister, I have a suit to you.
DUCHESS   To me, sir?
FERDINAND A gentleman here, Daniel de Bosola: 205
One that was in the galleys.
DUCHESS   Yes, I know him.
FERDINAND A worthy fellow he's. Pray let me entreat for
The provisorship of your horse.
DUCHESS   Your knowledge of him
Commends him, and prefers him.
FERDINAND   Call him hither.
        [*Exit Attendant*]
We are now upon parting. Good Lord Silvio,   210
Do us commend to all our noble friends

At the leaguer.

SILVIO   Sir, I shall.

DUCHESS   You are for Milan?

SILVIO I am.

DUCHESS Bring the caroches; we'll bring you down to the haven.
      [*Exeunt all except Cardinal and Ferdinand.*]

CARDINAL Be sure you entertain that Bosola   215
      For your intelligence. I would not be seen in't;°
      And therefore many times I have slighted him
      When he did court our furtherance, as this morning.

FERDINAND Antonio, the great master of her household,
      Had been far fitter.

CARDINAL   You are deceived in him,   220
      His nature is too honest for such business.
            [*Enter Bosola.*]
      He comes: I'll leave you.
            [*Exit Cardinal*]

BOSOLA   I was lured to you.

FERDINAND My brother here, the Cardinal, could never
      Abide you.

BOSOLA   Never since he was in my debt.

FERDINAND Maybe some oblique character in your face   225
      Made him suspect you?

BOSOLA   Doth he study physiognomy?
      There's no more credit to be given to th'face
      Than to a sick man's urine, which some call
      The physician's whore, because she cozens him.
      He did suspect me wrongfully.

FERDINAND   For that   230
      You must give great men leave to take their times.
      Distrust doth cause us seldom be deceived;
      You see, the oft shaking of the cedar-tree
      Fastens it more at root.

BOSOLA   Yet take heed:°
      For to suspect a friend unworthily   235
      Instructs him the next way to suspect you,°
      And prompts him to deceive you.

FERDINAND   There's gold.

BOSOLA   So:
      What follows? Never rained such show'rs as these
      Without thunderbolts in the tail of them.°

Whose throat must I cut?   240

FERDINAND Your inclination to shed blood rides post
  Before my occasion to use you. I give you that
  To live i'th' court, here, and observe the Duchess:
  To note all the particulars of her 'haviour,
  What suitors do solicit her for marriage   245
  And whom she best affects: she's a young widow,
  I would not have her marry again.

BOSOLA   No, sir?

FERDINAND Do not you ask the reason, but be satisfied
  I say I would not.

BOSOLA   It seems you would create me
  One of your familiars.

FERDINAND   Familiar! What's that?   250

BOSOLA Why, a very quaint invisible devil, in flesh:
  An intelligencer.

FERDINAND   Such a kind of thriving thing
  I would wish thee, and ere long thou may'st arrive
  At a higher place by't.

BOSOLA   Take your devils
  Which hell calls angels. These cursed gifts would make   255
  You a corrupter, me an impudent traitor,
  And should I take these they'd take me to hell.

FERDINAND Sir, I'll take nothing from you that I have given.
  There is a place that I procured for you
  This morning, the provisorship o'th' horse;   260
  Have you heard on't?

BOSOLA   No.

FERDINAND   'Tis yours. Is't not worth thanks?

BOSOLA I would have you curse yourself now, that your bounty,
  Which makes men truly noble, e'er should make
  Me a villain. O, that to avoid ingratitude
  For the good deed you have done me, I must do   265
  All the ill man can invent. Thus the devil
  Candies all sins o'er; and what heaven terms vile,
  That names he complimental.

FERDINAND   Be yourself:
  Keep your old garb of melancholy; 'twill express
  You envy those that stand above your reach,   270
  Yet strive not to come near 'em. This will gain
  Access to private lodgings, where yourself

May, like a politic dormouse—
BOSOLA   As I have seen some
Feed in a lord's dish, half asleep, not seeming°
To listen to any talk; and yet these rogues   275
Have cut his throat in a dream. What's my place?
The provisorship o'th' horse? Say then my corruption
Grew out of horse-dung. I am your creature.
FERDINAND Away.
BOSOLA Let good men, for good deeds, covet good fame,   280
Since place and riches oft are bribes of shame;
Sometimes the devil doth preach.
        Exit Bosola. [Enter Duchess and Cardinal]
CARDINAL We are to part from you; and your own discretion
Must now be your director.
FERDINAND   You are a widow:
You know already what man is, and therefore   285
Let not youth, high promotion, eloquence—
CARDINAL No, nor anything without the addition, honour,
Sway your high blood.
FERDINAND   Marry? They are most luxurious
Will wed twice.
CARDINAL   O fie!
FERDINAND   Their livers are more spotted°
Than Laban's sheep.
DUCHESS   Diamonds are of most value,°   290
They say, that have passed through most jewellers' hands.
FERDINAND Whores, by that rule, are precious.
DUCHESS   Will you hear me?
I'll never marry.
CARDINAL   So most widows say,
But commonly that motion lasts no longer
Than the turning of an hour-glass; the funeral sermon   295
And it, end both together.
FERDINAND   Now hear me:
You live in a rank pasture here, i'th' court;
There is a kind of honey-dew that's deadly:
'Twill poison your fame; look to't; be not cunning,
For they whose faces do belie their hearts   300
Are witches, ere they arrive at twenty years;
Ay, and give the devil suck.
DUCHESS This is terrible good counsel.

FERDINAND Hypocrisy is woven of a fine small thread,
    Subtler than Vulcan's engine; yet, believe't,°   305
    Your darkest actions, nay, your privat'st thoughts,
    Will come to light.
CARDINAL   You may flatter yourself,
    And take your own choice: privately be married
    Under the eaves of night.
FERDINAND   Think't the best voyage°
    That e'er you made like the irregular crab,   310
    Which, though't goes backward, thinks that it goes right,
    Because it goes its own way. But observe,
    Such weddings may more properly be said
    To be executed, than celebrated.
CARDINAL The marriage night   315
    Is the entrance into some prison.
FERDINAND   And those joys,
    Those lustful pleasures, are like heavy sleeps
    Which do fore-run man's mischief.
CARDINAL   Fare you well.
    Wisdom begins at the end: remember it.°
       [Exit Cardinal]
DUCHESS I think this speech between you both was studied,   320
    It came so roundly off.
FERDINAND   You are my sister,
    This was my father's poniard: do you see?
    I'd be loth to see't look rusty, 'cause 'twas his.
    I would have you to give o'er these chargeable revels;
    A visor and a mask are whispering-rooms   325
    That were ne'er built for goodness: fare ye well:
    And women like that part which, like the lamprey,
    Hath ne'er a bone in't.
DUCHESS   Fie, sir!
FERDINAND   Nay,
    I mean the tongue: variety of courtship.
    What cannot a neat knave with a smooth tale   330
    Make a woman believe? Farewell, lusty widow.
       [Exit Ferdinand]
DUCHESS Shall this move me? If all my royal kindred
    Lay in my way unto this marriage,
    I'd make them my low footsteps; and even now,
    Even in this hate, as men in some great battles,   335

By apprehending danger, have achieved
Almost impossible actions (I have heard soldiers say so)
So I, through frights, and threatenings, will assay
This dangerous venture. Let old wives report
I winked and chose a husband. Cariola,°   340
    [Enter Cariola]
To thy known secrecy I have given up
More than my life, my fame.

CARIOLA   Both shall be safe:
For I'll conceal this secret from the world
As warily as those that trade in poison
Keep poison from their children.

DUCHESS   Thy protestation   345
Is ingenious and hearty: I believe it.
Is Antonio come?

CARIOLA   He attends you.

DUCHESS   Good dear soul,
Leave me, but place thyself behind the arras,
Where thou may'st overhear us. Wish me good speed
For I am going into a wilderness,   350
Where I shall find nor path, nor friendly clew
To be my guide.
    [Cariola withdraws behind the arras. Enter Antonio]
           I sent for you: sit down,
Take pen and ink, and write. Are you ready?

ANTONIO   Yes.

DUCHESS What did I say?

ANTONIO   That I should write somewhat.

DUCHESS O, I remember.   355
After these triumphs, and this large expense,
It's fit, like thrifty husbands, we inquire°
What's laid up for tomorrow.

ANTONIO So please your beauteous excellence.

DUCHESS   Beauteous?
Indeed I thank you: I look young for your sake.   360
You have ta'en my cares upon you.

ANTONIO   I'll fetch your grace
The particulars of your revenue and expense.

DUCHESS O, you are an upright treasurer; but you mistook,
For when I said I meant to make inquiry
What's laid up for tomorrow, I did mean   365

What's laid up yonder for me.
ANTONIO   Where?
DUCHESS   In heaven.
  I am making my will, as 'tis fit princes should
  In perfect memory; and I pray, sir, tell me
  Were not one better make it smiling, thus,
  Than in deep groans, and terrible ghastly looks,   370
  As if the gifts we parted with procured
  That violent distraction?
ANTONIO   O, much better.
DUCHESS If I had a husband now, this care were quit;
  But I intend to make you overseer.
  What good deed shall we first remember? Say.   375
ANTONIO Begin with that first good deed began i'th' world
  After man's creation, the sacrament of marriage;
  I'd have you first provide for a good husband,
  Give him all.
DUCHESS   All?
ANTONIO   Yes, your excellent self.
DUCHESS In a winding sheet?
ANTONIO   In a couple.°   380
DUCHESS Saint Winifred, that were a strange will!°
ANTONIO 'Twere strange if there were no will in you
  To marry again.
DUCHESS   What do you think of marriage?
ANTONIO I take't, as those that deny purgatory:
  It locally contains or heaven or hell;   385
  There's no third place in't.
DUCHESS   How do you affect it?
ANTONIO My banishment, feeding my melancholy,
  Would often reason thus:—
DUCHESS   Pray let's hear it.
ANTONIO Say a man never marry, nor have children,
  What takes that from him? Only the bare name   390
  Of being a father, or the weak delight
  To see the little wanton ride a-cock-horse
  Upon a painted stick, or hear him chatter
  Like a taught starling.
DUCHESS   Fie, fie, what's all this?
  One of your eyes is bloodshot; use my ring to't,   395
  They say 'tis very sovereign: 'twas my wedding ring,

And I did vow never to part with it,
But to my second husband.
ANTONIO You have parted with it now
DUCHESS Yes, to help your eyesight.
ANTONIO   You have made me stark blind.   400
DUCHESS How?
ANTONIO There is a saucy and ambitious devil
Is dancing in this circle.
DUCHESS   Remove him.
ANTONIO   How?
DUCHESS There needs small conjuration, when your finger
May do it: thus, is it fit?
      [*She puts her ring upon his finger*]. *He kneels*
ANTONIO   What said you?
DUCHESS   Sir,   405
This goodly roof of yours is too low built;
I cannot stand upright in't, nor discourse,
Without I raise it higher: raise yourself,
Or if you please, my hand to help you: so.
      [*Raises him*]
ANTONIO Ambition, madam, is a great man's madness,   410
That is not kept in chains, and close-pent rooms,
But in fair lightsome lodgings, and is girt
With the wild noise of prattling visitants,
Which makes it lunatic, beyond all cure.
Conceive not I am so stupid but I aim   415
Whereto your favours tend; but he's a fool
That, being a-cold, would thrust his hands i'th' fire
To warm them.
DUCHESS   So, now the ground's broke,
You may discover what a wealthy mine
I make you lord of.
ANTONIO   O, my unworthiness.   420
DUCHESS You were ill to sell yourself;
This darkning of your worth is not like that
Which tradesmen use i'th' city: their false lights
Are to rid bad wares off; and I must tell you,
If you will know where breathes a complete man   425
(I speak it without flattery) turn your eyes
And progress through yourself.°
ANTONIO Were there nor heaven nor hell,

I should be honest, I have long served virtue,
And ne'er ta'en wages of her.

DUCHESS   Now she pays it.   430
The misery of us that are born great:
We are forced to woo, because none dare woo us;°
And as a tyrant doubles with his words,
And fearfully equivocates, so we
Are forced to express our violent passions   435
In riddles, and in dreams, and leave the path
Of simple virtue, which was never made
To seem the thing it is not. Go, go brag
You have left me heartless: mine is in your bosom,
I hope 'twill multiply love there. You do tremble: 440
Make not your heart so dead a piece of flesh
To fear more than to love me. Sir, be confident;
What is't distracts you? This is flesh, and blood, sir;
'Tis not the figure cut in alabaster
Kneels at my husband's tomb. Awake, awake, man.   445
I do here put off all vain ceremony,
And only do appear to you a young widow
That claims you for her husband, and like a widow
I use but half a blush in't.

ANTONIO   Truth speak for me:
I will remain the constant sanctuary   450
Of your good name.

DUCHESS   I thank you, gentle love,
And 'cause you shall not come to me in debt,
Being now my steward, here upon your lips
I sign your *Quietus est.*°
        [*Kisses him*]
This you should have begged now.   455
I have seen children oft eat sweetmeats thus,
As fearful to devour them too soon.

ANTONIO But for your brothers?

DUCHESS   Do not think of them.
All discord, without this circumference,°
Is only to be pitied, and not feared;   460
Yet, should they know it, time will easily
Scatter the tempest.

ANTONIO   These words should be mine,
And all the parts you have spoke, if some part of it

Would not have savoured flattery.

DUCHESS Kneel.   465

    [*They kneel. Cariola comes from behind the arras*]

ANTONIO Hah?

DUCHESS Be not amazed, this woman's of my counsel.
  I have heard lawyers say, a contract in a chamber
  Per verba de presenti is absolute marriage.°
  Bless, heaven, this sacred Gordian, which let violence°   470
  Never untwine.

ANTONIO And may our sweet affections, like the spheres,°
  Be still in motion.

DUCHESS   Quickening, and make°
  The like soft music.

ANTONIO That we may imitate the loving palms,   475
  Best emblem of a peaceful marriage,
  That ne'er bore fruit divided.°

DUCHESS What can the church force more?

ANTONIO That Fortune may not know an accident,
  Either of joy or sorrow, to divide   480
  Our fixèd wishes.

DUCHESS   How can the church build faster?
  We now are man and wife, and 'tis the church
  That must but echo this.—Maid, stand apart—
  I now am blind.

ANTONIO   What's your conceit in this?°

DUCHESS I would have you lead your fortune by the hand,   485
  Unto your marriage bed
  (You speak in me this, for we now are one):
  We'll only lie, and talk together, and plot
  T'appease my humorous kindred; and if you please,
  Like the old tale, in 'Alexander and Lodovic',°   490
  Lay a naked sword between us, keep us chaste.
  O, let me shroud my blushes in your bosom,
  Since 'tis the treasury of all my secrets.

    [*Exeunt Duchess and Antonio*]

CARIOLA Whether the spirit of greatness or of woman
  Reign most in her, I know not, but it shows   495
  A fearful madness; I owe her much of pity.

    [*Exit*]

2.1

[*Enter Bosola and Castruccio*]

BOSOLA You say you would fain be taken for an eminent courtier?

CASTRUCCIO 'Tis the very main of my ambition.

BOSOLA Let me see, you have a reasonable good face for't already, and your night-cap expresses your ears sufficient largely;° I would have you learn to twirl the strings of your band with a good grace; and in a set speech, at th'end of every sentence, to hum, three or four times, or blow your nose, till it smart again, to recover your memory. When you come to be a president in criminal causes, if you smile upon a prisoner, hang him, but if you frown upon him and threaten him, let him be sure to 'scape the gallows.

CASTRUCCIO I would be a very merry president.

BOSOLA Do not sup o' nights, 'twill beget you an admirable wit.

CASTRUCCIO Rather it would make me have a good stomach to quarrel, for they say your roaring boys eat meat seldom, and that makes them so valiant. But how shall I know whether the people take me for an eminent fellow?

BOSOLA I will teach a trick to know it: give out you lie a-dying, and if you hear the common people curse you, be sure you are taken for one of the prime night-caps.

[*Enter an Old Lady*]

You come from painting now?

OLD LADY From what?

BOSOLA Why, from your scurvy face-physic. To behold thee not painted inclines somewhat near a miracle. These, in thy face here, were deep ruts and foul sloughs the last progress. There was a lady in France that, having had the smallpox, flayed the skin off her face, to make it more level; and whereas before she looked like a nutmeg-grater, after she resembled an abortive hedgehog.

OLD LADY Do you call this painting?

BOSOLA No, no, but careening of an old morphewed lady, to make her disembogue° again. There's rough-cast phrase to your plastic.

OLD LADY It seems you are well acquainted with my closet.

BOSOLA One would suspect it for a shop of witchcraft, to find in it the fat of serpents, spawn of snakes, Jews' spittle, and their young children's ordures, and all these for the face. I would sooner eat a dead pigeon, taken from the soles of the feet of one sick of the plague,° than kiss one of you fasting.° Here are two of you, whose

sin of your youth° is the very patrimony of the physician, makes
him renew his footcloth with the spring and change his high-
prized° courtezan with the fall of the leaf: I do wonder you do not
loathe yourselves. Observe my meditation now: 40
What thing is in this outward form of man
To be beloved? We account it ominous
If nature do produce a colt, or lamb,
A fawn, or goat, in any limb resembling
A man; and fly from't as a prodigy.   45
Man stands amazed to see his deformity
In any other creature but himself.
But in our own flesh, though we bear diseases
Which have their true names only ta'en from beasts,
As the most ulcerous wolf, and swinish measle;   50
Though we are eaten up of lice and worms,
And though continually we bear about us
A rotten and dead body, we delight
To hide it in rich tissue. All our fear,
Nay, all our terror, is lest our physician   55
Should put us in the ground, to be made sweet.
Your wife's gone to Rome: you two couple, and get you
To the wells at Lucca, to recover your aches.
        [*Exeunt Castruccio and Old Lady*]
I have other work on foot. I observe our Duchess
Is sick o' days, she pukes, her stomach seethes,   60
The fins of her eyelids look most teeming blue,
She wanes i'th' cheek, and waxes fat i'th' flank;
And, contrary to our Italian fashion,
Wears a loose-bodied gown: there's somewhat in't!°
I have a trick may chance discover it,   65
A pretty one; I have bought some apricots,
The first our spring yields.
        [*Enter Antonio and Delio in conversation apart*]
DELIO   And so long since married?
    You amaze me.
ANTONIO   Let me seal your lips for ever,
For did I think that anything but th'air
Could carry these words from you, I should wish   70
You had no breath at all.
[*To Bosola*] Now, sir, in your contemplation? You are studying to
become a great wise fellow?

BOSOLA O sir, the opinion of wisdom is a foul tetter that runs all over a man's body: if simplicity direct us to have no evil, it directs 75 us to a happy being, for the subtlest folly proceeds from the subtlest wisdom. Let me be simply honest.

ANTONIO I do understand your inside.

BOSOLA Do you so?

ANTONIO Because you would not seem to appear to th' world puffed 80 up with your preferment, you continue this out-of-fashion° melancholy. Leave it, leave it.

BOSOLA Give me leave to be honest in any phrase, in any compliment whatsoever. Shall I confess myself to you? I look no higher than I can reach. They are the gods that must ride on winged 85 horses; a lawyer's mule of a slow pace will both suit my disposition and business; for mark me, when a man's mind rides faster than his horse can gallop, they quickly both tire.

ANTONIO You would look up to heaven, but I think
The devil, that rules i'th' air, stands in your light. 90

BOSOLA O sir, you are lord of the ascendant,° chief man with the Duchess, a Duke was your cousin-german removed. Say you were lineally descended from King Pepin,° or he himself, what of this? Search the heads of the greatest rivers in the world, you shall find them but bubbles of water. Some would think the souls of princes 95 were brought forth by some more weighty cause than those of meaner persons. They are deceived; there's the same hand to them, the like passions sway them: the same reason that makes a vicar go to law for a tithe-pig and undo his neighbours, makes them spoil a whole province, and batter down goodly cities with the cannon. 100

[*Enter Duchess with Cariola and Old Lady*]

DUCHESS Your arm, Antonio: do I not grow fat?
I am exceeding short-winded. Bosola,
I would have you, sir, provide for me a litter,
Such a one as the Duchess of Florence rode in.

BOSOLA The Duchess used one when she was great with child. 105

DUCHESS I think she did. [*To Old Lady*] Come hither, mend my ruff.
Here, when? Thou art such a tedious lady, and
Thy breath smells of lemon pills. Would thou hadst done!
Shall I swoon under thy fingers? I am
So troubled with the mother.

BOSOLA [*aside*]   I fear too much.° 110

DUCHESS I have heard you say that the French courtiers

Wear their hats on 'fore the King.
ANTONIO   I have seen it.
DUCHESS In the presence?
ANTONIO Yes.
DUCHESS   Why should not we bring up that fashion?°   115
    'Tis ceremony more than duty, that consists
    In the removing of a piece of felt.
    Be you the example to the rest o'th' court,
    Put on your hat first.
ANTONIO   You must pardon me:
    I have seen, in colder countries than in France,
    Nobles stand bare to th'Prince; and the distinction°   120
    Methought showed reverently.
BOSOLA I have a present for your grace.
DUCHESS   For me, sir?
BOSOLA Apricots, madam.
DUCHESS   O sir, where are they?
    I have heard of none to-year.
BOSOLA [aside]   Good, her colour rises.°
DUCHESS Indeed I thank you; they are wondrous fair ones.   125
    What an unskilful fellow is our gardener!
    We shall have none this month.
BOSOLA Will not your grace pare them?
DUCHESS No, they taste of musk, methinks; indeed they do.
BOSOLA I know not; yet I wish your grace had pared 'em.   130
DUCHESS Why?
BOSOLA   I forgot to tell you the knave gardener
    Only to raise his profit by them the sooner,
    Did ripen them in horse-dung.
DUCHESS   O you jest.
    [To Antonio] You shall judge: pray taste one.
ANTONIO   Indeed, madam,
    I do not love the fruit.
DUCHESS   Sir, you are loth   135
    To rob us of our dainties: 'tis a delicate fruit,
    They say they are restorative.
BOSOLA   'Tis a pretty art,
    This grafting.
DUCHESS   'Tis so: a bettering of nature.°
BOSOLA To make a pippin grow upon a crab,°
    A damson on a blackthorn. [Aside] How greedily she eats them!   140

A whirlwind strike off these bawd farthingales,
For, but for that, and the loose-bodied gown,
I should have discovered apparently°
The young springal cutting a caper in her belly.

DUCHESS I thank you, Bosola, they were right good ones—   145
If they do not make me sick.

ANTONIO   How now, madam?

DUCHESS This green fruit and my stomach are not friends.
How they swell me!

BOSOLA [*aside*]   Nay, you are too much swelled already.

DUCHESS O, I am in an extreme cold sweat!

BOSOLA I am very sorry.   150

DUCHESS Lights to my chamber. O good Antonio,
I fear I am undone.
        Exit [*Duchess*]

DELIO   Lights there, lights!
        [*Exeunt all except Antonio and Delio*]

ANTONIO O my most trusty Delio, we are lost.
I fear she's fallen in labour, and there's left
No time for her remove.

DELIO   Have you prepared   155
Those ladies to attend her? and procured
That politic safe conveyance for the midwife
Your Duchess plotted?

ANTONIO I have.

DELIO   Make use then of this forced occasion.
Give out that Bosola hath poisoned her   160
With these apricots: that will give some colour
For her keeping close.

ANTONIO   Fie, fie, the physicians
Will then flock to her.

DELIO   For that you may pretend
She'll use some prepared antidote of her own,
Lest the physicians should repoison her.   165

ANTONIO I am lost in amazement, I know not what to think on't.
        Exeunt

2.2

[Enter Bosola]

BOSOLA So, so: there's no question but her tetchiness and most vulturous eating of the apricots are apparent signs of breeding.

[Enter Old Lady. Bosola intercepts her]

OLD LADY Now? I am in haste, sir.

BOSOLA There was a young waiting-woman had a monstrous desire to see the glass-house.°   5

OLD LADY Nay, pray let me go.

BOSOLA And it was only to know what strange instrument it was should swell up a glass to the fashion of a woman's belly.

OLD LADY I will hear no more of the glass-house; you are still abusing women!   10

BOSOLA Who I? No, only, by the way now and then, mention your frailties. The orange tree bears ripe and green fruit, and blossoms all together, and some of you give entertainment for pure love, but more, for more precious reward. The lusty spring smells well; but drooping autumn tastes well. If we have the same golden showers 15 that rained in the time of Jupiter the Thunderer, you have the same Danäes° still, to hold up their laps to receive them. Didst thou never study the mathematics?

OLD LADY What's that, sir?

BOSOLA Why, to know the trick how to make a many lines meet 20 in one centre.° Go, go: give your foster-daughters° good counsel: tell them that the devil takes delight to hang at a woman's girdle, like a false rusty watch, that she cannot discern how the time passes.

[Exit Old Lady. Enter Antonio, Delio, Roderigo, Grisolan]

ANTONIO Shut up the court gates.

RODERIGO   Why, sir? What's the danger? 25

ANTONIO Shut up the posterns presently, and call
     All the officers o'th' court.

GRISOLAN   I shall instantly.

[Exit Grisolan]

ANTONIO Who keeps the key o'th' park gate?

RODERIGO   Forobosco.°

ANTONIO Let him bring't presently.

[Exit Roderigo. Enter Grisolan with Officers.]

FIRST OFFICER O, gentlemen o'th' court, the foulest treason! 30

BOSOLA [*aside*] If that these apricots should be poisoned now,
    Without my knowledge!
FIRST OFFICER There was taken even now a Switzer° in the
    Duchess' bedchamber.
SECOND OFFICER A Switzer?   35
FIRST OFFICER With a pistol° in his great cod-piece.
BOSOLA Ha, ha, ha!
FIRST OFFICER The cod-piece was the case for't.
SECOND OFFICER There was a cunning traitor. Who would have
    searched his cod-piece?   40
FIRST OFFICER True, if he had kept out of the ladies' chambers: and
    all the moulds of his buttons were leaden bullets.
SECOND OFFICER O, wicked cannibal—a fire-lock in's cod-piece!
FIRST OFFICER 'Twas a French plot, upon my life.°
SECOND OFFICER To see what the devil can do!   45
ANTONIO All the officers here?
OFFICERS We are.
ANTONIO Gentlemen,
    We have lost much plate you know; and but this evening
    Jewels, to the value of four thousand ducats,   50
    Are missing in the Duchess' cabinet.
    Are the gates shut?
OFFICERS   Yes.
ANTONIO   'Tis the Duchess' pleasure
    Each officer be locked into his chamber
    Till the sun-rising; and to send the keys
    Of all their chests, and of their outward doors,   55
    Into her bedchamber. She is very sick.
RODERIGO At her pleasure.
ANTONIO She entreats you take 't not ill; the innocent
    Shall be the more approved by it.
BOSOLA [*to the Officer*] Gentleman o'th' wood-yard, where's your   60
    Switzer now?
FIRST OFFICER By this hand, 'twas credibly reported by one o' the
    blackguard.
        [*Exeunt all except Antonio and Delio*]
DELIO How fares it with the Duchess?
ANTONIO   She's exposed
    Unto the worst of torture, pain, and fear.   65
DELIO Speak to her all happy comfort.
ANTONIO How I do play the fool with mine own danger!

You are this night, dear friend, to post to Rome;
My life lies in your service.

DELIO   Do not doubt me.

ANTONIO   O, 'tis far from me, and yet fear presents me   70
Somewhat that looks like danger.

DELIO   Believe it,
'Tis but the shadow of your fear, no more.
How superstitiously we mind our evils!
The throwing down salt, or crossing of a hare,
Bleeding at nose, the stumbling of a horse,   75
Or singing of a cricket, are of pówer
To daunt whole man in us. Sir, fare you well.°
I wish you all the joys of a blessed father;
And, for my faith, lay this unto your breast:°
Old friends, like old swords, still are trusted best.°   80
     [*Exit Delio. Enter Cariola*]

CARIOLA   Sir, you are the happy father of a son;
Your wife commends him to you.

ANTONIO   Blessed comfort!
For heaven' sake tend her well; I'll presently
Go set a figure for's nativity.°
     Exeunt

2.3

     [*Enter Bosola with a dark lantern*°]

BOSOLA   Sure I did hear a woman shriek: list, ha?
And the sound came, if I received it right,
From the Duchess' lodgings. There's some stratagem
In the confining all our courtiers
To their several wards. I must have part of it,   5
My intelligence will freeze else. List again!°
It may be 'twas the melancholy bird,
Best friend of silence and of solitariness,
The owl, that screamed so.
     [*Enter Antonio*]
                   Ha, Antonio!

ANTONIO   I heard some noise. Who's there? What art thou? Speak.   10

BOSOLA   Antonio? Put not your face nor body

To such a forced expression of fear:
I am Bosola, your friend.
ANTONIO   Bosola!.
[*Aside*] This mole does undermine me. [*To him*] Heard you not
A noise even now?
BOSOLA   From whence?
ANTONIO   From the Duchess' lodging.   15
BOSOLA Not I. Did you?
ANTONIO   I did: or else I dreamed.
BOSOLA Let's walk towards it.
ANTONIO   No: it may be 'twas
But the rising of the wind.
BOSOLA   Very likely.
Methinks 'tis very cold, and yet you sweat.
You look wildly.
ANTONIO   I have been setting a figure   20
For the Duchess' jewels.
BOSOLA   Ah, and how falls your question?°
Do you find it radical?
ANTONIO   What's that to you?
'Tis rather to be questioned what design,
When all men were commanded to their lodgings,
Makes you a night-walker.
BOSOLA   In sooth I'll tell you: 25
Now all the court's asleep, I thought the devil
Had least to do here; I came to say my prayers.
And if it do offend you I do so,
You are a fine courtier.
ANTONIO [*aside*]   This fellow will undo me.
[*To him*] You gave the Duchess apricots today;   30
Pray heaven they were not poisoned!
BOSOLA   Poisoned! A Spanish fig°
For the imputation.
ANTONIO   Traitors are ever confident,
Till they are discovered. There were jewels stol'n too;
In my conceit, none are to be suspected
More than yourself.
BOSOLA   You are a false steward.   35
ANTONIO Saucy slave! I'll pull thee up by the roots.
BOSOLA Maybe the ruin will crush you to pieces.
ANTONIO You are an impudent snake indeed, sir;

Are you scarce warm, and do you show your sting?° 40
[BOSOLA] . . .
ANTONIO You libel well, sir.
BOSOLA   No, sir, copy it out,
    And I will set my hand to't.
ANTONIO [*aside*]   My nose bleeds.
        [*He draws an initialled handkerchief*]
    One that were superstitious would count
    This ominous, when it merely comes by chance:
    Two letters, that are wrought here for my name, 45
    Are drowned in blood!
    Mere accident. [*To him*] For you, sir, I'll take order:
    I'th'morn you shall be safe. [*Aside*] 'Tis that must colour°
    Her lying-in. [*To him*] Sir, this door you pass not:
    I do not hold it fit that you come near 50
    The Duchess' lodgings, till you have quit yourself.
    [*Aside*] The great are like the base, nay, they are the same,
    When they seek shameful ways to avoid shame.
        Exit [Antonio]
BOSOLA Antonio hereabout did drop a paper;
    Some of your help, false friend. O, here it is:° 55
    What's here? A child's nativity calculated!
    [*Reads*] 'The Duchess was delivered of a son, 'tween the hours
    twelve and one, in the night: Anno Dom. 1504'—that's this
    year—'decimo nono Decembris'—that's this night—'taken accord-
    ing to the meridian of Malfi'—that's our Duchess: happy dis- 60
    covery!—'The lord of the first house, being combust in the
    ascendant, signifies short life; and Mars being in a human sign,
    joined to the tail of the Dragon, in the eighth house, doth threaten
    a violent death; caetera non scrutantur.'°
    Why now 'tis most apparent. This precise fellow 65
    Is the Duchess' bawd. I have it to my wish.
    This is a parcel of intelligency
    Our courtiers were cased up for! It needs must follow
    That I must be committed on pretence
    Of poisoning her; which I'll endure, and laugh at. 70
    If one could find the father now; but that
    Time will discover. Old Castruccio
    I'th' morning posts to Rome; by him I'll send
    A letter, that shall make her brothers' galls
    O'erflow their livers. This was a thrifty way. 75

Though lust do mask in ne'er so strange disguise,
She's oft found witty, but is never wise.
   [*Exit*]

2.4

[*Enter Cardinal and Julia*]

CARDINAL   Sit, thou art my best of wishes. Prithee tell me
  What trick didst thou invent to come to Rome
  Without thy husband.

JULIA   Why, my lord, I told him
  I came to visit an old anchorite
  Here, for devotion.

CARDINAL   Thou art a witty false one:°   5
  I mean to him.

JULIA   You have prevailed with me
  Beyond my strongest thoughts; I would not now
  Find you inconstant.

CARDINAL   Do not put thyself
  To such a voluntary torture, which proceeds
  Out of your own guilt.

JULIA   How, my lord?

CARDINAL   You fear   10
  My constancy, because you have approved
  Those giddy and wild turnings in yourself.

JULIA   Did you e'er find them?

CARDINAL   Sooth, generally for women.
  A man might strive to make glass malleable,
  Ere he should make them fixèd.

JULIA   So, my lord.   15

CARDINAL   We had need go borrow that fantastic glass°
  Invented by Galileo the Florentine,
  To view another spacious world i'th' moon,
  And look to find a constant woman there.

JULIA   This is very well, my lord.

CARDINAL   Why do you weep?   20
  Are tears your justification? The self-same tears
  Will fall into your husband's bosom, lady,
  With a loud protestation that you love him

Above the world. Come, I'll love you wisely,
That's jealously, since I am very certain   25
You cannot me make cuckold.

JULIA   I'll go home
To my husband.

CARDINAL   You may thank me, lady,
I have taken you off your melancholy perch,
Bore you upon my fist, and showed you game,
And let you fly at it. I pray thee, kiss me.°   30
When thou wast with thy husband, thou wast watched
Like a tame elephant: still you are to thank me.°
Thou hadst only kisses from him, and high feeding,
But what delight was that? 'Twas just like one
That hath a little fingering on the lute,   35
Yet cannot tune it: still you are to thank me.

JULIA You told me of a piteous wound i'th' heart,
And a sick liver, when you wooed me first,
And spake like one in physic.

CARDINAL [calling off-stage]   Who's that?°
Rest firm: for my affection to thee,   40
Lightning moves slow to't.
        [Enter Servant]

SERVANT   Madam, a gentleman,°
That's come post from Malfi, desires to see you.

CARDINAL Let him enter, I'll withdraw.
        Exit [Cardinal]

SERVANT   He says,
Your husband, old Castruccio, is come to Rome,
Most pitifully tired with riding post.   45
        [Exit Servant. Enter Delio]

JULIA Signor Delio! [Aside] 'Tis one of my old suitors.

DELIO I was bold to come and see you.

JULIA   Sir, you are welcome.

DELIO Do you lie here?

JULIA   Sure, your own experience
Will satisfy you, no: our Roman prelates
Do not keep lodging for ladies.

DELIO   Very well.   50
I have brought you no commendations from your husband,
For I know none by him.

JULIA   I hear he's come to Rome?

DELIO I never knew man and beast, of a horse and a knight,
    So weary of each other. If he had had a good back,°
    He would have undertook to have borne his horse, 55
    His breech was so pitifully sore.
JULIA   Your laughter
    Is my pity.
DELIO   Lady, I know not whether
    You want money, but I have brought you some.
JULIA From my husband?
DELIO   No, from mine own allowance.
JULIA I must hear the condition, ere I be bound to take it. 60
DELIO Look on't, 'tis gold: hath it not a fine colour?
JULIA I have a bird more beautiful.
DELIO Try the sound on't.
JULIA   A lute-string far exceeds it.
    It hath no smell, like cassia or civet,
    Nor is it physical, though some fond doctors 65
    Persuade us seethe 't in cullises. I'll tell you,
    This is a creature bred by—
        [Enter Servant]
SERVANT   Your husband's come,
    Hath delivered a letter to the Duke of Calabria,
    That, to my thinking, hath put him out of his wits.
        [Exit Servant]
JULIA Sir, you hear: 70
    Pray let me know your business and your suit,
    As briefly as can be.
DELIO   With good speed. I would wish you,
    At such time as you are non-resident
    With your husband, my mistress.
JULIA Sir, I'll go ask my husband if I shall, 75
    And straight return your answer.
        Exit [Julia]
DELIO   Very fine.
    Is this her wit or honesty that speaks thus?
    I heard one say the Duke was highly moved
    With a letter sent from Malfi: I do fear
    Antonio is betrayed. How fearfully 80
    Shows his ambition now! Unfortunate fortune!
    They pass through whirlpools and deep woes do shun,
    Who the event weigh, ere the action's done.
        Exit

2.5

[Enter] Cardinal, and Ferdinand with a letter

FERDINAND I have this night digged up a mandrake.

CARDINAL   Say you?

FERDINAND And I am grown mad with't.

CARDINAL   What's the prodigy?

FERDINAND Read there, a sister damned; she's loose i'th' hilts,°
  Grown a notorious strumpet.

CARDINAL   Speak lower.

FERDINAND   Lower?
  Rogues do not whisper 't now, but seek to publish 't,   5
  As servants do the bounty of their lords,
  Aloud; and with a covetous searching eye
  To mark who note them. O confusion seize her!
  She hath had most cunning bawds to serve her turn,
  And more secure conveyances for lust   10
  Than towns of garrison for service.

CARDINAL   Is't possible?°
  Can this be certain?

FERDINAND   Rhubarb, O for rhubarb°
  To purge this choler! Here's the cursèd day
  To prompt my memory, and here 't shall stick°
  Till of her bleeding heart I make a sponge   15
  To wipe it out.

CARDINAL   Why do you make yourself
  So wild a tempest?

FERDINAND   Would I could be one,
  That I might toss her palace 'bout her ears,
  Root up her goodly forests, blast her meads,
  And lay her general territory as waste   20
  As she hath done her honours.

CARDINAL   Shall our blood,
  The royal blood of Aragon and Castile,
  Be thus attainted?

FERDINAND   Apply desperate physic—
  We must not now use balsamum, but fire,°
  The smarting cupping-glass, for that's the mean   25
  To purge infected blood, such blood as hers.
  There is a kind of pity in mine eye,
  I'll give it to my handkercher; and now 'tis here,

I'll bequeath this to her bastard.

CARDINAL   What to do?

FERDINAND Why, to make soft lint for his mother's wounds,   30
When I have hewed her to pieces.

CARDINAL   Cursed creature!
Unequal nature, to place women's hearts°
So far upon the left side!

FERDINAND   Foolish men,°
That e'er will trust their honour in a bark
Made of so slight, weak bulrush as is woman,   35
Apt every minute to sink it!

CARDINAL Thus ignorance, when it hath purchased honour,
It cannot wield it.

FERDINAND   Methinks I see her laughing,
Excellent hyena! Talk to me somewhat, quickly,
Or my imagination will carry me   40
To see her in the shameful act of sin.

CARDINAL With whom?

FERDINAND   Haply with some strong thighed bargeman,
Or one o'th' wood-yard, that can quoit the sledge,°
Or toss the bar, or else some lovely squire
That carries coals up to her privy lodgings.°   45

CARDINAL You fly beyond your reason.

FERDINAND   Go to, mistress!
'Tis not your whore's milk that shall quench my wild-fire,
But your whore's blood.

CARDINAL How idly shows this rage! which carries you,
As men conveyed by witches, through the air   50
On violent whirlwinds. This intemperate noise
Fitly resembles deaf men's shrill discourse,
Who talk aloud, thinking all other men
To have their imperfection.

FERDINAND   Have not you
My palsy?

CARDINAL   Yes, I can be angry   55
Without this rupture. There is not in nature
A thing that makes man so deformed, so beastly,
As doth intemperate anger. Chide yourself.
You have divers men who never yet expressed
Their strong desire of rest, but by unrest,   60
By vexing of themselves. Come, put yourself

In tune.

FERDINAND So, I will only study to seem
    The thing I am not. I could kill her now,
    In you, or in myself, for I do think   65
    It is some sin in us heaven doth revenge
    By her.

CARDINAL Are you stark mad?

FERDINAND   I would have their bodies
    Burnt in a coal-pit, with the ventage stopped,
    That their cursed smoke might not ascend to heaven;   70
    Or dip the sheets they lie in, in pitch or sulphur,
    Wrap them in't, and then light them like a match;
    Or else to boil their bastard to a cullis,
    And give 't his lecherous father, to renew
    The sin of his back.

CARDINAL   I'll leave you.   75

FERDINAND Nay, I have done.
    I am confident, had I been damned in hell
    And should have heard of this, it would have put me
    Into a cold sweat. In, in, I'll go sleep.
    Till I know who leaps my sister, I'll not stir: 80
    That known, I'll find scorpions to string my whips,
    And fix her in a general eclipse.°
      Exeunt

3.1

[Enter Antonio and Delio]

ANTONIO Our noble friend, my most beloved Delio,
  O, you have been a stranger long at court.
  Came you along with the Lord Ferdinand?

DELIO I did, sir; and how fares your noble Duchess?

ANTONIO Right fortunately well. She's an excellent   5
  Feeder of pedigrees: since you last saw her,
  She hath had two children more, a son and daughter.

DELIO Methinks 'twas yesterday. Let me but wink,
  And not behold your face, which to mine eye
  Is somewhat leaner, verily I should dream   10
  It were within this half-hour.

ANTONIO You have not been in law, friend Delio,
  Nor in prison, nor a suitor at the court,
  Nor begged the reversion of some great man's place,°
  Nor troubled with an old wife, which doth make   15
  Your time so insensibly hasten.

DELIO   Pray, sir, tell me,
  Hath not this news arrived yet to the ear
  Of the Lord Cardinal?

ANTONIO   I fear it hath.
  The Lord Ferdinand, that's newly come to court,
  Doth bear himself right dangerously.

DELIO   Pray why?   20

ANTONIO He is so quiet, that he seems to sleep
  The tempest out, as dormice do in winter.
  Those houses that are haunted are most still,
  Till the devil be up.

DELIO   What say the common people?

ANTONIO The common rabble do directly say   25
  She is a strumpet.

DELIO   And your graver heads,
  Which would be politic, what censure they?

ANTONIO They do observe I grow to infinite purchase
  The left-hand way, and all suppose the Duchess°
  Would amend it, if she could. For, say they,   30
  Great princes, though they grudge their officers

Should have such large and unconfinèd means
To get wealth under them, will not complain
Lest thereby they should make them odious
Unto the people; for other obligation   35
Of love, or marriage, between her and me,
They never dream of.
      [Enter Ferdinand and Duchess]
DELIO   The Lord Ferdinand
  Is going to bed.
FERDINAND   I'll instantly to bed,
  For I am weary. *[To the Duchess]* I am to bespeak
  A husband for you.
DUCHESS   For me, sir! Pray who is't?   40
FERDINAND The great Count Malateste.
DUCHESS   Fie upon him,
  A count! He's a mere stick of sugar-candy,
  You may look quite thorough him. When I choose
  A husband, I will marry for your honour.
FERDINAND You shall do well in't. How is't, worthy Antonio?°   45
DUCHESS But, sir, I am to have private conference with you
  About a scandalous report is spread
  Touching mine honour.
FERDINAND   Let me be ever deaf to't:
  One of Pasquil's paper bullets, court-calumny,°
  A pestilent air which princes' palaces   50
  Are seldom purg'd of. Yet, say that it were true,
  I pour it in your bosom, my fixed love
  Would strongly excuse, extenuate, nay, deny
  Faults, were they apparent in you. Go, be safe
  In your own innocency.
DUCHESS   O blessed comfort!   55
  This deadly air is purg'd.
      Exeunt [all except Ferdinand]
FERDINAND   Her guilt treads on
  Hot-burning coulters.
      [Enter Bosola]
              Now, Bosola,°
  How thrives our intelligence?
BOSOLA   Sir, uncertainly.
  'Tis rumoured she hath had three bastards, but
  By whom, we may go read i'th' stars.

FERDINAND   Why, some   60
   Hold opinion all things are written there.
BOSOLA Yes, if we could find spectacles to read them.
   I do suspect there hath been some sorcery
   Used on the Duchess.
FERDINAND   Sorcery, to what purpose?
BOSOLA To make her dote on some desertless fellow   65
   She shames to acknowledge.
FERDINAND   Can your faith give way
   To think there's power in potions, or in charms,
   To make us love, whether we will or no?
BOSOLA Most certainly.
FERDINAND Away, these are mere gulleries, horrid things   70
   Invented by some cheating mountebanks
   To abuse us. Do you think that herbs or charms
   Can force the will? Some trials have been made
   In this foolish practice; but the ingredients
   Were lenitive poisons, such as are of force   75
   To make the patient mad; and straight the witch
   Swears, by equivocation, they are in love.
   The witchcraft lies in her rank blood. This night
   I will force confession from her. You told me
   You had got, within these two days, a false key   80
   Into her bedchamber.
BOSOLA   I have.
FERDINAND   As I would wish.
BOSOLA What do you intend to do?
FERDINAND   Can you guess?
BOSOLA   No.
FERDINAND Do not ask then.
   He that can compass me, and know my drifts,
   May say he hath put a girdle 'bout the world   85
   And sounded all her quicksands.
BOSOLA   I do not
   Think so.
FERDINAND What do you think then, pray?
BOSOLA   That you
   Are your own chronicle too much, and grossly
   Flatter yourself.
FERDINAND   Give me thy hand; I thank thee.
   I never gave pension but to flatterers,   90

Till I entertained thee. Farewell;
That friend a great man's ruin strongly checks,
Who rails into his belief all his defects.
    Exeunt

3.2

    [*Enter Duchess, Antonio and Cariola*]
DUCHESS [*to Cariola*] Bring me the casket hither, and the glass;
  You get no lodging here tonight, my lord.
ANTONIO Indeed, I must persuade one.
DUCHESS   Very good.
  I hope in time 'twill grow into a custom
  That noblemen shall come with cap and knee,°   5
  To purchase a night's lodging of their wives.
ANTONIO I must lie here.
DUCHESS   Must? You are a lord of misrule.°
ANTONIO Indeed, my rule is only in the night.
DUCHESS To what use will you put me?
ANTONIO   We'll sleep together.
DUCHESS Alas, what pleasure can two lovers find in sleep?   10
    [*Cariola gives the Duchess the casket and a mirror*]
CARIOLA My lord, I lie with her often, and I know
  She'll much disquiet you.
ANTONIO   See, you are complained of.
CARIOLA For she's the sprawling'st bedfellow.
ANTONIO I shall like her the better for that.
CARIOLA Sir, shall I ask you a question?   15
ANTONIO I pray thee, Cariola.
CARIOLA Wherefore still when you lie with my lady
  Do you rise so early?
ANTONIO   Labouring men
  Count the clock oftenest Cariola,
  Are glad when their task's ended.
DUCHESS   I'll stop your mouth.   20
    [*Kisses him*]
ANTONIO Nay, that's but one: Venus had two soft doves
  To draw her chariot—I must have another.
    [*Kisses her*]

When wilt thou marry, Cariola?
CARIOLA   Never, my lord.
ANTONIO O fie upon this single life. Forgo it.
We read how Daphne, for her peevish flight,   25
Became a fruitless bay-tree; Syrinx turned
To the pale empty reed; Anaxarete°
Was frozen into marble: whereas those
Which married, or proved kind unto their friends,
Were, by a gracious influence, transshaped   30
Into the olive, pomegranate, mulberry:°
Became flowers, precious stones, or eminent stars.
CARIOLA This is a vain poetry. But I pray you tell me,
If there were proposed me wisdom, riches, and beauty,
In three several young men, which should I choose?   35
ANTONIO 'Tis a hard question. This was Paris' case
And he was blind in't, and there was great cause:
For how was't possible he could judge right,
Having three amorous goddesses in view,
And they stark naked? 'Twas a motion°   40
Were able to benight the apprehension
Of the severest counsellor of Europe.
Now I look on both your faces, so well formed,
It puts me in mind of a question I would ask.
CARIOLA What is't?
ANTONIO   I do wonder why hard-favoured ladies,   45
For the most part, keep worse-favoured waiting-women
To attend them, and cannot endure fair ones.
DUCHESS O, that's soon answered.
Did you ever in your life know an ill painter
Desire to have his dwelling next door to the shop   50
Of an excellent picture-maker? 'Twould disgrace
His face-making, and undo him. I prithee,
When were we so merry? My hair tangles.
ANTONIO [aside to Cariola] Pray thee, Cariola, let's steal forth the
     room
And let her talk to herself. I have divers times   55
Served her the like, when she hath chafed extremely.
I love to see her angry. Softly, Cariola.
          Exeunt [Antonio and Cariola]
DUCHESS Doth not the colour of my hair 'gin to change?
When I wax grey, I shall have all the court

Powder their hair with orris, to be like me.   60
You have cause to love me: I entered you into my heart
   [*Enter Ferdinand behind*]
Before you would vouchsafe to call for the keys.
We shall one day have my brothers take you napping.
Methinks his presence, being now in court,
Should make you keep your own bed; but you'll say   65
Love mixed with fear is sweetest. I'll assure you
You shall get no more children till my brothers
Consent to be your gossips: have you lost your tongue?°
   [*Sees Ferdinand who holds a poniard*]
'Tis welcome:
For know, whether I am doomed to live or die,   70
I can do both like a prince.
   Ferdinand gives her a poniard

FERDINAND   Die then, quickly.
Virtue, where art thou hid? What hideous thing
Is it that doth eclipse thee?°

DUCHESS   Pray, sir, hear me.

FERDINAND Or is it true, thou art but a bare name,
And no essential thing?

DUCHESS   Sir—

FERDINAND   Do not speak.

DUCHESS   No, sir.   75
I will plant my soul in mine ears to hear you.

FERDINAND O most imperfect light of human reason,
That mak'st us so unhappy, to foresee
What we can least prevent. Pursue thy wishes,
And glory in them: there's in shame no comfort   80
But to be past all bounds, and sense of shame.

DUCHESS I pray, sir, hear me: I am married.

FERDINAND   So.

DUCHESS Haply, not to your liking; but for that,
Alas, your shears do come untimely now
To clip the bird's wings that's already flown.   85
Will you see my husband?

FERDINAND   Yes, if I could change
Eyes with a basilisk.

DUCHESS   Sure you came hither°
By his confederacy.

FERDINAND   The howling of a wolf

Is music to thee, screech-owl; prithee peace.°
Whate'er thou art, that hast enjoyed my sister   90
(For I am sure thou hear'st me), for thine own sake
Let me not know thee. I came hither prepared
To work thy discovery, yet am now persuaded
It would beget such violent effects
As would damn us both. I would not for ten millions   95
I had beheld thee; therefore use all means
I never may have knowledge of thy name.
Enjoy thy lust still, and a wretched life,
On that condition. And for thee, vile woman,
If thou do wish thy lecher may grow old   100
In thy embracements, I would have thee build
Such a room for him as our anchorites
To holier use inhabit. Let not the sun
Shine on him, till he's dead. Let dogs and monkeys
Only converse with him, and such dumb things   105
To whom nature denies use to sound his name.°
Do not keep a paraquito, lest she learn it.
If thou do love him, cut out thine own tongue
Lest it bewray him.
DUCHESS   Why might not I marry?
I have not gone about, in this, to create   110
Any new world, or custom.
FERDINAND   Thou art undone;
And thou hast ta'en that massy sheet of lead
That hid thy husband's bones, and folded it
About my heart.
DUCHESS   Mine bleeds for't.
FERDINAND   Thine? Thy heart?
What should I name't, unless a hollow bullet°   115
Filled with unquenchable wild-fire?
DUCHESS   You are, in this,
Too strict; and were you not my princely brother
I would say too wilful. My reputation
Is safe.
FERDINAND Dost thou know what reputation is?   120
I'll tell thee, to small purpose, since th' instruction
Comes now too late:
Upon a time, Reputation, Love, and Death
Would travel o'er the world; and it was concluded

That they should part, and take three several ways.   125
Death told them, they should find him in great battles,
Or cities plagued with plagues. Love gives them counsel
To inquire for him 'mongst unambitious shepherds,
Where dowries were not talked of, and sometimes
'Mongst quiet kindred that had nothing left   130
By their dead parents. 'Stay', quoth Reputation,
'Do not forsake me; for it is my nature,
If once I part from any man I meet,
I am never found again.' And so, for you:
You have shook hands with Reputation,   135
And made him invisible. So fare you well.
I will never see you more.
DUCHESS   Why should only I,
Of all the other princes of the world,
Be cased up, like a holy relic? I have youth,   140
And a little beauty.
FERDINAND   So you have some virgins°
That are witches. I will never see thee more.
          Exit [Ferdinand. Enter Antonio with a Pistol, and Cariola]
DUCHESS You saw this apparition?
ANTONIO   Yes: we are
Betrayed. How came he hither? [*To Cariola*] I should turn
This to thee, for that.
CARIOLA   Pray, sir, do; and when°   145
That you have cleft my heart, you shall read there
Mine innocence.
DUCHESS   That gallery gave him entrance.
ANTONIO I would this terrible thing would come again,
That, standing on my guard, I might relate
My warrantable love.
          [*The Duchess*] *shows the poniard*
                              Ha, what means this?   150
DUCHESS He left this with me.
ANTONIO   And it seems did wish
You would use it on yourself?
DUCHESS   His action seemed
To intend so much.
ANTONIO   This hath a handle to't
As well as a point. Turn it towards him,
And so fasten the keen edge in his rank gall:—   155

[*Knocking within*]
How now! Who knocks? More earthquakes?
DUCHESS   I stand
  As if a mine beneath my feet were ready
  To be blown up.
CARIOLA   'Tis Bosola.
DUCHESS   Away!°
  O misery, methinks unjust actions
  Should wear these masks and curtains, and not we.   160
  You must instantly part hence; I have fashioned it already.
        Exit Antonio. Enter Bosola
BOSOLA The Duke your brother is ta'en up in a whirlwind,
  Hath took horse, and's rid post to Rome.
DUCHESS   So late?
BOSOLA He told me, as he mounted into th' saddle,
  You were undone.
DUCHESS   Indeed, I am very near it.   165
BOSOLA What's the matter?
DUCHESS Antonio, the master of our household,
  Hath dealt so falsely with me, in's accounts.
  My brother stood engaged with me for money°
  Ta'en up of certain Neapolitan Jews,   170
  And Antonio lets the bonds be forfeit.
BOSOLA Strange! [*Aside*] This is cunning.
DUCHESS   And hereupon
  My brother's bills at Naples are protested
  Against. Call up our officers.
BOSOLA   I shall.
        Exit [Bosola. Enter Antonio]
DUCHESS The place that you must fly to is Ancona.   175
  Hire a house there. I'll send after you
  My treasure and my jewels. Our weak safety
  Runs upon enginous wheels; short syllables°
  Must stand for periods. I must now accuse you
  Of such a feignèd crime as Tasso calls   180
  Magnanima menzogna: a noble lie,°
  'Cause it must shield our honours. Hark!, they are coming.
        [*Enter Bosola and Officers*]
ANTONIO Will your grace hear me?
DUCHESS I have got well by you: you have yielded me
  A million of loss. I am like to inherit   185

The people's curses for your stewardship.
You had the trick in audit-time to be sick,
Till I had signed your *quietus*; and that cured you
Without help of a doctor. Gentlemen,
I would have this man be an example to you all: 190
So shall you hold my favour. I pray let him;°
For he's done that, alas, you would not think of,°
And, because I intend to be rid of him,
I mean not to publish. [*To Antonio*] Use your fortune elsewhere.

ANTONIO I am strongly armed to brook my overthrow,   195
As commonly men bear with a hard year.
I will not blame the cause on't, but do think
The necessity of my malevolent star
Procures this, not her humour. O the inconstant
And rotten ground of service! You may see.   200
'Tis even like him that, in a winter night,
Takes a long slumber o'er a dying fire,
As loth to part from't, yet parts thence as cold
As when he first sat down.

DUCHESS   We do confiscate,
Towards the satisfying of your accounts,   205
All that you have.

ANTONIO I am all yours, and 'tis very fit
All mine should be so.

DUCHESS   So, sir; you have your pass.

ANTONIO You may see, gentlemen, what 'tis to serve
A prince with body and soul.   210

          Exit [*Antonio*]

BOSOLA Here's an example for extortion: what moisture is drawn out
of the sea, when foul weather comes, pours down and runs into
the sea again.

DUCHESS I would know what are your opinions of this Antonio.

SECOND OFFICER He could not abide to see a pig's head gaping; I   215
thought your grace would find him a Jew.

THIRD OFFICER I would you had been his officer, for your own
sake.

FOURTH OFFICER You would have had more money.

FIRST OFFICER He stopped his ears with black wool; and to those   220
came to him for money, said he was thick of hearing.

SECOND OFFICER Some said he was an hermaphrodite, for he could
not abide a woman.

FOURTH OFFCER How scurvy proud he would look, when the
   treasury was full! Well, let him go.   225
FIRST OFFICER Yes, and the chippings of the buttery° fly after him,
   to scour his gold chain.°
DUCHESS Leave us.
      Exeunt [Officers]
   What do you think of these?
BOSOLA That these are rogues, that in's prosperity,   230
   But to have waited on his fortune, could have wished
   His dirty stirrup riveted through their noses,
   And followed after's mule, like a bear in a ring;
   Would have prostituted their daughters to his lust;
   Made their first-born intelligencers; thought none happy   235
   But such as were born under his blessed planet,
   And wore his livery: and do these lice drop off now?
   Well, never look to have the like again.
   He hath left a sort of flattering rogues behind him;
   Their doom must follow. Princes pay flatterers   240
   In their own money. Flatterers dissemble their vices,
   And they dissemble their lies: that's justice.
   Alas, poor gentleman!
DUCHESS Poor? He hath amply filled his coffers.
BOSOLA   Sure
   He was too honest. Pluto, the god of riches,°   245
   When he's sent by Jupiter to any man
   He goes limping, to signify that wealth
   That comes on God's name comes slowly; but when he's sent
   On the devil's errand, he rides post and comes in by scuttles.°
   Let me show you what a most unvalued jewel   250
   You have, in a wanton humour, thrown away,
   To bless the man shall find him. He was an excellent
   Courtier, and most faithful, a soldier that thought it
   As beastly to know his own value too little
   As devilish to acknowledge it too much.   255
   Both his virtue and form deserved a far better fortune.
   His discourse rather delighted to judge itself, than show itself.
   His breast was filled with all perfection,
   And yet it seemed a private whisp'ring-room,
   It made so little noise of 't.
DUCHESS   But he was basely descended.   260
BOSOLA Will you make yourself a mercenary herald,°

Rather to examine men's pedigrees than virtues?
You shall want him,
For know an honest statesman to a prince
Is like a cedar, planted by a spring: 265
The spring bathes the tree's root, the grateful tree
Rewards it with his shadow. You have not done so.
I would sooner swim to the Bermudes on°
Two politicians' rotten bladders, tied
Together with an intelligencer's heart-string,   270
Than depend on so changeable a prince's favour.
Fare thee well, Antonio; since the malice of the world
Would needs down with thee, it cannot be said yet
That any ill happened unto thee,
Considering thy fall was accompanied with virtue.   275

DUCHESS O, you render me excellent music.
BOSOLA   Say you?
DUCHESS This good one that you speak of, is my husband.
BOSOLA Do I not dream? Can this ambitious age
Have so much goodness in't, as to prefer
A man merely for worth, without these shadows   280
Of wealth, and painted honours? Possible?
DUCHESS I have had three children by him.
BOSOLA   Fortunate lady,
For you have made your private nuptial bed
The humble and fair seminary of peace.
No question but many an unbeneficed scholar°   285
Shall pray for you for this deed, and rejoice
That some preferment in the world can yet
Arise from merit. The virgins of your land,
That have no dowries, shall hope your example
Will raise them to rich husbands. Should you want   290
Soldiers, 'twould make the very Turks and Moors
Turn Christians, and serve you for this act.
Last, the neglected poets of your time,
In honour of this trophy of a man,
Raised by that curious engine, your white hand,   295
Shall thank you, in your grave, for't, and make that
More reverend than all the cabinets
Of living princes. For Antonio,
His fame shall likewise flow from many a pen,
When heralds shall want coats to sell to men.°   300

DUCHESS As I taste comfort in this friendly speech,
   So would I find concealment.
BOSOLA O, the secret of my Prince,
   Which I will wear on th' inside of my heart.
DUCHESS You shall take charge of all my coin and jewels,   305
   And follow him, for he retires himself
   To Ancona.
BOSOLA   So.
DUCHESS   Whither, within few days,
   I mean to follow thee.
BOSOLA   Let me think:
   I would wish your grace to feign a pilgrimage
   To our Lady of Loreto, scarce seven leagues   310
   From fair Ancona; so may you depart
   Your country with more honour, and your flight
   Will seem a princely progress, retaining
   Your usual train about you.
DUCHESS   Sir, your direction
   Shall lead me by the hand.
CARIOLA   In my opinion,   315
   She were better progress to the baths
   At Lucca, or go visit the Spa°
   In Germany, for, if you will believe me,
   I do not like this jesting with religion,
   This feignèd pilgrimage.   320
DUCHESS Thou art a superstitious fool.
   Prepare us instantly for our departure.
   Past sorrows, let us moderately lament them,
   For those to come, seek wisely to prevent them.
         Exit [Duchess with Cariola]
BOSOLA A politician is the devil's quilted anvil: 325
   He fashions all sins on him, and the blows
   Are never heard; he may work in a lady's chamber,
   As here for proof. What rests, but I reveal°
   All to my lord? O, this base quality
   Of intelligencer! Why, every quality i'th' world   330
   Prefers but gain or commendation.
   Now, for this act I am certain to be raised,
   And men that paint weeds to the life are praised.
         Exit

3.3

[Enter] Cardinal, Malateste; Ferdinand with Delio, Silvio,
[and] Pescara, [apart]

CARDINAL Must we turn soldier then?

MALATESTE   The Emperor,
  Hearing your worth that way, ere you attained
  This reverend garment, joins you in commission
  With the right fortunate soldier, the Marquis of Pescara,
  And the famous Lannoy.

CARDINAL   He that had the honour°   5
  Of taking French King prisoner?

MALATESTE   The same.
  Here's a plot drawn for a new fortification
  At Naples.
    [Malateste unfolds a map]

FERDINAND This great Count Malateste, I perceive,
  Hath got employment?

DELIO   No employment, my lord;   10
  A marginal note in the muster-book, that he is
  A voluntary lord.

FERDINAND   He's no soldier?°

DELIO He has worn gunpowder in's hollow tooth,
  For the toothache.

SILVIO He comes to the leaguer with a full intent   15
  To eat fresh beef and garlic, means to stay
  Till the scent be gone, and straight return to court.

DELIO He hath read all the late service
  As the City Chronicle relates it,
  And keeps two painters going, only to express   20
  Battles in model.

SILVIO   Then he'll fight by the book?°

DELIO By the almanac, I think,
  To choose good days, and shun the critical.°
  That's his mistress' scarf.

SILVIO   Yes, he protests
  He would do much for that taffeta.   25

DELIO I think he would run away from a battle

To save it from taking prisoner.

SILVIO   He is horribly afraid°
Gunpowder will spoil the perfume on't.

DELIO I saw a Dutchman break his pate once
For calling him pot-gun; he made his head   30
Have a bore in't, like a musket.

SILVIO I would he had made a touch-hole to't.
He is indeed a guarded sumpter-cloth,
Only for the remove of the court.°

> [*Enter Bosola, who speaks to Ferdinand and the Cardinal
> aside*]

PESCARA Bosola arrived! What should be the business?°   35
Some falling out amongst the cardinals.
These factions amongst great men, they are like
Foxes: when their heads are divided
They carry fire in their tails, and all the country
About them goes to wrack for't.

SILVIO   What's that Bosola?°   40

DELIO I knew him in Padua: a fantastical scholar, like such who
study to know how many knots was in Hercules' club, of what
colour Achilles' beard was, or whether Hector were not troubled
with the toothache. He hath studied himself half blear-eyed to
know the true symmetry of Caesar's nose by a shoeing-horn; and   45
this he did to gain the name of a speculative man.

PESCARA Mark Prince Ferdinand,
A very salamander lives in's eye,°
To mock the eager violence of fire.

SILVIO That Cardinal hath made more bad faces with his oppression   50
than ever Michelangelo made good ones; he lifts up's nose, like a
foul porpoise before a storm.°

PESCARA The Lord Ferdinand laughs.

DELIO   Like a deadly cannon
That lightens ere it smokes.

PESCARA These are your true pangs of death,   55
The pangs of life that struggle with great statesmen.°

DELIO In such a deformèd silence, witches whisper
Their charms.

> [*The Cardinal, Ferdinand and Bosola come forward*]

CARDINAL Doth she make religion her riding hood
To keep her from the sun and tempest?

FERDINAND   That.   60

That damns her. Methinks her fault and beauty,
Blended together, show like leprosy,
The whiter, the fouler. I make it a question
Whether her beggarly brats were ever christened.

CARDINAL I will instantly solicit the state of Ancona   65
To have them banished.

FERDINAND   You are for Loreto?
I shall not be at your ceremony; fare you well.
Write to the Duke of Malfi, my young nephew
She had by her first husband, and acquaint him°
With's mother's honesty.

BOSOLA   I will.

FERDINAND   Antonio: 70
A slave, that only smelled of ink and counters,
And ne'er in's life looked like a gentleman,
But in the audit-time. Go, go presently,
Draw me out an hundred and fifty of our horse,
And meet me at the fort-bridge.   75

　　　　Exeunt

3.4

[*Enter*] *Two Pilgrims to the Shrine of Our Lady of Loreto*

FIRST PILGRIM I have not seen a goodlier shrine than this,
Yet I have visited many.

SECOND PILGRIM The Cardinal of Aragon
Is this day to resign his cardinal's hat.
His sister Duchess likewise is arrived   5
To pay her vow of pilgrimage. I expect
A noble ceremony.

FIRST PILGRIM   No question. They come.

*Here the ceremony of the Cardinal's instalment in the habit of
a soldier, performed in delivering up his cross, hat, robes and
ring at the shrine, and investing him with sword, helmet,
shield and spurs. Then Antonio, the Duchess and their
Children, having presented themselves at the shrine, are (by a
form of banishment in dumb show expressed towards them by
the Cardinal and the state of Ancona) banished. During all
which ceremony, this ditty is sung to very solemn music, by*

divers Churchmen; and then exeunt [all, except the Two
Pilgrims].

CHURCHMEN   *Arms and honours deck thy story*
To thy fame's eternal glory;
Adverse fortune ever fly thee,   10
No disastrous fate come nigh thee.

I alone will sing thy praises,
Whom to honour virtue raises;
And thy study that divine is,
Bent to martial discipline is.   15
Lay aside all those robes lie by thee,
Crown thy arts with arms, they'll beautify thee.

O worthy of worthiest name, adorned in this manner,
Lead bravely thy forces on under war's warlike
      banner.
O, may'st thou prove fortunate in all martial courses,   20
Guide thou still by skill, in arts and forces.
Victory attend thee nigh whilst Fame sings loud thy
      powers,
Triumphant conquest crown thy head, and blessings
      pour down showers.°

FIRST PILGRIM   Here's a strange turn of state: who would have
   thought
So great a lady would have matched herself   25
Unto so mean a person? Yet the Cardinal
Bears himself much too cruel.
SECOND PILGRIM   They are banished.
FIRST PILGRIM   But I would ask what power hath this state
Of Ancona to determine of a free prince?
SECOND PILGRIM   They are a free state, sir, and her brother
   showed   30
How that the Pope, forehearing of her looseness,
Hath seized into th' protection of the church
The dukedom which she held as dowager.
FIRST PILGRIM   But by what justice?
SECOND PILGRIM   Sure I think by none,
Only her brother's instigation.   35
FIRST PILGRIM   What was it with such violence he took
Off from her finger?
SECOND PILGRIM   'Twas her wedding ring,

Which he vowed shortly he would sacrifice
To his revenge.
FIRST PILGRIM   Alas, Antonio!
If that a man be thrust into a well,   40
No matter who sets hand to't, his own weight°
Will bring him sooner to th' bottom. Come, let's hence.
Fortune makes this conclusion general:
All things do help th' unhappy man to fall.
    Exeunt

3.5

    [*Enter*] *Antonio, Duchess, Children, Cariola, Servants*
DUCHESS Banished Ancona!
ANTONIO   Yes, you see what power
Lightens in great men's breath.
DUCHESS   Is all our train
Shrunk to this poor remainder?
ANTONIO   These poor men,
Which have got little in your service, vow
To take your fortune; but your wiser buntings,   5
Now they are fledged, are gone.
DUCHESS   They have done wisely.
This puts me in mind of death: physicians thus,
With their hands full of money, use to give o'er
Their patients.
ANTONIO   Right the fashion of the world:
From decayed fortunes every flatterer shrinks,   10
Men cease to build where the foundation sinks.
DUCHESS I had a very strange dream tonight.
ANTONIO   What was't?
DUCHESS Methought I wore my coronet of state,
And on a sudden all the diamonds
Were changed to pearls.
ANTONIO   My interpretation   15
Is, you'll weep shortly, for to me, the pearls
Do signify your tears.
DUCHESS The birds that live i'th' field
On the wild benefit of nature, live°

Happier than we; for they may choose their mates,   20
And carol their sweet pleasures to the spring.
　　　[*Enter Bosola with a letter*]
BOSOLA   You are happily o'erta'en.
DUCHESS   From my brother?
BOSOLA   Yes, from the Lord Ferdinand, your brother,
All love and safety.
DUCHESS   Thou dost blanch mischief,
Wouldst make it white. See, see, like to calm weather   25
At sea, before a tempest, false hearts speak fair
To those they intend most mischief.
　　　[*She reads the*] letter
'Send Antonio to me; I want his head in a business:'
A politic equivocation!°
He doth not want your counsel, but your head;   30
That is, he cannot sleep till you be dead.
And here's another pitfall that's strewed o'er
With roses; mark it, 'tis a cunning one:
'I stand engaged for your husband, for several debts at Naples;
let not that trouble him: I had rather have his heart than his   35
money.'
And I believe so too.
BOSOLA   What do you believe?
DUCHESS   That he so much distrusts my husband's love,
He will by no means believe his heart is with him
Until he see it. The devil is not cunning enough   40
To circumvent us in riddles.
BOSOLA   Will you reject that noble and free league
Of amity and love which I present you?
DUCHESS   Their league is like that of some politic kings:
Only to make themselves of strength and pow'r   45
To be our after-ruin. Tell them so.
BOSOLA   And what from you?
ANTONIO   Thus tell him: I will not come.
BOSOLA   And what of this?
ANTONIO   My brothers have dispersed°
Bloodhounds abroad; which till I hear are muzzled,
No truce, though hatched with ne'er such politic skill,   50
Is safe, that hangs upon our enemies' will.
I'll not come at them.
BOSOLA   This proclaims your breeding.

Every small thing draws a base mind to fear,
As the adamant draws iron. Fare you well, sir,
You shall shortly hear from's.   55
    Exit [Bosola]
DUCHESS I suspect some ambush:
Therefore, by all my love, I do conjure you
To take your eldest son, and fly towards Milan.
Let us not venture all this poor remainder
In one unlucky bottom.
ANTONIO   You counsel safely.°   60
Best of my life, farewell. Since we must part
Heaven hath a hand in't; but no otherwise
Than as some curious artist takes in sunder
A clock or watch when it is out of frame,
To bring 't in better order.   65
DUCHESS I know not which is best,
To see you dead, or part with you. [*To her son*] Farewell, boy,
Thou art happy, that thou hast not understanding
To know thy misery, for all our wit
And reading brings us to a truer sense   70
Of sorrow. [*To Antonio*] In the eternal church, sir,°
I do hope we shall not part thus.
ANTONIO   O, be of comfort!
Make patience a noble fortitude,
And think not how unkindly we are used:°
Man, like to cassia, is proved best, being bruised.   75
DUCHESS Must I, like to a slave-born Russian,
Account it praise to suffer tyranny?
And yet, O Heaven, thy heavy hand is in't.
I have seen my little boy oft scourge his top
And compared myself to't: nought made me e'er   80
Go right but heaven's scourge-stick.
ANTONIO   Do not weep:
Heaven fashioned us of nothing, and we strive
To bring ourselves to nothing. Farewell, Cariola,
And thy sweet armful. [*To the Duchess*] If I do never see thee
    more,
Be a good mother to your little ones,   85
And save them from the tiger: fare you well.
DUCHESS Let me look upon you once more, for that speech
Came from a dying father. Your kiss is colder

Than that I have seen an holy anchorite
Give to a dead man's skull.   90
ANTONIO My heart is turned to a heavy lump of lead,
   With which I sound my danger: fare you well.
     Exit [Antonio with his elder Son]
DUCHESS My laurel is all withered.°
CARIOLA Look, madam, what a troop of armèd men
   Make toward us.
     Enter Bosola with a guard of soldiers, [all wearing] vizards.
DUCHESS   O, they are very welcome.°   95
   When Fortune's wheel is overcharged with princes,
   The weight makes it move swift. I would have my ruin
   Be sudden. I am your adventure, am I not?
BOSOLA You are: you must see your husband no more.
DUCHESS What devil art thou, that counterfeits heaven's thunder?   100
BOSOLA Is that terrible? I would have you tell me
   Whether is that note worse that frights the silly birds
   Out of the corn, or that which doth allure them
   To the nets? You have hearkened to the last too much.
DUCHESS O misery! Like to a rusty o'ercharged cannon,   105
   Shall I never fly in pieces? Come: to what prison?
BOSOLA To none.
DUCHESS   Whither then?
BOSOLA   To your palace.
DUCHESS   I have heard
   That Charon's boat serves to convey all o'er°
   The dismal lake, but brings none back again.
BOSOLA Your brothers mean you safety and pity.
DUCHESS   Pity?   110
   With such a pity men preserve alive
   Pheasants and quails, when they are not fat enough
   To be eaten.
BOSOLA These are your children?
DUCHESS   Yes.
BOSOLA   Can they prattle?
DUCHESS   No:
   But I intend, since they were born accursed,   115
   Curses shall be their first language.
BOSOLA   Fie, madam,
   Forget this base, low fellow.
DUCHESS   Were I a man

I'd beat that counterfeit face into thy other.°
BOSOLA One of no birth.
DUCHESS   Say that he was born mean:
   Man is most happy when's own actions   120
   Be arguments and examples of his virtue.
BOSOLA A barren, beggarly virtue.
DUCHESS I prithee, who is greatest? Can you tell?
   Sad tales befit my woe: I'll tell you one.
   A salmon, as she swam unto the sea,   125
   Met with a dog-fish, who encounters her
   With this rough language: 'Why art thou so bold
   To mix thyself with our high state of floods,
   Being no eminent courtier, but one
   That for the calmest and fresh time o'th' year   130
   Dost live in shallow rivers, rank'st thyself
   With silly smelts and shrimps? And darest thou
   Pass by our dog-ship, without reverence?'
   'O', quoth the salmon, 'sister, be at peace;
   Thank Jupiter we both have passed the net.   135
   Our value never can be truly known
   Till in the fisher's basket we be shown;
   I'th' market then my price may be the higher,
   Even when I am nearest to the cook and fire.'°
   So, to great men, the moral may be stretched: 140
   Men oft are valued high, when th'are most wretch'd.
   But come: whither you please; I am armed 'gainst misery,
   Bent to all sways of the oppressor's will.
   There's no deep valley, but near some great hill.°
    Exeunt

4.1

[*Enter Ferdinand and Bosola*]

FERDINAND How doth our sister Duchess bear herself
  In her imprisonment?

BOSOLA   Nobly. I'll describe her:
  She's sad, as one long used to't, and she seems
  Rather to welcome the end of misery
  Than shun it; a behaviour so noble   5
  As gives a majesty to adversity.
  You may discern the shape of loveliness
  More perfect in her tears than in her smiles;
  She will muse four hours together, and her silence,
  Methinks, expresseth more than if she spake.   10

FERDINAND Her melancholy seems to be fortified
  With a strange disdain.

BOSOLA   'Tis so; and this restraint,
  Like English mastiffs, that grow fierce with tying,
  Makes her too passionately apprehend
  Those pleasures she's kept from.

FERDINAND   Curse upon her!   15
  I will no longer study in the book
  Of another's heart. Inform her what I told you.°
     Exit [*Ferdinand. Enter Duchess*°]

BOSOLA All comfort to your grace.

DUCHESS   I will have none.
  Pray thee, why dost thou wrap thy poisoned pills
  In gold and sugar?   20

BOSOLA Your elder brother, the Lord Ferdinand,°
  Is come to visit you, and sends you word,
  'Cause once he rashly made a solemn vow
  Never to see you more, he comes i'th' night;
  And prays you, gently, neither torch nor taper°   25
  Shine in your chamber. He will kiss your hand,
  And reconcile himself; but, for his vow,
  He dares not see you.

DUCHESS   At his pleasure.
  Take hence the lights;
     [*Bosola removes the lights and walks apart. Enter Ferdinand*]
               he's come

FERDINAND   Where are you?
DUCHESS   Here, sir.°
FERDINAND This darkness suits you well.
DUCHESS   I would ask you pardon.   30
FERDINAND You have it;
   For I account it the honourabl'st revenge,
   Where I may kill, to pardon. Where are your cubs?
DUCHESS Whom?
FERDINAND Call them your children,   35
   For though our national law distinguish bastards
   From true legitimate issue, compassionate nature
   Makes them all equal.
DUCHESS   Do you visit me for this?
   You violate a sacrament o'th' church
   Shall make you howl in hell for't.
FERDINAND   It had been well,   40
   Could you have lived thus always; for indeed
   You were too much i'th' light. But no more,°
   I come to seal my peace with you: here's a hand,
     Gives her a dead man's hand
   To which you have vowed much love; the ring upon't°
   You gave.
DUCHESS   I affectionately kiss it.   45
FERDINAND Pray do, and bury the print of it in your heart.
   I will leave this ring with you for a love-token;
   And the hand, as sure as the ring; and do not doubt
   But you shall have the heart too. When you need a friend
   Send it to him that owed it; you shall see°   50
   Whether he can aid you.
DUCHESS   You are very cold.
   I fear you are not well after your travel.
   Ha! Lights!
     [*Bosola brings up lights*]
       O horrible!
FERDINAND   Let her have lights enough.
     Exit [*Ferdinand*]
DUCHESS What witchcraft doth he practise that he hath left
   A dead man's hand here?   55
     [*A curtain opens*]. *Here is discovered,*° *behind a traverse,*
     the figures° *of Antonio and his children,*° *appearing as if*
     they were dead
BOSOLA Look you: here's the piece from which 'twas ta'en.

He doth present you this sad spectacle
That, now you know directly they are dead,
Hereafter you may wisely cease to grieve
For that which cannot be recoverèd.   60

DUCHESS There is not between heaven and earth one wish
    I stay for after this. It wastes me more
    Than were't my picture, fashioned out of wax,
    Stuck with a magical needle, and then buried
    In some foul dunghill; and yon's an excellent property   65
    For a tyrant, which I would account mercy.

BOSOLA What's that?

DUCHESS If they would bind me to that lifeless trunk,°
    And let me freeze to death.

BOSOLA   Come, you must live.

DUCHESS That's the greatest torture souls feel in hell,   70
    In hell: that they must live, and cannot die.
    Portia, I'll new-kindle thy coals again,°
    And revive the rare and almost dead example
    Of a loving wife.

BOSOLA   O fie! Despair? Remember
    You are a Christian.

DUCHESS   The church enjoins fasting: 75
    I'll starve myself to death.

BOSOLA   Leave this vain sorrow.
    Things being at the worst begin to mend.
    The bee when he hath shot his sting into your hand
    May then play with your eyelid.

DUCHESS Good comfortable fellow,   80
    Persuade a wretch that's broke upon the wheel°
    To have all his bones new set; entreat him live
    To be executed again. Who must despatch me?
    I account this world a tedious theatre,
    For I do play a part in't 'gainst my will.   85

BOSOLA Come, be of comfort, I will save your life.

DUCHESS Indeed I have not leisure to tend so small a business.

BOSOLA Now, by my life, I pity you.

DUCHESS   Thou art a fool then,
    To waste thy pity on a thing so wretch'd
    As cannot pity itself. I am full of daggers.   90
    Puff! Let me blow these vipers from me.°
        [Enter Servant]

What are you?
SERVANT   One that wishes you long life.°
DUCHESS I would thou wert hanged for the horrible curse
    Thou hast given me:
        [*Exit Servant*]
                              I shall shortly grow one
Of the miracles of pity. I'll go pray; no,   95
I'll go curse.
BOSOLA   O fie!
DUCHESS   I could curse the stars.
BOSOLA   O fearful!
DUCHESS And those three smiling seasons of the year
    Into a Russian winter, nay the world
    To its first chaos.
BOSOLA Look you, the stars shine still.
DUCHESS   O, but you must   100
    Remember, my curse hath a great way to go.
    Plagues, that make lanes through largest families,
    Consume them!
BOSOLA   Fie, lady!
DUCHESS   Let them, like tyrants,
    Never be remembered, but for the ill they have done;
    Let all the zealous prayers of mortified   105
    Churchmen forget them!
BOSOLA   O uncharitable!°
DUCHESS Let heaven, a little while, cease crowning martyrs,
    To punish them!
    Go, howl them this, and say I long to bleed:°
    It is some mercy, when men kill with speed.   110
        Exit [*Duchess. Enter Ferdinand*]
FERDINAND Excellent; as I would wish; she's plagued in art.
    These presentations are but framed in wax,
    By the curious master in that quality,°
    Vincentio Lauriola, and she takes them°
    For true substantial bodies.   115
BOSOLA Why do you do this?
FERDINAND   To bring her to despair.
BOSOLA Faith, end here,
    And go no farther in your cruelty.
    Send her a penitential garment to put on
    Next to her delicate skin, and furnish her   120

With beads and prayer-books.

FERDINAND   Damn her! That body of hers,
While that my blood ran pure in't, was more worth
Than that which thou wouldst comfort, called a soul.
I will send her masques of common courtesans,
Have her meat served up by bawds and ruffians,   125
And, 'cause she'll needs be mad, I am resolved
To remove forth the common hospital
All the mad-folk, and place them near her lodging;
There let them practise together, sing, and dance,
And act their gambols to the full o'th' moon:°   130
If she can sleep the better for it, let her.
Your work is almost ended.

BOSOLA Must I see her again?

FERDINAND   Yes.

BOSOLA   Never.

FERDINAND   You must.

BOSOLA Never in mine own shape;
That's forfeited by my intelligence,°   135
And this last cruel lie. When you send me next,
The business shall be comfort.

FERDINAND   Very likely.
Thy pity is nothing of kin to thee. Antonio
Lurks about Milan; thou shalt shortly thither
To feed a fire, as great as my revenge,   140
Which ne'er will slack, till it have spent his fuel:
Intemperate agues make physicians cruel.
        Exeunt

4.2

[Enter Duchess and Cariola]

DUCHESS What hideous noise was that?

CARIOLA   'Tis the wild consort
Of madmen, lady, which your tyrant brother
Hath placed about your lodging. This tyranny,
I think, was never practised till this hour.

DUCHESS Indeed I thank him: nothing but noise and folly   5
Can keep me in my right wits, whereas reason

And silence make me stark mad. Sit down,
Discourse to me some dismal tragedy.

CARIOLA O, 'twill increase your melancholy.

DUCHESS   Thou art deceived;
To hear of greater grief would lessen mine.   10
This is a prison?

CARIOLA   Yes, but you shall live
To shake this durance off.

DUCHESS   Thou art a fool;
The robin redbreast, and the nightingale,
Never live long in cages.

CARIOLA   Pray dry your eyes.
What think you of, madam?

DUCHESS   Of nothing: 15
When I muse thus, I sleep.

CARIOLA Like a madman, with your eyes open?

DUCHESS Dost thou think we shall know one another,
In th'other world?

CARIOLA   Yes, out of question.

DUCHESS O that it were possible we might   20
But hold some two days' conference with the dead,
From them I should learn somewhat, I am sure
I never shall know here. I'll tell thee a miracle:
I am not mad yet, to my cause of sorrow.
Th' heaven o'er my head seems made of molten brass, 25
The earth of flaming sulphur, yet I am not mad.
I am acquainted with sad misery,
As the tanned galley-slave is with his oar.
Necessity makes me suffer constantly,
And custom makes it easy. Who do I look like now?   30

CARIOLA Like to your picture in the gallery,
A deal of life in show, but none in practice;
Or rather like some reverend monument
Whose ruins are even pitied.

DUCHESS   Very proper;°
And Fortune seems only to have her eyesight   35
To behold my tragedy. How now!°
What noise is that?
        [*Enter Servant*]

SERVANT   I am come to tell you
Your brother hath intended you some sport.

A great physician, when the Pope was sick
Of a deep melancholy, presented him   40
With several sorts of madmen, which wild object,
Being full of change and sport, forced him to laugh,
And so th' imposthume broke. The self-same cure
The duke intends on you.

DUCHESS   Let them come in.

SERVANT There's a mad lawyer, and a secular priest,°   45
A doctor that hath forfeited his wits
By jealousy; an astrologian
That in his works said such a day o'th' month
Should be the day of doom, and failing of't,
Ran mad; an English tailor, crazed i'th' brain   50
With the study of new fashion; a gentleman usher
Quite beside himself, with care to keep in mind
The number of his lady's salutations,
Or 'How do you', she employed him in each morning;
A farmer too, an excellent knave in grain,°   55
Mad 'cause he was hindered transportation;°
And let one broker that's mad loose to these,°
You'd think the devil were among them.

DUCHESS Sit, Cariola.—Let them loose when you please,
For I am chained to endure all your tyranny.°   60
    [Enter Madmen]
   Here, by a Madman, this song is sung to a dismal kind of music.

MADMAN (sings) O, let us howl some heavy note,
                Some deadly dogged howl,
                Sounding as from the threatening throat
                    Of beasts, and fatal fowl.   65
                As ravens, screech-owls, bulls, and bears,
                    We'll bill and bawl our parts,
                Till irksome noise have cloyed your ears
                    And corrosived your hearts.
                At last when as our choir wants breath,   70
                    Our bodies being blest,
                We'll sing like swans, to welcome death,
                    And die in love and rest.°

MAD ASTROLOGER° Doomsday not come yet? I'll draw it nearer by
a perspective, or make a glass that shall set all the world on fire   75
upon an instant. I cannot sleep, my pillow is stuffed with a litter
of porcupines.

MAD LAWYER Hell is a mere glass-house, where the devils are continually blowing up women's souls, on hollow irons, and the fire never goes out.   80

MAD PRIEST I will lie with every woman in my parish the tenth night; I will tithe them over, like haycocks.

MAD DOCTOR Shall my pothecary outgo me, because I am a cuckold? I have found out his roguery: he makes alum of his wife's urine, and sells it to puritans that have sore throats with over-straining.   85

MAD ASTROLOGER I have skill in heraldry.

MAD LAWYER Hast?

MAD ASTROLOGER You do give for your crest a woodcock's° head, with the brains picked out on't. You are a very ancient gentleman.

MAD PRIEST Greek is turned Turk; we are only to be saved by the   90
Helvetian translation.°

MAD ASTROLOGER [to the mad lawyer] Come on sir, I will lay° the law to you.

MAD LAWYER O, rather lay° a corrosive; the law will eat to the bone.

MAD PRIEST He that drinks but to satisfy nature is damned.   95

MAD DOCTOR If I had my glass° here, I would show a sight should make all the women here call me mad doctor.

MAD ASTROLOGER [pointing at the mad priest] What's he, a rope-maker?

MAD LAWYER No, no, no, a snuffling knave, that while he shows the   100
tombs, will have his hand in a wench's placket.

MAD PRIEST Woe to the caroche that brought home my wife from the masque, at three o'clock in the morning; it had a large featherbed° in it.

MAD DOCTOR I have pared the devil's nails forty times, roasted them   105
in raven's eggs, and cured agues with them.

MAD PRIEST Get me three hundred milch-bats to make possets to procure sleep.

MAD DOCTOR All the college may throw their caps at me,° I have made a soap-boiler costive.° It was my master-piece.   110

    Here the dance, consisting of eight Madmen, with music
    answerable thereunto; after which Bosola, like an old man,
    enters [and the madmen leave]

DUCHESS Is he mad too?

SERVANT   Pray question him; I'll leave you.

    [*Exit Servant*]

BOSOLA I am come to make thy tomb.

DUCHESS   Ha, my tomb!

Thou speak'st as if I lay upon my death-bed,
Gasping for breath. Dost thou perceive me sick?

BOSOLA Yes, and the more dangerously, since thy sickness is insensible.   115

DUCHESS Thou art not mad, sure; dost know me?

BOSOLA Yes.

DUCHESS Who am I?

BOSOLA Thou art a box of worm seed,° at best, but a salvatory of green mummy.° What's this flesh? A little curded milk, fantastical   120 puff-paste; our bodies are weaker than those paper prisons boys use to keep flies in; more contemptible, since ours is to preserve earth-worms. Didst thou ever see a lark in a cage? Such is the soul in the body: this world is like her little turf of grass, and the heaven o'er our heads, like her looking-glass, only gives us a miserable   125 knowledge of the small compass of our prison.

DUCHESS Am not I thy Duchess?

BOSOLA Thou art some great woman, sure, for riot begins to sit on thy forehead, clad in grey hairs, twenty years sooner than on a merry milkmaid's. Thou sleep'st worse than if a mouse should be   130 forced to take up her lodging in a cat's ear; a little infant that breeds its teeth, should it lie with thee, would cry out, as if thou wert the more unquiet bedfellow.

DUCHESS I am Duchess of Malfi still.

BOSOLA That makes thy sleeps so broken: 135
Glories, like glow-worms, afar off shine bright,
But looked to near, have neither heat, nor light.

DUCHESS Thou art very plain.

BOSOLA My trade is to flatter the dead, not the living; I am a tomb-maker.   140

DUCHESS And thou com'st to make my tomb?

BOSOLA Yes.

DUCHESS Let me be a little merry:
Of what stuff wilt thou make it?

BOSOLA Nay, resolve me first, of what fashion?   145

DUCHESS Why, do we grow fantastical in our death-bed?
Do we affect fashion in the grave?

BOSOLA Most ambitiously. Princes' images on their tombs do not lie, as they were wont, seeming to pray up to heaven, but with their hands under their cheeks, as if they died of the tooth-ache. They   150 are not carved with their eyes fixed upon the stars, but as their minds were wholly bent upon the world, the selfsame way they seem to turn their faces.

DUCHESS Let me know fully therefore the effect
  Of this thy dismal preparation,   155
  This talk fit for a charnel.
BOSOLA   Now I shall.
    [*Enter Executioners with*] *a coffin, cords and a bell.*
  Here is a present from your princely brothers,
  And may it arrive welcome, for it brings
  Last benefit, last sorrow.
DUCHESS   Let me see it.
  I have so much obedience in my blood,   160
  I wish it in their veins, to do them good.
BOSOLA This is your last presence-chamber.
CARIOLA O my sweet lady!
DUCHESS   Peace, it affrights not me.
BOSOLA I am the common bellman°
  That usually is sent to condemned persons   165
  The night before they suffer.
DUCHESS   Even now thou said'st
  Thou wast a tomb-maker.
BOSOLA   'Twas to bring you
  By degrees to mortification. Listen:°
    [*Bosola rings the bell*]
      Hark, now everything is still,
      The screech-owl and the whistler shrill   170
      Call upon our dame, aloud,
      And bid her quickly don her shroud.
      Much you had of land and rent,
      Your length in clay's now competent.
      A long war disturbed your mind,   175
      Here your perfect peace is signed.
      Of what is't fools make such vain keeping?
      Sin their conception, their birth weeping;
      Their life a general mist of error,
      Their death a hideous storm of terror.   180
      Strew your hair with powders sweet,
      Don clean linen, bathe your feet,
      And, the foul fiend more to check,
      A crucifix let bless your neck.
      Tis now full tide 'tween night and day: 185
      End your groan, and come away.
    [*Executioners approach*]

CARIOLA Hence villains, tyrants, murderers! Alas,
　　What will you do with my lady?—Call for help.
DUCHESS To whom? To our next neighbours? They are mad-
　　folks.   190
BOSOLA Remove that noise.
　　　　　[*Executioners seize Cariola*]
DUCHESS   Farewell, Cariola.
　　In my last will I have not much to give;
　　A many hungry guests have fed upon me,
　　Thine will be a poor reversion.
CARIOLA   I will die with her.
DUCHESS I pray thee look thou giv'st my little boy   195
　　Some syrup for his cold, and let the girl
　　Say her prayers, ere she sleep.
　　　　　[*Executioners force Cariola off*]
　　　　　　　　　　　　　Now what you please:
　　What death?
BOSOLA   Strangling: here are your executioners.
DUCHESS I forgive them:
　　The apoplexy, catarrh, or cough o'th' lungs   200
　　Would do as much as they do.
BOSOLA Doth not death fright you?
DUCHESS   Who would be afraid on't,
　　Knowing to meet such excellent company
　　In th'other world?
BOSOLA Yet, methinks,   205
　　The manner of your death should much afflict you,
　　This cord should terrify you?
DUCHESS   Not a whit.
　　What would it pleasure me to have my throat cut
　　With diamonds? or to be smothered
　　With cassia? or to be shot to death with pearls?   210
　　I know death hath ten thousand several doors
　　For men to take their exits; and 'tis found°
　　They go on such strange geometrical hinges,
　　You may open them both ways. Any way, for heaven' sake,°
　　So I were out of your whispering. Tell my brothers   215
　　That I perceive death, now I am well awake,
　　Best gift is they can give, or I can take.
　　I would fain put off my last woman's fault,°
　　I'd not be tedious to you.

diff. from T (margin note beside lines 203–204)

EXECUTIONER   We are ready.

DUCHESS Dispose my breath how please you, but my body   220
    Bestow upon my women, will you?

EXECUTIONER   Yes.

DUCHESS Pull, and pull strongly, for your able strength
    Must pull down heaven upon me.
    Yet stay; heaven' gates are not so highly arched
    As princes' palaces; they that enter there   225
    Must go upon their knees. [*Kneels*] Come, violent death,
    Serve for mandragora to make me sleep.°
    Go tell my brothers, when I am laid out,
    They then may feed in quiet.
       They strangle her

BOSOLA Where's the waiting-woman?   230
    Fetch her. Some other strangle the children.
    [*Executioners bring Cariola, and some go to strangle the*
    children.]
    Look you, there sleeps your mistress.

CARIOLA   O, you are damned
    Perpetually for this. My turn is next,
    Is't not so ordered?

BOSOLA   Yes, and I am glad
    You are so well prepared for't.

CARIOLA   You are deceived sir,   235
    I am not prepared for't, I will not die;
    I will first come to my answer, and know°
    How I have offended.

BOSOLA   Come, despatch her.
    You kept her counsel, now you shall keep ours.

CARIOLA I will not die, I must not, I am contracted   240
    To a young gentleman.

EXECUTIONER [*showing the noose*] Here's your wedding ring.

CARIOLA Let me but speak with the Duke. I'll discover
    Treason to his person.

BOSOLA   Delays: throttle her.

EXECUTIONER She bites, and scratches.

CARIOLA   If you kill me now
    I am damned: I have not been at confession   245
    This two years.

BOSOLA   When!

CARIOLA   I am quick with child.

BOSOLA   Why then,°
Your credit's saved.
    [*The Executioners strangle Cariola*]
           Bear her into th'next room;°
Let this lie still.
    [*Exeunt Executioners with the body of Cariola. Enter*
    Ferdinand]
FERDINAND   Is she dead?
BOSOLA   She is what°
You'd have her. But here begin your pity:
    [*Bosola draws a traverse and*] *shows the children strangled*
Alas, how have these offended?
FERDINAND   The death   250
Of young wolves is never to be pitied.
BOSOLA Fix your eye here.
FERDINAND   Constantly.
BOSOLA   Do you not weep?
Other sins only speak; murder shrieks out.
The element of water moistens the earth,
But blood flies upwards, and bedews the heavens.°   255
FERDINAND Cover her face: mine eyes dazzle: she died young.°
BOSOLA I think not so; her infelicity
Seemed to have years too many.
FERDINAND She and I were twins;
And should I die this instant, I had lived   260
Her time to a minute.
BOSOLA   It seems she was born first.
You have bloodily approved the ancient truth,
That kindred commonly do worse agree
Than remote strangers.
FERDINAND   Let me see her face again.
Why didst not thou pity her? What an excellent   265
Honest man might'st thou have been
If thou hadst borne her to some sanctuary!
Or, bold in a good cause, opposed thyself
With thy advancèd sword above thy head,
Between her innocence and my revenge!   270
I bade thee, when I was distracted of my wits,
Go kill my dearest friend, and thou hast done't.
For let me but examine well the cause:
What was the meanness of her match to me?

Only I must confess, I had a hope,   275
Had she continued widow, to have gained
An infinite mass of treasure by her death;
And that was the main cause. Her marriage,
That drew a stream of gall quite through my heart.
For thee (as we observe in tragedies   280
That a good actor many times is cursed
For playing a villain's part), I hate thee for't:
And for my sake say thou hast done much ill well.

BOSOLA Let me quicken your memory; for I perceive
You are falling into ingratitude. I challenge   285
The reward due to my service.

FERDINAND   I'll tell thee
What I'll give thee.

BOSOLA   Do.

FERDINAND   I'll give thee a pardon
For this murder.

BOSOLA   Ha?

FERDINAND   Yes: and 'tis
The largest bounty I can study to do thee.
By what authority didst thou execute   290
This bloody sentence?

BOSOLA   By yours.

FERDINAND   Mine? Was I her judge?
Did any ceremonial form of law
Doom her to not-being? Did a complete jury
Deliver her conviction up i'th' court?
Where shalt thou find this judgement registered   295
Unless in hell? See: like a bloody fool
Thou'st forfeited thy life, and thou shalt die for't.

BOSOLA The office of justice is perverted quite
When one thief hangs another. Who shall dare
To reveal this?

FERDINAND   O, I'll tell thee: 300
The wolf shall find her grave, and scrape it up;
Not to devour the corpse, but to discover
The horrid murder.

BOSOLA   You, not I, shall quake for't.°

FERDINAND Leave me.

BOSOLA   I will first receive my pension.

FERDINAND You are a villain.

BOSOLA   When your ingratitude   305
  Is judge, I am so.
FERDINAND   O horror!
  That not the fear of him which binds the devils
  Can prescribe man obedience.
  Never look upon me more.
BOSOLA   Why, fare thee well.
  Your brother and yourself are worthy men;   310
  You have a pair of hearts are hollow graves,
  Rotten, and rotting others; and your vengeance,
  Like two chained bullets, still goes arm in arm,
  You may be brothers; for treason, like the plague,
  Doth take much in a blood. I stand like one°   315
  That long hath ta'en a sweet and golden dream:
  I am angry with myself, now that I wake.
FERDINAND Get thee into some unknown part o'th' world
  That I may never see thee.
BOSOLA   Let me know
  Wherefore I should be thus neglected. Sir,   320
  I served your tyranny, and rather strove
  To satisfy yourself, than all the world;
  And though I loathed the evil, yet I loved
  You that did counsel it, and rather sought
  To appear a true servant than an honest man.   325
FERDINAND I'll go hunt the badger by owl-light:
  'Tis a deed of darkness.
    Exit [Ferdinand]
BOSOLA He's much distracted. Off my painted honour!°
  While with vain hopes our faculties we tire,
  We seem to sweat in ice, and freeze in fire.   330
  What would I do, were this to do again?
  I would not change my peace of conscience
  For all the wealth of Europe. She stirs; here's life.
  Return, fair soul, from darkness, and lead mine
  Out of this sensible hell. She's warm, she breathes.°   335
  Upon thy pale lips I will melt my heart
  To store them with fresh colour. Who's there?
  Some cordial drink! Alas, I dare not call:
  So pity would destroy pity; her eye opes,°
  And heaven in it seems to ope, that late was shut,   340
  To take me up to mercy.

DUCHESS Antonio.
BOSOLA   Yes, madam, he is living;
  The dead bodies you saw were but feigned statues;
  He's reconciled to your brothers; the Pope hath wrought
  The atonement.
DUCHESS   Mercy.   345
      She dies
BOSOLA O, she's gone again; there the cords of life broke.°
  O sacred innocence, that sweetly sleeps
  On turtles' feathers, whilst a guilty conscience
  Is a black register, wherein is writ
  All our good deeds, and bad, a perspective   350
  That shows us hell. That we cannot be suffered
  To do good when we have a mind to it!
  [*He weeps*] This is manly sorrow:
  These tears, I am very certain, never grew
  In my mother's milk. My estate is sunk   355
  Below the degree of fear; where were
  These penitent fountains while she was living?
  O, they were frozen up. Here is a sight
  As direful to my soul as is the sword
  Unto a wretch hath slain his father. Come,   360
  I'll bear thee hence,
  And execute thy last will; that's deliver
  Thy body to the reverent dispose
  Of some good women; that the cruel tyrant
  Shall not deny me. Then I'll post to Milan   365
  Where somewhat I will speedily enact
  Worth my dejection.
      Exit [with the body]

5.1

[*Enter Antonio and Delio*]

ANTONIO What think you of my hope of reconcilement
To the Aragonian brethren?

DELIO   I misdoubt it,
For though they have sent their letters of safe conduct
For your repair to Milan, they appear
But nets to entrap you. The Marquis of Pescara,   5
Under whom you hold certain land in cheat,°
Much 'gainst his noble nature, hath been moved
To seise those lands, and some of his dependents°
Are at this instant making it their suit
To be invested in your revenues.   10
I cannot think they mean well to your life
That do deprive you of your means of life,
Your living.

ANTONIO   You are still an heretic
To any safety I can shape myself.

        [*Enter Pescara*]

DELIO Here comes the Marquis. I will make myself   15
Petitioner for some part of your land,
To know whither it is flying.

ANTONIO   I pray do.

        [*Antonio retires*]

DELIO Sir, I have a suit to you.

PESCARA   To me?

DELIO   An easy one.
There is the Citadel of Saint Benet,°
With some demesnes, of late in the possession   20
Of Antonio Bologna; please you bestow them on me?

PESCARA You are my friend; but this is such a suit,
Nor fit for me to give, nor you to take.

DELIO No, sir?

PESCARA   I will give you ample reason for't
Soon in private.

        [*Enter Julia*]

               Here's the Cardinal's mistress.   25

JULIA My lord, I am grown your poor petitioner,

And should be an ill beggar, had I not
A great man's letter here, the Cardinal's,
To court you in my favour.
[*Gives Pescara a letter which he reads*]

PESCARA He entreats for you
The Citadel of Saint Benet, that belonged
To the banished Bologna.

JULIA Yes.

PESCARA I could not have thought of a friend I could
Rather pleasure with it: 'tis yours.

JULIA Sir, I thank you;
And he shall know how doubly I am engaged
Both in your gift, and speediness of giving,
Which makes your grant the greater.
Exit [*Julia*]

ANTONIO [*aside*] How they fortify
Themselves with my ruin!

DELIO Sir, I am
Little bound to you.

PESCARA Why?

DELIO Because you denied this suit to me, and gave't
To such a creature.

PESCARA Do you know what it was?
It was Antonio's land; not forfeited
By course of law, but ravished from his throat
By the Cardinal's entreaty. It were not fit
I should bestow so main a piece of wrong
Upon my friend; 'tis a gratification
Only due to a strumpet, for it is injustice.
Shall I sprinkle the pure blood of innocents
To make those followers I call my friends
Look ruddier upon me? I am glad
This land, ta'en from the owner by such wrong,
Returns again unto so foul an use
As salary for his lust. Learn, good Delio,
To ask noble things of me, and you shall find
I'll be a noble giver.

DELIO You instruct me well.

ANTONIO [*aside*] Why, here's a man now, would fright impudence
From sauciest beggars.

PESCARA Prince Ferdinand's come to Milan

Sick, as they give out, of an apoplexy;
But some say 'tis a frenzy; I am going
To visit him.

    Exit [Pescara]

ANTONIO [*advancing*] 'Tis a noble old fellow.   60

DELIO What course do you mean to take, Antonio?

ANTONIO This night I mean to venture all my fortune,
Which is no more than a poor lingering life,
To the Cardinal's worst of malice. I have got
Private access to his chamber, and intend   65
To visit him, about the mid of night,
As once his brother did our noble Duchess.
It may be that the sudden apprehension
Of danger (for I'll go in mine own shape),
When he shall see it fraught with love and duty,   70
May draw the poison out of him, and work
A friendly reconcilement; if it fail,
Yet it shall rid me of this infamous calling,
For better fall once, than be ever falling.

DELIO I'll second you in all danger; and howe'er,   75
My life keeps rank with yours.

ANTONIO You are still my loved and best friend.

    Exeunt

5.2

    [*Enter Pescara and a Doctor*]

PESCARA Now, doctor, may I visit your patient?

DOCTOR If't please your lordship; but he's instantly
To take the air here in the gallery,
By my direction.

PESCARA   Pray thee, what's his disease?

DOCTOR A very pestilent disease, my lord,   5
They call lycanthropia.

PESCARA   What's that?°
I need a dictionary to't.

DOCTOR   I'll tell you:
In those that are possessed with't there o'erflows
Such melancholy humour, they imagine
Themselves to be transformèd into wolves,   10

Steal forth to churchyards in the dead of night,
And dig dead bodies up; as two nights since
One met the Duke, 'bout midnight in a lane
Behind Saint Mark's church, with the leg of a man
Upon his shoulder; and he howled fearfully;   15
Said he was a wolf, only the difference
Was a wolf's skin was hairy on the outside,
His on the inside; bade them take their swords,
Rip up his flesh, and try. Straight I was sent for,
And having ministered to him, found his grace   20
Very well recoverèd.
PESCARA   I am glad on't.
DOCTOR Yet not without some fear
  Of a relapse. If he grow to his fit again
  I'll go a nearer way to work with him°
  Than ever Paracelsus dreamed of. If°   25
  They'll give me leave, I'll buffet his madness out of him.
      [*Enter Ferdinand, Malateste, and Cardinal; Bosola apart*]
  Stand aside, he comes.
FERDINAND Leave me.
MALATESTE Why doth your lordship love this solitariness?
FERDINAND Eagles commonly fly alone. They are crows, daws,   30
  and starlings that flock together. Look, what's that follows
  me?
MALATESTE Nothing, my lord.
FERDINAND Yes.
MALATESTE 'Tis your shadow.   35
FERDINAND Stay it, let it not haunt me.
MALATESTE Impossible, if you move, and the sun shine.
FERDINAND I will throttle it.
      [*Throws himself upon his shadow*]
MALATESTE O, my lord, you are angry with nothing.
FERDINAND You are a fool. How is't possible I should catch my 40
  shadow unless I fall upon't? When I go to hell, I mean to carry a
  bribe; for look you, good gifts evermore make way for the worst
  persons.
PESCARA Rise, good my lord.
FERDINAND I am studying the art of patience.   45
PESCARA 'Tis a noble virtue.
FERDINAND To drive six snails before me, from this town to
  Moscow;° neither use goad nor whip to them, but let them take

their own time (the patient'st man i'th' world match me for an
experiment), and I'll crawl after like a sheep-biter.°   50

CARDINAL   Force him up.
       [*They raise him*]

FERDINAND   Use me well, you were best. What I have done, I have
done; I'll confess nothing.

DOCTOR   Now let me come to him. Are you mad, my lord? Are you
out of your princely wits?   55

FERDINAND   What's he?

PESCARA   Your doctor.

FERDINAND   Let me have his beard sawed off, and his eyebrows filed
more civil.

DOCTOR   I must do mad tricks with him, for that's the only way on't.   60
I have brought your grace a salamander's skin,° to keep you from
sun-burning.

FERDINAND   I have cruel sore eyes.

DOCTOR   The white of a cockatrice's° egg is present remedy.

FERDINAND   Let it be a new-laid one, you were best.   65
Hide me from him. Physicians are like kings,
They brook no contradiction.

DOCTOR   Now he begins to fear me, now let me alone with him.
       [*Ferdinand tries to undress; the Cardinal restrains him*]

CARDINAL   How now, put off your gown?

DOCTOR   Let me have some forty urinals filled with rose-water: he   70
and I'll go pelt one another with them, now he begins to fear me.
Can you fetch a frisk,° sir? Let him go, let him go upon my peril.
I find by his eye, he stands in awe of me; I'll make him as tame as
a dormouse.
       [*Cardinal releases Ferdinand*]

FERDINAND   Can you fetch your frisks, sir? I will stamp him into a   75
cullis, flay off his skin, to cover one of the anatomies this rogue
hath set i'th' cold yonder, in Barber-Chirurgeons' Hall.° Hence,
hence, you are all of you like beasts for sacrifice; there's nothing
left of you, but tongue and belly,° flattery and lechery.
       [*Exit Ferdinand*]

PESCARA   Doctor, he did not fear you throughly.°   80

DOCTOR   True, I was somewhat too forward.
       [*Exit Doctor*]

BOSOLA [*aside*]   Mercy upon me, what a fatal judgement
Hath fallen upon this Ferdinand!

PESCARA   Knows your grace

What accident hath brought unto the Prince
This strange distraction?   85
CARDINAL [aside] I must feign somewhat. [To them] Thus they say
   it grew:
You have heard it rumoured for these many years,
None of our family dies, but there is seen
The shape of an old woman, which is given
By tradition to us to have been murdered   90
By her nephews, for her riches. Such a figure
One night, as the Prince sat up late at's book,
Appeared to him when, crying out for help,
The gentlemen of's chamber found his grace
All on a cold sweat, alter'd much in face   95
And language. Since which apparition,
He hath grown worse and worse, and I much fear
He cannot live.
BOSOLA [to the Cardinal] Sir, I would speak with you.
PESCARA   We'll leave your grace,
Wishing to the sick Prince, our noble lord,   100
All health of mind and body.
CARDINAL   You are most welcome.
   [Exeunt all except Cardinal and Bosola]
Are you come? So; [aside] this fellow must not know
By any means I had intelligence
In our Duchess' death; for, though I counselled it,
The full of all th'engagement seemed to grow°   105
From Ferdinand. [To him] Now, sir, how fares our sister?
I do not think but sorrow makes her look
Like to an oft-dyed garment. She shall now°
Taste comfort from me. Why do you look so wildly?
O, the fortune of your master here, the Prince,   110
Dejects you, but be you of happy comfort:
If you'll do one thing for me I'll entreat,
Though he had a cold tombstone o'er his bones,
I'd make you what you would be.
BOSOLA   Anything;
Give it me in a breath, and let me fly to 't.   115
They that think long, small expedition win,
For musing much o'th' end, cannot begin.
   [Enter Julia]
JULIA Sir, will you come in to supper?

CARDINAL   I am busy, leave me.
JULIA [*aside*] What an excellent shape hath that fellow!
        [*Exit Julia*]
CARDINAL 'Tis thus: Antonio lurks here in Milan;   120
    Inquire him out, and kill him. While he lives
    Our sister cannot marry, and I have thought
    Of an excellent match for her. Do this, and style me°
    Thy advancement.
BOSOLA   But by what means shall I find him out?
CARDINAL There is a gentleman, called Delio,   125
    Here in the camp, that hath been long approved
    His loyal friend. Set eye upon that fellow,
    Follow him to mass; maybe Antonio,
    Although he do account religion
    But a school-name, for fashion of the world   130
    May accompany him; or else go inquire out
    Delio's confessor, and see if you can bribe
    Him to reveal it. There are a thousand ways
    A man might find to trace him; as to know
    What fellows haunt the Jews for taking up   135
    Great sums of money, for sure he's in want;
    Or else to go to th' picture-makers, and learn
    Who brought her picture lately: some of these°
    Happily may take.
BOSOLA   Well, I'll not freeze i'th' business;
    I would see that wretched thing, Antonio,   140
    Above all sights i'th' world.
CARDINAL   Do, and be happy.
        Exit [*Cardinal*]
BOSOLA This fellow doth breed basilisks in's eyes.
    He's nothing else but murder; yet he seems
    Not to have notice of the Duchess' death.
    'Tis his cunning. I must follow his example;   145
    There cannot be a surer way to trace°
    Than that of an old fox.
        [*Enter Julia holding a pistol*]
JULIA   So, sir, you are well met.
BOSOLA How now?
JULIA   Nay, the doors are fast enough.
    Now, sir, I will make you confess your treachery.
BOSOLA Treachery?

JULIA   Yes, confess to me   150
  Which of my women 'twas you hired, to put
  Love-powder into my drink?
BOSOLA   Love-powder!
JULIA   Yes,
  When I was at Malfi.
  Why should I fall in love with such a face else?
  I have already suffered for thee so much pain,   155
  The only remedy to do me good
  Is to kill my longing.
BOSOLA   Sure your pistol holds
  Nothing but perfumes, or kissing-comfits.
  Excellent lady,
  You have a pretty way on't to discover   160
  Your longing. Come, come, I'll disarm you,   '
  And arm you thus [*embraces her*]; yet this is wondrous strange.
JULIA Compare thy form and my eyes together,
  You'll find my love no such great miracle.
  Now you'll say   165
  I am wanton. This nice modesty in ladies
  Is but a troublesome familiar
  That haunts them.
BOSOLA Know you me, I am a blunt soldier.
JULIA   The better;
  Sure there wants fire where there are no lively sparks 170
  Of roughness.
BOSOLA   And I want compliment.
JULIA   Why, ignorance
  In courtship cannot make you do amiss,
  If you have a heart to do well.
BOSOLA   You are very fair.
JULIA Nay, if you lay beauty to my charge,
  I must plead unguilty.
BOSOLA   Your bright eyes   175
  Carry a quiver of darts in them, sharper
  Than sunbeams.
JULIA   You will mar me with commendation,
  Put yourself to the charge of courting me,
  Whereas now I woo you.
BOSOLA [*aside*] I have it, I will work upon this creature. 180
  [*To her*] Let us grow most amorously familiar.

> If the great Cardinal now should see me thus,
> Would he not count me a villain?

JULIA No, he might count me a wanton,
> Not lay a scruple of offence on you;   185
> For if I see and steal a diamond,
> The fault is not i'th' stone, but in me the thief
> That purloins it. I am sudden with you;
> We that are great women of pleasure use to cut off
> These uncertain wishes, and unquiet longings,   190
> And in an instant join the sweet delight
> And the pretty excuse together; had you been i'th' street,
> Under my chamber window, even there
> I should have courted you.

BOSOLA   O, you are an excellent lady.

JULIA Bid me do somewhat for you presently   195
> To express I love you.

BOSOLA   I will, and if you love me,
> Fail not to effect it.
> The Cardinal is grown wondrous melancholy;
> Demand the cause; let him not put you off
> With feigned excuse, discover the main ground on't.   200

JULIA Why would you know this?

BOSOLA   I have depended on him,
> And I hear that he is fallen in some disgrace
> With the Emperor. If he be, like the mice
> That forsake falling houses, I would shift
> To other dependance.   205

JULIA You shall not need follow the wars;
> I'll be your maintenance.

BOSOLA   And I your loyal servant;
> But I cannot leave my calling.

JULIA   Not leave
> An ungrateful general for the love of a sweet lady?
> You are like some, cannot sleep in feather-beds,   210
> But must have blocks for their pillows.

BOSOLA   Will you do this?

JULIA Cunningly.

BOSOLA   Tomorrow I'll expect th'intelligence.

JULIA Tomorrow? Get you into my cabinet,
> You shall have it with you; do not delay me,
> No more than I do you. I am like one   215

That is condemned: I have my pardon promised,
But I would see it sealed. Go, get you in,
You shall see me wind my tongue about his heart,
Like a skein of silk.
          [*Bosola withdraws. Enter Cardinal, attended by Servants*]
CARDINAL Where are you?
SERVANTS   Here.
CARDINAL   Let none upon your lives   220
Have conference with the Prince Ferdinand,
Unless I know it.
          [*Exeunt Servants*]
                    [*Aside*] In this distraction
He may reveal the murder.
Yon's my lingering consumption:
I am weary of her, and by any means   225
Would be quit of.
JULIA   How now, my lord?
What ails you?
CARDINAL   Nothing.
JULIA   O, you are much altered:
Come, I must be your secretary, and remove
This lead from off your bosom: what's the matter?
CARDINAL I may not tell you.   230
JULIA Are you so far in love with sorrow,
You cannot part with part of it? Or think you
I cannot love your grace when you are sad,
As well as merry? Or do you suspect
I, that have been a secret to your heart   235
These many winters, cannot be the same
Unto your tongue?
CARDINAL   Satisfy thy longing,
The only way to make thee keep my counsel
Is not to tell thee.
JULIA   Tell your echo this,
Or flatterers that, like echoes, still report   240
What they hear (though most imperfect), and not me;
For, if that you be true unto yourself,
I'll know.
CARDINAL   Will you rack me?
JULIA   No, judgement shall
Draw it from you. It is an equal fault

To tell one's secrets unto all, or none.   245
CARDINAL The first argues folly.
JULIA   But the last tyranny.
CARDINAL Very well. Why, imagine I have committed
  Some secret deed, which I desire the world
  May never hear of.
JULIA   Therefore may not I know it?
  You have concealed for me as great a sin   250
  As adultery. Sir, never was occasion
  For perfect trial of my constancy
  Till now. Sir, I beseech you.
CARDINAL   You'll repent it.
JULIA   Never.
CARDINAL It hurries thee to ruin. I'll not tell thee.
  Be well advised, and think what danger 'tis   255
  To receive a prince's secrets; they that do,
  Had need have their breasts hooped with adamant
  To contain them. I pray thee yet be satisfied
  Examine thine own frailty; 'tis more easy
  To tie knots, than unloose them; 'tis a secret   260
  That, like a ling'ring poison, may chance lie
  Spread in thy veins, and kill thee seven year hence.
JULIA Now you dally with me.
CARDINAL   No more, thou shalt know it.
  By my appointment the great Duchess of Malfi,
  And two of her young children, four nights since,   265
  Were strangled.
JULIA   O heaven! Sir, what have you done?
CARDINAL How now? How settles this? Think you your bosom
  Will be a grave dark and obscure enough
  For such a secret?
JULIA   You have undone yourself, sir.
CARDINAL Why?
JULIA   It lies not in me to conceal it.
CARDINAL   No?   270
  Come, I will swear you to't upon this book.
        [*He holds out a bible*]
JULIA Most religiously.
CARDINAL   Kiss it.
        [*She kisses it*]
  Now you shall never utter it; thy curiosity

Hath undone thee: thou'rt poisoned with that book;
Because I knew thou couldst not keep my counsel,   275
I have bound thee to't by death.
    [*Enter Bosola*]

BOSOLA For pity' sake, hold!

CARDINAL   Ha, Bosola!

JULIA   I forgive you
This equal piece of justice you have done,
For I betrayed your counsel to that fellow;
He overheard it; that was the cause I said   280
It lay not in me to conceal it.

BOSOLA O foolish woman,
    Couldst not thou have poisoned him?

JULIA   'Tis weakness
Too much to think what should have been done. I go,
I know not whither.
    [*Julia dies*]

CARDINAL   Wherefore com'st thou hither?   285

BOSOLA That I might find a great man, like yourself,
    Not out of his wits, as the Lord Ferdinand,
    To remember my service.

CARDINAL   I'll have thee hewed in pieces.

BOSOLA Make not yourself such a promise of that life
    Which is not yours to dispose of.

CARDINAL   Who placed thee here?   290

BOSOLA Her lust, as she intended.

CARDINAL   Very well;
Now you know me for your fellow murderer.

BOSOLA And wherefore should you lay fair marble colours
    Upon your rotten purposes to me?°
    Unless you imitate some that do plot great treasons,   295
    And when they have done, go hide themselves i'th' graves
    Of those were actors in't?

CARDINAL No more, there is a fortune attends thee.

BOSOLA Shall I go sue to Fortune any longer?
    'Tis the fool's pilgrimage.

CARDINAL   I have honours in store for thee.   300

BOSOLA There are a many ways that conduct to seeming
    Honour, and some of them very dirty ones.

CARDINAL Throw to the devil
    Thy melancholy. The fire burns well,

What need we keep a-stirring of 't, and make   305
A greater smother? Thou wilt kill Antonio?
BOSOLA Yes.
CARDINAL   Take up that body
BOSOLA   I think I shall
Shortly grow the common bier for churchyards.
CARDINAL I will allow thee some dozen of attendants
To aid thee in the murder.   310
BOSOLA O, by no means: physicians that apply horse-leeches to any
rank swelling use to cut off their tails, that the blood may run
through them the faster. Let me have no train when I go to shed
blood, lest it make me have a greater when I ride to the gallows.
CARDINAL Come to me after midnight, to help to remove that   315
body
To her own lodging; I'll give out she died o'th' plague;
'Twill breed the less inquiry after her death.
BOSOLA Where's Castruccio, her husband?
CARDINAL He's rode to Naples to take possession
Of Antonio's citadel.   320
BOSOLA Believe me, you have done a very happy turn.
CARDINAL Fail not to come. There is the master-key
Of our lodgings; and by that you may conceive
What trust I plant in you.
BOSOLA   You shall find me ready.
     Exit [Cardinal]
O poor Antonio, though nothing be so needful   325
To thy estate as pity, yet I find
Nothing so dangerous. I must look to my footing.
In such slippery ice-pavements, men had need
To be frost-nailed well: they may break their necks else.
The precedent's here afore me: how this man   330
Bears up in blood! seems fearless! Why, 'tis well:°
Security some men call the suburbs of hell,
Only a dead wall between. Well, good Antonio,°
I'll seek thee out, and all my care shall be
To put thee into safety from the reach   335
Of these most cruel biters, that have got
Some of thy blood already. It may be
I'll join with thee in a most just revenge.
The weakest arm is strong enough, that strikes
With the sword of justice. Still methinks the Duchess   340

Haunts me; there, there:
'Tis nothing but my melancholy.
O penitence, let me truly taste thy cup,
That throws men down, only to raise them up.
     Exit [with the body]

5.3

*[Enter Antonio and Delio]. There is an echo from the
Duchess' grave*

DELIO Yon's the Cardinal's window. This fortification
    Grew from the ruins of an ancient abbey,
    And to yond side o'th' river lies a wall,
    Piece of a cloister, which in my opinion
    Gives the best echo that you ever heard: 5
    So hollow, and so dismal, and withal
    So plain in the distinction of our words,
    That many have supposed it is a spirit
    That answers.
ANTONIO   I do love these ancient ruins:
    We never tread upon them but we set   10
    Our foot upon some reverend history.
    And questionless, here in this open court,
    Which now lies naked to the injuries
    Of stormy weather, some men lie interred
    Loved the church so well, and gave so largely to't,   15
    They thought it should have canopied their bones
    Till doomsday. But all things have their end:
    Churches and cities, which have diseases like to men,
    Must have like death that we have.
ECHO   Like death that we have.
DELIO Now the echo hath caught you.
ANTONIO   It groaned, methought, and gave   20
    A very deadly accent.
ECHO   Deadly accent.
DELIO I told you 'twas a pretty one. You may make it
    A huntsman, or a falconer, a musician,
    Or a thing of sorrow.
ECHO   A thing of sorrow.

ANTONIO Ay, sure: that suits it best.
ECHO   That suits it best.   25
ANTONIO 'Tis very like my wife's voice.
ECHO   Ay, wife's voice.
DELIO Come, let's us walk farther from't.
   I would not have you go to th' Cardinal's tonight:
   Do not.
ECHO   Do not.
DELIO Wisdom doth not more moderate wasting sorrow   30
   Than time: take time for't; be mindful of thy safety.
ECHO Be mindful of thy safety.
ANTONIO   Necessity compels me:
   Make scrutiny throughout the passes
   Of your own life, you'll find it impossible
   To fly your fate.
ECHO   O, fly your fate.   35
DELIO Hark, the dead stones seem to have pity on you
   And give you good counsel.
ANTONIO Echo, I will not talk with thee,
   For thou art a dead thing.
ECHO   Thou art a dead thing.
ANTONIO My Duchess is asleep now,   40
   And her little ones, I hope, sweetly. O heaven,
   Shall I never see her more?
ECHO   Never see her more.
ANTONIO I marked not one repetition of the echo
   But that; and on the sudden, a clear light
   Presented me a face folded in sorrow.   45
DELIO Your fancy, merely.
ANTONIO Come, I'll be out of this ague;
   For to live thus is not indeed to live:
   It is a mockery, and abuse of life.
   I will not henceforth save myself by halves;   50
   Lose all, or nothing.
DELIO   Your own virtue save you.
   I'll fetch your eldest son, and second you;
   It may be that the sight of his own blood,
   Spread in so sweet a figure, may beget
   The more compassion.
ANTONIO   However, fare you well.   55
   Though in our miseries Fortune have a part,

Yet in our noble suff'rings she hath none:
Contempt of pain, that we may call our own.
    Exeunt

5.4

    [*Enter*] *Cardinal, Pescara, Malateste, Roderigo, Grisolan*
CARDINAL You shall not watch tonight by the sick Prince,
    His grace is very well recovered.
MALATESTE Good my lord, suffer us.
CARDINAL   O, by no means;
    The noise and change of object in his eye
    Doth more distract him. I pray, all to bed,   5
    And though you hear him in his violent fit,
    Do not rise, I entreat you.
PESCARA So sir, we shall not.
CARDINAL   Nay, I must have you promise
    Upon your honours, for I was enjoined to't
    By himself; and he seemed to urge it sensibly.   10
PESCARA Let our honours bind this trifle.
CARDINAL Nor any of your followers.
MALATESTE   Neither.
CARDINAL It may be, to make trial of your promise
    When he's asleep, myself will rise and feign
    Some of his mad tricks, and cry out for help,   15
    And feign myself in danger.
MALATESTE   If your throat were cutting,
    I'd not come at you, now I have protested against it.
CARDINAL Why, I thank you.
    [*Cardinal withdraws*]
GRISOLAN   'Twas a foul storm tonight.
RODERIGO The Lord Ferdinand's chamber shook like an osier.
MALATESTE 'Twas nothing but pure kindness in the devil   20
    To rock his own child.
    Exeunt [*all except the Cardinal*]
CARDINAL The reason why I would not suffer these
    About my brother, is because at midnight
    I may with better privacy convey
    Julia's body to her own lodging. O, my conscience!   25

I would pray now, but the devil takes away my heart
For having any confidence in prayer.
About this hour I appointed Bosola
To fetch the body. When he hath served my turn,
He dies.   30

    Exit [Cardinal. Enter Bosola]

BOSOLA Ha? 'Twas the Cardinal's voice. I heard him name
Bosola, and my death. Listen, I hear one's footing.

    [Enter Ferdinand]

FERDINAND Strangling is a very quiet death.

BOSOLA *[aside]* Nay then, I see I must stand upon my guard.

FERDINAND What say' to that? Whisper, softly: do you agree to't?   35
So it must be done i'th' dark: the Cardinal
Would not for a thousand pounds the doctor should see it.

    Exit [Ferdinand]

BOSOLA My death is plotted; here's the consequence of murder:
We value not desert, nor Christian breath,
When we know black deeds must be cured with death.   40

    [Enter Antonio and Servant]

SERVANT Here stay, sir, and be confident, I pray.
I'll fetch you a dark lantern.

    Exit [Servant]

ANTONIO   Could I take him
At his prayers, there were hope of pardon.

BOSOLA Fall right my sword!

    [Stabs Antonio]

I'll not give thee so much leisure as to pray.   45

ANTONIO O, I am gone. Thou hast ended a long suit
In a minute.

BOSOLA   What art thou?

ANTONIO   A most wretched thing,
That only have thy benefit in death,
To appear myself.°

    [Enter Servant with a lantern]

SERVANT   Where are you, sir?

ANTONIO Very near my home:—Bosola?

SERVANT   O, misfortune.   50

BOSOLA *[to Servant]* Smother thy pity, thou art dead
    else.—Antonio!
The man I would have saved 'bove mine own life!
We are merely the stars' tennis balls, struck and bandied°

Which way please them.—O good Antonio,
I'll whisper one thing in thy dying ear   55
Shall make thy heart break quickly: thy fair Duchess
And two sweet children—

ANTONIO   Their very names
Kindle a little life in me.

BOSOLA   Are murdered!

ANTONIO Some men have wished to die
At the hearing of sad tidings: I am glad   60
That I shall do't in sadness; I would not now°
Wish my wounds balmed, nor healed, for I have no use
To put my life to. In all our quest of greatness,
Like wanton boys whose pastime is their care,
We follow after bubbles, blown in th'air.   65
Pleasure of life, what is't? Only the good hours
Of an ague; merely a preparative to rest,
To endure vexation. I do not ask
The process of my death; only commend me
To Delio.   70

BOSOLA Break heart!

ANTONIO   And let my son fly the courts of princes.
          [Antonio dies]

BOSOLA Thou seem'st to have loved Antonio?

SERVANT   I brought him hither,
To have reconciled him to the Cardinal.

BOSOLA I do not ask thee that.
Take him up, if thou tender thine own life,   75
And bear him where the Lady Julia
Was wont to lodge.
          [Servant picks up the corpse]
                    O, my fate moves swift!
I have this Cardinal in the forge already,
Now I'll bring him to th' hammer. O direful misprision!
I will not imitate things glorious,   80
No more than base: I'll be mine own example.
[To Servant] On, on, and look thou represent, for silence,
The thing thou bear'st.°
          Exeunt [with the Servant carrying Antonio's body]

5.5

[*Enter*] *Cardinal, with a book*

CARDINAL I am puzzled in a question about hell.
　He says, in hell there's one material fire,°
　And yet it shall not burn all men alike.
　Lay him by. How tedious is a guilty conscience!°
　When I look into the fishponds, in my garden,　　　　　5
　Methinks I see a thing armed with a rake
　That seems to strike at me.
　　　[*Enter Bosola, and Servant with Antonio's body*]
　　　　　　　　　　　　Now? art thou come?
　Thou look'st ghastly:
　There sits in thy face some great determination,
　Mixed with some fear.
BOSOLA　　　　　　　　Thus it lightens into action:　　10
　I am come to kill thee.
CARDINAL　　　　　　　Ha? Help! our guard!
BOSOLA Thou art deceived:
　They are out of thy howling.
CARDINAL Hold, and I will faithfully divide
　Revenues with thee.
BOSOLA　　　　　　　Thy prayers and proffers　　　　15
　Are both unseasonable.
CARDINAL　　　　　　　Raise the watch!
　We are betrayed!
BOSOLA　　　　　I have confined your flight:
　I'll suffer your retreat to Julia's chamber,
　But no further.
CARDINAL　　　Help! We are betrayed!
　　　[*Enter above, Pescara, Malateste, Roderigo and Grisolan*]
MALATESTE　　　　　　　　　　Listen.
CARDINAL My dukedom for rescue!
RODERIGO　　　　　　　　Fie upon his counterfeiting!　　20
MALATESTE Why, 'tis not the Cardinal.
RODERIGO　　　　　　　　Yes, yes, 'tis he,
　But I'll see him hanged, ere I'll go down to him.
CARDINAL Here's a plot upon me; I am assaulted! I am lost,
　Unless some rescue!
GRISOLAN　　　　　He doth this pretty well;

But it will not serve to laugh me out of mine honour.   25
CARDINAL The sword's at my throat!
RODERIGO   You would not bawl so loud then.
MALATESTE Come, come,
    Let's go to bed; he told us thus much aforehand.
PESCARA He wished you should not come at him; but believe't,
    The accent of the voice sounds not in jest.   30
    I'll down to him, howsoever, and with engines°
    Force ope the doors.
            [*Exit Pescara*]
RODERIGO   Let's follow him aloof,
    And note how the Cardinal will laugh at him.
            [*Exeunt all above*]
BOSOLA There's for you first,
            He kills the Servant
    'Cause you shall not unbarricade the door°   35
    To let in rescue.
CARDINAL What cause hast thou to pursue my life?
BOSOLA   Look there.
CARDINAL Antonio?
BOSOLA   Slain by my hand unwittingly.
    Pray, and be sudden; when thou killed'st thy sister,
    Thou took'st from Justice her most equal balance,   40
    And left her naught but her sword.
CARDINAL   O, mercy!
BOSOLA Now it seems thy greatness was only outward,
    For thou fall'st faster of thyself than calamity
    Can drive thee. I'll not waste longer time: there!
            [*Stabs the Cardinal*]
CARDINAL Thou hast hurt me.
BOSOLA   Again!
            [*Stabs him again*]
CARDINAL   Shall I die like a leveret   45
    Without any resistance? Help, help, help!
    I am slain!
            [*Enter Ferdinand*]
FERDINAND   Th'alarum! Give me a fresh horse:
    Rally the vanguard, or the day is lost.
    [*Threatens the Cardinal*] Yield, yield! I give you the honour of
        arms,°
    Shake my sword over you, will you yield?   50

CARDINAL Help me, I am your brother.
FERDINAND   The devil?
My brother fight upon the adverse party?
There flies your ransom.

He wounds the Cardinal, and in the scuffle gives Bosola his
death wound

CARDINAL   O Justice!°
I suffer now for what hath former been:
Sorrow is held the eldest child of sin.   55
FERDINAND Now you're brave fellows. Caesar's fortune was harder
than Pompey's: Caesar died in the arms of prosperity, Pompey at
the feet of disgrace;° you both died in the field. The pain's
nothing; pain many times is taken away with the apprehension of
greater, as the toothache with the sight of a barber that comes to   60
pull it out: there's philosophy for you.
BOSOLA Now my revenge is perfect.

He kills Ferdinand

                              Sink, thou main cause
Of my undoing! The last part of my life
Hath done me best service.
FERDINAND Give me some wet hay, I am broken-winded.   65
I do account this world but a dog-kennel;
I will vault credit, and affect high pleasures,°
Beyond death.
BOSOLA   He seems to come to himself,
Now he's so near the bottom.
FERDINAND My sister! O my sister! There's the cause on't: 70
Whether we fall by ambition, blood, or lust,
Like diamonds, we are cut with our own dust.°

[Ferdinand dies]

CARDINAL Thou hast thy payment too.
BOSOLA Yes, I hold my weary soul in my teeth;
'Tis ready to part from me. I do glory   75
That thou, which stood'st like a huge pyramid
Begun upon a large and ample base,
Shalt end in a little point, a kind of nothing.

[Enter Pescara, Malateste, Roderigo, and Grisolan]

PESCARA How now, my lord?
MALATESTE   O sad disaster!
RODERIGO   How comes this?
BOSOLA Revenge, for the Duchess of Malfi, murderèd   80

198

By th'Aragonian brethren; for Antonio,
Slain by this hand; for lustful Julia,
Poisoned by this man; and lastly, for myself,
That was an actor in the main of all
Much 'gainst mine own good nature, yet i'th' end   85
Neglected.

PESCARA   How now, my lord?

CARDINAL   Look to my brother:
He gave us these large wounds, as we were struggling
Here i'th' rushes: And now, I pray, let me°
Be laid by, and never thought of.
    [The Cardinal dies]

PESCARA How fatally, it seems, he did withstand   90
His own rescue!

MALATESTE   Thou wretched thing of blood,
How came Antonio by his death?

BOSOLA In a mist: I know not how;
Such a mistake as I have often seen
In a play. O, I am gone.   95
We are only like dead walls, or vaulted graves,°
That, ruined, yields no echo. Fare you well.
It may be pain, but no harm to me to die
In so good a quarrel. O, this gloomy world!
In what a shadow, or deep pit of darkness,   100
Doth, womanish and fearful, mankind live!
Let worthy minds ne'er stagger in distrust
To suffer death, or shame for what is just:
Mine is another voyage.
    [Bosola dies]

PESCARA The noble Delio, as I came to th' palace,   105
Told me of Antonio's being here, and showed me
A pretty gentleman, his son and heir.
    [Enter Delio, with Antonio's son]

MALATESTE O sir, you come too late!

DELIO   I heard so, and
Was armed for't ere I came. Let us make noble use
Of this great ruin; and join all our force   110
To establish this young, hopeful gentleman
In's mother's right. These wretched eminent things
Leave no more fame behind 'em than should one
Fall in a frost, and leave his print in snow;

As soon as the sun shines, it ever melts,   115
Both form and matter. I have ever thought
Nature doth nothing so great for great men,
As when she's pleased to make them lords of truth:
Integrity of life is fame's best friend,°
Which nobly, beyond death, shall crown the end.   120
    Exeunt

THE DEVIL'S LAW-CASE

THE PERSONS OF THE PLAY

Romelio, *a merchant, and brother of Jolenta*
Leonora, *a widow and mother of Romelio and Jolenta, and in love with Contarino*
Jolenta, *sister of Romelio*
Winifred, *a Waiting-Woman of Leonora*
Contarino, *a nobleman in love with Jolenta*
Ercole, *a Knight of Malta also in love with Jolenta*
Crispiano, *a civil lawyer from Seville*
Sanitonella, *companion of Crispiano; later a lawyer's clerk*
Julio, *the spendthrift son of Crispiano*
Ariosto, *an advocate, later a judge*
Contilupo, *a dapper, unscrupulous lawyer*
Prospero, *a Neapolitan gentleman*
Baptista, *a rich merchant*
Angiolella, *a young nun*
A Capuchin
Two Surgeons
Lawyers and Judges
Register of the Court
Bellmen
Marshal
Herald
Servants

[Dedication]

To the right worthy, and all-accomplished Gentleman, Sir
Thomas Finch,° Knight Baronet

Sir, let it not appear strange that I do aspire to your patronage.
Things that taste of any goodness love to be sheltered near
goodness. Nor do I flatter in this (which I hate), only touch at the
original copy° of your virtues. Some of my other works, as *The
White Devil*, *The Duchess of Malfi*, *Guise*,° and others, you have   5
formerly seen; I present this humbly to kiss your hands, and to
find your allowance. Nor do I much doubt it, knowing the greatest
of the Cæsars have cheerfully entertained less° poems than this;
and had I thought it unworthy, I had not inquired after so worthy
a patronage. Yourself I understand to be all courtesy. I doubt not   10
therefore of your acceptance, but resolve that my election is happy.
For which favour done me, I shall ever rest

Your Worship's humbly devoted,

JOHN WEBSTER

To the Judicious Reader

I hold it, in these kind of poems, with that of Horace: *Sapientia prima, stultitia caruisse,*° to be free from those vices which proceed from ignorance; of which I take it, this play will ingeniously acquit itself. I do chiefly therefore expose it to the judicious. *Locus est, et pluribus umbris,*° others have leave to sit down, and read it, who come unbidden. But to these, should a man present them with the most excellent music, it would delight them no more than *Auriculas citharae collecta sorde dolentes.*° I will not further insist upon the approvement of it, for I am so far from praising myself, that I have not given way to divers of my friends, whose unbegged commendatory verses offered themselves to do me service in the front of this poem. A great part of the grace of this, I confess, lay in action;° yet can no action ever be gracious, where the decency of the language, and ingenious structure of the scene, arrive not to make up a perfect harmony. What I have failed of this, you that have approved my other works, when you have read this, tax me of. For the rest, *Non ego ventosae plebis, suffragia venor.*°

The Devil's Law-Case
or
When Women go to Law, the Devil is full of Business

[1.1]

Enter Romelio and Prospero

PROSPERO You have shown a world of wealth; I did not think
    There had been a merchant lived in Italy
    Of half your substance.
ROMELIO   I'll give the King of Spain
    Ten thousand ducats yearly, and discharge
    My yearly custom. The Hollanders scarce trade°   5
    More generally than I. My factors' wives
    Wear chaperons of velvet, and my scriveners,
    Merely through my employment, grow so rich
    They build their palaces and belvederes°
    With musical water-works. Never in my life°   10
    Had I a loss at sea. They call me on th'Exchange
    The Fortunate Young Man and make great suit
    To venture with me. Shall I tell you, sir,
    Of a strange confidence in my way of trading?
    I reckon it as certain as the gain   15
    In erecting a lottery.
PROSPERO   I pray, sir, what do you think°
    Of Signor Baptista's estate?
ROMELIO   A mere beggar:
    He's worth some fifty thousand ducats.
PROSPERO   Is not that well?
ROMELIO How 'well'? For a man to be melted to snow-
    water,
    With toiling in the world from three-and-twenty   20
    Till threescore, for poor fifty thousand ducats.
PROSPERO To your estate 'tis little, I confess;°

You have the spring-tide of gold.

ROMELIO   Faith, and for silver,°
    Should I not send it packing to th'East Indies,
    We should have a glut on't.   25
        Enter Servant
SERVANT Here's the great lord Contarino.
        [*Exit Servant*]
PROSPERO   O, I know
    His business; he's a suitor to your sister.
ROMELIO Yes, sir, but to you,
    As my most trusted friend, I utter it:
    I will break the alliance.
PROSPERO   You are ill advised then;   30
    There lives not a completer gentleman
    In Italy, nor of a more ancient house.
ROMELIO What tell you me of gentry? 'Tis nought else
    But a superstitious relic of time past;
    And sift it to the true worth, it is nothing   35
    But ancient riches; and in him you know
    They are pitifully in the wane. He makes his colour
    Of visiting us so often, to sell land,
    And thinks, if he can gain my sister's love,
    To recover the treble value.
PROSPERO   Sure he loves her   40
    Entirely, and she deserves it.
ROMELIO   Faith, though she were
    Crook'd shouldered, having such a portion,°
    She would have noble suitors. But truth is,
    I would wish my noble venturer take heed:
    It may be whiles he hopes to catch a gilt-head,   45
    He may draw up a gudgeon.
        Enter Contarino
PROSPERO   He's come. Sir, I will leave you.°
        [*Exit Prospero*]
CONTARINO I sent you the evidence of the piece of land
    I motioned to you for the sale.
ROMELIO   Yes.
CONTARINO Has your counsel perused it?
ROMELIO   Not yet, my lord. Do you
    Intend to travel?
CONTARINO   No.

ROMELIO   O then you lose   50
  That which makes man most absolute.
CONTARINO   Yet I have heard
  Of divers that, in passing of the Alps,
  Have but exchanged their virtues at dear rate
  For others' vices.
ROMELIO   O my lord, lie not idle.°
  The chiefest action for a man of great spirit   55
  Is never to be out of action. We should think
  The soul was never put into the body,
  Which has so many rare and curious pieces
  Of mathematical motion, to stand still.
  Virtue is ever sowing of her seeds: 60
  In the trenches for the soldier, in the wakeful study
  For the scholar, in the furrows of the sea
  For men of our profession, of all which
  Arise and spring up honour. Come, I know
  You have some noble great design in hand,   65
  That you levy so much money.
CONTARINO   Sir, I'll tell you:
  The greatest part of it I mean to employ
  In payment of my debts, and the remainder
  Is like to bring me into greater bonds,°
  As I aim it.
ROMELIO   How, sir?
CONTARINO   I intend it   70
  For the charge of my wedding.
ROMELIO Are you to be married, my lord?
CONTARINO Yes, sir; and I must now entreat your pardon
  That I have concealed from you a business,
  Wherein you had at first been called to counsel,   75
  But that I thought it a less fault in friendship,
  To engage myself thus far without your knowledge
  Than to do it against your will. Another reason
  Was, that I would not publish to the world,
  Nor have it whispered scarce, what wealthy voyage°   80
  I went about, till I had got the mine
  In mine own possession.
ROMELIO   You are dark to me yet.°
CONTARINO I'll now remove the cloud. Sir, your sister and I
  Are vowed each other's, and there only wants

Her worthy mother's and your fair consents   85
To style it marriage; this is a way,
Not only to make a friendship, but confirm it
For our posterities. How do you look upon't?
ROMELIO Believe me, sir, as on the principal column
 To advance our house. Why, you bring honour with you,   90
Which is the soul of wealth. I shall be proud
To live to see my little nephews ride
O'th' upper hand of their uncle's, and the daughters°
Be ranked by heralds at solemnities
Before the mother: all this derived   95
From your nobility. Do not blame me, sir,
If I be taken with't exceedingly,
For this same honour, with us citizens,
Is a thing we are mainly fond of, especially°
When it comes without money, which is very seldom.   100
But as you do perceive my present temper,
Be sure I am yours—[aside] fired with scorn and laughter
At your over-confident purpose—[aloud] and no doubt,
My mother will be of your mind.
CONTARINO   'Tis my hope, sir.
 Exit Romelio
I do observe how this Romelio   105
Has very worthy parts, were they not blasted
By insolent vainglory. There rests now
The mother's approbation to the match,
Who is a woman of that state and bearing,
Though she be city-born, both in her language,   110
Her garments, and her table, she excels
Our ladies of the court. She goes not gaudy;
Yet have I seen her wear one diamond,
Would have bought twenty gay ones out of their clothes,°
And some of them, without the greater grace,°   115
Out of their honesties.
 Enter Leonora
       She comes. I will try
How she stands affected to me, without relating°
My contract with her daughter.
LEONORA Sir, you are nobly welcome, and presume°
You are in a place that's wholly dedicated   120
To your service.

CONTARINO   I am ever bound to you
For many special favours.

LEONORA   Sir, your fame
Renders you most worthy of it.

CONTARINO   It could never have got
A sweeter air to fly in than your breath.

LEONORA You have been strange a long time. You are weary°   125
Of our unseasonable time of feeding;
Indeed th'Exchange bell makes us dine so late;
I think the ladies of the court from us°
Learn to lie so long abed.°

CONTARINO They have a kind of Exchange among them too;   130
Marry, unless it be to hear of news, I take it
Theirs is like the New Burse, thinly furnished°
With tires and new fashions. I have a suit to you.

LEONORA I would not have you value it the less,
If I say 'tis granted already.

CONTARINO   You are all bounty.   135
'Tis to bestow your picture on me.

LEONORA   O sir,
Shadows are coveted in summer, and with me°
'Tis fall o'th' leaf.

CONTARINO   You enjoy the best of time.
This latter spring of yours shows in my eye
More fruitful, and more temperate withal,   140
Than that whose date is only limited
By the music of the cuckoo.

LEONORA   Indeed, sir, I dare tell you,
My looking-glass is a true one, and as yet
It does not terrify me. Must you have my picture?

CONTARINO So please you, lady, and I shall preserve it   145
As a most choice object.

LEONORA You will enjoin me to a strange punishment.
With what a compelled face a woman sits
While she is drawing! I have noted divers°
Either to feign smiles, or suck in the lips   150
To have a little mouth; ruffle the cheeks
To have the dimple seen, and so disorder
The face with affectation, at next sitting
It has not been the same. I have known others
Have lost the entire fashion of their face   155

In half an hour's sitting.

CONTARINO   How?

LEONORA   In hot weather,
The painting on their face has been so mellow,
They have left the poor man harder work by half,
To mend the copy he wrought by. But indeed,
If ever I would have mine drawn to th'life,   160
I would have a painter steal it at such a time
I were devoutly kneeling at my prayers;
There is then a heavenly beauty in't, the soul
Moves in the superficies.

CONTARINO   Excellent lady,
Now you teach beauty a preservative,   165
More than 'gainst fading colours; and your judgement
Is perfect in all things.

LEONORA   Indeed, sir, I am a widow,
And want the addition to make it so;
For man's experience has still been held
Woman's best eyesight. I pray, sir, tell me,   170
You are about to sell a piece of land
To my son, I hear.

CONTARINO   'Tis truth.

LEONORA   Now I could rather wish
That noblemen would ever live i'th' country,
Rather than make their visits up to th'city
About such business. O sir, noble houses°   175
Have no such goodly prospects any way,
As into their own land; the decay of that,°
Next to their begging church-land, is a ruin°
Worth all men's pity. Sir, I have forty thousand crowns
Sleep in my chest, shall waken when you please,   180
And fly to your commands. Will you stay supper?

CONTARINO I cannot, worthy lady.

LEONORA I would not have you come hither, sir, to sell,
But to settle your estate. I hope you understand
Wherefore I make this proffer; so I leave you.   185

        Exit Leonora

CONTARINO What a treasury have I pierced! 'I hope
You understand wherefore I make this proffer'.
She has got some intelligence how I intend to marry
Her daughter, and ingeniously perceived

That by her picture, which I begged of her,   190
I meant the fair Jolenta. Here's a letter
Which gives express charge not to visit her
Till midnight: [*reads*] 'Fail not to come, for 'tis a business
That concerns both our honours.
                Yours in danger to be lost, Jolenta.'   195
'Tis a strange injunction. What should be the business?
She is not changed, I hope. I'll thither straight,
For women's resolutions in such deeds,
Like bees, light oft on flowers, and oft on weeds.
    Exit

[1.2]

    Enter Ercole, Romelio, Jolenta

ROMELIO O sister, come, the tailor must to work,
  To make your wedding clothes.
JOLENTA   The tomb-maker,
  To take measure of my coffin.
ROMELIO   Tomb-maker?
  Look you, the King of Spain greets you.
    [*He gives her a paper*]
JOLENTA   What does this mean?
  Do you serve process on me?
ROMELIO   Process? come,°   5
  You would be witty now.
JOLENTA   Why, what's this, I pray?
ROMELIO Infinite grace to you: it is a letter
  From His Catholic Majesty, for the commends
  Of this gentleman for your husband.
JOLENTA   In good season;
  I hope he will not have my allegiance stretched   10
  To the undoing of myself.
ROMELIO Undo yourself? He does proclaim him here—
JOLENTA Not for a traitor, does he?
ROMELIO   You are not mad—
  For one of the noblest gentlemen.
JOLENTA   Yet kings many times
  Know merely but men's outsides. Was this commendation   15

Voluntary, think you?
ROMELIO   Voluntary? What mean you by that?
JOLENTA Why, I do not think but he begged it of the king,
    And it may fortune to be out of 's way:
    Some better suit, that would have stood his lordship
    In far more stead. Letters of commendations!   20
    Why, 'tis reported that they are grown stale,
    When places fall i'th' university.°
    I pray you return his pass; for to a widow
    That longs to be a courtier, this paper
    May do knight's service.°   25
ERCOLE Mistake not, excellent mistress; these commends
    Express His Majesty of Spain has given me
    Both addition of honour, as you may perceive
    By my habit, and a place here to command
    O'er thirty galleys. This your brother shows,   30
    As wishing that you would be partner
    In my good fortune.
ROMELIO [to Jolenta]   I pray come hither:
    Have I any interest in you?
JOLENTA   You are my brother.°
ROMELIO I would have you then use me with that respect
    You may still keep me so, and to be swayed   35
    In this main business of life, which wants
    Greatest consideration, your marriage,
    By my direction. Here's a gentleman—
JOLENTA Sir, I have often told you,
    I am so little my own to dispose that way,   40
    That I can never be his.
ROMELIO   Come, too much light
    Makes you moon-eyed. Are you in love with title?°
    I will have a herald, whose continual practice
    Is all in pedigree, come a-wooing to you,
    Or an antiquary in old buskins.
ERCOLE   Sir, you have done me°   45
    The mainest wrong that e'er was offered°
    To a gentleman of my breeding.
ROMELIO   Why, sir?
ERCOLE   You have led me
    With a vain confidence that I should marry
    Your sister; have proclaimed it to my friends,

Employed the greatest lawyers of our state   50
To settle her a jointure, and the issue°
Is that I must become ridiculous
Both to my friends and enemies. I will leave you,
Till I call to you for a strict account
Of your unmanly dealing.

ROMELIO   Stay, my lord.   55
    [*Aside to Jolenta*] Do you long to have my throat cut?—Good
        my lord,
    Stay but a little, till I have removed
    This court-mist from her eyes, till I wake her°
    From this dull sleep, wherein she'll dream herself
    To a deformed beggar. [*To Jolenta*] You would marry   60
    The great lord Contarino—
            Enter Leonora

LEONORA   Contarino
    Were you talking of? He lost last night at dice
    Five thousand ducats; and when that was gone,
    Set at one throw a lordship that twice trebled
    The former loss.

ROMELIO   And that flew after.

LEONORA   And most carefully   65
    Carried the gentleman in his caroche
    To a lawyer's chamber, there most legally
    To put him in possession; was this wisdom?

ROMELIO Oh yes, their credit in the way of gaming
    Is the main thing they stand on; that must be paid,   70
    Though the brewer bawl for's money. And this lord
    Does she prefer i'th' way of marriage
    Before our choice here, noble Ercole.

LEONORA [*to Jolenta*] You'll be advised I hope. Know for your
        sakes
    I married, that I might have children;   75
    And for your sakes, if you'll be ruled by me,
    I will never marry again. Here's a gentleman
    Is noble, rich, well-featured, but 'bove all,
    He loves you entirely. His intents are aimed
    For an expedition 'gainst the Turk,   80
    Which makes the contract cannot be delayed.

JOLENTA Contract? You must do this without my knowledge.
    Give me some potion to make me mad,

And happily, not knowing what I speak,
I may then consent to't.

ROMELIO   Come, you are mad already,   85
And I shall never hear you speak good sense,
Till you name him for husband.

ERCOLE   Lady, I will do
A manly office for you; I will leave you
To the freedom of your own soul. May it move whither
Heaven and you please.

JOLENTA   Now you express yourself   90
Most nobly.

ROMELIO   Stay, sir, what do you mean to do?

LEONORA [*kneels*] Hear me: if thou dost marry Contarino,
All the misfortune that did ever dwell
In a parent's curse light on thee!

ERCOLE   O rise, lady,
Certainly heaven never intended kneeling   95
To this fearful purpose.

JOLENTA Your imprecation has undone me for ever.

ERCOLE Give me your hand.

JOLENTA   No, sir.

ROMELIO   Give't me then.
[*Takes her hand*] O, what rare workmanship have I seen this
To finish with your needle, what excellent music   100
Have these struck upon the viol! Now I'll teach
A piece of art.

JOLENTA   Rather a damnable cunning,
To have me go about to give't away,
Without consent of my soul.
        [*Jolenta starts to weep*]

ROMELIO   Kiss her, my lord.
If crying had been regarded, maidenheads   105
Had ne'er been lost; at least some appearance of crying,
As an April shower i'th' sunshine.
        [*Ercole embraces and kisses Jolenta*]

LEONORA   She is yours.

ROMELIO [*to Ercole*] Nay, continue your station, and deal you in
        dumb show;°
Kiss this doggedness out of her.

LEONORA   To be contracted
In tears is but fashionable.

ROMELIO   Yet suppose   110
  That they were hearty.
LEONORA   Virgins must seem unwilling.°
ROMELIO O what else? And you remember, we observe
  The like in greater ceremonies than these contracts;
  At the consecration of prelates, they use ever°
  Twice to say nay, and take it.
JOLENTA   O brother!   115
ROMELIO [*to Ercole*] Keep your possession, you have the door by
    th'ring;
  That's livery and seisin in England. But, my lord,°
  Kiss that tear from her lip, you'll find the rose
  The sweeter for the dew.
JOLENTA   Bitter as gall.
ROMELIO Ay, ay, all you women,   120
  Although you be of never so low stature,
  Have gall in you most abundant; it exceeds
  Your brains by two ounces. I was saying somewhat—
  O, do but observe i'th' city, and you'll find
  The thriftiest bargains that were ever made,   125
  What a deal of wrangling ere they could be brought
  To an upshot.
LEONORA Great persons do not ever come together—
ROMELIO With revelling faces, nor is it necessary
  They should; the strangeness and unwillingness   130
  Wears the greater state, and gives occasion that°
  The people may buzz and talk of 't, though the bells
  Be tongue-tied at the wedding.
LEONORA And truly I have heard say,
  To be a little strange to one another   135
  Will keep your longing fresh.
ROMELIO   Ay, and make you beget
  More children when you're married: some doctors
  Are of that opinion. You see, my lord, we are merry
  At the contract; your sport is to come hereafter.
ERCOLE [*to Jolenta*] I will leave you, excellent lady, and withal   140
  Leave a heart with you so entirely yours,
  That I protest, had I the least of hope
  To enjoy you, though I were to wait the time
  That scholars do in taking their degree°
  In the noble arts, 'twere nothing; howsoe'er,   145

He parts from you, that will depart from life,
To do you any service; and so, humbly,
I take my leave.
JOLENTA   Sir, I will pray for you.
          Exit Ercole
ROMELIO Why, that's well; 'twill make your prayer complete,
To pray for your husband.
JOLENTA   Husband?
LEONORA   This is   150
The happiest hour that I ever arrived at.
          [*Exit Leonora*]
ROMELIO Husband, ay, husband. Come, you peevish thing,
Smile me a thank for the pains I have ta'en.
JOLENTA I hate myself for being thus enforced;
You may soon judge then what I think of you   155
Which are the cause of it.
          Enter [Winifred, the] waiting-woman
ROMELIO You, lady of the laundry, come hither.
WINIFRED   Sir?°
          [*Romelio and Winifred talk apart*]
ROMELIO Look, as you love your life, you have an eye
Upon your mistress. I do henceforth bar her
All visitants. I do hear there are bawds abroad,   160
That bring cut-works, and mantoons, and convey letters
To such young gentlewomen, and there are others
That deal in corn-cutting, and fortune-telling.
Let none of these come at her, on your life,
Nor Deuce-ace, the wafer-woman, that prigs abroad   165
With musk melons, and melocotons
Nor the Scotchwoman with the cittern, do you mark;
Nor a dancer by any means, though he ride on's foot-cloth,°
Nor a hackney coachman, if he can speak French.°
WINIFRED Why, sir?
ROMELIO   By no means; no more words!   170
Nor the woman with the marrowbone puddings. I have heard
Strange juggling tricks have been conveyed to a woman
In a pudding. You are apprehensive?°
WINIFRED O good sir, I have travelled.
ROMELIO   When you had a bastard,
You travelled indeed. But my precious chaperoness,°   175
I trust thee the better for that; for I have heard

There is no warier keeper of a park,
To prevent stalkers, or your night-walkers,
Than such a man as in his youth has been
A most notorious deer-stealer.

WINIFRED   Very well, sir,   180
You may use me at your pleasure.

ROMELIO By no means, Winifred; that were the way
To make thee travel again. Come, be not angry,
I do but jest; thou knowest, wit and a woman
Are two very frail things; and so I leave you.   185
    [*Exit Romelio*]

WINIFRED [*to Jolenta*] I could weep with you; but 'tis no matter,
I can do that at any time: I have now
A greater mind to rail a little. Plague of these
Unsanctified matches; they make us loathe
The most natural desire our grandam Eve ever left us.   190
Force one to marry against their will! Why, 'tis
A more ungodly work than enclosing the commons.°

JOLENTA Prithee, peace.
This is indeed an argument so common,
I cannot think of matter new enough   195
To express it bad enough.

WINIFRED   Here's one I hope
Will put you out of 't.
    Enter Contarino°

CONTARINO   How now, sweet mistress?
You have made sorrow look lovely of late:
You have wept.

WINIFRED She has done nothing else these three days. Had you stood   200
behind the arras, to have heard her shed so much salt water as I
have done, you would have thought she had been turned fountain.

CONTARINO I would fain know the cause can be worthy this
Thy sorrow.

JOLENTA [*to Winifred*] Reach me the caskanet. I am studying, sir,°   205
To take an inventory of all that's mine.

CONTARINO What to do with it, lady?

JOLENTA   To make you a deed of gift.

CONTARINO That's done already; you are all mine.

WINIFRED Yes, but the devil would fain put in for's share, in likeness
of a separation.   210

JOLENTA O sir, I am bewitched.

217

CONTARINO   Ha?
JOLENTA   Most certain: I am forespoken°
   To be married to another; can you ever think
   That I shall ever thrive in't? Am I not then bewitched?
   All comfort I can teach myself is this:
   There is a time left for me to die nobly,   215
   When I cannot live so!
CONTARINO   Give me, in a word, to whom,
   Or by whose means are you thus torn from me?
JOLENTA By Lord Ercole, my mother, and my brother.
CONTARINO I'll make his bravery fitter for a grave
   Than for a wedding.
JOLENTA   So you will beget   220
   A far more dangerous and strange disease
   Out of the cure. You must love him again
   For my sake, for the noble Ercole
   Had such a true compassion of my sorrow.
   Hark in your ear, I'll show you his right worthy   225
   Demeanour to me.
     [She whispers to him, and he turns and embraces her]
WINIFRED *[aside]*   O you pretty ones!
   I have seen this lord many a time and oft
   Set her in's lap, and talk to her of love
   So feelingly, I do protest it has made me
   Run out of myself to think on't. O sweet-breathed monkey!°   230
   How they grow together! Well, 'tis my opinion,
   He was no woman's friend that did invent
   A punishment for kissing.°
CONTARINO If he bear himself so nobly,
   The manliest office I can do for him   235
   Is to afford him my pity, since he's like
   To fail of so dear a purchase. For your mother,
   Your goodness quits her ill. For your brother,
   He that vows friendship to a man, and proves
   A traitor, deserves rather to be hanged,   240
   Than he that counterfeits money; yet, for your sake,
   I must sign his pardon too. Why do you tremble?
   Be safe, you are now free from him.
JOLENTA   O but, sir,
   The intermission from a fit of an ague
   Is grievous; for indeed it doth prepare us.   245

To entertain torment next morning.

CONTARINO Why, he's gone to sea.

JOLENTA   But he may return too soon.

CONTARINO To avoid which, we will instantly be married.

WINIFRED To avoid which, get you instantly to bed together;
   Do, and I think no civil lawyer for his fee   250
   Can give you better counsel.

JOLENTA Fie upon thee, prithee leave us.
       [*Exit Winifred*]

CONTARINO Be of comfort, sweet mistress.

JOLENTA On one condition: we may have no quarrel°
   About this.

CONTARINO Upon my life, none.

JOLENTA   None,   255
   Upon your honour?

CONTARINO   With whom? With Ercole?
   You have delivered him guiltless. With your brother?
   He's part of yourself. With your complimental mother?
   I use not fight with women. Tomorrow we'll°
   Be married. Let those that would oppose this union   260
   Grow ne'er so subtle, and entangle themselves
   In their own work like spiders, while we two
   Haste to our noble wishes, and presume
   The hindrance of it will breed more delight,
   As black copartiments shows gold more bright.   265
       Exeunt

[2.1]

Enter Crispiano [disguised as a merchant], Sanitonella

CRISPIANO Am I well habited?

SANITONELLA Exceeding well; any man would take you for a
merchant. But pray, sir, resolve me, what should be the reason,
that you, being one of the most eminent civil lawyers in Spain, and
but newly arrived from the East Indies, should take this habit of a   5
merchant upon you?

CRISPIANO Why, my son lives here in Naples, and in's riot
Doth far exceed the exhibition I allowed him.

SANITONELLA So then; and in this disguise you mean to trace
him?

CRISPIANO Partly for that, but there is other business   10
Of greater consequence.°

SANITONELLA Faith, for his expense, 'tis nothing to your estate.
What, to Don Crispiano, the famous corregidor° of Seville,° who
by his mere practice of the law, in less time than half a jubilee,°
hath gotten thirty thousand ducats a year?   15

CRISPIANO Well, I will give him line, let him
Run on in's course of spending.

SANITONELLA   Freely?

CRISPIANO   Freely;
For I protest, if that I could conceive,
My son would take more pleasure or content,
By any course of riot, in the expense   20
Than I took joy, nay, soul's felicity,
In the getting of it, should all the wealth I have
Waste to as small an atomy as flies
I'th' sun, I do protest on that condition
It should not move me.   25

SANITONELLA How's this? Cannot he take more pleasure in spend-
ing it riotously than you have done by scraping it together? O ten
thousand times more, and I make no question, five hundred young
gallants will be of my opinion.
Why, all the time of your collectionship°   30
Has been a perpetual calendar. Begin first°
With your melancholy study of the law°
Before you come to finger the ruddocks; after that

The tiring importunity of clients,
To rise so early, and sit up so late,   35
You made yourself half ready in a dream,°
And never prayed but in your sleep. Can I think
That you have half your lungs left with crying out
For judgements, and days of trial. Remember, sir,
How often have I borne you on my shoulder,   40
Among a shoal or swarm of reeking night-caps,
When that your worship has bepissed yourself,
Either with vehemency of argument,
Or being out from the matter. I am merry.°

CRISPIANO Be so.   45

SANITONELLA You could not eat like a gentleman, at leisure,
But swallowed it like flap-dragons, as if you had lived°
With chewing the cud after.

CRISPIANO No pleasure in the world was comparable to't.

SANITONELLA Possible?

CRISPIANO   He shall never taste the like,   50
Unless he study law.

SANITONELLA   What, not in wenching, sir?
'Tis a court game, believe it, as familiar
As gleek, or any other.

CRISPIANO Wenching? O fie, the disease follows it.°
Beside, can the fingering taffetas, or lawns,   55
Or a painted hand, or a breast, be like the pleasure
In taking clients' fees, and piling them
In several goodly rows before my desk?
And according to the bigness of each heap,
Which I took by a leer (for lawyers do not tell them),°   60
I vailed my cap, and withal gave great hope°
The cause should go on their sides.

SANITONELLA   What think you then
Of a good cry of hounds? It has been known°
Dogs have hunted lordships to a fault.

CRISPIANO   Cry of curs?°
The noise of clients at my chamber door   65
Was sweeter music far, in my conceit,
Than all the hunting in Europe.

SANITONELLA   Pray stay, sir;
Say he should spend it in good housekeeping.

CRISPIANO Ay, marry, sir, to have him keep a good house,

And not sell't away, I'd find no fault with that.   70
But his kitchen I'd have no bigger than a saw-pit;
For the smallness of a kitchen, without question,
Makes many noblemen in France and Spain
Build the rest of the house the bigger.

SANITONELLA   Yes, mock-beggars.°

CRISPIANO Some sevenscore chimneys, but half of them   75
Have no tunnels.

SANITONELLA   A pox upon them kickshaws,°
That beget such monsters without fundaments.

CRISPIANO Come, come, leave citing other vanities;
For neither wine, nor lust, nor riotous feasts,
Rich clothes, nor all the pleasure that the devil   80
Has ever practised with to raise a man
To a devil's likeness, e'er brought man that pleasure
I took in getting my wealth: so I conclude.
If he can out-vie me, let it fly to th'devil.
Yon's my son: what company keeps he?   85

    Enter Romelio [*and*] *Julio* [*in conversation;*] *Ariosto* [*and*]
    Baptista°

SANITONELLA The gentleman he talks with is Romelio
The merchant.

CRISPIANO   I never saw him till now.
A has a brave sprightly look; I knew his father,
And sojourned in his house two years together,
Before this young man's birth. I have news to tell him   90
Of certain losses happened him at sea,
That will not please him.

SANITONELLA   What's that dapper fellow
In the long stocking? I do think 'twas he
Came to your lodging this morning.

CRISPIANO   'Tis the same.
There he stands, but a little piece of flesh;   95
But he is the very miracle of a lawyer,
One that persuades men to peace, and compounds quarrels
Among his neighbours, without going to law.

SANITONELLA And is he a lawyer?

CRISPIANO   Yes, and will give counsel
In honest causes gratis; never in his life   100
Took fee, but he came and spake for't; is a man

Of extreme practice, and yet all his longing°
Is to become a judge.

SANITONELLA Indeed that's a rare longing with men of his profession;°

I think he'll prove the miracle of a lawyer indeed.   105

ROMELIO [*introducing Crispiano*] Here's the man brought word your
father died i'th' Indies.

    [*Romelio turns to talk to Ariosto*]

JULIO He died in perfect memory, I hope,°
And made me his heir.

CRISPIANO   Yes, sir.

JULIO He's gone the right way, then, without question. Friend, in   110
time of mourning, we must not use any action that is but accessory
to the making men merry; I do therefore give you nothing for your
good tidings.

CRISPIANO Nor do I look for it, sir.

JULIO Honest fellow, give me thy hand. I do not think but thou hast   115
carried New Year's gifts to th'court in thy days, and learned'st
there to be so free of thy pains-taking.

ROMELIO Here's an old gentleman says he was chamber-fellow to
your father, when they studied the law together at Barcelona.

JULIO Do you know him?   120

ROMELIO Not I, he's newly come to Naples.

JULIO And what's his business?

ROMELIO A says he's come to read you good counsel.

CRISPIANO (*aside* [*to Ariosto*]) To him, rate him soundly.

    [*Crispiano and Sanitonella walk apart, watching*]

JULIO And what's your counsel?   125

ARIOSTO Why, I would have you leave your whoring.

JULIO He comes hotly upon me at first: 'whoring'?

ARIOSTO O young quat, incontinence is plagued
In all the creatures of the world.

JULIO When did you ever hear that a cocksparrow   130
Had the French pox?

ARIOSTO When did you ever know any of them fat, but in the nest? Ask
all your cantharide-mongers° that question; remember yourself, sir.

JULIO A very fine naturalist! A physician, I take you, by your round
slop; for 'tis just of the bigness, and no more, of the case for a   135
urinal;° 'tis concluded, you are a physician. [*Ariosto removes his
hat*] What do you mean, sir? You'll take cold.

ARIOSTO 'Tis concluded you are a fool, a precious one; you are a
mere stick of sugar candy: a man may look quite through you.
  [*Julio removes his hat*]

JULIO You are a very bold gamester.   140

ARIOSTO I can play at chess, and know how to handle a rook.°

JULIO Pray preserve your velvet from the dust.

ARIOSTO Keep your hat upon the block, sir, 'twill continue fashion
the longer.°

JULIO I was never so abused with the hat in the hand   145
In my life.
  [*Julio replaces his hat*]

ARIOSTO I will put on.
  [*He replaces his hat*]
                    Why, look you,°
Those lands that were the client's are now become
The lawyer's; and those tenements that were
The country gentleman's are now grown   150
To be his tailor's.

JULIO Tailor's?

ARIOSTO Yes, tailors in France, they grow to great abominable
purchase, and become great officers. How many ducats think you
he has spent within a twelvemonth, besides his father's allowance?   155

JULIO Besides my father's allowance? Why, gentleman, do you think
an auditor begat me? Would you have me make even at year's
end?

ROMELIO A hundred ducats a month in breaking Venice glasses.°

ARIOSTO He learnt that of an English drunkard, and a knight too, as   160
I take it. This comes of your numerous wardrobe.

ROMELIO Ay, and wearing cut-work, a pound a purl.

ARIOSTO Your dainty embroidered stockings, with overblown
roses,° to hide your gouty ankles.

ROMELIO And wearing more taffeta for a garter than would serve the   165
galley dung-boat for streamers.°

ARIOSTO Your switching up at the horse-race, with the *illustrissimi*.

ROMELIO And studying a puzzling arithmetic° at the cock-pit.

ARIOSTO Shaking your elbow at the table-board.

ROMELIO And resorting to your whore in hired velvet, with a   170
spangled copper fringe at her netherlands.°

ARIOSTO Whereas if you had stayed at Padua,° and fed upon
cow-trotters, and fresh beef to supper—

JULIO How I am baited!

ARIOSTO Nay, be not you so forward with him neither, for 'tis 175
   thought you'll prove a main part of his undoing.

JULIO I think this fellow is a witch.

ROMELIO Who, I, sir?

ARIOSTO You have certain rich city chuffs that, when they have no
   acres of their own, they will go and plough up fools, and turn them 180
   into excellent meadow; besides some enclosures for the first
   cherries in the spring, and apricots to pleasure a friend at court
   with. You have pothecaries deal in selling commodities° to young
   gallants, will put four or five coxcombs into a sieve, and so drum
   with them upon their counter, they'll searce them through like 185
   Guinea pepper;° they cannot endure to find a man like a pair of
   terriers;° they would° undo him in a trice.°

ROMELIO Maybe there are such.

ARIOSTO O terrible exactors, fellows with six hands, and three
   heads.° 190

JULIO Ay, those are hell-hounds.

ARIOSTO Take heed of them, they'll rend thee like tenterhooks.°
   Hark in your ear: there is intelligence upon° you; the report goes,
   there has been gold conveyed beyond the sea° in hollow anchors.
   Farewell, you shall know me better; I will do thee more good than 195
   thou art aware of.
      Exit Ariosto

JULIO He's a mad fellow.

SANITONELLA He would have made an excellent barber, he does so
   curry it with his tongue.°
      Exit [Sanitonella]

CRISPIANO Sir, I was directed to you. 200

ROMELIO From whence?

CRISPIANO From the East Indies.

ROMELIO You are very welcome.

CRISPIANO Please you walk apart,
   I shall acquaint you with particulars 205
   Touching your trading i'th' East Indies.

ROMELIO Willingly; pray walk, sir.
      Exeunt Crispiano, Romelio. Enter Ercole

ERCOLE [*to Julio and Baptista*] O my right worthy friends, you
   have stayed me long.°
   One health, and then aboard, for all the galleys
   Are come about.
      Enter Contarino

CONTARINO   Signor Ercole,°   210
  The wind has stood my friend, sir, to prevent
  Your putting to sea.
ERCOLE   Pray why, sir?
CONTARINO   Only love, sir,
  That I might take my leave, sir, and withal,
  Entreat from you a private recommends
  To a friend in Malta; 'twould be delivered   215
  To your bosom, for I had no time to write.
ERCOLE Pray leave us, gentlemen.
        Exeunt [Julio and Baptista]
                    Wilt please you sit?
    They sit down
CONTARINO Sir, my love to you has proclaimed you one,
  Whose word was still led by a noble thought,
  And that thought followed by as fair a deed.   220
  Deceive not that opinion; we were students
  At Padua together, and have long
  To th'world's eye shown like friends.
  Was it hearty on your part to me?
ERCOLE   Unfeigned.
CONTARINO   You are false
  To the good thought I held of you, and now   225
  Join the worst part of man to you, your malice,
  To uphold that falsehood; sacred innocence
  Is fled your bosom. Signor, I must tell you,
  To draw the picture of unkindness truly
  Is to express two that have dearly loved,   230
  And fall'n at variance. 'Tis a wonder to me,
  Knowing my interest in the fair Jolenta,°
  That you should love her.
ERCOLE Compare her beauty and my youth together,
  And you will find the fair effects of love   235
  No miracle at all.
CONTARINO   Yes, it will prove
  Prodigious to you. I must stay your voyage.
ERCOLE Your warrant must be mighty.
CONTARINO   It's a seal
  From heaven to do it, since you would ravish from me
  What's there entitled mine. And yet I vow,   240
  By the essential front of spotless virtue,

I have compassion of both our youths;
To approve which, I have not ta'en the way,
Like an Italian, to cut your throat°
By practice, that had given you now for dead,   245
And never frowned upon you.
ERCOLE   You deal fair, sir.
CONTARINO Quit me of one doubt, pray, sir.
ERCOLE   Move it.
CONTARINO   'Tis this:
  Whether her brother were a main instrument
  In her design for marriage.
ERCOLE   If I tell truth,
  You will not credit me.
CONTARINO   Why?
ERCOLE   I will tell you truth,   250
  Yet show some reason you have not to believe me.
  Her brother had no hand in't: is't not hard
  For you to credit this? For you may think
  I count it baseness to engage another
  Into my quarrel, and for that take leave°   255
  To dissemble the truth. Sir, if you will fight
  With any but myself, fight with her mother:
  She was the motive.
CONTARINO I have no enemy in the world then, but yourself;
  You must fight with me.
ERCOLE   I will, sir.
CONTARINO   And instantly.   260
ERCOLE I will haste before you; point whither.
CONTARINO Why, you speak nobly; and for this fair dealing,
  Were the rich jewel which we vary for°
  A thing to be divided, by my life,
  I would be well content to give you half;   265
  But since 'tis vain to think we can be friends,
  'Tis needful one of us be ta'en away
  From being the other's enemy.
ERCOLE   Yet methinks.
  This looks not like a quarrel.
CONTARINO   Not a quarrel?
ERCOLE You have not apparelled your fury well;   270
  It goes too plain, like a scholar.
CONTARINO   It is an ornament

Makes it more terrible; and you shall find it
A weighty injury, and attended on
By discreet valour, because I do not strike you,
Or give you the lie; such foul preparatives   275
Would show like the stale injury of wine.°
I reserve my rage to sit on my sword's point,
Which a great quantity of your best blood
Cannot satisfy.

ERCOLE   You promise well to yourself.
Shall's have no seconds?

CONTARINO   None, for fear of prevention.   280

ERCOLE The length of our weapons?

CONTARINO   We'll fit them by the way.°
So, whether our time calls us to live or die,
Let us do both like noble gentlemen,
And true Italians.

ERCOLE   For that let me embrace you.
        [*They embrace*]

CONTARINO Methinks, being an Italian, I trust you   285
To come somewhat too near me;
But your jealousy gave that embrace to try
If I were armèd, did it not?

ERCOLE   No, believe me,
I take your heart to be sufficient proof,
Without a privy coat; and for my part,°   290
A taffeta is all the shirt of mail
I am armed with.

CONTARINO   You deal equally.
        Exeunt [*Contarino and Ercole*]. *Enter Julio and Servant*

JULIO Where are these gallants, the brave Ercole,
And noble Contarino?

SERVANT   They are newly gone, sir,
And bade me tell you that they will return   295
Within this half hour.
        Enter Romelio

JULIO   Met you the Lord Ercole?

ROMELIO No, but I met the devil in villainous tidings.

JULIO Why, what's the matter?

ROMELIO   O, I am poured out,
Like water; the greatest rivers i'th' world
Are lost in the sea, and so am I. Pray leave me.   300

Where's Lord Ercole?

JULIO   You were scarce gone hence,
But in came Contarino.

ROMELIO   Contarino?

JULIO And entreated some private conference with Ercole;
And on the sudden they have given's the slip.

ROMELIO One mischief never comes alone: they are   305
Gone to fight.

JULIO   To fight?

ROMELIO   An you be gentlemen,
Do not talk, but make haste after them.

JULIO Let's take several ways then,
And if't be possible, for women's sakes,
For they are proper men, use our endeavours   310
That the prick do not spoil them.
         Exeunt

[2.2]

         Enter Ercole, Contarino

CONTARINO You'll not forgo your interest in my mistress?

ERCOLE My sword shall answer that. Come, are you ready?

CONTARINO Before you fight, sir, think upon your cause,
It is a wondrous foul one, and I wish
That all your exercise these four days past   5
Had been employed in a most fervent prayer,
And the foul sin for which you are to fight
Chiefly remembered in't.

ERCOLE   I'd as soon take
Your counsel in divinity at this present,
As I would take a kind direction from you   10
For the managing my weapon; and indeed,
Both would show much alike.
Come, are you ready?

CONTARINO   Bethink yourself
How fair the object is that we contend for.

ERCOLE O, I cannot forget it.
         They fight [and Contarino wounds Ercole]

CONTARINO   You are hurt.   15

ERCOLE Did you come hither only to tell me so,
 Or to do it? I mean well, but 'twill not thrive.°
CONTARINO Your cause, your cause, sir:
 Will you yet be a man of conscience, and make
 Restitution for your rage upon your death-bed?   20
ERCOLE Never, till the grave gather one of us.
  [They] fight. [Contarino wounds Ercole again]
CONTARINO That was fair, and home, I think.°
ERCOLE You prate as if you were in a fence-school.
CONTARINO Spare your youth, have compassion on yourself.
ERCOLE When I am all in pieces! I am now unfit   25
 For any lady's bed; take the rest with you.
   Contarino, wounded, falls upon Ercole
CONTARINO I am lost in too much daring: yield your sword.
ERCOLE To the pangs of death I shall, not to thee.
CONTARINO You are now at my repairing, or confusion:°
 Beg your life.
ERCOLE   O most foolishly demanded,   30
 To bid me beg that which thou canst not give.
  [Ercole loses consciousness]. Enter Romelio, Prospero,
  Baptista, Ariosto, Julio
PROSPERO See, both of them are lost; we come too late.
ROMELIO Take up the body, and convey it
 To Saint Sebastian's monastery.°
  [Contarino takes Ercole's sword]
CONTARINO I will not part with his sword, I have won't.
JULIO   You shall not.° 35
 Take him up gently; so, and bow his body,
 For fear of bleeding inward.
 Well, these are perfect lovers.
PROSPERO   Why, I pray?
JULIO It has been ever my opinion
 That there are none love perfectly indeed,   40
 But those that hang or drown themselves for love.
 Now these have chose a death next to beheading:
 They have cut one another's throats, brave valiant lads.
PROSPERO Come, you do ill to set the name of valour
 Upon a violent and mad despair.   45
 Hence may all learn, that count such actions well,
 The roots of fury shoot themselves to hell.
  Exeunt

[2.3]

Enter Romelio, Ariosto

ARIOSTO Your losses, I confess, are infinite,
  Yet, sir, you must have patience.

ROMELIO   Sir, my losses
  I know, but you I do not.

ARIOSTO   'Tis most true.
  I am but a stranger to you, but am wished,
  By some of your best friends, to visit you,   5
  And out of my experience in the world,
  To instruct you patience.

ROMELIO   Of what profession are you?

ARIOSTO Sir, I am a lawyer.

ROMELIO   Of all men living,
  You lawyers I account the only men
  To confirm patience in us; your delays   10
  Would make three parts of this little Christian world
  Run out of their wits else. Now I remember,
  You read lectures to Julio. Are you such a leech
  For patience?

ARIOSTO   Yes, sir, I have had some crosses.

ROMELIO You are married then, I am certain.

ARIOSTO   That I am, sir.   15

ROMELIO And have you studied patience?

ARIOSTO   You shall find I have.

ROMELIO Did you ever see your wife make you cuckold?

ARIOSTO Make me cuckold?

ROMELIO I ask it seriously; an you have not seen that,
  Your patience has not ta'en the right degree   20
  Of wearing scarlet; I should rather take you°
  For a Bachelor in the Art, than for a Doctor.

ARIOSTO You are merry.

ROMELIO   No, sir, with leave of your patience,
  I am horrible angry.

ARIOSTO   What should move you
  Put forth that harsh interrogatory, if these eyes   25
  Ever saw my wife do the thing you wot of?

ROMELIO Why, I'll tell you:
  Most radically to try your patience,

And the mere question shows you but a dunce in't.
It has made you angry; there's another lawyer's beard   30
In your forehead, you do bristle.

ARIOSTO You are very conceited.
    But come, this is not the right way to cure you.
    I must talk to you like a divine.

ROMELIO   I have heard
    Some talk of it very much, and many times   35
    To their auditors' impatience; but I pray,
    What practice do they make of't in their lives?
    They are too full of choler with living honest,
    And some of them not only impatient
    Of their own slightest injuries, but stark mad   40
    At one another's preferment. Now to you, sir:
    I have lost three goodly carracks.

ARIOSTO   So I hear.

ROMELIO The very spice in them,
    Had they been shipwrecked here upon our coast,
    Would have made all our sea a drench.   45

ARIOSTO All the sick horses in Italy
    Would have been glad of your loss then.

ROMELIO You are conceited too.

ARIOSTO   Come, come, come,
    You gave those ships most strange, most dreadful, and
    Unfortunate names: I never looked they'd prosper.°   50

ROMELIO Is there any ill omen in giving names to ships?

ARIOSTO Did you not call one *The Storm's Defiance*;
    Another, *The Scourge of the Sea*; and the third, *The Great
    Leviathan*?

ROMELIO   Very right, sir.

ARIOSTO   Very devilish names
    All three of them; and surely I think they were cursed   55
    In their very cradles; I do mean, when they
    Were upon their stocks.

ROMELIO   Come, you are superstitious.°
    I'll give you my opinion, and 'tis serious:
    I am persuaded there came not cuckolds enough
    To the first launching of them, and 'twas that   60
    Made them thrive the worse for't. O your cuckold's handsel°
    Is prayed for i'th' city.

ARIOSTO   I will hear no more.

Give me thy hand. My intent of coming hither.
Was to persuade you to patience; as I live,
If ever I do visit you again,   65
It shall be to entreat you to be angry; sure I will,
I'll be as good as my word, believe it.
    Exit [Ariosto]. Enter Leonora
ROMELIO So, sir.
    [*Sound of a bell ringing repeatedly*]
           How now?
Are the screech-owls abroad already?
LEONORA What a dismal noise yon bell makes;   70
Sure some great person's dead.
ROMELIO   No such matter;
It is the common bellman goes about,°
To publish the sale of goods.
LEONORA   Why do they ring
Before my gate thus? [*To a servant off-stage*] Let them into
    th'court;
I cannot understand what they say.   75
    Enter two Bellmen and a Capuchin
CAPUCHIN For pity's sake, you that have tears to shed,
Sigh a soft requiem, and let fall a bead,°
For two unfortunate nobles, whose sad fate
Leaves them both dead and excommunicate.
No churchman's prayer to comfort their last groans,   80
No sacred seed of earth to hide their bones;
But as their fury wrought them out of breath,
The canon speaks them guilty of their own death.°
LEONORA What noblemen, I pray, sir?
CAPUCHIN   The Lord Ercole,
And the noble Contarino, both of them   85
Slain in single combat.
LEONORA   O, I am lost for ever!
ROMELIO Denied Christian burial! I pray what does that,
Or the dead lazy march in the funeral,
Or the flattery in the epitaphs, which shows
More sluttish far than all the spiders' webs   90
Shall ever grow upon it—what do these
Add to our well-being after death?
CAPUCHIN Not a scruple.
ROMELIO   Very well then.

I have a certain meditation,
If I can think of't, somewhat to this purpose;   95
I'll say it to you, while my mother there
Numbers her beads.
You that dwell near these graves and vaults,
Which oft do hide physicians' faults,
Note what a small room does suffice   100
To express men's good; their vanities
Would fill more volume in small hand
Than all the evidence of church-land.
Funerals hide men in civil wearing,°
And are to the drapers a good hearing,°   105
Make the heralds laugh in their black raiment,
And all die worthies die worth payment°
To the altar offerings, though their fame,
And all the charity of their name,
'Tween heaven and this yield no more light   110
Than rotten trees, which shine i'th' night.°
O look the last act be the best i'th' play,
And then rest, gentle bones; yet pray,
That when by the precise you are viewed,°
A supersedeas be not sued,°   115
To remove you to a place more airy,
That in your stead they may keep chary
Stockfish, or seacoal, for the abuses
Of sacrilege have turned graves to viler uses.
How then can any monument say,   120
'Here rest these bones till the last day',
When time, swift both of foot and feather,
May bear them the sexton kens not whither?
What care I then, though my last sleep
Be in the desert or in the deep,   125
No lamp nor taper, day and night,
To give my charnel chargeable light?
I have there like quantity of ground,
And at the last day I shall be found.
Now I pray leave me.
CAPUCHIN   I am sorry for your losses.   130
ROMELIO Um, sir, the more spacious that the tennis court is,
   The more large is the hazard.
   I dare the spiteful Fortune do her worst,

I can now fear nothing.

CAPUCHIN   O sir, yet consider,
He that is without fear is without hope,   135
And sins from presumption. Better thoughts attend you.
    Exit Capuchin [with Bellmen]
ROMELIO Poor Jolenta! Should she hear of this,
She would not after the report keep fresh
So long as flowers in graves.
    Enter Prospero

                            How now, Prospero?
PROSPERO Contarino has sent you here his will,   140
Wherein a has made your sister his sole heir.
ROMELIO Is he not dead?
PROSPERO   He's yet living.
ROMELIO   Living? The worse luck.
LEONORA The worse? I do protest it is the best
That ever came to disturb my prayers.
ROMELIO   How?
LEONORA Yet I would have him live   145
To satisfy public justice for the death
Of Ercole. O go visit him, for heaven's sake.
I have within my closet a choice relic,
Preservative 'gainst swooning, and some earth
Brought from the Holy Land, right sovereign   150
To staunch blood. Has he skilful surgeons, think you?
PROSPERO The best in Naples!
ROMELIO   How oft has he been dressed?
PROSPERO But once.
LEONORA   I have some skill this way;
The second or third dressing will show clearly
Whether there be hope of life. I pray be near him,   155
If there be any soul can bring me word,
That there is hope of life.
ROMELIO Do you prize his life so?
LEONORA   That he may live, I mean,
To come to his trial, to satisfy the law.
ROMELIO O, is't nothing else?
LEONORA   I shall be the happiest woman.   160
    Exeunt Leonora, Prospero
ROMELIO Here is cruelty apparelled in kindness.
I am full of thoughts, strange ones, but they're no good ones.

I must visit Contarino; upon that
Depends an engine shall weigh up my losses,°
Were they sunk as low as hell. Yet let me think   165
How I am impaired in an hour, and the cause of 't
Lost in security. O how this wicked world bewitches,
Especially made insolent with riches!
So sails with fore-winds stretched do soonest break,°
And pyramids a'th' top are still most weak.   170

    Exit

[2.4]

    Enter Capuchin, Ercole led between two [Monks]

CAPUCHIN Look up, sir,
  You are preservèd beyond natural reason:
  You were brought dead out o'th' field, the surgeons
  Ready to have embalmed you.
ERCOLE I do look on my action with a thought of terror;   5
  To do ill and dwell in 't is unmanly.°
CAPUCHIN You are divinely informed, sir.
ERCOLE I fought for one, in whom I have no more right.
  Than false executors here in orphans' goods
  They cozen them of; yet though my cause were naught,   10
  I rather chose the hazard of my soul
  Than forgo the compliment of a choleric man.°
  I pray continue the report of my death, and give out,
  'Cause the church denied me Christian burial,
  The vice-admiral of my galleys took my body,   15
  With purpose to commit it to the earth,
  Either in Sicil or Malta.
CAPUCHIN   What aim you at
  By this rumour of your death?
ERCOLE   There is hope of life
  In Contarino; and he has my prayers
  That he may live to enjoy what is his own,   20
  The fair Jolenta; where, should it be thought°
  That I were breathing, happily her friends
  Would oppose it still.
CAPUCHIN   But if you be supposed dead,

The law will strictly prosecute his life
For your murder.
ERCOLE   That's prevented thus: 25
There does belong a noble privilege
To all his family, ever since his father
Bore from the worthy Emperor Charles the Fifth
An answer to the French king's challenge, at such time
The two noble princes were engaged to fight,   30
Upon a frontier arm o'th' sea in a flat-bottomed boat,°
That if any of his family should chance
To kill a man i'th' field, in a noble cause,
He should have his pardon. Now, sir, for his cause,
The world may judge if it were not honest.   35
Pray help me in speech, 'tis very painful to me.
CAPUCHIN Sir, I shall.
ERCOLE The guilt of this lies in Romelio.
And as I hear, to second this good contract,°
He has got a nun with child.
CAPUCHIN   There are crimes   40
That either must make work for speedy repentance,
Or for the devil.
ERCOLE   I have much compassion on him,
For sin and shame are ever tied together
With Gordian knots, of such a strong thread spun,°
They cannot without violence be undone.   45
    Exeunt

3.1

Enter Ariosto, Crispiano

ARIOSTO Well, sir, now I must claim
  Your promise, to reveal to me the cause
  Why you live thus clouded.

CRISPIANO   Sir, the King of Spain
  Suspects that your Romelio here, the merchant,
  Has discovered some gold-mine to his own use   5
  In the West Indies, and for that employs me
  To discover in what part of Christendom
  He vents this treasure. Besides, he is informed°
  What mad tricks has been played of late by ladies.

ARIOSTO Most true, and I am glad the king has heard on't.   10
  Why, they use their lords as if they were their wards;
  And as your Dutchwomen in the Low Countries
  Take all and pay all, and do keep their husbands
  So silly all their lives of their own estates,°
  That when they are sick, and come to make their will,   15
  They know not precisely what to give away
  From their wives, because they know not what they are worth:
  So here, should I repeat what factions,
  What bat-fowling for offices
  (As you must conceive their game is all i'th' night)   20
  What calling in question one another's honesties,
  Withal what sway they bear i'th' viceroy's court,
  You'd wonder at it.
  'Twill do well shortly, can we keep them off
  From being of our council of war.

CRISPIANO   Well, I have vowed   25
  That I will never sit upon the bench more,°
  Unless it be to curb the insolencies
  Of these women.

ARIOSTO   Well, take it on my word then,
  Your place will not long be empty.
        Exeunt

[3.2]

Enter Romelio in the habit of a Jew°

ROMELIO Excellently well habited! Why, methinks
That I could play with mine own shadow now,
And be a rare Italianated Jew:
To have as many several change of faces
As I have seen carved upon one cherrystone;   5
To wind about a man like rotten ivy,
Eat into him like quicksilver, poison a friend
With pulling but a loose hair from's beard, or give a drench,
He should linger of't nine years, and ne'er complain
But in the spring and fall, and so the cause   10
Imputed to the disease natural. For slight villainies,°
As to coin money, corrupt ladies' honours,
Betray a town to th'Turk, or make a bonfire
O'th' Christian navy, I could settle to't,
As if I had eat a politician,   15
And digested him to nothing but pure blood.
But stay, I lose myself; this is the house.
Within there!

Enter two Surgeons

FIRST SURGEON Now, sir?

ROMELIO You are the men of art that, as I hear,
Have the Lord Contarino under cure.   20

SECOND SURGEON Yes, sir, we are his surgeons,
But he is past all cure.

ROMELIO   Why, is he dead?

FIRST SURGEON He is speechless, sir, and we do find his wound
So festered near the vitals, all our art
By warm drinks cannot clear th'impostumation;   25
And he's so weak, to make incision
By the orifice were present death to him.

ROMELIO He has made a will, I hear.

FIRST SURGEON   Yes, sir.

ROMELIO And deputed Jolenta his heir.

SECOND SURGEON   He has, we are witness to't.

ROMELIO Has not Romelio been with you yet,   30
To give you thanks and ample recompense
For the pains you have ta'en?

FIRST SURGEON   Not yet.
ROMELIO Listen to me, gentlemen, for I protest,
    If you will seriously mind your own good,
    I am come about a business shall convey   35
    Large legacies from Contarino's will
    To both of you.
SECOND SURGEON How, sir? Why, Romelio has the will,
    And in that he has given us nothing.
ROMELIO I pray attend me: I am a physician.°   40
SECOND SURGEON A physician? Where do you practise?
ROMELIO In Rome.
FIRST SURGEON   O then you have store of patients.
ROMELIO Store? Why, look you, I can kill my twenty a month
    And work but i'th' forenoons. You will give me leave
    To jest and be merry with you. But as I said,   45
    All my study has been physic; I am sent
    From a noble Roman that is near akin
    To Contarino, and that ought indeed,
    By the law of alliance, be his only heir,
    To practise his good and yours.
BOTH SURGEONS   How, I pray, sir?   50
ROMELIO I can by an extraction which I have,°
    Though he were speechless, his eyes set in's head,
    His pulses without motion, restore to him
    For half an hour's space the use of sense,
    And perhaps a little speech. Having done this,   55
    If we can work him, as no doubt we shall,
    To make another will, and therein assign
    This gentleman his heir, I will assure you,
    'Fore I depart this house, ten thousand ducats;
    And then we'll pull the pillow from his head,   60
    And let him e'en go whither the religion sends him
    That he died in.
FIRST SURGEON   Will you give's ten thousand ducats?
ROMELIO Upon my Jewism.
SECOND SURGEON   'Tis a bargain, sir, we are yours.
    [*They draw a traverse and discover*] Contarino in a bed
    Here is the subject you must work on.
ROMELIO Well said, you are honest men,   65
    And go to the business roundly. But, gentlemen,
    I must use my art singly.

FIRST SURGEON   O sir, you shall have all privacy.

ROMELIO And the doors locked to me.

SECOND SURGEON   At your best pleasure.
  [*aside*] Yet for all this, I will not trust this Jew.

FIRST SURGEON [*aside*] Faith, to say truth,   70
  I do not like him neither; he looks like a rogue.
  This is a fine toy: fetch a man to life°
  To make a new will! There's some trick in't.
  I'll be near you, Jew.
      Exeunt Surgeons

ROMELIO Excellent, as I would wish: these credulous fools   75
  Have given me freely what I would have bought
  With a great deal of money. Softly, here's breath yet.
  Now, Ercole, for part of the revenge
  Which I have vowed for thy untimely death,
  Besides this politic working of my own,   80
  That scorns precedent. Why, should this great man live,
  And not enjoy my sister—as I have vowed
  He never shall—O, he may alter's will
  Every new moon if he please; to prevent which,
  I must put in a strong caveat. Come forth then,   85
  My desperate stiletto, that may be worn
  In a woman's hair, and ne'er discovered,
  And either would be taken for a bodkin
  Or a curling-iron at most. Why, 'tis an engine
  That's only fit to put in execution   90
  Bermuda pigs; a most unmanly weapon,°
  That steals into a man's life he knows not how.
  O that great Caesar, he that passed the shock°
  Of so many armèd pikes, and poisoned darts,
  Swords, slings, and battleaxes, should at length,   95
  Sitting at ease on a cushion, come to die
  By such a shoemaker's awl as this, his soul let forth
  At a hole no bigger than the incision
  Made for a wheal. Ud's foot, I am horribly angry
  That he should die so scurvily; yet wherefore   100
  Do I condemn thee thereof so cruelly,°
  Yet shake him by the hand? 'Tis to express
  That I would never have such weapons used,
  But in a plot like this, that's treacherous.
  Yet this shall prove most merciful to thee,   105

For it shall preserve thee
From dying on a public scaffold, and withal
Bring thee an absolute cure, thus.
    Stabs him

                         So, 'tis done;°
And now for my escape.
    Enter Surgeons
FIRST SURGEON   You rogue mountebank,
  I will try whether your inwards can endure°   110
  To be washed in scalding lead.°
ROMELIO Hold, I turn Christian.°
SECOND SURGEON Nay, prithee be a Jew still;
  I would not have a Christian be guilty
  Of such a villainous act as this is.   115
ROMELIO I am Romelio the merchant.
FIRST SURGEON Romelio! You have proved yourself
  A cunning merchant indeed.
ROMELIO   You may read why
  I came hither.
SECOND SURGEON Yes, in a bloody Roman letter.°
ROMELIO I did hate this man; each minute of his breath   120
  Was torture to me.
FIRST SURGEON   Had you forborne this act,
  He had not lived this two hours.
ROMELIO   But he had died then,
  And my revenge unsatisfied. Here's gold.
  Never did wealthy man purchase the silence
  Of a terrible scolding wife at a dearer rate.   125
  Than I will pay for yours; here's your earnest
  In a bag of double ducats.
SECOND SURGEON Why, look you, sir, as I do weigh this business,
  This cannot be counted murder in you by no means.
  Why, 'tis no more than should I go and choke   130
  An Irishman, that were three quarters drowned,
  With pouring usquebaugh in's throat.
ROMELIO You will be secret?
FIRST SURGEON   As your soul.
ROMELIO The West Indies shall sooner want gold than you then.
SECOND SURGEON That protestation has the music of the mint
  in't.   135
ROMELIO [*aside*] How unfortunately was I surprised!

I have made myself a slave perpetually
To these two beggars.
    Exit [Romelio]

FIRST SURGEON Excellent! By this act he has made his estate ours.

SECOND SURGEON I'll presently grow a lazy surgeon, and ride on my   140
    foot-cloth.° I'll fetch from him every eight days a policy for a
    hundred double ducats; if he grumble, I'll peach.

FIRST SURGEON But let's take heed he do not poison us.

SECOND SURGEON O, I will never eat nor drink with him,
    Without unicorn's horn in a hollow tooth.°   145

CONTARINO O!

FIRST SURGEON Did he not groan?

SECOND SURGEON   Is the wind in that door still?°

FIRST SURGEON Ha! come hither, note a strange accident:
    His steel has lighted in the former wound,
    And made free passage for the congealed blood;
    Observe in what abundance it delivers   150
    The putrefaction.

SECOND SURGEON   Methinks he fetches
    His breath very lively.

FIRST SURGEON   The hand of heaven is in't,
    That his intent to kill him should become
    The very direct way to save his life.

SECOND SURGEON Why, this is like one I have heard of in Eng-
    land,   155
    Was cured o'th' gout, by being racked i'th' Tower.
    Well, if we can recover him, here's reward
    On both sides. Howsoever, we must be secret.

FIRST SURGEON We are tied to't.
    When we cure gentlemen of foul diseases,   160
    They give us so much for the cure, and twice as much
    That we do not blab on't. Come, let's to work roundly,
    Heat the lotion, and bring the searing.
    Exeunt

[3.3]

A table [is] set forth with two tapers, a death's head, a book.
[Enter] Jolenta in mourning, Romelio sits by her

ROMELIO Why do you grieve thus? Take a looking-glass,
And see if this sorrow become you; that pale face
Will make men think you used some art before,
Some odious painting. Contarino's dead.

JOLENTA O that he should die so soon.

ROMELIO   Why, I pray tell me,   5
Is not the shortest fever the best? And are not bad plays
The worse for their length?

JOLENTA   Add not to the ill you've done
An odious slander. He stuck i'th' eyes o'th' court
As the most choice jewel there.

ROMELIO   O, be not angry.
Indeed the court to well-composèd nature   10
Adds much to perfection; for it is, or should be,
As a bright crystal mirror to the world
To dress itself; but I must tell you, sister,
If th'excellency of the place could have wrought salvation,
The devil had ne'er fallen from heaven: he was proud—   15
        [*Jolenta rises indignantly, as if to go*]
Leave us, leave us?
Come, take your seat again. I have a plot,
If you will listen to it seriously,
That goes beyond example; it shall breed,
Out of the death of these two noblemen,   20
The advancement of our house.

JOLENTA   O take heed,
A grave is a rotten foundation.

ROMELIO   Nay, nay, hear me.
'Tis somewhat indirectly, I confess;
But there is much advancement in the world
That comes in indirectly. I pray mind me: 25
You are already made by absolute will°
Contarino's heir; now, if it can be proved
That you have issue by Lord Ercole,
I will make you inherit his land too.

JOLENTA   How's this?

Issue by him, he dead, and I a virgin!   30
ROMELIO I knew you would wonder how it could be done,
    But I have laid the case so radically,
    Not all the lawyers in Christendom
    Shall find any the least flaw in't. I have a mistress
    Of the Order of St Clare, a beauteous nun,°   35
    Who being cloistered ere she knew the heat
    Her blood would arrive to, had only time enough
    To repent, and idleness sufficient
    To fall in love with me; and to be short,
    I have so much disordered the holy Order,   40
    I have got this nun with child.
JOLENTA   Excellent work,
    Made for a dumb midwife!
ROMELIO   I am glad you grow thus pleasant.
    Now will I have you presently give out
    That you are full two months quickened with child
    By Ercole, which rumour can beget   45
    No scandal to you, since we will affirm
    The precontract was so exactly done,°
    By the same words used in the form of marriage,
    That with a little dispensation,
    A money matter, it shall be registered   50
    Absolute matrimony.
JOLENTA   So then, I conceive you:
    My conceivèd child must prove your bastard.
ROMELIO   Right;
    For at such time my mistress falls in labour,
    You must feign the like.
JOLENTA   'Tis a pretty feat, this,
    But I am not capable of it.
ROMELIO   Not capable?   55
JOLENTA No, for the thing you would have me counterfeit
    Is most essentially put in practice: nay 'tis done,°
    I am with child already.
ROMELIO   Ha, by whom?
JOLENTA By Contarino. Do not knit the brow;
    The precontract shall justify it, it shall.   60
    Nay, I will get some singular fine churchman,
    Or though he be a plural one, shall affirm.°
    He coupled us together.

ROMELIO   O misfortune!
  Your child must then be reputed Ercole's.
JOLENTA Your hopes are dashed then, since your votary's issue   65
  Must not inherit the land.
ROMELIO   No matter for that,
  So I preserve her fame. I am strangely puzzled.
  Why, suppose that she be brought abed before you,
  And we conceal her issue till the time
  Of your delivery, and then give out   70
  That you had two at a birth: ha, were't not excellent?
JOLENTA And what resemblance, think you, would they have
  To one another? Twins are still alike.
  But this is not your aim: you would have your child
  Inherit Ercole's land. O my sad soul,   75
  Have you not made me yet wretched enough,
  But after all this frosty age in youth,°
  Which you have witched upon me, you will seek
  To poison my fame?
ROMELIO   That's done already.
JOLENTA No, sir, I did but feign it,   80
  To a fatal purpose, as I thought.
ROMELIO   What purpose?
JOLENTA If you had loved or tendered my dear honour,
  You would have locked your poniard in my heart,
  When I named I was with child; but I must live
  To linger out, till the consumption   85
  Of my own sorrow kill me.
ROMELIO [aside]   This will not do.
  The devil has on the sudden furnished me
  With a rare charm, yet a most unnatural falsehood.
  No matter, so 'twill take.
  Stay, sister, I would utter to you a business,   90
  But I am very loath; a thing indeed,
  Nature would have compassionately concealed
  Till my mother's eyes be closed.
JOLENTA Pray what's that, sir?
ROMELIO   You did observe
  With what a dear regard our mother tendered°   95
  The Lord Contarino, yet how passionately
  She sought to cross the match. Why, this was merely
  To blind the eye o'th' world, for she did know

That you would marry him, an he was capable.°
My mother doted upon him, and it was plotted   100
Cunningly between them, after you were married,
Living all three together in one house,
A thing I cannot whisper without horror:
Why, the malice scarce of devils would suggest.
Incontinence 'tween them two.

JOLENTA   I remember since his hurt   105
She has been very passionately inquiring
After his health.

ROMELIO   Upon my soul, this jewel,
With a piece of the holy cross in't, this relic
Valued at many thousand crowns, she would have sent him,
Lying upon his death-bed.

JOLENTA   Professing, as you say,   110
Love to my mother, wherefore did he make
Me his heir?

ROMELIO His will was made afore he went to fight,
When he was first a suitor to you.

JOLENTA To fight: O, well remembered!   115
If he loved my mother, wherefore did he lose
His life in my quarrel?°

ROMELIO For the affront sake, a word you understand not:
Because Ercole was pretended rival to him,
To clear your suspicion. I was gulled in't too.   120
Should he not have fought upon't, he had undergone
The censure of a coward.°

JOLENTA How came you by this wretched knowledge?

ROMELIO His surgeon overheard it,
As he did sigh it out to his confessor,   125
Some half-hour 'fore he died.

JOLENTA I would have the surgeon hanged
For abusing confession, and for making me
So wretched by th'report. Can this be truth?

ROMELIO No, but direct falsehood°   130
As ever was banished the court. Did you ever hear
Of a mother that has kept her daughter's husband
For her own tooth? He fancied you in one kind,
For his lust,
And he loved our mother in another kind,   135
For her money—

The gallant's fashion right. But come, ne'er think on't;
Throw the fowl to the devil that hatched it, and let this°
Bury all ill that's in't; she is our mother.

JOLENTA I never did find anything i'th' world   140
Turn my blood so much as this; here's such a conflict
Between apparent presumption and unbelief
That I shall die in't.
O, if there be another world i'th' moon,
As some fantastics dream, I could wish all men,   145
The whole race of them, for their inconstancy,
Sent thither to people that. Why, I protest,°
I now affect the Lord Ercole's memory
Better than the other's.

ROMELIO But were Contarino living—

JOLENTA   I do call anything to witness   150
That the divine law prescribed us to strengthen
An oath: were he living and in health, I would never
Marry with him. Nay, since I have found the world
So false to me, I'll be as false to it:
I will mother this child for you.

ROMELIO   Ha?   155

JOLENTA Most certainly; it will beguile part of my sorrow.

ROMELIO O most assuredly; make you smile to think
How many times i'th' world lordships descend
To divers men that might, an truth were known,
Be heir, for anything belongs to th'flesh,°   160
As well to the Turk's richest eunuch.

JOLENTA   But do you not think
I shall have a horrible strong breath now?

ROMELIO   Why?

JOLENTA O, with keeping your counsel, 'tis so terrible foul.

ROMELIO Come, come, come,
You must leave these bitter flashes.   165

JOLENTA Must I dissemble dishonesty? You have divers
Counterfeit honesty; but I hope here's none
Will take exceptions. I now must practise
The art of a great-bellied woman, and go feign
Their qualms and swoonings.

ROMELIO   Eat unripe fruit and oatmeal,   170
To take away your colour.

JOLENTA   Dine in my bed

Some two hours after noon.
ROMELIO   And when you are up,
  Make to your petticoat a quilted preface°
  To advance your belly.
JOLENTA   I have a strange conceit now.°
  I have known some women, when they were with child,   175
  Have longed to beat their husbands; what if I,
  To keep decorum, exercise my longing
  Upon my tailor that way, and noddle him soundly?
  He'll make the larger bill for't.
ROMELIO I'll get one shall be as tractable to't as stockfish.°   180
JOLENTA O my fantastical sorrow! Cannot I now
  Be miserable enough, unless I wear
  A pied fool's coat? Nay, worse, for when our passions
  Such giddy and uncertain changes breed,
  We are never well, till we are mad indeed.   185
     Exit [Jolenta]
ROMELIO So; nothing in the world could have done this,
  But to beget in her a strong distaste
  Of the Lord Contarino. O jealousy,
  How violent, especially in women,
  How often has it raised the devil up   190
  In form of a law-case! My especial care
  Must be to nourish craftily this fiend
  'Tween the mother and the daughter, that the deceit
  Be not perceived. My next task, that my sister,
  After this supposèd childbirth, be persuaded   195
  To enter into religion: 'tis concluded
  She must never marry; so I am left guardian
  To her estate. And lastly, that my two surgeons
  Be waged to the East Indies; let them prate°
  When they are beyond the line: the calenture,°   200
  Or the scurvy, or the Indian pox, I hope,
  Will take order for their coming back.°
     Enter Leonora
  O here's my mother. I ha' strange news for you:
  My sister is with child.
LEONORA   I do look now
  For some great misfortunes to follow; for indeed mischiefs   205
  Are like the visits of Franciscan friars,
  They never come to prey upon us single.

In what estate left you Contarino?

ROMELIO   Strange that you
Can skip from the former sorrow to such a question!
I'll tell you: in the absence of his surgeon,   210
My charity did that for him in a trice,
They would have done at leisure and been paid for't.
I have killed him.

LEONORA   I am twenty years elder
Since you last opened your lips.

ROMELIO   Ha?

LEONORA You have given him the wound you speak of   215
Quite through your mother's heart.

ROMELIO I will heal it presently, mother, for this sorrow
Belongs to your error. You would have him live
Because you think he's father of the child;
But Jolenta vows by all the rights of truth.   220
'Tis Ercole's. It makes me smile to think
How cunningly my sister could be drawn
To the contract, and yet how familiarly°
To his bed. Doves never couple without
A kind of murmur.

LEONORA   O, I am very sick.   225

ROMELIO Your old disease: when you are grieved, you are troubled
With the mother.

LEONORA [aside]   I am rapt with the mother indeed°
That I ever bore such a son.

ROMELIO   Pray tend my sister;
I am infinitely full of business.

LEONORA   Stay, you will mourn
For Contarino.

ROMELIO   O by all means, 'tis fit: 230
My sister is his heir.
         Exit [Romelio]

LEONORA I will make you chief mourner, believe it.
Never was woe like mine. O that my care
And absolute study to preserve his life
Should be his absolute ruin. Is he gone then?   235
There is no plague i'th' world can be compared
To impossible desire, for they are plagued°
In the desire itself; never, O never
Shall I behold him living, in whose life

I lived far sweetlier than in mine own. 240
A precise curiosity has undone me: why did I not°
Make my love known directly? 'T had not been
Beyond example for a matron to affect
I'th' honourable way of marriage
So youthful a person. O I shall run mad 245
For, as we love our youngest children best,
So the last fruit of our affection,
Wherever we bestow it, is most strong,
Most violent, most unresistible,
Since 'tis indeed our latest harvest-home,° 250
Last merriment 'fore winter; and we widows,
As men report of our best picture-makers,
We love the piece we are in hand with better
Than all the excellent work we have done before.
And my son has deprived me of all this. Ha, my son! 255
I'll be a Fury to him. Like an Amazon lady,
I'd cut off this right pap that gave him suck,°
To shoot him dead. I'll no more tender him°
Than had a wolf stol'n to my teat i'th' night,
And robbed me of my milk; nay, such a creature 260
I should love better far. Ha, ha, what say you?
I do talk to somewhat, methinks; it may be
My evil genius. Do not the bells ring?
I have a strange noise in my head: O fly in pieces!°
Come, age, and wither me into the malice 265
Of those that have been happy: let me have
One property more than the devil of hell;
Let me envy the pleasure of youth heartily;
Let me in this life fear no kind of ill,
That have no good to hope for; let me die 270
In the distraction of that worthy princess
Who loathèd food, and sleep, and ceremony,
For thought of losing that brave gentleman
She would fain have saved, had not a false conveyance
Expressed him stubborn-hearted. Let me sink° 275
Where neither man, nor memory may ever find me.
     [*Leonora*] *falls down*. [*Enter Capuchin and Ercole*]
CAPUCHIN This is a private way which I command,
    As her confessor. I would not have you seen yet,
    Till I prepare her. [*Ercole retires*] Peace to you, lady.

LEONORA   Ha?

CAPUCHIN You are well employed, I hope; the best pillow i'th'
    world   280
  For this your contemplation is the earth,
  And the best object heaven.

LEONORA I am whispering to a dead friend.

CAPUCHIN   And I am come
  To bring you tidings of a friend was dead,
  Restored to life again.

LEONORA   Say, sir.   285

CAPUCHIN One whom I dare presume, next to your children,
  You tendered above life.

LEONORA   Heaven will not suffer me
  Utterly to be lost.

CAPUCHIN   For he should have been
  Your son-in-law; miraculously saved,
  When surgery gave him o'er.

LEONORA   O, may you live°   290
  To win many souls to heaven, worthy sir,
  That your crown may be the greater. Why, my son
  Made me believe he stole into his chamber,
  And ended that which Ercole began
  By a deadly stab in's heart.

ERCOLE [aside]   Alas, she mistakes,   295
  'Tis Contarino she wishes living; but I must fasten
  On her last words, for my own safety.

LEONORA   Where,
  O where shall I meet this comfort?

ERCOLE [coming forward] Here in the vowed comfort of your
    daughter.°

LEONORA O I am dead again. Instead of the man, you present me   300
  The grave swallowed him.

ERCOLE   Collect yourself, good lady.
  Would you behold brave Contarino living?
  There cannot be a nobler chronicle
  Of his good than myself. If you would view him dead,
  I will present him to you bleeding fresh   305
  In my penitency.

LEONORA   Sir, you do only live
  To redeem another ill you have committed:
  That my poor innocent daughter perish not

By your vile sin, whom you have got with child.

ERCOLE Here begin all my compassion. O poor soul. 310
    She is with child by Contarino; and he dead,
    By whom should she preserve her fame to th' world,
    But by myself that loved her 'bove the world?
    There never was a way more honourable
    To exercise my virtue than to father it, 315
    And preserve her credit, and to marry her.
    I'll suppose her Contarino's widow, bequeathed to me
    Upon his death; for sure she was his wife,
    But that the ceremony o'th' church was wanting.
    Report this to her, madam, and withal 320
    That never father did conceive more joy
    For the birth of an heir than I to understand
    She had such confidence in me. I will not now
    Press a visit upon her, till you have prepared her,
    For I do read in your distraction, 325
    Should I be brought o'th' sudden to her presence,
    Either the hasty fright, or else the shame
    May blast the fruit within her. I will leave you
    To commend as loyal faith and service to her
    As e'er heart harboured. By my hope of bliss, 330
    I never lived to do good act but this.

CAPUCHIN [*aside to Ercole*] Withal, an you be wise,
    Remember what the mother has revealed
    Of Romelio's treachery.
        Exeunt Ercole, Capuchin

LEONORA A most noble fellow! In his loyalty 335
    I read what worthy comforts I have lost
    In my dear Contarino, and all adds
    To my despair.—Within there!
        Enter Winifred
                Fetch the picture
    Hangs in my inner closet.
        Exit Winifred
                I remember
    I let a word slip of Romelio's practice 340
    At the surgeons'. No matter, I can salve it.
    I have deeper vengeance that's preparing for him.
    To let him live and kill him: that's revenge
    I meditate upon.

Enter Winifred [with] the picture
                    So, hang it up.
[*Aside*] I was enjoined by the party ought that picture,°   345
Forty years since, ever when I was vexed
To look upon that. What was his meaning in't
I know not, but methinks upon the sudden
It has furnished me with mischief, such a plot
As never mother dreamt of. Here begins   350
My part i'th' play: my son's estate is sunk
By loss at sea, and he has nothing left
But the land his father left him. 'Tis concluded,
The law shall undo him. [*To Winifred*] Come hither,
I have a weighty secret to impart,   355
But I would have thee first confirm to me
How I may trust that thou canst keep my counsel
Beyond death.
WINIFRED   Why, mistress, 'tis your only way
To enjoin me first that I reveal to you
The worst act I e'er did in all my life;   360
So one secret shall bind another.
LEONORA   Thou instruct'st me
Most ingeniously; for indeed it is not fit,
Where any act is plotted that is naught,
Any of counsel to it should be good;
And in a thousand ills have happed i'th' world,   365
The intelligence of one another's shame
Have wrought far more effectually than the tie
Of conscience or religion.
WINIFRED   But think not, mistress,
That any sin which ever I committed
Did concern you; for proving false in one thing,   370
You were a fool, if ever you would trust me
In the least matter of weight.
LEONORA   Thou hast lived with me
These forty years; we have grown old together,
As many ladies and their women do,
With talking nothing, and with doing less;   375
We have spent our life in that which least concerns life,
Only in putting on our clothes. And now I think on't,
I have been a very courtly mistress to thee:°
I have given thee good words, but no deeds; now's the time

To requite all. My son has six lordships left him.   380
WINIFRED 'Tis truth.
LEONORA   But he cannot live four days to enjoy them.
WINIFRED Have you poisoned him?
LEONORA   No, the poison is yet but brewing.
WINIFRED You must minister it to him with all privacy.°
LEONORA Privacy? It shall be given him
In open court; I'll make him swallow it   385
Before the judge's face. If he be master
Of poor ten arpents of land forty hours longer,°
Let the world repute me an honest woman.
WINIFRED So 'twill, I hope.
LEONORA   O thou canst not conceive
My unimitable plot. Let's to my ghostly father,   390
Where first I will have thee make a promise
To keep my counsel, and then I will employ thee
In such a subtle combination,
Which will require, to make the practice fit,
Four devils, five advocates, to one woman's wit.   395
      Exeunt

[4.1]

Enter Leonora, Sanitonella° at one door, [with] Winifred,
Register; at the other, Ariosto

SANITONELLA [*to Register*] Take her into your office, sir; she has
    that in her belly
Will dry up your ink, I can tell you.
    [*Exeunt Register and Winifred*]
[*To Leonora*] This is the man that is your learned counsel,
A fellow that will troll it off with tongue;
He never goes without restorative powder   5
Of the lungs of fox in's pocket, and Malaga raisins°
To make him long-winded.—Sir, this gentlewoman
Entreats your counsel in an honest cause,
Which, please you, sir, this brief, my own poor labour,
Will give you light of.
    [*He gives the brief to Ariosto*]
ARIOSTO   Do you call this a brief?   10
Here's, as I weigh them, some fourscore sheets of paper.
What would they weigh if there were cheese wrapped in them,
Or fig-dotes?
SANITONELLA Joy come to you, you are merry.
We call this but a brief in our office.
The scope of the business lies i'th' margin.   15
ARIOSTO Methinks you prate too much.
I never could endure an honest cause
With a long prologue to't.
LEONORA   You trouble him.
ARIOSTO [*studies the brief*] What's here? O strange; I have lived
    this sixty years,
Yet in my practice never did shake hands°   20
With a cause so odious. Sirrah, are you her knave?
SANITONELLA No, sir, I am a clerk.
ARIOSTO   Why, you whoreson fogging rascal,
Are there not whores enough for presentations,°
Of overseers, wrong the will o'th' dead,°
Oppressions of widows or young orphans,   25
Wicked divorces, or your vicious cause
Of *plus quam satis*, to content a woman,°

But you must find new stratagems, new purse-nets?
O women, as the ballad lives to tell you,
What will you shortly come to?   30
SANITONELLA Your fee is ready, sir.
ARIOSTO   The devil take such fees,
And all such suits i'th' tail of them! See, the slave
Has writ false Latin. Sirrah Ignoramus,
Were you ever at the university?
SANITONELLA   Never, sir,
But 'tis well known to divers I have commenced°   35
In a pew of our office.
ARIOSTO   Where, in a pew of your office?°
SANITONELLA I have been dry-foundered in't this four years,°
Seldom found non-resident from my desk.°
ARIOSTO Non-resident subsumner!°
I'll tear your libel for abusing that word,°   40
By virtue of the clergy.°
          [*Tears up the brief*]
SANITONELLA   What do you mean, sir?
It cost me four nights' labour.
ARIOSTO   Hadst thou been drunk
So long, th'hadst done our court better service.
LEONORA   Sir,
You do forget your gravity, methinks.
ARIOSTO Cry ye mercy, do I so?   45
And as I take it, you do very little remember
Either womanhood, or Christianity.
Why do ye meddle
With that seducing knave, that's good for nought,
Unless't be to fill the office full of fleas,   50
Or a winter itch, wears that spacious ink-horn
All a vacation only to cure tetters,
And his penknife to weed corns from the splay toes
Of the right worshipful of the office?
LEONORA You make bold with me, sir.   55
ARIOSTO Woman, you're mad, I'll swear't, and have more need
Of a physician than a lawyer.
The melancholy humour flows in your face;
Your painting cannot hide it. Such vile suits
Disgrace our courts, and these make honest lawyers   60
Stop their own ears whilst they plead; and that's the reason

Your younger men that have good conscience
Wear such large nightcaps. Go, old woman, go pray°
For lunacy, or else the devil himself
Has ta'en possession of thee. May like cause   65
In any Christian court never find name:
Bad suits, and not the law, bred the law's shame.
    Exit [Ariosto]
LEONORA Sure the old man's frantic.
SANITONELLA   Plague on's gouty fingers!
Were all of his mind, to entertain no suits
But such they thought were honest, sure our lawyers   70
Would not purchase half so fast.
    Enter Contilupo, a spruce lawyer
                     But here's the man,
Learned Signor Contilupo, here's a fellow
Of another piece, believe't; I must make shift
With the foul copy.
    [He approaches Contilupo and offers him the documents]
CONTILUPO   Business to me?°
SANITONELLA To you, sir, from this lady.
CONTILUPO   She is welcome.   75
SANITONELLA 'Tis a foul copy, sir, you'll hardly read it.
There's twenty double ducats, can you read, sir?
CONTILUPO Exceeding well; very, very exceeding well.
SANITONELLA *[aside]* This man will be saved: he can read. Lord,
    Lord,°
To see what money can do; be the hand never so foul,   80
Somewhat will be picked out on't.
CONTILUPO   Is not this
'*Vivere honeste*'?
SANITONELLA   No, that's struck out, sir;°
And wherever you find '*Vivere honeste*' in these papers,
Give it a dash, sir.°
CONTILUPO   I shall be mindful of it.
In troth, you write a pretty secretary;   85
Your secretary hand ever takes best in mine opinion.°
SANITONELLA Sir, I have been in France,
And there, believe't, your court hand generally°
Takes beyond thought.
CONTILUPO   Even as a man is traded in't.

SANITONELLA That I could not think of this virtuous gentleman   90
    Before I went to th'tother hog-rubber!
    Why, this was wont to give young clerks half fees,
    To help him to clients.—Your opinion in the case, sir?
CONTILUPO I am struck with wonder, almost ecstasied,
    With this most goodly suit.   95
LEONORA It is the fruit of a most hearty penitence.
CONTILUPO 'Tis a case shall leave a precedent to all the world.
    In our succeeding annals, and deserves
    Rather a spacious public theatre
    Than a pent court for audience; it shall teach°   100
    All ladies the right path to rectify their issue.°
SANITONELLA Lo you, here's a man of comfort.
CONTILUPO And you shall go unto a peaceful grave,
    Discharged of such a guilt as would have lain
    Howling for ever at your wounded heart,   105
    And rose with you to Judgement.
SANITONELLA O give me such a lawyer, as will think
    Of the Day of Judgement!
LEONORA You must urge the business against him
    As spitefully as may be.   110
CONTILUPO Doubt not. What, is he summoned?
SANITONELLA Yes, and the court will sit within this half hour;
    Peruse your notes, you have very short warning.
CONTILUPO Never fear you that.
    Follow me, worthy lady, and make account°   115
    This suit is ended already.
        Exeunt

[4.2]

Enter Officers preparing seats for the Judges; to them Ercole
muffled

FIRST OFFICER You would have a private seat, sir?
ERCOLE   Yes, sir.
SECOND OFFICER Here's a closet belongs to th'court,
    Where you may hear all unseen.
ERCOLE I thank you; there's money.

SECOND OFFICER I give you your thanks again, sir.   5
  [*Ercole withdraws*]. *Enter Contarino,* [*disguised as a Dane*],
  the Surgeons, disguised
CONTARINO Is't possible Romelio's persuaded,
 You are gone to the East Indies?
FIRST SURGEON   Most confidently.
CONTARINO But do you mean to go?
SECOND SURGEON   How? Go to the East Indies?
 And so many Hollanders gone to fetch sauce for their pickled
 herrings?° Some have been peppered there too lately. But I pray,   10
 being thus well recovered of your wounds, why do you not reveal
 yourself?
CONTARINO That my fair Jolenta should be rumoured
 To be with child by noble Ercole
 Makes me expect to what a violent issue°   15
 These passages will come. I hear her brother
 Is marrying the infant she goes with,
 'Fore it be born; as, if it be a daughter,
 To the Duke of Austria's nephew; if a son,°
 Into the noble ancient family   20
 Of the Palavafini. He's a subtle devil.°
 And I do wonder what strange suit in law
 Has happed between him and's mother.
FIRST SURGEON 'Tis whispered 'mong the lawyers,
 'Twill undo him for ever.   25
  Enter Sanitonella, Winifred
SANITONELLA Do you hear, officers?
 You must take special care that you let in
 No brachygraphy men to take notes.
FIRST OFFICER   No, sir?
SANITONELLA   By no means;
 We cannot have a cause of any fame,
 But you must have scurvy pamphlets, and lewd ballads   30
 Engendered of it presently. [*To Winifred*] Have you broke fast
 yet?
WINIFRED Not I, sir.
SANITONELLA   'Twas very ill done of you,
 For this cause will be long a-pleading. But no matter,
 I have a modicum in my buckram bag
 To stop your stomach.
WINIFRED   What is't? Green ginger?   35

SANITONELLA Green ginger, nor pellitory of Spain neither;°
  Yet 'twill stop a hollow tooth better than either of them.
WINIFRED Pray what is't?
SANITONELLA   Look you, [*produces a pie from his bag*]
  It is a very lovely pudding-pie,
  Which we clerks find great relief in.
WINIFRED   I shall have no stomach.   40
SANITONELLA No matter; an you have not, I may pleasure
  Some of our learned counsel with 't; I have done it
  Many a time and often, when a cause
  Has proved like an after-game at Irish.°
       Enter Crispiano like a Judge, with another Judge [on a dais];
       Contilupo, and another Lawyer at one bar; Romelio, Ariosto,
       at another; Leonora with a black veil over her, and Julio
CRISPIANO 'Tis a strange suit. Is Leonora come?   45
CONTILUPO She's here, my lord; make way there for the lady.
CRISPIANO Take off her veil; it seems she is ashamed
  To look her cause i'th' face.
CONTILUPO   She's sick, my lord.
ARIOSTO She's mad, my lord, and would be kept more dark.°
  [*To Romelio*] By your favour, sir, I have now occasion   50
  To be at your elbow, and within this half hour
  Shall entreat you to be angry, very angry.
CRISPIANO Is Romelio come?
ROMELIO I am here, my lord, and called, I do protest,
  To answer what I know not, for as yet   55
  I am wholly ignorant of what the court
  Will charge me with.
CRISPIANO   I assure you, the proceeding
  Is most unequal then, for I perceive°
  The counsel of the adverse party furnished
  With full instruction.   60
ROMELIO Pray my lord, who is my accuser?
CRISPIANO   'Tis your mother.
ROMELIO [*aside*] She has discovered Contarino's murder.
  If she prove so unnatural to call
  My life in question, I am armed to suffer°
  This to end all my losses.
CRISPIANO   Sir, we will do you   65
  This favour: you shall hear the accusation,
  Which being known, we will adjourn the court

Till a fortnight hence; you may provide your counsel.

ARIOSTO I advise you, take their proffer,

Or else the lunacy runs in a blood,°   70

You are more mad than she.

ROMELIO   What are you, sir?

ARIOSTO An angry fellow that would do thee good,°

For goodness' sake itself, I do protest,

Neither for love nor money.

ROMELIO Prithee stand further, I shall gall your gout else.   75

ARIOSTO Come, come, I know you for an East Indy merchant;

You have a spice of pride in you still.

ROMELIO [to Contarino] My lord, I am so strengthened in my in-
    nocence

For any the least shadow of a crime

Committed 'gainst my mother, or the world,   80

That she can charge me with, here do I make it

My humble suit, only this hour and place

May give it as full hearing, and as free

And unrestrained a sentence.

CRISPIANO   Be not too confident;

You have cause to fear.

ROMELIO   Let fear dwell with earthquakes,   85

Shipwrecks at sea, or prodigies in heaven;°

I cannot set myself so many fathom

Beneath the height of my true heart as fear.°

ARIOSTO Very fine words, I assure you, if they were

To any purpose.

CRISPIANO   Well, have your entreaty;   90

And if your own credulity undo you,

Blame not the court hereafter. [To Contilupo] Fall to your plea.

CONTILUPO May it please your lordship, and the reverend court,

To give me leave to open to you a case

So rare, so altogether void of precedent,   95

That I do challenge all the spacious volumes

Of the whole civil law to show the like.

We are of counsel for this gentlewoman;

We have received our fee, yet the whole course

Of what we are to speak is quite against her;   100

Yet we'll deserve our fee too. There stands one,

Romelio the merchant; I will name him to you

Without either title or addition,

For those false beams of his supposèd honour,°
As void of true heat as are all painted fires   105
Or glow-worms in the dark, suit him all basely,
As if he had bought his gentry from the herald
With money got by extortion. I will first
Produce this Aesop's crow, as he stands forfeit°
For the long use of his gay borrowed plumes,   110
And then let him hop naked. I come to th'point.
It's been a dream in Naples, very near°
This eight-and-thirty years, that this Romelio
Was nobly descended; he has ranked himself
With the nobility, shamefully usurped   115
Their place, and in a kind of saucy pride,
Which, like to mushrooms, ever grow most rank
When they do spring from dunghills, sought to o'ersway
The Fieschi, the Grimaldi, Doria°,
And all the ancient pillars of our state.   120
View now what he is come to: this poor thing
Without a name, this cuckoo hatched i'th' nest
Of a hedge-sparrow.
ROMELIO Speaks he all this to me?
ARIOSTO   Only to you, sir.
ROMELIO I do not ask thee; prithee hold thy prating.   125
ARIOSTO Why, very good, you will be presently
    As angry as I could wish.
CONTILUPO What title shall I set to this base coin?
    He has no name, and for's aspect he seems
    A giant in a May-game that within°   130
    Is nothing but a porter. I'll undertake,
    He had as good have travelled all his life
    With gipsies. I will sell him to any man
    For an hundred chequeens, and he that buys him of me
    Shall lose by th'hand too.
ARIOSTO   Lo, what you are come to:°   135
    You that did scorn to trade in anything
    But gold or spices, or your cochineal,
    He rates you now at poor John.
ROMELIO   Out upon thee,°
    I would thou wert of his side.
ARIOSTO   Would you so?
ROMELIO The devil and thee together on each hand,   140

To prompt the lawyer's memory when he founders.

CRISPIANO Signor Contilupo, the court holds it fit
　　You leave this stale declaiming 'gainst the person,
　　And come to the matter.

CONTILUPO　　　　　　　　Now I shall, my lord.

CRISPIANO It shows a poor malicious eloquence,　　　　　145
　　And it is strange, men of your gravity
　　Will not forgo it. Verily, I presume,
　　If you but heard yourself speaking with my ears,
　　Your phrase would be more modest.

CONTILUPO　　　　　　　　　Good my lord, be assured,
　　I will leave all circumstance, and come to th'purpose:　150
　　This Romelio is a bastard.

ROMELIO　　　　　　　How, a bastard!
　　O mother, now the day begins grow hot
　　On your side.

CONTILUPO　　　Why, she is your accuser.

ROMELIO I had forgot that. Was my father married
　　To any other woman at the time　　　　　155
　　Of my begetting?

CONTILUPO　　　　　That's not the business.

ROMELIO I turn me then to you that were my mother,
　　But by what name I am to call you now,
　　You must instruct me: were you ever married
　　To my father?

LEONORA　　　　To my shame I speak it, never.　　　　160

CRISPIANO Not to Francisco Romelio?

LEONORA　　　　　　　　May it please your lordships,
　　To him I was, but he was not his father.

CONTILUPO Good my lord, give us leave in a few words
　　To expound the riddle, and to make it plain,
　　Without the least of scruple: for I take it　　　　165
　　There cannot be more lawful proof i'th' world
　　Than the oath of the mother.

CRISPIANO　　　　　　　Well then, to your proofs,
　　And be not tedious.

CONTILUPO　　　　　I'll conclude in a word.
　　Some nine-and-thirty years since, which was the time
　　This woman was married, Francisco Romelio,　　　　170
　　This gentleman's putative father and her husband,
　　Being not married to her past a fortnight,

Would needs go travel; did so, and continued
In France and the Low Countries eleven months:
Take special note o'th' time, I beseech your lordship,   175
For it makes much to th' business. In his absence
He left behind to sojourn at his house
A Spanish gentleman, a fine spruce youth
By the lady's confession, and you may be sure
He was no eunuch neither; he was one   180
Romelio loved very dearly, as oft haps,
No man alive more welcome to the husband
Than he that makes him cuckold.
This gentleman, I say,
Breaking all laws of hospitality,   185
Got his friend's wife with child, a full two months
Fore the husband returned.

SANITONELLA [*aside*]   Good sir, forget not the lambskin.
CONTILUPO [*aside*] I warrant thee.
SANITONELLA [*aside*]   I will pinch by the buttock
To put you in mind of't.
CONTILUPO [*aside*]   Prithee hold thy prating.
What's to be practised now, my lord? Marry, this: 190
Romelio being a young novice, not acquainted
With this precedence, very innocently
Returning home from travel, finds his wife
Grown an excellent good housewife°, for she had set
Her women to spin flax, and to that use   195
Had, in a study which was built of stone,°
Stored up at least an hundredweight of flax;
Marry, such a thread as was to be spun from the flax,
I think the like was never heard of.
CRISPIANO   What was that?
CONTILUPO You may be certain she would lose no time   200
In bragging that her husband had got up
Her belly; to be short, at seven months' end,
Which was the time of her delivery,
And when she felt herself to fall in travail,
She makes her waiting-woman, as by mischance,   205
Set fire to the flax, the fright whereof,
As they pretend, causes this gentlewoman
To fall in pain, and be deliverèd
Eight weeks afore her reckoning.

SANITONELLA [*aside to Contilupo*] Now, sir, remember the lamb-
    skin.   210
CONTILUPO The midwife straight howls out there was no hope
    Of th'infant's life, swaddles it in a flayed lambskin,
    As a bird hatched too early, makes it up
    With three-quarters of a face, that made it look
    Like a changeling, cries out to Romelio°   215
    To have it christened, lest it should depart
    Without that it came for; and thus are many served°
    That take care to get gossips for those children,°
    To which they might be godfathers themselves,
    And yet be no arch-puritans neither.
CRISPIANO   No more.°   220
ARIOSTO Pray, my lord, give him way, you spoil his oratory else;
    Thus would they jest, were they fee'd to open
    Their sisters' cases.
CRISPIANO   You have urged enough;°
    You first affirm her husband was away from her
    Eleven months.
CONTILUPO   Yes, my lord.   225
CRISPIANO And at seven months' end,
    After his return, she was deliverèd
    Of this Romelio, and had gone her full time.
CONTILUPO True, my lord.
CRISPIANO So by this account this gentleman was begot   230
    In his supposèd father's absence?
CONTILUPO   You have it fully.
CRISPIANO A most strange suit this. 'Tis beyond example,
    Either time past, or present, for a woman
    To publish her own dishonour voluntarily,
    Without being called in question, some forty years   235
    After the sin committed, and her counsel
    To enlarge the offence with as much oratory
    As ever I did hear them in my life
    Defend a guilty woman. 'Tis most strange,
    Or why with such a poisoned violence   240
    Should she labour her son's undoing? We observe
    Obedience of creatures to the law of nature
    Is the stay of the whole world. Here that law is broke,
    For though our civil law makes difference°
    'Tween the base and the legitimate, compassionate nature   245

Makes them equal; nay, she many times prefers them.
I pray resolve me, sir, have not you and your mother
Had some suit in law together lately?

ROMELIO None, my lord.

CRISPIANO No? No contention about parting your goods?   250

ROMELIO Not any.

CRISPIANO   No flaw, no unkindness?

ROMELIO None that ever arrived at my knowledge.

CRISPIANO Bethink yourself, this cannot choose but savour
    Of a woman's malice deeply; and I fear
    You're practised upon most devilishly. How happed,   255
    Gentlewoman, you revealed this no sooner?

LEONORA While my husband lived, my lord, I durst not.

CRISPIANO I should rather ask you, why you reveal it now?

LEONORA Because, my lord, I loathed that such a sin
    Should lie smothered with me in my grave; my penitence,   260
    Though to my shame, prefers the revealing of it
    'Bove worldly reputation.

CRISPIANO   Your penitence?
    Might not your penitence have been as hearty,°
    Though it had never summoned to the court
    Such a conflux of people?   265

LEONORA Indeed I might have confessed it privately
    To th'church, I grant; but you know repentance
    Is nothing without satisfaction.°

CRISPIANO Satisfaction? Why, your husband's dead,
    What satisfaction can you make him?   270

LEONORA The greatest satisfaction in the world, my lord:
    To restore the land to th'right heir, and that's
    My daughter.

CRISPIANO   O, she's straight begot then.

ARIOSTO Very well, may it please this honourable court,
    If he be a bastard, and must forfeit his land for't,   275
    She has proved herself a strumpet, and must lose
    Her dower; let them go a-begging together.°

SANITONELLA Who shall pay us our fees then?

CRISPIANO Most just.

ARIOSTO   You may see now what an old house°
    You are like to pull over your head, dame.   280

ROMELIO Could I conceive this publication
    Grew from a hearty penitence, I could bear

My undoing the more patiently; but, my lord,
There is no reason, as you said even now,
To satisfy me but this suit of hers   285
Springs from a devilish malice, and her pretence
Of a grieved conscience, and religion,
Like to the horrid powder-treason in England,°
Has a most bloody unnatural revenge
Hid under it. O the violencies of women!   290
Why, they are creatures made up and compounded
Of all monsters, poisonèd minerals,
And sorcerous herbs that grows.
ARIOSTO   Are you angry yet?
ROMELIO Would man express a bad one, let him forsake
All natural example, and compare°   295
One to another: they have no more mercy
Than ruinous fires in great tempests.
ARIOSTO Take heed you do not crack your voice, sir.
ROMELIO Hard-hearted creatures, good for nothing else
But to wind dead bodies.
ARIOSTO   Yes, to weave seaming lace   300
With the bones of their husbands that were long since buried,°
And curse them when they tangle.
ROMELIO   Yet why do I
Take bastardy so distastefully, when i'th' world
A many things that are essential parts
Of greatness are but by-slips, and are fathered   305
On the wrong parties;
Preferment in the world a many times
Basely begotten? Nay, I have observed
The immaculate justice of a poor man's cause,
In such a court as this, has not known whom   310
To call father, which way to direct itself
For compassion. But I forget my temper.
Only, that I may stop that lawyer's throat,
I do beseech the court, and the whole world,
They will not think the baselier of me   315
For the vice of a mother; for that woman's sin,
To which you all dare swear when it was done,
I would not give my consent.
CRISPIANO   Stay, here's an accusation,
But here's no proof. What was the Spaniard's name

You accuse of adultery?

CONTILUPO   Don Crispiano, my lord.   320

CRISPIANO What part of Spain was he born in?

CONTILUPO   In Castile.

JULIO [aside] This may prove my father.

SANITONELLA [aside]   And my master;
My client's spoiled then.

CRISPIANO I knew that Spaniard well. If you be a bastard,
Such a man being your father, I dare vouch you   325
A gentleman; and in that, Signor Contilupo,
Your oratory went a little too far.
When do we name Don John of Austria,°
The emperor's son, but with reverence?
And I have known, in divers families,   330
The bastards the greater spirits. But to th'purpose:
What time was this gentleman begot? And be sure
You lay your time right.

ARIOSTO   Now the metal comes
To the touchstone.

CONTILUPO   In anno seventy-one, my lord.

CRISPIANO Very well, seventy-one; the battle of Lepanto°   335
Was fought in't, a most remarkable time:°
'Twill lie for no man's pleasure. And what proof is there,
More than the affirmation of the mother,
Of this corporal dealing?°

CONTILUPO   The deposition
Of a waiting-woman served her the same time.   340

CRISPIANO Where is she?

CONTILUPO   Where is our solicitor
With the waiting-woman?

ARIOSTO   Room for the bag and baggage!°

SANITONELLA Here my lord, ore tenus.

CRISPIANO   And what can you say, gentlewoman?°

WINIFRED Please your lordship, I was the party that dealt in the
business, and brought them together.   345

CRISPIANO Well.

WINIFRED And conveyed letters between them.

CRISPIANO What needed letters, when 'tis said he lodged in her
house?

WINIFRED A running° ballad now and then to her viol, for he was   350
never well but when he was fiddling.°

CRISPIANO Speak to the purpose: did you ever know them in bed
together?

WINIFRED No, my lord, but I have brought him to the bed-side.

CRISPIANO That was somewhat near to the business. And what, did   355
you help him off with his shoes?

WINIFRED He wore no shoes, an't please you, my lord.

CRISPIANO No? what then, pumps?

WINIFRED Neither.

CRISPIANO Boots were not fit for his journey.   360

WINIFRED He wore tennis-court woollen slippers, for fear of creak-
ing, sir, and making a noise to wake the rest o'th' house.

CRISPIANO Well, and what did he there, in his tennis-court woollen
slippers?

WINIFRED Please your lordship, question me in Latin, for the cause   365
is very foul; the examiner o'th' court was fain to get it out of me
alone i'th' counting-house, 'cause he would not spoil the youth
o'th' office.

ARIOSTO Here's a Latin° spoon, and a long one, to feed with the devil.

WINIFRED I'd be loth to be ignorant° that way, for I hope to marry   370
a proctor, and take my pleasure abroad at the commencements
with him.

ARIOSTO Come closer to the business.

WINIFRED I will come as close as modesty will give me leave. Truth
is, every morning when he lay with her, I made a caudle for him,   375
by the appointment of my mistress, which he would still refuse,
and call for small drink.

CRISPIANO Small drink?°

ARIOSTO For a julep.

WINIFRED And said he was wondrous thirsty.   380

CRISPIANO What's this to the purpose?

WINIFRED Most effectual, my lord. I have heard them laugh together
extremely, and the curtainrods fall from the tester of the bed, and
he ne'er came from her, but he thrust money in my hand; and
once, in truth, he would have had some dealing with me which I   385
took; he thought 'twould be the only way i'th' world to make me
keep counsel the better.

SANITONELLA [aside] That's a stinger;° 'tis a good wench, be not
daunted.

CRISPIANO Did you ever find the print of two in the bed?   390

WINIFRED What a question's that to be asked! May it please your
lordship, 'tis to be thought he lay nearer to her than so.

CRISPIANO What age are you of, gentlewoman?

WINIFRED About six-and-forty, my lord.

CRISPIANO   Anno seventy-one,
And Romelio is thirty-eight. By that reckoning,   395
You were a bawd at eight year old; now verily,
You fell to the trade betimes.

SANITONELLA [aside]   There you're from the bias.°

WINIFRED I do not know my age directly. Sure I am elder; I can
remember two great frosts, and three great plagues, and the loss of
Calais, and the first coming up of the breeches with the great   400
cod-piece.° And I pray what age do you take me of then?

SANITONELLA [aside] Well come off again!

ARIOSTO An old hunted hare, she has all her doubles.°

ROMELIO For your own gravities,
And the reverence of the court, I do beseech you,   405
Rip up the cause no further, but proceed
To sentence.

CRISPIANO   One question more and I have done.
Might not this Crispiano, this Spaniard,
Lie with your mistress at some other time,
Either afore or after, than i'th' absence   410
Of her husband?

LEONORA   Never.

CRISPIANO   Are you certain of that?

LEONORA On my soul, never.

CRISPIANO   That's well; he never lay with her,
But in anno seventy-one, let that be remembered.
Stand you aside a while.—Mistress, the truth is,
I knew this Crispiano, lived in Naples   415
At the same time, and loved the gentleman
As my bosom friend; and as I do remember,
The gentleman did leave his picture with you,
If age or neglect have not in so long time ruined it.

LEONORA I preserve it still, my lord.

CRISPIANO   I pray let me see't,   420
Let me see the face I then loved so much to look on.

LEONORA Fetch it.

WINIFRED   I shall, my lord.

CRISPIANO   No, no, gentlewoman,
I have other business for you.

        [Exit an Officer for the picture]

FIRST SURGEON [*aside to Contarino*] Now were the time to cut
    Romelio's throat,
  And accuse him for your murder.
CONTARINO [*aside to the Surgeons*]   By no means.   425
SECOND SURGEON [*aside to Contarino*] Will you not let us be men
    of fashion,
  And down with him now he's going?°
CONTARINO [*aside to the Surgeons*] Peace, let's attend the sequel.
CRISPIANO [*To Leonora*]   I commend you, lady;
  There was a main matter of conscience.
  How many ills spring from adultery!   430
  First, the supreme law, that is violated°
  Nobility oft stained with bastardy,
  Inheritance of land falsely possessed,
  The husband scorned, wife shamed, and babes unblessed.
       The picture [*is brought in by an Officer*]
  So, hang it up i'th' court. You have heard   435
  What has been urgèd 'gainst Romelio.
  Now, my definitive sentence in this cause
  Is, I will give no sentence at all.
ARIOSTO   No?
CRISPIANO No, I cannot, for I am made a party.
SANITONELLA [*aside*] How, a party? Here are fine cross tricks.°   440
  What the devil will he do now?
CRISPIANO Signor Ariosto, His Majesty of Spain
  Confers my place upon you by this patent,
  Which till this urgent hour I have kept
  From your knowledge. May you thrive in't, noble sir,   445
  And do that which but few in our place do,
  Go to their grave uncursed.
ARIOSTO [*taking Crispiano's place*] This law business
  Will leave me so small leisure to serve God,
  I shall serve the king the worse.
SANITONELLA [*aside*]   Is he a judge?
  We must then look for all conscience, and no law: 450
  He'll beggar all his followers.
CRISPIANO [*to Romelio*] Sir, I am of your counsel, for the cause in
    hand
  Was begun at such a time, 'fore you could speak;
  You had need therefore have one speak for you.
ARIOSTO Stay, I do here first make protestation,   455

I ne'er took fee of this Romelio
For being of his counsel, which may free me,
Being now his judge, for the imputation
Of taking a bribe. Now, sir, speak your mind.

CRISPIANO I do first entreat that the eyes of all here present 460
May be fixed upon this.°

LEONORA O, I am confounded: this is Crispiano!

JULIO [aside] This is my father; how the judges have bleared him!°

WINIFRED [aside] You may see truth will out in spite of the devil.

CRISPIANO Behold, I am the shadow of this shadow; 465
Age has made me so. Take from me forty years,
And I was such a summer fruit as this—
At least the painter feigned so; for indeed,
Painting and epitaphs are both alike:
They flatter us, and say we have been thus. 470
But I am the party here that stands accused
For adultery with this woman, in the year
Seventy-one. Now I call you, my lord, to witness
Four years before that time I went to th'Indies,
And till this month did never set my foot since 475
In Europe; and for any former incontinence,
She has vowed there was never any. What remains then,
But this is a mere practice 'gainst her son;
And I beseech the court it may be sifted,
And most severely punished.

SANITONELLA [aside]   Ud's foot, we are spoiled; 480
Why, my client's proved an honest woman.

WINIFRED [aside to Sanitonella] What do you think will become of
me now?

SANITONELLA [aside] You'll be made dance lachrymae, I fear,
At a cart's tail.°

ARIOSTO   You, mistress, where are you now?
Your tennis-court slips, and your ta'en drink° 485
In a morning for your hot liver? Where's the man°
Would have had some dealing with you that you might
Keep counsel the better?

WINIFRED May it please the court, I am but a young thing, and was
drawn arsy-varsy into the business.° 490

ARIOSTO How young? Of five-and-forty?

WINIFRED Five-and-forty, an't shall please you! I am not five-and-
twenty. She made me colour my hair with bean-flour to seem elder

than I was; and then my rotten teeth, with eating sweetmeats; why, should a farrier look in my mouth, he might mistake my age. O mistress, mistress, you are an honest woman, and you may be ashamed on't, to abuse the court thus.   495

LEONORA Whatsoe'er I have attempted
  'Gainst my own fame, or the reputation
  Of that gentleman, my son, the Lord Contarino   500
  Was the cause of it.

CONTARINO [aside]   Who, I?

ARIOSTO He that should have married your daughter?
  It was a plot belike, then, to confer
  The land on her that should have been his wife.

LEONORA More than I have said already, all the world   505
  Shall ne'er extract from me; I entreat from both
  Your equal pardons.

JULIO   And I from you, sir.

CRISPIANO Sirrah, stand you aside;
  I will talk with you hereafter.

JULIO I could never away with after-reckonings.°   510

LEONORA And now, my lords, I do most voluntarily
  Confine myself unto a stricter prison
  And a severer penance than this court
  Can impose: I am entered into religion.

CONTARINO [aside] I the cause of this practice! This ungodly
    woman   515
  Has sold herself to falsehood; I will now
  Reveal myself.

ERCOLE [revealing himself] Stay, my lord, here's a window
  To let in more light to the court.

CONTARINO [aside] Mercy upon me! O, that thou art living   520
  Is mercy indeed!

FIRST SURGEON [aside to Contarino] Stay, keep in your shell
  A little longer!

ERCOLE   I am Ercole.

ARIOSTO A guard upon him for the death of Contarino!

ERCOLE I obey the arrest o'th' court.   525

ROMELIO O sir, you are happily restored to life,
  And to us your friends.

ERCOLE   Away, thou art the traitor
  I only live to challenge. This former suit
  Touched but thy fame; this accusation

Reaches to thy fame and life. The brave Contarino   530
Is generally supposed slain by this hand—
CONTARINO [*aside*] How knows he the contrary?
ERCOLE   But truth is,
Having received from me some certain wounds
Which were not mortal, this vile murderer
Being by will deputed overseer   535
Of the nobleman's estate to his sister's use,
That he might make him sure from surviving
To revoke that will, stole to him in's bed, and killed him.
ROMELIO Strange, unheard of! More practice yet!
ARIOSTO What proof of this?   540
ERCOLE The report of his mother delivered to me,
In distraction for Contarino's death.
CONTARINO [*aside*] For my death? I begin to apprehend
That the violence of this woman's love to me
Might practise the disinheriting of her son.   545
ARIOSTO What say you to this, Leonora?
LEONORA Such a thing I did utter out of my distraction;
But how the court will censure that report,
I leave to their wisdoms.
ARIOSTO   My opinion is
That this late slander urged against her son   550
Takes from her all manner of credit; she
That would not stick to deprive him of his living,
Will as little tender his life.
LEONORA   I beseech the court,
I may retire myself to my place of penance,
I have vowed myself and my woman.   555
ARIOSTO Go when you please.
        [*Exeunt Leonora and Winifred*]
[*To Ercole*]   What should move you be thus forward
In the accusation?
ERCOLE   My love to Contarino.
ARIOSTO O, it bore very bitter fruit at your last meeting.
ERCOLE 'Tis true: but I begun to love him
When I had most cause to hate him, when our bloods   560
Embraced each other; then I pitied
That so much valour should be hazarded
On the fortune of a single rapier,
And not spent against the Turk.

ARIOSTO   Stay, sir, be well advised.
  There is no testimony but your own   565
  [*Turning to Romelio*] To approve you slew him, therefore no
    other way
  To decide it, but by duel.
CONTARINO Yes, my lord, I dare affirm 'gainst all the world,
  This nobleman speaks truth.   570
ARIOSTO You will make yourself a party in the duel.
ROMELIO Let him, I will fight with them both, sixteen of them.
ERCOLE Sir, I do not know you.
CONTARINO   Yes, but you have forgot me;
  You and I have sweat in the breach together
  At Malta.
ERCOLE   Cry you mercy, I have known°   575
  Of your nation brave soldiers.°
JULIO [*aside*]   Now if my father
  Have any true spirit in him, I'll recover
  His good opinion. [*To Contarino*] Do you hear? Do not swear,
    sir,
  For I dare swear that you will swear a lie,   580
  A very filthy, stinking, rotten lie;
  And if the lawyers think not this sufficient,
  I'll give the lie in the stomach—
  That's somewhat deeper than the throat—°
  Both here, and all France over and over,   585
  From Marseilles, or Bayonne, to Calais sands,°
  And there draw my sword upon thee, and new scour it
  In the gravel of thy kidneys.
ARIOSTO   You the defendant
  Charged with the murder, and you second there,
  Must be committed to the custody
  Of the Knight Marshal; and the court gives charge°   590
  They be tomorrow ready in the lists
  Before the sun be risen.
ROMELIO I do entreat the court there be a guard
  Placed o'er my sister, that she enter not
  Into religion; she's rich, my lords,   595
  And the persuasions of friars, to gain
  All her possessions to their monasteries,
  May do much upon her.
ARIOSTO   We'll take order for her.

CRISPIANO There's a nun too you have got with child:
　　How will you dispose of her?   600
ROMELIO You question me, as if I were graved already.
　　When I have quenched this wild-fire in Ercole's
　　Tame blood, I'll tell you.
　　　　Exit [Romelio]
ERCOLE　　　　　　　　You have judged today
　　A most confusèd practice that takes end
　　In as bloody a trial; and we may observe   605
　　By these great persons, and their indirect
　　Proceedings shadowed in a veil of state,
　　Mountains are deformèd heaps, swelled up aloft,
　　Vales wholesomer, though lower, and trod on oft.
SANITONELLA Well, I will put up my papers,   610
　　And send them to France for a precedent,
　　That they may not say yet, but for one strange law-suit,
　　We come somewhat near them.
　　　　Exeunt

[5.1]

Enter Jolenta, and Angiolella great-bellied

JOLENTA How dost thou, friend? Welcome. Thou and I
  Were playfellows together, little children,
  So small a while ago, that I presume
  We are neither of us wise yet.

ANGIOLELLA   A most sad truth
  On my part.

JOLENTA   Why do you pluck your veil   5
  Over your face?

ANGIOLELLA   If you will believe truth,
  There's nought more terrible to a guilty heart
  Than the eye of a respected friend!

JOLENTA   Say, friend,
  Are you quick with child?

ANGIOLELLA Too sure.

JOLENTA   How could you know   10
  Of your first child, when you quickened?°

ANGIOLELLA How could you know, friend?
  'Tis reported you are in the same taking.

JOLENTA Ha, ha, ha, so 'tis given out;
  But Ercole's coming to life again has shrunk   15
  And made invisible my great belly; yes, faith,
  My being with child was merely in supposition,
  Not practice.

ANGIOLELLA   You are happy. What would I give
  To be a maid again!

JOLENTA   Would you? To what purpose?
  I would never give great purchase for that thing°   20
  Is in danger every hour to be lost. Pray thee, laugh:
  A boy or a girl, for a wager?

ANGIOLELLA   What heaven please.

JOLENTA Nay, nay, will you venture°
  A chain of pearl with me whether?

ANGIOLELLA   I'll lay nothing;
  I have ventured too much for't already, my fame.   25
  I make no question, sister, you have heard°
  Of the intended combat?

JOLENTA   O what else?
  I have a sweetheart in't, against a brother.
ANGIOLELLA And I a dead friend, I fear. What good counsel
  Can you minister unto me?
JOLENTA   Faith, only this: 30
  Since there's no means i'th' world to hinder it,
  Let thou and I, wench, get as far as we can
  From the noise of it.
ANGIOLELLA   Whither?
JOLENTA   No matter; any whither.
ANGIOLELLA Any whither, so you go not by sea:
  I cannot abide rough water.   35
JOLENTA Not endure to be tumbled? Say no more then;°
  We'll be land-soldiers for that trick. Take heart,°
  Thy boy shall be born a brave Roman.
ANGIOLELLA   O you mean
  To go to Rome then.
JOLENTA   Within there!
        Enter a Servant
                            Bear this letter
  To the Lord Ercole. Now, wench, I am for thee   40
  All the world over.
ANGIOLELLA   I, like your shade, pursue you.°
        Exeunt

[5.2]

        Enter Prospero and Sanitonella
PROSPERO Well, I do not think but to see you as pretty a piece of
  law-flesh.°
SANITONELLA In time I may. Marry, I am resolved to take a new
  way for't. You have lawyers take their clients' fees, and their backs
  are no sooner turned, but they call them fools, and laugh at them.   5
PROSPERO That's ill done of them.
SANITONELLA There's one thing too that has a vile abuse in't.
PROSPERO What's that?
SANITONELLA Marry, this: that no proctor in the term time be
  tolerated to go to the tavern above six times i'th' forenoon.°   10
PROSPERO Why, man?

SANITONELLA O sir, it makes their clients overtaken,° and become
    friends sooner than they would be.

        Enter Ercole with a letter, and Contarino, coming in friars'
        habits, as having been at the Bathanites',° a ceremony used
        afore these combats

ERCOLE Leave the room, gentlemen.

    [*Exeunt Prospero and Sanitonella*]

CONTARINO [*aside*] Wherefore should I with such an obstinacy   15
    Conceal myself any longer? I am taught
    That all the blood which will be shed tomorrow,
    Must fall upon my head; one question
    Shall fix it or untie it. [*To Ercole*] Noble brother,
    I would fain know how it is possible,   20
    When it appears you love the fair Jolenta
    With such a height of fervour, you were ready
    To father another's child and marry her,
    You would so suddenly engage yourself
    To kill her brother, one that ever stood   25
    Your loyal and firm friend?
ERCOLE   Sir, I'll tell you:
    My love, as I have formerly protested,
    To Contarino, whose unfortunate end
    The traitor wrought; and here is one thing more
    Deads all good thoughts of him, which I now received   30
    From Jolenta.

        [*He shows him a letter*]

CONTARINO   In a letter?
ERCOLE   Yes, in this letter;
    For having sent to her to be resolved
    Most truly who was father of the child,
    She writes back that the shame she goes withal
    Was begot by her brother.   35
CONTARINO O most incestuous villain!
ERCOLE   I protest,
    Before I thought 'twas Contarino's issue,
    And for that would have veiled her dishonour.
CONTARINO   No more.
    Has the armourer brought the weapons?
ERCOLE   Yes, sir.
CONTARINO I will no more think of her.
ERCOLE   Of whom?   40

CONTARINO Of my mother, I was thinking of my mother.
  Call the armourer.
    Exeunt

[5.3]

Enter [First] Surgeon, and Winifred

WINIFRED You do love me, sir, you say?
SURGEON   O most entirely.
WINIFRED And you will marry me?
SURGEON   Nay, I'll do more than that.
  The fashion of the world is many times
  To make a woman naught, and afterwards
  To marry her; but I, o'th' contrary,   5
  Will make you honest first, and afterwards
  Proceed to the wedlock.
WINIFRED   Honest? What mean you by that?
SURGEON I mean that your suborning the late law-suit°
  Has got you a filthy report; now there's no way,
  But to do some excellent piece of honesty,   10
  To recover your good name.
WINIFRED   How, sir?
SURGEON You shall straight go and reveal to your old mistress,
  For certain truth, Contarino is alive.
WINIFRED How, living?
SURGEON   Yes, he is living.
WINIFRED No, I must not tell her of it.
SURGEON   No, why?   15
WINIFRED For she did bind me yesterday by oath,
  Never more to speak of him.
SURGEON   You shall reveal it then
  To Ariosto the judge.
WINIFRED   By no means; he has heard me
  Tell so many lies i'th' court, he'll ne'er believe me.
  What if I told it to the Capuchin?
SURGEON   You cannot   20
  Think of a better; as for your young mistress
  Who, as you told me, has persuaded you
  To run away with her, let her have her humour.

I have a suit Romelio left i'th' house,
The habit of a Jew: that I'll put on,   25
And pretending I am robbed, by break of day,
Procure all passengers to be brought back,°
And by the way reveal myself, and discover
The comical event. They say she's a little mad;
This will help to cure her. Go, go presently,   30
And reveal it to the Capuchin.
WINIFRED   Sir, I shall.
        Exeunt

[5.4]

        Enter Julio, Prospero, and Sanitonella
JULIO A pox on't,
    I have undertaken the challenge very foolishly.
    What if I do not appear to answer it?
PROSPERO It would be absolute conviction
    Of cowardice and perjury; and the Dane°   5
    May, to your public shame, reverse your arms,°
    Or have them ignominiously fastened
    Under his horse-tail.
JULIO   I do not like that so well.
    I see then I must fight whether I will or no.
PROSPERO How does Romelio bear himself? They say   10
    He has almost brained one of the cunning'st fencers
    That practised with him.
JULIO Very certain; and now you talk of fencing,
    Do not you remember the Welsh gentleman
    That was travelling to Rome upon return?°   15
PROSPERO No, what of him?
JULIO There was a strange experiment of a fencer.
PROSPERO What was that?
JULIO The Welshman in's play, do what the fencer could,
    Hung still an arse—he could not for's life°   20
    Make him come on bravely—till one night at supper,
    Observing what a deal of Parma cheese
    His scholar devoured, goes ingeniously
    The next morning and makes a spacious button

For his foil of toasted cheese; and as sure as you live,°   25
That made him come on the braveliest.
PROSPERO   Possible!°
JULIO Marry, it taught him an ill grace in's play;
   It made him gape still, gape as he put in for't,°
   As I have seen some hungry usher.°
PROSPERO The toasting of it belike   30
   Was to make it more supple, had he chanced
   To have hit him o'th' chaps.
JULIO   Not unlikely. Who can tell me°
   If we may breathe in the duel?
PROSPERO   By no means.°
JULIO Nor drink?
PROSPERO   Neither.
JULIO That's scurvy; anger will make me very dry.   35
PROSPERO You mistake, sir, 'tis sorrow that is very dry.°
SANITONELLA Not always, sir; I have known sorrow very wet.
JULIO In rainy weather.
SANITONELLA No, when a woman has come dropping wet
   Out of a cucking-stool.
JULIO   Then 'twas wet indeed, sir.   40
      Enter Romelio very melancholy, and the Capuchin
CAPUCHIN [*aside*] Having from Leonora's waiting-woman
   Delivered a most strange intelligence
   Of Contarino's recovery, I am come
   To sound Romelio's penitence; that performed,
   To end these errors by discovering   45
   What she related to me. [*To Romelio*] Peace to you, sir.
   Pray, gentlemen, let the freedom of this room
   Be mine a little. [*To Julio*] Nay, sir, you may stay.°
      Exeunt Prospero [and] Sanitonella
   Will you pray with me?
ROMELIO   No, no, the world and I
   Have not made up our accounts yet.
CAPUCHIN   Shall I pray for you?   50
ROMELIO Whether you do or no, I care not.
CAPUCHIN O you have a dangerous voyage to take.
ROMELIO No matter, I will be mine own pilot;
   Do not you trouble your head with the business.
CAPUCHIN Pray tell me, do not you meditate of death?   55
ROMELIO Phew, I took out that lesson°

When I once lay sick of an ague; I do now
Labour for life, for life. Sir, can you tell me
Whether your Toledo, or your Milan blade
Be best tempered?

CAPUCHIN   These things, you know,   60
Are out of my practice.

ROMELIO   But these are things, you know,
I must practise with tomorrow.

CAPUCHIN   Were I in your case,
I should present to myself strange shadows.

ROMELIO Turn you: were I in your case, I should laugh°
At mine own shadow.   65
Who has hired you to make me coward?

CAPUCHIN   I would make you
A good Christian.

ROMELIO   Withal, let me continue
An honest man, which I am very certain
A coward can never be. You take upon you
A physician's place, rather than a divine's.   70
You go about to bring my body so low,
I should fight i'th' lists tomorrow like a dormouse,
And be made away in a slumber.

CAPUCHIN Did you murder Contarino?

ROMELIO That's a scurvy question now.

CAPUCHIN   Why, sir?   75

ROMELIO Did you ask it as a confessor, or as a spy?

CAPUCHIN As one that fain would jostle the devil
Out of your way.

ROMELIO   Um, you are but weakly made for't;
He's a cunning wrestler, I can tell you, and has broke
Many a man's neck.

CAPUCHIN   But to give him the foil°   80
Goes not by strength.

ROMELIO   Let it go by what it will;
Get me some good victuals to breakfast, I am hungry.

CAPUCHIN (*offering him a book*) Here's food for you.

ROMELIO   Pew, I am not to commence doctor,°
For then the word 'Devour that book!' were proper.°
I am to fight, to fight, sir, and I'll do't,   85
As I would feed, with a good stomach.

CAPUCHIN   Can you feed,°

And apprehend death?

ROMELIO   Why, sir? Is not death
A hungry companion? Say, is not the grave
Said to be a great devourer? Give me some victuals.
I knew a man that was to lose his head   90
Feed with an excellent good appetite,
To strengthen his heart, scarce half an hour before.
And if he did it, that only was to speak,°
What should I, that am to do?

CAPUCHIN   This confidence,°
If it be grounded upon truth, 'tis well.   95

ROMELIO You must understand that resolution
Should ever wait upon a noble death,°
As captains bring their soldiers out o'th' field,
And come off last; for, I pray, what is death?
The safest trench i'th' world to keep man free   100
From fortune's gunshot; to be afraid of that
Would prove me weaker than a teeming woman,
That does endure a thousand times more pain
In bearing of a child.

CAPUCHIN   O, I tremble for you,
For I do know you have a storm within you   105
More terrible than a sea-fight, and your soul
Being heretofore drowned in security,
You know not how to live, nor how to die;
But I have an object that shall startle you,
And make you know whither you are going.   110

ROMELIO I am armed for't.

Enter Leonora with two coffins borne by her servants, and two
winding-sheets stuck with flowers. [She] presents one to her
son, and the other to Julio

'Tis very welcome, this is a decent garment
Will never be out of fashion. I will kiss it.
All the flowers of the spring
Meet to perfume our burying;   115
These have but their growing prime,°
And man does flourish but his time.
Survey our progress from our birth:
We are set, we grow, we turn to earth.°

Soft music [off-stage]

Courts adieu, and all delights,   120

All bewitching appetites;
Sweetest breath, and clearest eye,
Like perfumes, go out and die;
And consequently this is done,°
As shadows wait upon the sun.   125
Vain the ambition of kings,
Who seek by trophies and dead things
To leave a living name behind,
And weave but nets to catch the wind.°
O you have wrought a miracle, and melted   130
A heart of adamant; you have comprised
In this dumb pageant a right excellent form
Of penitence.
CAPUCHIN   I am glad you so receive it.
ROMELIO This object does persuade me to forgive
The wrong she has done me, which I count the way   135
To be forgiven yonder; and this shroud°
Shows me how rankly we do smell of earth,
When we are in all our glory. [*To Leonora*] Will it please you
Enter that closet, where I shall confer
'Bout matters of most weighty consequence,   140
Before the duel?
        Exit Leonora
JULIO [*Wrapping himself in one of the winding-sheets*] Now I am
right in the bandoleer for th'gallows.°
What a scurvy fashion 'tis to hang one's coffin in a scarf!°
CAPUCHIN Why, this is well;   145
And now that I have made you fit for death,
And brought you even as low as is the grave,
I will raise you up again, speak comforts to you
Beyond your hopes, turn this intended duel
To a triumph.
ROMELIO   More divinity yet?   150
Good sir, do one thing first. There's in my closet
A prayer-book that is covered with gilt vellum;
Fetch it, and pray you certify my mother°
I'll presently come to her.
        [*Exit Capuchin to the closet; Romelio*] *locks him in*
                So, now you are safe.
JULIO What have you done?
ROMELIO   Why, I have locked them up   155

Into a turret of the castle, safe enough
For troubling us this four hours; an he please,
He may open up a casement, and whistle out to th'sea,
Like a boatswain; not any creature can hear him.
Wast not thou aweary of his preaching?   160
JULIO Yes. If he had had an hour-glass by him,
I would have wished he would have jogged it a little.
But your mother, your mother's locked in too.
ROMELIO So much the better;
I am rid of her howling at parting.   165
     [*Knocking off-stage*]
JULIO Hark, he knocks to be let out an he were mad.
ROMELIO Let him knock till his sandals fly in pieces.
JULIO Ha, what says he? Contarino living?
ROMELIO Ay, ay, he means he would have Contarino's living°
Bestowed upon his monastery; 'tis that   170
He only fishes for. So, 'tis break of day;
We shall be called to the combat presently.
JULIO I am sorry for one thing.
ROMELIO   What's that?
JULIO That I made not mine own ballad. I do fear
I shall be roguishly abused in metre,   175
If I miscarry. Well, if the young Capuchin
Do not talk o'th' flesh as fast now to your mother,
As he did to us o'th' spirit. If he do,
'Tis not the first time that the prison royal
Has been guilty of close committing.
ROMELIO   Now to th'combat.°   180
     [*Exeunt*]

[5.5]

     Enter Capuchin and Leonora above at a window
LEONORA Contarino living?
CAPUCHIN Yes, madam, he is living, and Ercole's second.
LEONORA Why has he locked us up thus?
CAPUCHIN   Some evil angel
Makes him deaf to his own safety. We are shut
Into a turret, the most desolate prison   5

Of all the castle; and his obstinacy,
Madness, or secret fate, has thus prevented
The saving of his life.
LEONORA   O the saving Contarino's!
His is worth nothing; for heaven's sake call louder.
CAPUCHIN To little purpose.
LEONORA   I will leap these battlements,   10
And may I be found dead time enough
To hinder the combat.
CAPUCHIN   O look upwards rather;
Their deliverance must come thence. To see how heaven
Can invert man's firmest purpose! His intent
Of murdering Contarino was a mean   15
To work his safety, and my coming hither
To save him is his ruin; wretches turn
The tide of their good fortune, and being drenched
In some presumptuous and hidden sins,
While they aspire to do themselves most right,   20
The devil that rules i'th' air hangs in their light.
LEONORA O they must not be lost thus; some good Christian
Come within our hearing! Ope the other casement
That looks into the city.
CAPUCHIN   Madam, I shall.
        Exeunt

[5.6]

The lists [are] set up. Enter the Marshal, Crispiano, and
Ariosto as judges; they sit. [Enter Sanitonella, a Herald and
Attendants]

MARSHAL Give the appellant his summons; do the like
To the defendant.
        Two tuckets° [are sounded] by several trumpets. Enter at one
        door, Ercole and Contarino, at the other, Romelio and Julio
Can any of you allege aught why the combat
Should not proceed?
COMBATANTS   Nothing.
ARIOSTO   Have the knights weighed
And measured their weapons?

MARSHAL   They have.   5
ARIOSTO Proceed then to the battle, and may heaven
    Determine the right.
HERALD *Soit la bataille, et victoire à ceux qui ont droit.°*
ROMELIO Stay, I do not well know whither I am going:
    'Twere needful therefore, though at the last gasp,   10
    To have some churchman's prayer. Run, I pray thee,
    To Castle Novo. This key will release
    A Capuchin and my mother, whom I shut
    Into a turret. Bid them make haste, and pray;
    I may be dead ere he comes.   15
        [*Exit an Attendant*]
    Now, *Victoire à ceux qui ont droit.*
ALL THE CHAMP° *Victoire à ceux qui ont droit.*
        The combat continued to a good length, when enters Leonora,
        and the Capuchin
LEONORA Hold, hold, for heaven's sake hold.
ARIOSTO What are these that interrupt the combat?
    Away to prison with them.
CAPUCHIN   We have been prisoners too long.   20
    O sir, what mean you? Contarino's living.
ERCOLE Living!
CAPUCHIN   Behold him living.
        [*Contarino reveals himself*]
ERCOLE You were but now my second; now I make you
    Myself for ever.
        [*They embrace*]
LEONORA   O, here's one between
    Claims to be nearer.
CONTARINO   And to you, dear lady,   25
    I have entirely vowed my life.
ROMELIO   If I do not
    Dream, I am happy too.
ARIOSTO   How insolently
    Has this high Court of Honour been abused!
        Enter Angiolella veiled, and Jolenta [dressed as a nun], her
        face coloured like a Moor, the two Surgeons, one of them like
        a Jew
    How now, who are these?
SECOND SURGEON A couple of strange fowl, and I the falconer   30
    That have sprung them. This is a white nun,°

Of the Order of St Clare; and this a black one,
You'll take my word for't.
    Discovers Jolenta
ARIOSTO   She's a black one indeed.
JOLENTA Like or dislike me, choose you whether.
  The down upon the raven's feather   35
  Is as gentle and as sleek
  As the mole on Venus' cheek.
  Hence vain show! I only care
  To preserve my soul most fair;
  Never mind the outward skin,   40
  But the jewel that's within;
  And though I want the crimson blood,°
  Angels boast my sisterhood.
  Which of us now judge you whiter:
  Her whose credit proves the lighter,°   45
  Or this black and ebon hue
  That, unstained, keeps fresh and true?
  For I proclaim't without control,
  There's no true beauty but i'th' soul.
ERCOLE O 'tis the fair Jolenta! To what purpose   50
  Are you thus eclipsed?
JOLENTA   Sir, I was running away
  From the rumour of the combat; I fled likewise
  From the untrue report my brother spread
  To his politic ends, that I was got with child.
LEONORA Cease here all further scrutiny; this paper   55
  Shall give unto the court each circumstance
  Of all these passages.
ARIOSTO No more. Attend the sentence of the court.
  Rareness and difficulty give estimation
  To all things are i'th' world. You have met both   60
  In these several passages; now it does remain
  That these so comical events be blasted
  With no severity of sentence. You, Romelio,
  Shall first deliver to that gentleman,
  Who stood your second, all those obligations   65
  Wherein he stands engaged to you, receiving
  Only the principal.
ROMELIO   I shall, my lord.
JULIO   I thank you.°

I have an humour now to go to sea
Against the pirates; and my only ambition
Is to have my ship furnished with a rare concert   70
Of music; and when I am pleased to be mad,
They shall play me *Orlando*.°
SANITONELLA You must lay wait for the fiddlers:
  They'll fly away from the press like watermen.°
ARIOSTO Next, you shall marry that nun.
ROMELIO   Most willingly.   75
ANGIOLELLA O sir, you have been unkind;
  But I do only wish that this my shame
  May warn all honest virgins not to seek
  The way to heaven, that is so wondrous steep,
  Through those vows they are too frail to keep.   80
ARIOSTO Contarino, and Romelio, and yourself,
  Shall for seven years maintain against the Turk
  Six galleys. Leonora, Jolenta,
  And Angiolella there, the beauteous nun,
  For their vows' breach unto the monastery,°   85
  Shall build a monastery. Lastly, the two surgeons,
  For concealing Contarino's recovery,
  Shall exercise their art at their own charge
  For a twelvemonth in the galleys. So we leave you,
  Wishing your future life may make good use   90
  Of these events, since that these passages,
  Which threatened ruin, built on rotten ground,
  Are with success beyond our wishes crowned.
     Exeunt

A CURE FOR A CUCKOLD

THE PERSONS OF THE PLAY

Compass, *a sailor who was thought lost at sea*
Urse, *Compass's wife*
Lessingham, *a young gentleman in love with Clare*
Bonvile, *a young gentleman married to Annabel*
Clare, *in love with Bonvile*
Annabel, *wife of Bonvile*
Franckford, *a rich merchant, and brother-in-law of Woodroff*
Nurse, *employed by Franckford*
Luce, *childless wife of Franckford*
Woodroff, *a justice of the peace, and father of Annabel*
Rochfield, *a younger son turned highwayman*
Rafe ⎫ *two boys*
Jack ⎭
Pettifog ⎫ *two lawyers*
Dodge ⎭
Raymond ⎫
Eustace ⎪
Lionel ⎬ *gallants at Annabel's wedding*
Grover ⎭
Counsellor
First Client
Second Client
Waiting-woman
Drawer
Servants
Sailor
Child

The Stationer to the Judicious Reader

Gentlemen

It was not long since I was only a book-reader, and not a bookseller, which quality, my former employment somewhat failing and I being unwilling to be idle, I have now lately taken on me. It hath been my fancy and delight, e'er since I knew anything, to converse with books; and the pleasure I have taken in those of this nature, viz. plays, hath 5
been so extraordinary that it hath been much to my cost, for I have been, as we term it, a gatherer of plays for some years, and I am confident I have more of several sorts than any man in England, bookseller or other. I can at any time show 700 in number, which is within a small matter all that were ever printed. Many of these I have 10
several times over, and intend, as I sell, to purchase more; all, or any of which, I shall be ready either to sell or lend to you upon reasonable considerations.

In order to the increasing of my store, I have now this term printed and published three, viz. this called *A Cure for a Cuckold*, and another 15
called *The Thracian Wonder*, and the third called *Gammer Gurton's Needle*.° Two of these three were never printed; the third, viz. *Gammer Gurton's Needle*, hath been formerly printed, but it is almost an hundred years since. As for this play, I need not speak anything in its commendation: the authors' names, Webster and Rowley,° are, 20
to knowing men, sufficient to declare its worth. Several persons remember the acting of it, and say that it then pleased generally well; and let me tell you, in my judgement it is an excellent old play. The expedient of curing a cuckold after the manner set down in this play hath been tried° to my knowledge, and therefore I may say *probatum* 25
est.° I should, I doubt, be too tedious, or else I would say somewhat in defence of this, and in commendation of plays in general. But I question not but you have read what abler pens than mine have writ in their vindication. Gentlemen, I hope you will so encourage me in my beginnings that I may be induced to proceed to do you service, 30
and that I may frequently have occasion in this nature to subscribe myself

Your Servant,
FRANCIS KIRKMAN°

A Cure for a Cuckold

1.1

[Music plays off-stage]. Enter Lessingham and Clare

LESSINGHAM This is a place of feasting and of joy,
And as in triumphs and ovations, here
Nothing save state and pleasure.

CLARE   'Tis confessed.

LESSINGHAM A day of mirth and solemn jubilee.

CLARE For such as can be merry.

LESSINGHAM   A happy nuptial,   5
Since a like pair of fortunes suitable,
Equality in birth, parity in years,
And in affection no way different,
Are this day sweetly coupled.

CLARE   'Tis a marriage.

LESSINGHAM True, lady, and a noble precedent,   10
Methinks, for us to follow. Why should these
Outstrip us in our loves, that have not yet
Outgone us in our time? If we thus lose
Our best and not-to-be-recovered hours,
Unprofitably spent, we shall be held   15
Mere truants in love's school.

CLARE   That's a study
In which I never shall ambition have
To become graduate.

LESSINGHAM   Lady, you are sad.
This jovial meeting puts me in a spirit
To be made such. We two are guests invited,   20
And meet by purpose, not by accident;
Where's then a place more opportunely fit,
In which we may solicit our own loves,
Than before this example?

CLARE   In a word,
I purpose not to marry.

LESSINGHAM   By your favour   25
(For as I ever to this present hour

Have studied your observance, so from henceforth°
I now will study plainness), I have loved you
Beyond myself, misspended for your sake
Many a fair hour, which might have been employed   30
To pleasure, or to profit; have neglected
Duty to them from whom my being came,
My parents; but my hopeful studies most.
I have stolen time from all my choice delights,
And robbed myself, thinking to enrich you.   35
Matches I have had offered—some have told me—
As fair as rich; I never thought them so,
And lost all these in hope to find out you.
Resolve me then for Christian charity.
Think you an answer of that frozen nature   40
Is a sufficient satisfaction for
So many more-than-needful services?

CLARE I have said, sir.

LESSINGHAM   Whence might this distaste arise?
Be at least so kind to perfect me in that.
Is it of some dislike lately conceived   45
Of this my person, which perhaps may grow
From calumny and scandal? If not that,
Some late receivèd melancholy in you;°
If neither, your perverse and peevish will
To which I most imply it.°   50

CLARE Be it what it can, or may be, thus it is,
And with this answer pray rest satisfied.
In all these travels, windings and indents,°
Paths, and by-paths which many have sought out,
There's but one only road, and that alone   55
To my fruition; which whoso finds out,°
'Tis like he may enjoy me; but that failing,
I ever am mine own.

LESSINGHAM   O name it, sweet.
I am already in a labyrinth
Until you guide me out.

CLARE   I'll to my chamber.   60
May you be pleased, unto your misspent time
To add but some few minutes. By my maid
You shall hear further from me.

LESSINGHAM   I'll attend you.

Exit Clare

What more can I desire than be resolved
Of such a long suspense? Here's now the period°   65
Of much expectation.

Enter Raymond, Eustace, Lionel and Grover, Gallants

RAYMOND What? You alone retired to privacy,
Of such a goodly confluence all prepared
To grace the present nuptials?

LESSINGHAM   I have heard some say
Men are ne'er less alone than when alone,   70
Such power hath meditation.

EUSTACE   O these choice beauties
That are this day assembled! But of all,
Fair mistress Clare, the bride excepted still,
She bears away the prize.

LIONEL   And worthily;
For, setting off her present melancholy,   75
She is without taxation.

GROVER   I conceive°
The cause of her so sudden discontent.

RAYMOND 'Tis far out of my way.

GROVER   I'll speak it then.
In all estates, professions, or degrees
In arts or sciences, there is a kind   80
Of emulation; likewise so in this.
There's a maid this day married, a choice beauty;
Now mistress Clare, a virgin of like age
And fortunes correspondent, apprehending
Time lost in her that's in another gained,   85
May upon this—for who knows women's thoughts?—
Grow into this deep sadness.

RAYMOND   Like enough.

LESSINGHAM You are pleasant, gentlemen, or else perhaps
Though I know many have pursued her love—

GROVER And you amongst the rest, with pardon, sir.   90
Yet she might cast some more peculiar eye°
On some that not respects her.

LESSINGHAM   That's my fear°
Which you now make your sport.

Enter Waiting-Woman [with a letter]

WOMAN [*aside, to Lessingham*]   A letter, sir.

LESSINGHAM From whom?
WOMAN   My mistress.
LESSINGHAM   She has kept her promise,
　And I will read it, though I in the same   95
　Know my own death included.
WOMAN   Fare you well, sir.
　　　Exit [*Woman*]
LESSINGHAM [*reads letter*] 'Prove all thy friends, find out the best
　　and nearest;°
　Kill for my sake that friend that loves thee dearest.'
　Her servant, nay her hand and character,
　All meeting in my ruin! Read again: 100
　'Prove all thy friends, find out the best and nearest;
　Kill for my sake that friend that loves thee dearest.'
　And what might that one be? 'Tis a strange difficulty,
　And it will ask much counsel.
　　　Exit Lessingham
RAYMOND   Lessingham
　Hath left us on the sudden.
EUSTACE   Sure the occasion   105
　Was of that letter sent him.
LIONEL   It may be
　It was some challenge.
GROVER   Challenge! Never dream it.
　Are such things sent by women?
RAYMOND   'Twere an heresy°
　To conceive but such a thought.
LIONEL   Tush, all the difference
　Begot this day must be at night decided   110
　Betwixt the bride and bridegroom. Here both come.
　　　Enter Woodroff, Annabel, Bonvile, Franckford, Luce, Nurse,
　　　[*and Servant*]
WOODROFF What did you call the gentleman we met
　But now in some distraction?
BONVILE   Lessingham,
　A most approved and noble friend of mine
　And one of our prime guests.
WOODROFF   He seemed to me   115
　Somewhat in mind distempered. What concern
　Those private humours our so public mirth
　In such a time of revels? Mistress Clare,

I miss her too. Why, gallants, have you suffered her°
Thus to be lost amongst you?
ANNABEL   Dinner done,   120
Unknown to any, she retired herself.
WOODROFF Sick of the maid perhaps, because she sees°
You, mistress bride, her school- and playfellow,
So suddenly turned wife.
FRANCKFORD   'Twas shrewdly guessed.
WOODROFF [to Servant] Go find her out.
      [Exit Servant]
                              Fie, gentlemen, within   125
The music plays unto the silent walls,
And no man there to grace it. When I was young,
At such a meeting I have so bestirred me,
Till I have made the pale green-sickness girls
Blush like the ruby, and drop pearls apace   130
Down from their ivory foreheads; in those days
I have cut capers thus high. Nay, in, gentlemen,
And single out the ladies.
RAYMOND   Well advised.
Nay, mistress bride, you shall along with us,
For without you all's nothing.
ANNABEL   Willingly,   135
With master bridegroom's leave.
BONVILE   O my best joy,
This day I am your servant.
      [Exeunt Raymond, Eustace, Lionel, Grover, Annabel, and
      Bonvile]
WOODROFF   True, this day;
She his her whole life after—so it should be:
Only this day a groom to do her service,
For which the full remainder of his age   140
He may write master. I have done it yet,
And so I hope still shall do. Sister Luce,
May I presume my brother Franckford can
Say as much, and truly?
LUCE   Sir, he may,
I freely give him leave.
WOODROFF   Observe that, brother: 145
She freely gives you leave. But who gives leave,
The master or the servant?

301

FRANCKFORD   You're pleasant,
  And it becomes you well, but this day most,
  That, having but one daughter, have bestowed her
  To your great hope and comfort.
WOODROFF   I have one—   150
  Would you could say so, sister; but your barrenness
  Hath given your husband freedom, if he please,
  To seek his pastime elsewhere.
LUCE   Well, well, brother,
  Though you may taunt me that have never yet
  Been blessed with issue, spare my husband, pray,   155
  For he may have a by-blow, or an heir°
  That you never heard of.
FRANCKFORD   O fie, wife, make not
  My fault too public.
LUCE   Yet himself keep within compass.°
FRANCKFORD If you love me, sweet—
LUCE   Nay, I have done.
WOODROFF   But if
  He have not, wench, I would he had; the hurt   160
  I wish you both. [*To Luce*] Prithee, thine ear a little.°
       [*They speak aside*]
NURSE [*to Franckford*] Your boy grows up, and 'tis a chopping° lad,
  a man even in the cradle.
FRANCKFORD [*whispers*] Softly, nurse.
NURSE [*whispers*] One of the forwardest infants: how it will crow and   165
  chirrup like a sparrow! I fear shortly it will breed teeth; you must
  provide him therefore a coral,° with a whistle and a chain.
FRANCKFORD He shall have anything.
NURSE He's now quite out of blankets.
       [*He gives her money*]
FRANCKFORD There's a piece;   170
  Provide him what he wants; only, good nurse,
  Prithee at this time be silent.
NURSE A charm to bind any nurse's tongue that's living.
WOODROFF [*coming forward with Luce*] Come, we are missed
  Among the younger fry; gravity oft-times°   175
  Becomes the sports of youth, especially
  At such solemnities; and it were sin
  Not in our age to show what we have been.
       Exeunt

[1.2]

Enter Lessingham sad, with a letter in his hand
LESSINGHAM 'Amicitia nihil dedit natura maius nec rarius',°
    So saith my author. If then powerful nature,°
    In all her bounties showered upon mankind,
    Found none more rare and precious than this one
    We call friendship, O to what a monster   5
    Would this transshape me, to be made that he°
    To violate such goodness! To kill any
    Had been a sad injunction, but a friend!
    Nay, of all friends the most approved! A task
    Hell till this day could never parallel;   10
    And yet this woman has a power of me
    Beyond all virtue—virtue! almost grace.
    What might her hidden purpose be in this?
    Unless she apprehend some fantasy
    That no such thing has being; and, as kindred   15
    And claims to crowns are worn out of the world,
    So the name friend? 'T may be 'twas her conceit.
    I have tried those that have professèd much
    For coin, nay, sometimes slighter courtesies,
    Yet found 'em cold enough; so perhaps she,   20
    Which makes her thus opinioned. If in the former
    And therefore better days 'twas held so rare,
    Who knows but in these last and worser times
    It may be now with justice banished th'earth?°
    I'm full of thoughts, and this my troubled breast   25
    Distempered with a thousand fantasies—
    Something I must resolve. I'll first make proof
    If such a thing there be; which having found,
    'Twixt love and friendship 'twill be a brave fight
    To prove in man which claims the greatest right.   30
    Enter Raymond, Eustace, Lionel, and Grover
RAYMOND What, Master Lessingham!
    You that were wont to be composed of mirth,
    All spirit and fire, alacrity itself,
    Like the lustre of a late bright-shining sun,
    Now wrapped in clouds and darkness!
LIONEL   Prithee be merry.   35

Thy dullness sads the half part of the house,
And deads the spirit which thou wast wont to quicken,
And, half spent, to give life to.

LESSINGHAM   Gentlemen,
Such as have cause for sport I shall wish ever
To make of it the present benefit°   40
While it exists. Content is still short-breathed.
When it was mine, I did so; if now yours,
I pray make your best use on't.

LIONEL   Riddles and paradoxes:
Come, come, some crotchet's come into thy pate,
And I will know the cause on't.

GROVER   So will I,   45
Or, I protest, ne'er leave thee.

LESSINGHAM   'Tis a business
Proper to myself; one that concerns
No second person.

GROVER   How's that? Not a friend?

LESSINGHAM Why, is there any such?

GROVER Do you question that? What do you take me for?   50

EUSTACE Ay, sir, or me? 'Tis many months ago
Since we betwixt us interchanged that name,
And of my part ne'er broken.

LIONEL   Troth, nor mine.

RAYMOND If you make question of a friend, I pray
Number not me the last in your account   55
That would be crowned in your opinion first.

LESSINGHAM You all speak nobly. But amongst you all
Can such a one be found?

RAYMOND   Not one amongst us,
But would be proud to wear the character
Of noble friendship. In the name of which,   60
And of all us here present, I entreat,
Expose to us the grief that troubles you.

LESSINGHAM I shall, and briefly: if ever gentleman
Sunk beneath scandal, or his reputation,
Never to be recovered, suffered, and   65
For want of one whom I may call a friend,
Then mine is now in danger.

RAYMOND   I'll redeem't
Though with my life's dear hazard.

EUSTACE   I pray, sir,
  Be to us open-breasted.

LESSINGHAM   Then 'tis thus:°
  There is to be performed a monomachy, 70
  Combat, or duel—time, place, and weapon
  Agreed betwixt us. Had it touched myself,
  And myself only, I had then been happy.
  But I by composition am engaged
  To bring with me my second, and he too, 75
  Not as the law of combat is—to stand
  Aloof and see fair play, bring off his friend—°
  But to engage his person; both must fight
  And either of them dangerous.

EUSTACE   Of all things°
  I do not like this fighting.

LESSINGHAM   Now gentlemen, 80
  Of this so great a courtesy I am
  At this instant merely destitute.

RAYMOND   The time?

LESSINGHAM By eight o'clock tomorrow.

RAYMOND   How unhappily
  Things may fall out. I am just at that hour,
  Upon some late conceivèd discontents,° 85
  To atone me to my father; otherwise,°
  Of all the rest you had commanded me
  Your second and your servant.

LIONEL   Pray, the place?

LESSINGHAM Calais sands.

LIONEL   It once was fatal to a friend of mine,°
  And a near kinsman, for which I vowed then, 90
  And deeply too, never to see that ground;
  But if it had been elsewhere, one of them
  Had before nine been worms' meat.

GROVER   What's the weapon?

LESSINGHAM Single sword.

GROVER   Of all that you could name°
  A thing I never practised. Had it been 95
  Rapier, or that and poniard, where men use
  Rather sleight than force, I had been then your man;
  Being young, I strained the sinews of my arm,
  Since then to me 'twas never serviceable.

EUSTACE In troth, sir, had it been a money-matter,   100
　　I could have stood your friend; but as for fighting
　　I was ever out at that.
LESSINGHAM   Well, farewell gentlemen.°
　　　　Exeunt [Raymond, Eustace, Lionel, and Grover]
　　But where's the friend in all this?
　　　　Enter Bonvile
　　　　　　　　　　　　Tush, she's wise,
　　And knows there's no such thing beneath the moon;
　　I now applaud her judgement.   105
BONVILE Why, how now, friend? This discontent, which now
　　Is so unseasoned, makes me question what°
　　I ne'er durst doubt before: your love to me.
　　Doth it proceed from envy of my bliss
　　Which this day crowns me with? Or have you been   110
　　A secret rival in my happiness,
　　And grieve to see me owner of those joys
　　Which you could wish your own?
LESSINGHAM   Banish such thoughts,
　　Or you shall wrong the truest faithful friendship
　　Man e'er could boast of. O mine honour, sir,   115
　　'Tis that which makes me wear this brow of sorrow;
　　Were that free from the power of calumny—
　　But pardon me that being now a-dying,
　　Which is so near to man, if part we cannot
　　With pleasant looks.
BONVILE   Do but speak the burden,°   120
　　And I protest to take it off from you°
　　And lay it on myself.
LESSINGHAM   'Twere a request
　　Impudence without blushing could not ask;
　　It bears with it such injury.
BONVILE   Yet must I know't.
LESSINGHAM Receive it then. But I entreat you, sir,   125
　　Not to imagine that I apprehend
　　A thought to further my intent by you:°
　　From you 'tis least suspected. 'Twas my fortune°
　　To entertain a quarrel with a gentleman,
　　The field betwixt us challenged, place and time,   130
　　And these to be performed not without seconds.
　　I have relied on many seeming friends,

But cannot bless my memory with one
Dares venture in my quarrel.

BONVILE   Is this all?

LESSINGHAM It is enough to make all temperature°   135
Convert to fury. Sir, my reputation,
The life and soul of honour, is at stake,
In danger to be lost, the word of coward
Still printed in the name of Lessingham.°

BONVILE Not while there is a Bonvile. May I live poor,   140
And die despised, not having one sad friend
To wait upon my hearse, if I survive
The ruin of that honour. Sir, the time?

LESSINGHAM Above all spare me that, for that once known,
You'll cancel this your promise and unsay   145
Your friendly proffer. Neither can I blame you;
Had you confirmed it with a thousand oaths,
The heavens would look with mercy, not with justice
On your offence, should you infringe 'em all.
Soon after sunrise, upon Calais sands,   150
Tomorrow we should meet. Now to defer
Time one half hour, I should but forfeit all.
But, sir, of all men living, this alas
Concerns you least: for shall I be the man
To rob you of this night's felicity,   155
And make your bride a widow, her soft bed
No witness of those joys this night expects?

BONVILE I still prefer my friend before my pleasure,
Which is not lost forever, but adjourned
For more mature employment.

LESSINGHAM   Will you go then?°   160

BONVILE I am resolved I will.

LESSINGHAM   And instantly?

BONVILE With all the speed celerity can make.

LESSINGHAM You do not weigh those inconveniences
This action meets with. Your departure hence
Will breed a strange distraction in your friends,   165
Distrust of love in your fair virtuous bride,
Whose eyes perhaps may never more be blessed
With your dear sight, since you may meet a grave,
And that not amongst your noble ancestors,
But amongst strangers, almost enemies.   170

BONVILE This were enough to shake a weak resolve;
It moves not me. Take horse as secretly
As you well may; my groom shall make mine ready
With all speed possible, unknown to any.
        Enter Annabel
LESSINGHAM But, sir, the bride.   175
ANNABEL Did you not see the key that's to unlock
My carcanet and bracelets? Now in troth,°
I am afraid 'tis lost.
BONVILE   No, sweet, I ha't.
I found it lie at random in your chamber,°
And knowing you would miss it, laid it by.   180
'Tis safe, I warrant you.
ANNABEL   Then my fear's past;
But till you give it back, my neck and arms
Are still your prisoners.
BONVILE   But you shall find°
They have a gentle gaoler.
ANNABEL   So I hope.
Within you're much enquired of.   185
BONVILE Sweet, I follow.
        [*Exit Annabel*]
   [*To Lessingham*]   Dover?
LESSINGHAM   Yes, that's the place.
BONVILE If you be there before me, hire a bark;
I shall not fail to meet you.
        [*Exit Bonvile*]
LESSINGHAM   Was ever known
A man so miserably blessed as I?
I have no sooner found the greatest good   190
Man in this pilgrimage of life can meet,
But I must make the womb where 'twas conceived
The tomb to bury it, and the first hour it lives
The last it must breathe. Yet there's a fate
That sways and governs above woman's hate.   195
        Exit

[2.1]

Enter Rochfield, a young gentleman

ROCHFIELD   A younger brother? 'Tis a poor calling:
   Though not unlawful, very hard to live on.
   The elder fool inherits all the lands,
   And we that follow, legacies of wit,
   And get 'em when we can too. Why should law,   5
   If we be lawful and legitimate,
   Leave us without an equal dividend?
   Or why compels it not our fathers else
   To cease from getting, when they want to give?°
   No, sure, our mothers will ne'er agree to that: 10
   They love to groan, although the gallows echo
   And groan together for us. From the first
   We travel forth, t'other's our journey's end.°
   I must forward; to beg is out of my way,
   And borrowing is out of date. The old road,   15
   The old highway 't must be, and I am in't.
   The place will serve for a young beginner, for
   This is the first day I set ope shop.
   Success then, sweet Laverna; I have heard°
   That thieves adore thee for a deity.   20
   I would not purchase by thee but to eat,
   And 'tis too churlish to deny me meat.
     Enter Annabel and a Servant
   Soft, here may be a booty.
     [*He hides*]

ANNABEL   Horsed, say'st thou?
SERVANT   Yes, mistress, with Lessingham.
ANNABEL   Alack, I know not what to doubt or fear.   25
   I know not well whether't be well or ill,
   But sure it is no custom for the groom
   To leave his bride upon the nuptial day.
   I am so young and ignorant a scholar—
   Yes, and it proves so: I talk away perhaps   30
   That might be yet recovered. Prithee run!°
   The forepath may advantage thee to meet 'em;°
   Or the ferry which is not two miles before

May trouble 'em until thou com'st in ken;
And if thou dost, prithee enforce thy voice   35
To overtake thine eyes, cry out, and crave
For me but one word 'fore his departure.
I will not stay him, say, beyond his pleasure,
Nor rudely ask the cause, if he be willing
To keep it from me. Charge him by all the love—   40
But I stay thee too long: run, run!
SERVANT If I had wings, I would spread 'em now, mistress.
    Exit [Servant]
ANNABEL I'll make the best speed after that I can;
Yet I am not well acquainted with the path.
My fears, I fear me, will misguide me too.   45
    Exit [Annabel]
ROCHFIELD [*coming forward*] There's good movables, I perceive,
    what'er°
The ready coin be—
Whoever owns her, she's mine now. The next ground
Has a most pregnant hollow for the purpose.
    Exit [Rochfield]

[2.2]

    *Enter Servant running over [the stage; exits]. Enter Annabel;
    after her Rochfield*
ANNABEL I'm at a doubt already where I am.
ROCHFIELD I'll help you, mistress. Well overtaken!
ANNABEL Defend me, goodness! What are you?
ROCHFIELD   A man.
ANNABEL An honest man, I hope.
ROCHFIELD In some degrees hot, not altogether cold   5
So far as rank poison, yet dangerous°
As I may be 'dressed: I am an honest thief.°
ANNABEL 'Honest' and 'thief' hold small affinity.
I never heard they were akin before;
Pray heaven I find it now.
ROCHFIELD   I tell you my name.   10
ANNABEL Then, honest thief, (since you have taught me so—
For I'll enquire no other) use me honestly.

ROCHFIELD Thus then I'll use you: first then, to prove me honest,
    I will not violate your chastity—
    That's no part yet of my profession— 15
    Be you wife or virgin.
ANNABEL   I am both, sir.
ROCHFIELD This then, it seems, should be your wedding-day,
    And these the hours of interim to keep you
    In that double state. Come then, I'll be brief,°
    For I'll not hinder your desirèd Hymen.° 20
    You have about you some superfluous toys,
    Which my lank hungry pockets would contrive
    With much more profit, and more privacy.
    You have an idle chain, which keeps your neck
    A prisoner; a manacle, I take it, 25
    About your wrist too. If these prove emblems
    Of the combinèd hemp to halter mine,°
    The fates take their pleasure! These are set down
    To be your ransom, and there the thief is proved.
ANNABEL I will confess both, and the last forget.° 30
    You shall be only honest in this deed.
    Pray you take it. I entreat you to it,
    And then you steal 'em not.
ROCHFIELD You may deliver 'em.
ANNABEL   Indeed I cannot.
    If you observe, sir, they are both locked about me, 35
    And the key I have not. Happily you are furnished
    With some instrument that may unloose 'em.
ROCHFIELD No, in troth, lady, I am but a freshman.
    I never read further than this book you see,
        [*Draws his sword*]
    And this very day is my beginning too. 40
    These picking laws I am to study yet.°
ANNABEL O, do not show me that, sir: 'tis too frightful.
    Good, hurt me not, for I do yield 'em freely.
    Use but your hands. Perhaps their strength will serve
    To tear 'em from me without much detriment: 45
    Somewhat I will endure.
        [*Rochfield sheathes his sword*]
ROCHFIELD   Well, sweet lady,
    You're the best patient for a young physician
    That I think ere was practised on. I'll use you

As gently as I can, as I'm an honest thief.
    [Tries to slip off her bracelet]
No? wilt not do? Do I hurt you, lady?

ANNABEL   Not much, sir.   50

ROCHFIELD I'd be loath at all; I cannot do't.
    She draws his sword

ANNABEL Nay then you shall not, sir. You a thief,
And guard yourself no better! No further read,
Yet out in your own book? A bad clerk, are you not?

ROCHFIELD Ay, by St Nicholas, lady, sweet lady.°   55

ANNABEL Sir, I have now a masculine vigour,
And will redeem myself with purchase, too.
What money have you?

ROCHFIELD Not a cross, by this foolish hand of mine.

ANNABEL No money. 'Twere pity then to take this from thee.   60
I know thou'lt use me ne'er the worse for this.
    [Returns his sword]
Take it again: I know not how to use it.
A frown had taken't from me, which thou hadst not.
And now hear and believe me,
    [She kneels]

                      on my knees
I make the protestation: forbear   65
To take what violence and danger must
Dissolve, if I forgo 'em now. I do assure°
You would not strike my head off for my chain,
Nor my hand for this. How to deliver 'em
Otherwise I know not. Accompany   70
Me back unto my house; 'tis not far off.
By all the vows which this day I have tied
Unto my wedded husband, the honour
Yet equal with my cradle purity°
—If you will tax me—to the hoped joys,°   75
The blessings of the bed, posterity,
Or what aught else by woman may be pledged,
I will deliver you in ready coin
The full and dear'st esteem of what you crave.

ROCHFIELD Ha, ready money is the prize I look for;   80
It walks without suspicion anywhere,
When chains and jewels may be stayed and called
Before the constable. But—

ANNABEL [*rising*]   But? Can you doubt?
  You saw I gave you my advantage up.
  Did you e'er think a woman to be true?   85
ROCHFIELD Thought's free. I have heard of some few, lady,
  Very few indeed.
ANNABEL   Will you add one more to your belief?
ROCHFIELD They were fewer than the articles of my belief;°
  Therefore I have room for you, and will believe you.
  Stay; you'll ransom your jewels with ready coin?   90
  So may you do, and then discover me.
ANNABEL Shall I reiterate the vows I made
  To this injunction, or new ones coin?
ROCHFIELD Neither, I'll trust you. If you do destroy
  A thief that never yet did robbery,   95
  Then farewell I, and mercy fall upon me.
  I knew one once fifteen years courtier-old,
  And he was buried ere he took a bribe.°
  It may be my case in the worser way.
  Come, you know your path back?
ANNABEL   Yes, I shall guide you.   100
ROCHFIELD Your arm; I'll lead with greater dread than will,
  Nor do you fear, though in thief's handling still.°
    Exeunt

[2.3]

Enter two boys, [Rafe and Jack, who holds] a child in his
arms

RAFE I say 'twas fair play.
JACK To snatch up stakes!° I say you should not say so, if the child
  were out of mine arms.
RAFE Ay, then thou'dst lay about like a man; but the child will not
  be out of thine arms this five years, and then thou hast a   5
  prenticeship° to serve to a boy afterwards.
    Enter Compass
JACK So, sir! You know you have the advantage of me.
RAFE I'm sure you have the odds of me: you are two to one. But soft,
  Jack, who comes here? If a point° will make us friends, we'll not
  fall out.   10

JACK O the pity, 'tis gaffer Compass! They said he was dead three years ago.

RAFE Did not he dance the hobby-horse in Hackney morris° once?

JACK Yes, yes, at Green-goose fair;° as honest and as poor a man—

COMPASS Blackwall, sweet Blackwall,° do I see thy white cheeks again? I have brought some brine from sea for thee; tears that might be tied in a true-love knot, for they're fresh salt indeed.° O beautiful Blackwall! If Urse, my wife, be living to this day, though she die tomorrow, sweet fates!

JACK Alas, let's put him out of his dumps, for pity sake.—Welcome home, gaffer Compass, welcome home, gaffer.

COMPASS My pretty youths, I thank you. [*To Jack*] Honest Jack! what a little man art thou grown since I saw thee! Thou hast got a child since, methinks.

JACK I am fain° to keep it, you see, whosoever got it, gaffer; it may be another man's case° as well as mine.

COMPASS Say'st true, Jack; and whose pretty knave is it?

JACK One that I mean to make a younger brother, if he live to't, gaffer. But I can tell you news: you have a brave boy of your own wife's; O, 'tis a shoat to this pig.

COMPASS Have I, Jack? I'll owe thee a dozen of points for this news.

JACK O, 'tis a chopping boy! It cannot choose, you know, gaffer, it was so long a-breeding.

COMPASS How long, Jack?

JACK You know 'tis four year ago since you went to sea, and your child is but a quarter old yet.

COMPASS What plaguy° boys are bred nowadays.

RAFE Pray gaffer, how long may a child be breeding before 'tis born?

COMPASS That is as things are and prove, child. The soil has a great hand in't too, the horizon, and the clime. These things you'll understand, when you go to sea. In some parts of London hard by, you shall have a bride married today, and brought to bed within a month after; sometimes within three weeks, a fortnight.

RAFE O horrible!

COMPASS True as I tell you, lads; in another place you shall have a couple of drones, do what they can—shift lodgings, beds, bedfellows—yet not a child in ten years.

JACK O pitiful!

COMPASS Now it varies again by that time you come to Wapping, Radcliff, Limehouse;° and here with us at Blackwall, our children come uncertainly, as the wind serves. Sometimes here we are supposed to be away three or four year together; 'tis nothing so: we are at home and gone again, when nobody knows on't. If you'll believe me, I have been at Surat° as this day; I have taken the long-boat—a fair gale with me—been here abed with my wife by twelve o'clock at night, up and gone again i'th' morning and no man the wiser, if you'll believe me.

JACK Yes, yes, gaffer, I have thought so many times: that you or somebody else, have been at home. I lie at next wall,° and I have heard a noise in your chamber all night long.

COMPASS Right, why, that was I, yet thou never saw'st me.

JACK No indeed, gaffer.

COMPASS No, I warrant thee, I was a thousand leagues off ere thou wert up. But, Jack, I have been loath to ask all this while for discomforting myself: how does my wife? is she living?

JACK O never better, gaffer, never so lusty;° and truly, she wears better clothes than she was wont in your days, especially on holidays: fair gowns, brave petticoats, and fine smocks, they say that have seen 'em; and some of the neighbours reports that they were taken up° at London.

COMPASS Like enough: they must be paid for, Jack.

JACK And good reason, gaffer.

COMPASS Well, Jack, thou shalt have the honour on't; go tell my wife the joyful tidings of my return.

JACK That I will, for she heard you were dead long ago.

Exit Jack

RAFE Nay, sir, I'll be as forward as you, by your leave.

Exit Rafe

COMPASS Well, wife, if I be one of the livery,° I thank thee. The horners° are a great company: there may be an alderman amongst us one day; 'tis but changing our copy,° and then we are no more to be called by our old brotherhood.

Enter Compass's wife Urse

URSE O my sweet Compass, art thou come again?

COMPASS O Urse, give me leave to shed. The fountains of love will have their course. Though I cannot sing at first sight,° yet I can cry before I see. I am new-come into the world, and children cry before they laugh,° a fair while.

URSE And so thou art, sweet Compass, new-born indeed,
For rumour laid thee out for dead long since.
I never thought to see this face again.
I heard thou wert dived to th'bottom of the sea,

And taken up a lodging in the sands,   90
Never to come to Blackwall again.

COMPASS I was going indeed, wife, but I turned back. I heard an ill
report of my neighbours, sharks and swordfishes, and the like,
whose companies I did not like. Come kiss my tears now, sweet
Urse, sorrow begins to ebb.   95

URSE A thousand times welcome home, sweet Compass.

COMPASS An ocean of thanks, and that will hold 'em. And Urse, how
goes all at home? Or cannot all go° yet? Lank° still? Wilt never be
full sea at our wharf?°

URSE Alas, husband.   100

COMPASS A lass or a lad, wench? I should be glad of both. I did look
for a pair of Compasses before this day.

URSE And you from home?

COMPASS I from home? Why, though I be from home, and other of
our neighbours from home, it is not fit all should be from home,   105
so the town might be left desolate, and our neighbours of Bow
might come further from the Hams,° and inhabit here.

URSE I'm glad you're merry, sweet husband.

COMPASS Merry? nay, I'll be merrier yet. Why should I be sorry? I
hope my boy's well, is he not? I looked for another by this time.   110

URSE What boy, husband?

COMPASS What boy? Why, the boy I got when I came home in the
cock-boat one night about a year ago! You have not forgotten, I
hope? I think I left behind for a boy, and a boy I must be answered.
I'm sure I was not drunk; it could be no girl.   115

URSE Nay then, I do perceive my fault is known. Dear man, your
pardon.

COMPASS Pardon? Why, thou hast not made away my boy, hast
thou? I'll hang thee, if there were ne'er a whore in London more,°
if thou hast hurt but his little toe.   120

URSE Your long absence, with rumour of your death—
After long battery, I was surprised.°

COMPASS Surprised? I cannot blame thee. Blackwall, if it were
double black-walled, can't hold out always, no more than Limehouse, or Shadwell,° or the strongest suburbs about London; and   125
when it comes to that, woe be to the City, too!

URSE Pursued by gifts and promises I yielded.
Consider husband, I am a woman,
Neither the first nor last of such offenders.
'Tis true, I have a child.   130

COMPASS Ha, you? And what shall I have then, I pray? Will not you
labour for me as I shall do for you? Because I was out o'th' way
when 'twas gotten, shall I lose my share? There's better law
amongst the players° yet, for a fellow shall have his share, though
he do not play that day. If you look for any part of my four years'   135
wages, I will have half the boy.

URSE If you can forgive me, I shall be joyed at it.

COMPASS Forgive thee? For what? For doing me a pleasure? And
what is he that would seem to father my child?

URSE A man, sir, whom in better courtesies   140
We have been beholding to:
The merchant, Master Franckford.

COMPASS I'll acknowledge no other courtesies. For this I am beholding to him, and I would requite it if his wife were young enough.
Though he be one of our merchants at sea, he shall give me leave   145
to be owner at home.° And where's my boy? Shall I see him?

URSE He's nursed at Bethnal Green: 'tis now too late.
Tomorrow I'll bring you to it, if you please.

COMPASS I would thou couldst bring me another by tomorrow.
Come, we'll eat and to bed; and if a fair gale come,   150
We'll hoist sheets and set forwards.°
Let fainting fools lie sick upon their scorns;
I'll teach a cuckold how to hide his horns.
        Exeunt

[2.4]

Enter Woodroff, Franckford, Raymond, Eustace, Grover,
Lionel, Clare, Luce

WOODROFF This wants a precedent: that a bridegroom
Should so discreet and decently observe
His forms, postures, all customary rites
Belonging to the table, and then hide himself
From his expected wages in the bed.   5

FRANCKFORD Let this be forgotten too, that it remain not
A first example.

RAYMOND [*aside to Eustace, Grover, and Lionel*]
            Keep it amongst us,
Lest it beget too much unfruitful sorrow.

Most likely 'tis that love to Lessingham
Hath fastened on him we all denied.   10
EUSTACE [*aside*] 'Tis more certain than likely. I know 'tis so.
GROVER [*aside*] Conceal, then. The event may be well enough.
WOODROFF The bride my daughter, she's hidden too;
  This last hour she hath not been seen with us.
RAYMOND Perhaps they are together.   15
EUSTACE And then we make too strict an inquisition.
  Under correction of fair modesty,
  Should they be stol'n away to bed together,
  What would you say to that?
WOODROFF   I would say, speed 'em well;
  And if no worse news comes, I'll never weep for't.   20
        Enter Nurse
  How now, hast thou any tidings?
NURSE Yes forsooth, I have tidings.
WOODROFF Of any one that's lost?
NURSE Of one that's found again, forsooth.
WOODROFF O, he was lost, it seems then?   25
FRANCKFORD This tidings comes to me, I guess, sir.
NURSE Yes, truly does it, sir.
        [*They confer apart*]
RAYMOND Ay, has old lads work for young nurses?
EUSTACE Yes, when they groan towards their second infancy.
CLARE [*aside*] I fear myself most guilty for the absence   30
  Of the bridegroom. What our wills will do
  With over-rash and headlong peevishness
  To bring our calm discretions to repentance!
  Lessingham's mistaken, quite out o'th' way
  Of my purpose too.   35
FRANCKFORD [*coming forward with Nurse*] Returned?°
NURSE And all discovered.
FRANCKFORD A fool! Rid him further off. Let him not
  Come near the child.
NURSE Nor see't, if it be your charge.   40
FRANCKFORD It is, and strictly.
NURSE Tomorrow morning, as I hear, he purposeth to come to
  Bethnal Green, his wife with him.
FRANCKFORD He shall be met there; yet if he forestall
  My coming, keep the child safe.   45
NURSE If he be the earlier up, he shall arrive at the proverb.°

Exit Nurse. Enter Rochfield and Annabel

WOODROFF So, so, there's some good luck yet: the bride's in sight
    again.

ANNABEL Father and gentlemen all, beseech you
    Entreat this gentleman with all courtesy.   50
    He is a loving kinsman of my Bonvile's,
    That kindly came to gratulate our wedding.°
    But, as the day falls out, you see alone
    I personate both groom and bride;°
    Only your help to make this welcome better.   55

WOODROFF Most dearly.

RAYMOND   To all, assure you, sir.

WOODROFF But where's the bridegroom, girl?
    We are all at a non-plus here, at a stand, quite out.°
    The music ceased, and dancing surbated,
    Not a light heel amongst us; my cousin Clare too,   60
    As cloudy here as on a washing day.

CLARE It is because you will not dance with me;
    I should then shake it off.

ANNABEL   'Tis I have cause
    To be the sad one now, if any be;
    But I have questioned with my meditations,   65
    And they have rendered well and comfortably°
    To the worst fear I found. Suppose this day
    He had long since appointed to his foe
    To meet, and fetch a reputation from him°
    —Which is the dearest jewel unto man.   70
    Say he do fight. I know his goodness such
    That all those powers that love it are his guard,
    And ill cannot betide him.

WOODROFF   Prithee peace.
    Thou'lt make us all cowards to hear a woman
    Instruct so valiantly. Come, the music!   75
        [*Music starts off-stage*]
    I'll dance myself rather than thus put down.°
    What, I am rife a little yet.

ANNABEL   Only this gentleman,°
    Pray you, be free in welcome to. I tell you°
    I was in a fear when first I saw him.

ROCHFIELD [*aside*] Ha! She'll tell.

ANNABEL   I had quite lost my way   80

In my first amazement, but he so fairly came°
To my recovery in his kind conduct,°
Gave me such loving comforts to my fears
('Twas he instructed me in what I spake)
And many better than I have told you yet;°   85
You shall hear more anon.

ROCHFIELD [*aside*]   So, she will out with't.

ANNABEL [*to Rochfield*] I must, I see, supply both places still;°
Come, when I have seen you back to your pleasure,
I will return to you, sir; we must discourse
More of my Bonvile yet.

ALL   A noble bride, 'faith.   90

CLARE [*aside*] You have your wishes, and you may be merry;
Mine have overgone me.

            Exeunt [Woodroff, Franckford, Raymond, Eustace, Lionel,
            Grover, Clare, Luce, Annabel. Rochfield remains]

ROCHFIELD It is the trembling'st trade to be a thief:
He'd need have all the world bound to the peace,
Besides the bushes, and the vanes of houses;   95
Everything that moves he goes in fear of's life on.
A fur-gowned cat, an meet her in the night,
She stares with a constable's eye upon him;
And every dog a watchman; a black cow
And a calf with a white face after her   100
Shows like a surly justice and his clerk;
And if the baby go but to the bag,
'Tis ink and paper for a *mittimus.*°
Sure I shall never thrive on't, and it may be
I shall need take no care. I may be now   105
At my journey's end, or but the gaol's distance.
And so to the t'other place. I trust a woman°
With a secret worth a hanging—is that well?
I could find in my heart to run away yet.
And that were base too: to run from a woman.   110
I can lay claim to nothing but her vows,
And they shall strengthen me.
            Enter Annabel

ANNABEL   See, sir, my promise:
There's twenty pieces, the full value, I vow,
Of what they cost.

ROCHFIELD   Lady, do not trap me

Like a sumpter horse, and then spur-gall me till   115
I break my wind. If the constable be at the door,°
Let his fair staff appear; perhaps I may
Corrupt him with this gold.
ANNABEL Nay then, if you mistrust me: father, gentlemen,
Master Raymond, Eustace!
    Enter all [i.e. Woodroff, Franckford, Clare, Luce, Raymond,
    Eustace, Lionel, Grover] as before, and a Sailor
WOODROFF   How now, what's the matter, girl?   120
ANNABEL For shame! Will you bid your kinsman welcome?
No one but I will lay a hand on him?°
Leave him alone, and all a-revelling?
WOODROFF O, is that it? Welcome, welcome heartily!
I thought the bridegroom had been returned.   125
But I have news, Annabel: this fellow brought it.
    [*Greets Rochfield*]
Welcome, sir. Why, you tremble methinks, sir.
ANNABEL Some agony of anger 'tis, believe it;
His entertainment is so cold and feeble.
RAYMOND Pray be cheered, sir.   130
ROCHFIELD I'm wondrous well, sir; 'twas the gentleman's mistake.
WOODROFF 'Twas my hand shook belike. Then you must pardon
Age; I was stiffer once. But as I was saying,°
I should by promise see the sea tomorrow:
'Tis meant for physic. As low as Leigh or Margate.°   135
I have a vessel riding forth, gentlemen:
'Tis called the God-speed too. Though I say't, a brave one,
Well and richly fraughted; and I can tell you
She carries a letter of mart in her mouth, too,°
And twenty roaring boys on both sides on her,   140
Starboard and larboard.°
What say you now to make you all adventurers?
You shall have fair dealing, that I'll promise you.
RAYMOND A very good motion, sir. I begin:
There's my ten pieces.
EUSTACE   I second 'em with these.   145
GROVER My ten in the third place.
ROCHFIELD And sir, if you refuse not a proffered love,
Take my ten pieces with you too.
WOODROFF   Yours above all the rest, sir.
ANNABEL Then make 'em above: venture ten more.°

ROCHFIELD Alas lady, 'tis a younger brother's portion,   150
  And all in one bottom.

ANNABEL   At my encouragement, sir.
  Your credit, if you want, sir, shall not sit down
  Under that sum returned.

ROCHFIELD   With all my heart, lady. There, sir.
  [*aside*] So, she has fished for her gold back, and caught it;
  I am no thief now.

WOODROFF   I shall make here a pretty assurance.   155

ROCHFIELD Sir, I shall have a suit to you.

WOODROFF You are likely to obtain it then, sir.

ROCHFIELD That I may keep you company to sea,
  And attend you back; I am a little travelled.

WOODROFF And heartily thank you too, sir.

ANNABEL   Why, that's well said.   160
  Pray you be merry. Though your kinsman be absent,
  I am here, the worst part of him. Yet that shall serve
  To give you welcome. Tomorrow may show you
  What this night will not; and be full assured,
  Unless your twenty pieces be ill lent,   165
  Nothing shall give you cause of discontent.
  There's ten more, sir.

ROCHFIELD [*aside*] Why should I fear? Foutre on't.
  I'll be merry now spite of the hangman.
      Exeunt

3.1

Enter Lessingham and Bonvile

BONVILE We are first i'th' field. I think your enemy
    Is stayed at Dover, or some other port;
    We hear not of his landing.

LESSINGHAM   I am confident
    He is come over.

BONVILE   You look, methinks, fresh-coloured.

LESSINGHAM Like a red morning, friend, that still foretells   5
    A stormy day to follow. But methinks,
    Now I observe your face, that you look pale:
    There's death in't already.

BONVILE   I could chide your error.
    Do you take me for a coward? A coward
    Is not his own friend, much less can he be   10
    Another man's. Know, sir, I am come hither
    To instruct you by my generous example
    To kill your enemy, whose name as yet
    I never questioned.

LESSINGHAM   Nor dare I name him yet,
    For disheartening you.

BONVILE   I do begin to doubt   15
    The goodness of your quarrel.

LESSINGHAM   Now you have't.
    For I protest that I must fight with one
    From whom, in the whole course of our acquaintance,
    I never did receive the least injury.

BONVILE It may be the forgetful wine begot°   20
    Some sudden blow, and thereupon this challenge.
    Howe'er, you are engaged; and for my part,
    I will not take your course, my unlucky friend,
    To say your conscience grows pale and heartless,
    Maintaining a bad course. Fight as lawyers plead,   25
    Who gain the best of reputation
    When they can fetch a bad cause smoothly off:°
    You are in, and must through.

LESSINGHAM   O my friend,
    The noblest ever man had! When my fate

Threw me upon this business, I made trial   30
Of divers had professed to me much love,
And found their friendship, like the effects that kept
Our company together, wine and riot,
Giddy and sinking. I had found 'em oft
Brave seconds at pluralities of healths,°   35
But when it came to th'proof, my gentlemen
Appeared to me as promising and failing
As cozening lotteries. But then I found
This jewel worth a thousand counterfeits.
I did but name my engagement, and you flew   40
Unto my succour with that cheerfulness,
As a great general hastes to a battle,
When that the chief of the adverse part
Is a man glorious of ample fame.°
You left your bridal bed to find your death bed,   45
And herein you most nobly expressed
That the affection 'tween two loyal friends
Is far beyond the love of man to woman,
And is more near allied to eternity.
What better friend's part could be showed i'th' world?   50
It transcends all! My father gave me life,
But you stand by my honour when 'tis falling,
And nobly underpropped it with your sword.
But now you have done me all this service,
How, how shall I requite this? How return   55
My grateful recompence for all this love?
For it am I come hither with full purpose
To kill you.
BONVILE   Ha?
LESSINGHAM   Yes, I have no opposite i'th' world
  But yourself. There, read the warrant for your death.
        [*Hands him Clare's letter*]
BONVILE 'Tis a woman's hand.
LESSINGHAM   And 'tis a bad hand too.   60
  The most of 'em speak fair, write foul, mean worse.
BONVILE Kill me! Away, you jest!
LESSINGHAM Such jest as your sharp-witted gallants use
  To utter, and lose their friends. Read there how I
  Am fettered in a woman's proud command.   65
  I do love madly, and must do madly.

Deadliest hellebore, or vomit of a toad
Is qualified poison to the malice of a woman.

BONVILE 'And kill that friend'? strange!

LESSINGHAM   You may see, sir,
Although the tenure by which land was held   70
In villeinage be quite extinct in England,°
Yet you have women there at this day living
Make a number of slaves.

BONVILE   'And kill that friend'? She mocks you,
Upon my life, she does equivocate.
Her meaning is you cherish in your breast   75
Either self-love, or pride, as your best friend,
And she wishes you'd kill that.

LESSINGHAM   Sure her command
Is more bloody, for she loathes me, and has put,
As she imagines, this impossible task,
For ever to be quit and free from me.   80
But such is the violence of my affection
That I must undergo it. Draw your sword,
And guard yourself. Though I fight in fury,
I shall kill you in cold blood, for I protest
'Tis done in heart-sorrow.

BONVILE   I'll not fight with you,   85
For I have much advantage. The truth is,
I wear a privy coat.°

LESSINGHAM Prithee put it off then, if thou be'st manly.

BONVILE The defence I mean is the justice of my cause
That would guard me and fly to thy destruction.   90
What confidence thou wearest in a bad cause!
I am likely to kill thee if I fight,
And then you fail to effect your mistress' bidding,
Or to enjoy the fruit of 't.
I have ever wished thy happiness, and vow   95
I now so much affect it in compassion
Of my friend's sorrow—make thy way to it.
        [Offers Lessingham his sword]

LESSINGHAM That were a cruel murder.

BONVILE Believe 't 'tis ne'er intended otherwise,
When 'tis a woman's bidding.   100

LESSINGHAM O the necessity of my fate!

BONVILE You shed tears.

LESSINGHAM [*draws*]   And yet must on in my cruel purpose.
A judge methinks looks loveliest when he weeps,
Pronouncing of death's sentence. How I stagger
In my resolve! Guard thee, for I came hither   105
To do, and not to suffer.
      [*Bonvile keeps his sword down*]
                          Wilt not yet
Be persuaded to defend thee? Turn the point,
Advance it from the ground above thy head,
And let it underprop thee otherwise
In a bold resistance.
BONVILE   Stay! Thy injunction was   110
Thou shouldst kill thy friend.
LESSINGHAM   It was.
BONVILE   Observe me:
He wrongs me most ought to offend me least;
And they that study man say of a friend,
There's nothing in the world that's harder found,
Nor sooner lost. Thou cam'st to kill thy friend,   115
And thou may'st brag thou hast done't. For here, for ever,
All friendship dies between us, and my heart,
For bringing forth any effects of love,
Shall be as barren to thee as this sand
We tread on, cruel and inconstant as   120
The sea that beats upon this beach. We now
Are severed: thus hast thou slain thy friend,
And satisfied what the witch thy mistress bade thee.
Go and report that thou hast slain thy friend.
LESSINGHAM I am served right.   125
BONVILE And now that I do cease to be thy friend,
I will fight with thee as thine enemy.
I came not over idly to do nothing.
LESSINGHAM   O friend!
BONVILE   Friend?
The naming of that word shall be the quarrel.
What do I know but that thou lov'st my wife,   130
And feigned'st this plot to divide me from her bed,
And that this letter here is counterfeit?
Will you advance, sir?
LESSINGHAM Not a blow.
'Twould appear ill in either of us to fight: 135

326

In you unmanly, for believe it, sir,
You have disarmed me already, done away
All power of resistance in me; it would show
Beastly to do wrong to the dead. To me you say
You are dead for ever, lost on Calais sands   140
By the cruelty of a woman. Yet remember
You had a noble friend, whose love to you
Shall continue after death. Shall I go over
In the same bark with you?
BONVILE   Not for yon town
Of Calais. You know 'tis dangerous living   145
At sea with a dead body.
LESSINGHAM   O you mock me.°
May you enjoy all your noble wishes.
BONVILE And may you find a better friend than I,
And better keep him.
        Exeunt

[3.2]

Enter Nurse, Compass, and his Wife

NURSE Indeed you must pardon me, goodman Compass. I have no
  authority to deliver, no, not to let you see the child. To tell you
  true, I have command unto the contrary.
COMPASS Command? From whom?
NURSE By the father of it.   5
COMPASS The father? Who am I?
NURSE Not the father sure. The civil law has found it otherwise.
COMPASS The civil law! Why then the uncivil law shall make it mine
  again. I'll be as dreadful as a Shrove Tuesday° to thee: I will tear
  thy cottage, but I will see my child.   10
NURSE Speak but half so much again, I'll call the constable and lay
  burglary to thy charge.
URSE My good husband, be patient; and prithee, nurse, let him see
  the child.
NURSE Indeed, I dare not. The father first delivered me the child.   15
  He pays me well, and weekly, for my pains; and to his use I keep
  it.
COMPASS Why, thou white° bastard-breeder, is not this the mother?

327

NURSE Yes, I grant you that.

COMPASS Dost thou? And I grant it too. And is not the child mine   20
own then by the wife's copyhold?°

NURSE The law must try that.

COMPASS Law? Dost think I'll be but a father in law?° All the law
betwixt Blackwall and Tothill Street°—and there's a pretty deal—
shall not keep it from me. Mine own flesh and blood! Who does   25
use to get my children but myself?

NURSE Nay, you must look to that. I ne'er knew you get any.

COMPASS Never? Put on a clean smock and try me, if thou darest:
three to one I get a bastard on thee tomorrow morning between
one and three.   30

NURSE I'll see thee hanged first.

COMPASS So thou shalt too.

Enter Franckford and Luce

NURSE O, here's the father. Now pray talk with him.

FRANCKFORD Good morning, neighbour, morrow to you both.

COMPASS Both? Morrow to you and your wife too.   35

FRANCKFORD I would speak calmly with you.

COMPASS I know what belongs to a calm, and a storm too. A cold
word with you: you have tied your mare° in my ground.

FRANCKFORD No, 'twas my nag.°

COMPASS I will cut off your nag's tail, and make his rump make   40
hair-buttons,° if e'er I take him there again.

FRANCKFORD Well, sir, but to the main.°

COMPASS Main? Yes, and I'll clip his mane too, and crop his ears
too, do you mark? And back-gall him, and spur-gall him, do you
note? And slit his nose, do you smell me now, sir? Unbreech his   45
barrel,° and discharge his bullets:° I'll gird him till he stinks°—you
smell me now, I'm sure.

FRANCKFORD You are too rough, neighbour, to maintain.°

COMPASS Maintain? You shall not maintain no child of mine, my
wife does not bestow her labour to that purpose.   50

FRANCKFORD You are too speedy: I will not maintain—

COMPASS No, marry shall you not.

FRANCKFORD —the deed to be lawful.
I have repented it, and to the law
Given satisfaction: my purse has paid for't.°   55

COMPASS Your purse? 'Twas my wife's purse! You brought in the
coin indeed, but it was found base and counterfeit.

FRANCKFORD I would treat colder with you, if you be pleased.

COMPASS Pleased? Yes, I am pleased well enough, serve me so still.
I am going again to sea one of these days; you know where I dwell.   60
Yet you'll but lose your labour; get as many children as you can,
you shall keep none of them.

FRANCKFORD You are mad.

COMPASS If I be horn-mad,° what's that to you?

FRANCKFORD I leave off milder phrase, and then tell you plain you   65
are a—

COMPASS A what? What am I?

FRANCKFORD A coxcomb.

COMPASS A coxcomb? I knew 'twould begin with a 'c'.

FRANCKFORD The child is mine. I am the father of it.   70
As it is past the deed, 'tis past the shame.
I do acknowledge, and will enjoy it.

COMPASS Yes, when you can get it again. Is it not my wife's labour?
I'm sure she's the mother. You may be as far off the father as I
am, for my wife's acquainted with more whoremasters besides   75
yourself, and crafty merchants too.

URSE No indeed, husband, to make my offence
Both least and most, I knew no other man.
He's the begetter, but the child is mine:
I bred and bore it, and I will not lose it.   80

LUCE The child's my husband's, dame, and he must have it.
I do allow my sufferance to the deed,
In lieu I never yet was fruitful to him,°
And in my barrenness excuse my wrong.

COMPASS Let him dung his own ground better at home. Then, if he   85
plant his radish roots in my garden, I'll eat 'em with bread and
salt, though I get no mutton° to 'em. What, though your husband
lent my wife your distaff, shall not the yarn be mine? I'll have the
head, let him carry the spindle home again.

FRANCKFORD Forbear more words; then let the law try it.   90
Meantime, nurse, keep the child; and to keep it better,
Here take more pay beforehand. There's money for thee.

COMPASS There's money for me too; keep it for me, nurse. Give him
both thy dugs at once: I pay for thy right dug.

NURSE I have two hands,° you see. Gentlemen, this does but show   95
how the law will hamper you: even thus you must be used.

FRANCKFORD The law shall show which is the worthier gender;

A schoolboy can do't.

COMPASS I'll whip that schoolboy that declines° the child from my
 wife and her heirs. Do not I know my wife's case the genitive case,   100
 and that's *huius*, as great a case as can be?

FRANCKFORD Well, fare you well, we shall meet in another place.
 Come, Luce.

 [*Exeunt Franckford and Luce*]

COMPASS Meet her in the same place again if you dare, and do your
 worst. Must we go to law for our children nowadays? No marvel,   105
 if the lawyers grow rich; but ere the law shall have a limb, a leg,
 a joint, a nail, I will spend more than a whole child in getting:
 Some win by play, and others by by-betting.°

 Exeunt

[3.3]

Enter Raymond, Eustace, Lionel, Grover, Annabel, Clare

LIONEL Whence was that letter sent?

ANNABEL   From Dover, sir.

LIONEL And does that satisfy you what was the cause
 Of his going over?

ANNABEL   It does; yet had he only
 Sent this, it had been sufficient.

RAYMOND   Why, what's that?

ANNABEL His will, wherein   5
 He has estated me in all his land.

EUSTACE [*whispers to Lionel*] He's gone to fight.

LIONEL [*whispers*] Lessingham's second, certain.

ANNABEL And I am lost, lost in't forever.

CLARE [*aside*] O fool Lessingham.   10
 Thou hast mistook my injunction utterly,
 Utterly mistook it; and I am mad, stark mad
 With my own thoughts, not knowing what event
 Their going o'er will come to. 'Tis too late
 Now for my tongue to cry my heart mercy.°   15
 Would I could be senseless till I hear
 Of their return. I fear me both are lost.

RAYMOND [*whispers to Eustace*] Who should it be Lessingham's gone
 to fight with?

EUSTACE [*whispers*] Faith, I cannot possibly conjecture.

ANNABEL Miserable creature! A maid, a wife,   20
    And widow in the compass of two days.

RAYMOND [*to Clare*] Are you sad too?

CLARE   I am not very well, sir.

RAYMOND [*taking hold of her*] I must put life in you.

CLARE   Let me go, sir.

RAYMOND I do love you in spite of your heart.

CLARE Believe it,   25
    There was never a fitter time to express it,
    For my heart has a great deal of spite in't.

RAYMOND I will discourse to you fine fancies.

CLARE Fine fooleries, will you not?

RAYMOND By this hand, I love you, and will court you.

CLARE   Fie,   30
    You can command your tongue, and I my ears
    To hear you no further.

RAYMOND [*aside*]   On my reputation,
    She's off o'th' hinges strangely.
       Enter Woodroff, Rochfield, and a Sailor

WOODROFF Daughter, good news.

ANNABEL   What, is my husband heard of?°

WOODROFF That's not the business. But you have here a cousin 35
    You may be mainly proud of, and I am sorry
    'Tis by your husband's kindred, not your own,
    That we might boast to have so brave a man
    In our alliance.

ANNABEL   What, so soon returned?
    You have made but a short voyage. Howsoever,   40
    You are to me most welcome.

ROCHFIELD   Lady, thanks;
    'Tis you have made me your own creature.
    Of all my being, fortunes, and poor fame—
    If I have purchased any, and of which
    I no way boast—next the high providence,   45
    You have been the sole creatress.

ANNABEL   O dear cousin,
    You are grateful above merit. What occasion
    Drew you so soon from sea?

WOODROFF   Such an occasion
    As I may bless heaven for, you thank their bounty,

And all of us be joyful.
ANNABEL   Tell us how.   50
WOODROFF Nay, daughter, the discourse will best appear
  In his relation. Where he fails, I'll help.
ROCHFIELD Not to molest your patience with recital
  Of every vain and needless circumstance,
  'Twas briefly thus. Scarce having reached to Margate,   55
  Bound on our voyage, suddenly in view
  Appeared to us three Spanish men of war.°
  These, having spied the English cross advance,°
  Salute us with a piece to have us strike;°
  Ours, better spirited and no way daunted   60
  At their unequal odds, though but one bottom,
  Returned 'em fire for fire. The fight begins,
  And dreadful on the sudden. Still they proferred
  To board us, still we bravely beat 'em off.
WOODROFF But, daughter, mark the event.   65
ROCHFIELD Sea-room we got; our ship being swift of sail,°
  It helped us much. Yet two unfortunate shot,
  One struck the captain's head off, and the other
  With an unlucky splinter laid the master
  Dead on the hatches. All our spirits then failed us.   70
WOODROFF Not all; you shall hear further, daughter.
ROCHFIELD For none was left to manage; nothing now
  Was talked of but to yield up ship and goods,
  And mediate for our peace.
WOODROFF   Nay, coz, proceed.
ROCHFIELD Excuse me, I entreat you, for what's more   75
  Hath already passed my memory.
WOODROFF But mine it never can. Then he stood up,
  And with his oratory made us again
  To recollect our spirits so late dejected.
ROCHFIELD Pray, sir!
WOODROFF   I'll speak't out. By unite consent°   80
  Then the command was his, and 'twas his place
  Now to bestir him. Down he went below,
  And put the linstocks in the gunners' hands—
  They ply their ordnance bravely—then again
  Up to the decks. Courage is there renewed,   85
  Fear now not found amongst us. Within less
  Than four hours' fight two of their ships were sunk,

Both foundered, and soon swallowed. Not long after,
The third begins to wallow, lies on the lee°
To stop her leaks. Then boldly we come on,   90
Boarded and took her; and she's now our prize.
SAILOR Of this we were eye-witnesses.
WOODROFF And many more brave boys of us besides,
    Myself for one. Never was, gentlemen,
    A sea-fight better managed.
ROCHFIELD   Thanks to heaven   95
    We have saved our own, damaged the enemy,
    And to our nation's glory we bring home
    Honour and profit.
WOODROFF   In which, cousin Rochfield,
    You as a venturer have a double share,
    Besides the name of captain, and in that   100
    A second benefit; but most of all,
    Way to more great employment.
ROCHFIELD [to Annabel]   Thus your bounty
    Hath been to me a blessing.
RAYMOND   Sir, we are all
    Indebted to your valour. This beginning
    May make us, of small venturers, to become°   105
    Hereafter wealthy merchants.
WOODROFF   Daughter and gentlemen,
    This is the man was born to make us all.
    Come, enter, enter; we will in and feast.
    He's in the bridegroom's absence my chief guest.
        Exeunt

4.1

Enter Compass, Wife, Lionel, and Pettifog the Attorney, and
[Jack. Tables are set out]

COMPASS 'Three Tuns'° do you call this tavern? It has a good
neighbour of Guildhall, Mr Pettifog. Show a room, boy.

JACK Welcome, gentlemen.

COMPASS What? art thou here, Hodge?

JACK I am glad you are in health, sir. 5

COMPASS This was the honest crack-rope first gave me tidings of my
wife's fruitfulness. Art bound prentice?

JACK Yes, sir.

COMPASS Mayest thou long jumble bastard° most artificially, to the
profit of thy master and pleasure of thy mistress. 10

JACK What wine drink ye, gentlemen?

LIONEL What wine relishes our palate, good Mr Pettifog?

PETTIFOG Nay, ask the woman.

COMPASS Alicant for her: I know her diet.

PETTIFOG Believe me, I con her thank° for't. I am of her side. 15

COMPASS Marry, and reason, sir, we have entertained you for our
attorney.

JACK A cup of neat alicant?

COMPASS Yes, but do not make it speak Welsh,° boy.

JACK How mean you? 20

COMPASS Put no Metheglin in't, ye rogue.

They sit down. Pettifog pulls out papers

JACK Not a drop, as I am true Briton.

[Exit Jack.] Enter Franckford, Eustace, [Raymond],
Luce, and Mr Dodge, a Lawyer, to another table, and a
Drawer

FRANCKFORD Show a private room, drawer.

DRAWER Welcome, gentlemen.

EUSTACE As far as you can from noise, boy. 25

DRAWER Further this way then, sir, for in the next room there are
three or four fish-wives taking up a brabbling business.

FRANCKFORD Let's not sit near them by any means.

DODGE Fill canary, sirrah.

[Drawer fills glasses, and exits]

FRANCKFORD And what do you think of my cause, Mr Dodge? 30

DODGE O we shall carry it most indubitably. You have money to go
through with the business; and ne'er fear it, but we'll trounce 'em.
You are the true father.

LUCE The mother will confess as much.

DODGE Yes, mistress, we have taken her affidavit. Look you, sir,   35
here's the answer to his declaration.

FRANCKFORD You may think strange, sir, that I am at charge
To call a charge upon me; but 'tis truth.
I made a purchase lately, and in that
I did estate the child, 'bout which I'm sued,   40
Joint purchaser in all the land I bought.
Now that's one reason that I should have care,
Besides the tie of blood, to keep the child
Under my wing, and see it carefully
Instructed in those fair abilities   45
May make it worthy hereafter to be mine,
And enjoy the land I have provided for't.

LUCE Right, and I counselled you to make that purchase,
And therefore I'll not have the child brought up
By such a coxcomb as now sues for him.   50
He'd bring him up only to be a swabber.
He was born a merchant and a gentleman,
And he shall live and die so.

DODGE Worthy mistress, I drink to you. You are a good woman, and
but few of so noble a patience.   55

    Enter Jack

[JACK] [*to Tapster off-stage*] Score a quart of alicant to th'woodcock.°

    Enter Rafe like a musician

RAFE Will you have any music, gentlemen?

COMPASS Music amongst lawyers? Here's nothing but discord.
What, Rafe! Here's another of my young cuckoos I heard last
April, before I heard the nightingale.° No music, good Rafe. Here,   60
boy, your father was a tailor, and methinks by your leering eye you
should take after him. A good boy: make a leg handsomely, scrape
yourself out of our company.

    [*Exit Rafe*]

And what do you think of my suit, sir?

PETTIFOG Why, look you, sir: the defendant was arrested first by   65
Latitat° in an action of trespass.

COMPASS And a lawyer told me it should have been an action of the
case,° should it not, wife?

335

URSE I have no skill in law, sir, but you heard a lawyer say so.

PETTIFOG Ay, but your action of the case is in that point too   70
ticklish.

COMPASS But what do you think? Shall I overthrow my adversary?

PETTIFOG Sans question. The child is none of yours: what of that?
I marry a widow possessed of a ward; shall not I have the tuition
of that ward? Now, sir, you lie at a stronger ward,° for *partus*   75
sequitur ventrem,° says the civil law; and if you were within compass
of the four seas, as the common law goes, the child shall be yours
certain.

COMPASS There's some comfort in that yet. O your attorneys in
Guildhall have a fine time on't.   80

LIONEL You are in effect both judge and jury yourselves.

COMPASS And how you will laugh at your clients, when you sit in a
tavern, and call them coxcombs, and whip up a cause, as a barber
trims his customers on a Christmas Eve: a snip, a wipe, and away!

PETTIFOG That's ordinary,° sir. You shall have the like at a *Nisi*   85
Prius.°

        Enter First Client.

O, you are welcome, sir.

FIRST CLIENT Sir, you'll be mindful of my suit?

PETTIFOG As I am religious, I'll drink to you.

FIRST CLIENT I thank you. [*To Urse*] By your favour, mistress. I   90
have much business and cannot stay, but there's money for a quart
of wine.

COMPASS By no means.

FIRST CLIENT I have said, sir.

        Exit [First Client]

PETTIFOG He's my client, sir, and he must pay. This is my tribute.   95
Custom is not more truly paid in the Sound of Denmark.°

        Enter Second Client

SECOND CLIENT Good sir, be careful of my business.

PETTIFOG Your declaration's drawn, sir; I'll drink to you.

SECOND CLIENT I cannot drink this morning, but there's money for
a pottle° of wine.   100

PETTIFOG O good sir!

SECOND CLIENT I have done, sir. Morrow, gentlemen.

        Exit [Second Client]

COMPASS We shall drink good cheap, Master Pettifog.

PETTIFOG An we sat here long, you'd say so. I have sat here in this
tavern but one half hour, drunk but three pints of wine, and what   105

with the offering of my clients in that short time, I have got nine
shillings clear, and paid all the reckoning.

LIONEL Almost a counsellor's° fee.

PETTIFOG And a great one, as the world goes in Guildhall; for now
our young clerks share with 'em, to help 'em to clients.   110

COMPASS I don't think but that the cucking-stool is an enemy to a
number of brabbles that would else be determined by law.

PETTIFOG 'Tis so indeed, sir. My client that came in now sues his
neighbour for kicking his dog, and using the defamatory speeches:
'Come out, cuckold's cur!'   115

LIONEL And what? shall you recover upon this speech?°

PETTIFOG In Guildhall, I assure you. The other that came in was an
informer, a precious knave.

COMPASS Will not the ballad of Flood° that was pressed make them
leave their knavery?   120

PETTIFOG I'll tell you how he was served: this informer comes into
Turnbull Street to a victualling-house, and there falls in league
with a wench—

COMPASS A tweak, or bronstrops:° I learnt that name in a play.

PETTIFOG —had belike some private dealings with her, and there got   125
a goose.°

COMPASS I would he had got two, I cannot away with an informer.

PETTIFOG Now, sir, this fellow, in revenge of this, informs against
the bawd that kept the house, that she used cans in her house; but
the cunning jade comes me into th'court, and there deposes that   130
she gave him true Winchester measure.°

COMPASS Marry, I thank her with all my heart for't.

    Enter Drawer

DRAWER Here's a gentleman, one Justice Woodroff, enquires for
Master Franckford.

    [Exit Drawer]

FRANCKFORD O, my brother and the other compromiser come to   135
take up the business.

    Enter Counsellor and Woodroff

WOODROFF We have conferred and laboured for your peace,
Unless your stubborness prohibit it;
And be assured, as we can determine it,
The law will end, for we have sought the cases.°   140

COMPASS If the child fall to my share, I am content to end upon any
conditions. The law shall run on headlong else.

FRANCKFORD Your purse must run by like a footman then.

337

COMPASS My purse shall run open-mouthed at thee.

COUNSELLOR My friend, be calm, you shall hear the reasons.   145
  I have stood up for you, pleaded your cause,
  But am overthrown; yet no further yielded
  Than your own pleasure. You may go on in law,
  If you refuse our censure.

COMPASS I will yield to nothing but my child.   150

COUNSELLOR 'Tis then as vain in us to seek your peace.
  Yet take the reasons with you. This gentleman
  First speaks, a justice, to me; and observe it:
  A child that's base and illegitimate born,
  The father found, who, if the need require it,   155
  Secures the charge and damage of the parish
  But the father? Who charged with education
  But the father? Then, by clear consequence,
  He ought for what he pays for to enjoy.
  Come to the strength of reason, upon which   160
  The law is grounded. The earth brings forth,
  This ground or that, her crop of wheat or rye:
  Whether shall the seedsman enjoy the sheaf,
  Or leave it to the earth that brought it forth?
  The summer tree brings forth her natural fruit,   165
  Spreads her large arms: who but the lord of it
  Shall pluck apples, or command the lops?
  Or shall they sink into the root again?
  'Tis still most clear upon the father's part.

COMPASS All this law I deny, and will be mine own lawyer. Is not   170
  the earth our mother? And shall not the earth have all her children
  again? I would see that law durst° keep any of us back! She'll have
  lawyers and all first, though they be none of her best children. My
  wife is the mother, and so much for the civil law. Now I come
  again, and you're gone at the common law.° Suppose this is my   175
  ground; I keep a sow upon it, as it might be my wife; you keep
  a boar, as it might be my adversary here; your boar comes
  foaming° into my ground, jumbles with my sow and wallows in
  her mire; my sow cries 'week', as if she had pigs in her belly: who
  shall keep these pigs? He the boar, or she the sow?   180

WOODROFF Past other alteration I am changed.
  The law is on the mother's part.

COUNSELLOR For me, I am strong in your opinion;
  I never knew my judgement err so far.

I was confirmed upon the other part,   185
And now am flat against it.

WOODROFF [to Franckford] Sir, you must yield.
Believe it, there's no law can relieve you.

FRANCKFORD I found it in myself. Well, sir,
The child's your wife's; I'll strive no further in it,   190
And being so near unto agreement, let us go
Quite through to't. Forgive my fault, and I
Forgive my charges, nor will I take back
The inheritance I made unto it.

COMPASS Nay, there you shall find me kind too. I have a pottle of   195
claret and a capon to supper for you; but no more mutton for you,
not a bit.

RAYMOND Yes, a shoulder, and we'll be there too—or a leg opened,
with venison sauce?°

COMPASS No legs opened, by your leave, nor no such sauce.   200

WOODROFF Well, brother and neighbour, I am glad you are friends.

OMNES All, all joy at it.

          Exeunt Woodroff, Franckford, [Luce] and Lawyers

COMPASS Urse, come kiss, Urse, all friends!

RAYMOND Stay, sir. One thing I would advise you: 'tis counsel worth
a fee, though I be no lawyer. 'Tis physic indeed, and cures   205
cuckoldry, to keep that spiteful brand out of your forehead, that it
shall not dare to meet or look out at any window to you. 'Tis better
than an onion to a green wound° i'th' left hand made by fire: it
takes out scar and all.

COMPASS This were a rare receipt. I'll content you for your skill.   210

RAYMOND Make here a flat divorce between yourselves;
Be you no husband, nor let her be no wife.
Within two hours you may salute again,
Woo and wed afresh; and then the cuckold's blotted.
This medicine is approved.   215

COMPASS Excellent, and I thank you. Urse, I renounce thee, and I
renounce myself from thee. Thou art a widow, Urse. I will go hang
myself two hours, and so long thou shalt drown thyself. Then will
we meet again in the Pease-field by Bishop's Hall,° and as the
swads and the cods° shall instruct us, we'll talk of a new matter.   220

URSE I will be ruled. Fare you well, sir.

COMPASS Farewell, widow. Remember time and place; change your
clothes too, do ye hear, widow?

          Exit Urse

[*To Raymond*] Sir, I am beholding to your good counsel.

RAYMOND But you'll not follow your own so far, I hope? You said   225
you'd hang yourself.

COMPASS No, I have devised a better way: I will go drink myself
dead for an hour; then, when I awake again, I am a fresh new man,
and so I go a-wooing.

RAYMOND That's handsome; and I'll lend thee a dagger.   230

COMPASS For the long weapon let me alone then.

    Exeunt

[4.2]

    Enter Lessingham and Clare

CLARE O sir, are you returned? I do expect
To hear strange news now.

LESSINGHAM   I have none to tell you.
I am only to relate I have done ill
At a woman's bidding. That's, I hope, no news.
Yet wherefore do I call that ill begets   5
My absolute happiness? You now are mine;
I must enjoy you solely.

CLARE   By what warrant?

LESSINGHAM By your condition. I have been at Calais;
Performed your will, drawn my revengeful sword,
And slain my nearest and best friend i'th' world   10
I had, for your sake.

CLARE   Slain your friend for my sake?

LESSINGHAM A most sad truth.

CLARE   And your best friend?

LESSINGHAM   My chiefest.

CLARE Then of all men you are most miserable,
Nor have you aught furthered your suit in this,
Though I enjoined you to't; for I had thought   15
That I had been the best esteemèd friend
You had i'th' world.

LESSINGHAM   Ye did not wish, I hope,
That I should have murdered you?

CLARE   You shall perceive
More of that hereafter. But I pray, sir, tell me—

For I do freeze with expectation of it,   20
It chills my heart with horror till I know—
What friend's blood you have sacrificed to your fury,
And to my fatal sport, this bloody riddle.
Who is it you have slain?
LESSINGHAM   Bonvile the bridegroom.
CLARE   Say?
O you have struck him dead thorough my heart;   25
In being true to me, you have proved in this
The falsest traitor. O, I am lost for ever.
Yet wherefore am I lost? Rather recovered
From a deadly witchcraft, and upon his grave
I will not gather rue, but violets°   30
To bless my wedding strewings. Good sir, tell me,°
Are you certain he is dead?
LESSINGHAM   Never, never
To be recovered.
CLARE   Why now, sir, I do love you
With an entire heart. I could dance, methinks.
Never did wine or music stir in woman   35
A sweeter touch of mirth. I will marry you,
Instantly marry you.
LESSINGHAM [aside] This woman has strange changes. [To Clare]
      You are ta'en
Strangely with his death.
CLARE   I'll give the reason
I have to be thus ecstasied with joy: 40
Know, sir, that you have slain my dearest friend,
And fatalest enemy.
LESSINGHAM   Most strange!
CLARE   'Tis true.
You have ta'en a mass of lead from off my heart
For ever would have sunk it in despair.
When you beheld me yesterday, I stood   45
As if a merchant walking on the Downs
Should see some goodly vessel of his own
Sunk 'fore his face i'th' harbour; and my heart
Retained no more heat than a man that toils
And vainly labours to put out the flames   50
That burns his house to th'bottom. I will tell you
A strange concealment, sir, and till this minute

Never revealed, and I will tell it now,
Smiling and not blushing: I did love that Bonvile,
Not as I ought, but as a woman might   55
That's beyond reason. I did dote upon him,
Though he ne'er knew of't, and beholding him
Before my face wedded unto another,
And all my interest in him forfeited,
I fell into despair; and at that instant   60
You urging your suit to me, and I thinking
That I had been your only friend i'th' world,
I heartily did wish you would have killed
That friend yourself to have ended all my sorrow;
And had prepared it that, unwittingly,   65
You should have done't by poison.

LESSINGHAM   Strange amazement!

CLARE Th'effects of a strange love.

LESSINGHAM   'Tis a dream, sure.

CLARE No 'tis real, sir, believe it.

LESSINGHAM   Would it were not.

CLARE What, sir? You have done bravely. 'Tis your mistress
That tells you you have done so.

LESSINGHAM   But my conscience   70
Is of counsel 'gainst you, and pleads otherwise.
Virtue in her past actions glories still,
But vice throws loathèd looks on former ill.
But did you love this Bonvile?

CLARE   Strangely, sir,
Almost to a degree of madness.

LESSINGHAM [aside]   Trust a woman?   75
Never henceforward! I will rather trust
The winds which Lapland witches sell to men.°
All that they have is feigned: their teeth, their hair,
Their blushes, nay their conscience too is feigned.
Let 'em paint, load themselves with cloth of tissue,   80
They cannot yet hide woman; that will appear
And disgrace all. The necessity of my fate!
Certain this woman has bewitched me here,
For I cannot choose but love her. O how fatal
This might have proved! I would it had for me.   85
It would not grieve me, though my sword had split
His heart in sunder: I had then destroyed

One that may prove my rival. O, but then
What had my horror been, my guilt of conscience!
I know some do ill at women's bidding   90
I'th' dog-days, and repent all the winter after.
No, I account it treble happiness
That Bonvile lives, but 'tis my chiefest glory
That our friendship is divided.

CLARE   Noble friend,
Why do you talk to yourself?

LESSINGHAM   Should you do so,   95
You'd talk to an ill woman; fare you well,
For ever fare you well. [*Aside*] I will do somewhat
To make as fatal breach and difference
In Bonvile's love as mine. I am fixed in't;
My melancholy and the devil shall fashion't.   100

CLARE You will not leave me thus?

LESSINGHAM   Leave you forever,
And may my friend's blood whom you loved so dearly
For ever lie impostumed in your breast,
And i'th' end choke you. Woman's cruelty
This black and fatal thread hath ever spun: 105
It must undo, or else it is undone.
        Exit [*Lessingham*]

CLARE I am every way lost, and no means to raise me
But blest repentance. What two unvalued jewels
Am I at once deprived of? Now I suffer
Deservedly. There's no prosperity settled: 110
Fortune plays ever with our good or ill,
Like cross and pile, and turns up which she will.°
        Enter Bonvile
Friend! O, you are the welcomest under heaven!
Lessingham did but fright me, yet I fear
That you are hurt to danger.

BONVILE   Not a scratch.   115

CLARE Indeed, you look exceeding well, methinks.

BONVILE I have been sea-sick lately, and we count
That excellent physic. How does my Annabel?

CLARE As well, sir, as the fear of such a loss
As your esteemèd self will suffer her.   120

BONVILE Have you seen Lessingham since he returned?

CLARE He departed hence but now, and left with me

A report had almost killed me.

BONVILE   What was that?

CLARE That he had killed you.

BONVILE   So he has.

CLARE   You mock me.

BONVILE He has killed me for a friend, for ever silenced   125
All amity between us. You may now
Go and embrace him, for he has fulfilled
The purpose of that letter.

> *[Bonvile] gives her a letter*

CLARE   O I know't.

> *She gives him another*

And had you known this which I meant to have sent you
An hour 'fore you were married to your wife,   130
The riddle had been construed.

BONVILE   Strange! This expresses
That you did love me.

CLARE   With a violent affection.

BONVILE Violent indeed, for it seems it was your purpose
To have ended it in violence on your friend;
The unfortunate Lessingham unwittingly   135
Should have been the executioner.

CLARE   'Tis true.

BONVILE And do you love me still?

CLARE   I may easily
Confess it, since my extremity is such
That I must needs speak or die.

BONVILE   And you would enjoy me
Though I am married?

CLARE   No, indeed not I, sir.   140
You are to sleep with a sweet bedfellow
Would knit the brow at that.

BONVILE Come, come, a woman's telling truth makes amends
For her playing false. You would enjoy me?

CLARE If you were a bachelor or widower,   145
Afore all the great ones living.

BONVILE   But 'tis impossible
To give you present satisfaction, for
My wife is young and healthful; and I like
The summer and the harvest of our love,
Which yet I have not tasted of, so well   150

That, an you'll credit me, for me her days
Shall ne'er be shortened. Let your reason therefore
Turn you another way, and call to mind,
With best observance, the accomplished graces
Of that brave gentleman whom late you sent   155
To his destruction; a man so every way
Deserving, no one action of his
In all his lifetime e'er degraded him
From the honour he was born to. Think how observant
He'll prove to you in nobler request that so   160
Obeyed you in a bad one; and remember
That afore you engaged him to an act
Of horror, to the killing of his friend,
He bore his steerage true in every part,°
Led by the compass of a noble heart.   165

CLARE Why do you praise him thus? You said but now
He was utterly lost to you. Now 't appears
You are friends, else you'd not deliver of him
Such a worthy commendation.

BONVILE   You mistake,
Utterly mistake that I am friends with him   170
In speaking this good of him. To what purpose
Do I praise him? Only to this fatal end,
That you might fall in love and league with him;
And what worse office can I do i'th' world
Unto my enemy than to endeavour   175
By all means possible to marry him
Unto a whore? And there I think she stands.

CLARE Is whore a name to be beloved? If not,
What reason have I ever to love that man
Puts it upon me falsely? You have wrought   180
A strange alteration in me; were I a man,
I would drive you with my sword into the field,
And there put my wrong to silence. Go, you're not worthy
To be a woman's friend in the least part
That concerns honourable reputation,   185
For you are a liar.

BONVILE   I will love you now
With a noble observance, if you will continue
This hate unto me. Gather all those graces
From whence you have fall'n yonder, where you have left 'em

345

In Lessingham, he that must be your husband;   190
And though henceforth I cease to be his friend,
I will appear his noblest enemy,
And work reconcilement 'tween you.

CLARE   No, you shall not.
You shall not marry him to a strumpet. For that word
I shall ever hate you.

[BONVILE]   And for that one deed   195
I shall ever love you. Come, convert your thoughts
To him that best deserves 'em, Lessingham.
It's most certain you have done him wrong.
But your repentance and compassion now
May make amends. Disperse this melancholy,   200
And on that turn of fortune's wheel depend,
When all calamities will mend, or end.

    Exeunt

[4.3]

Enter Compass, Raymond, Eustace, Lionel, Grover

COMPASS Gentlemen, as you have been witness to our divorce, you
    shall now be evidence to our next meeting, which I look for every
    minute, if you please, gentlemen.

RAYMOND We came for the same purpose, man.

COMPASS I do think you'll see me come off° with as smooth a   5
    forehead, make my wife as honest a woman once more, as a man
    sometimes would desire; I mean, of her rank, and a teeming
    woman as she has been. Nay, surely I do think to make the child
    as lawful a child, too, as a couple of unmarried people can beget,
    and let it be° begotten when the father is beyond sea, as this was.   10
    Do but note.

    Enter Urse

EUSTACE 'Tis what we wait for.

COMPASS You have waited the good hour. See, she comes. A little
    room, I beseech you; silence and observation.

RAYMOND All your own, sir.   15

    [*They withdraw a little*]

COMPASS Good morrow, fair maid.

URSE Mistaken in both, sir: neither fair, nor maid.

COMPASS No? a married woman?

URSE That's it I was, sir—a poor widow now.

COMPASS A widow? Nay, then I must make a little bold with you.   20
'Tis akin to mine own case: I am a wifeless husband too. How
long have you been a widow, pray?

    [*Urse weeps*]

Nay, do not weep.

URSE I cannot choose to think the loss I had.

COMPASS He was an honest man to thee it seems.   25

URSE 'Honest', quotha—o!

COMPASS By my feck, and those are great losses. An honest man is
not to be found in every hole, nor every street. If I took a whole
parish in sometimes, I might say true, for stinking mackerel may
be cried for new.°   30

RAYMOND [*aside*] Somewhat sententious.

EUSTACE [*aside*] O, silence was an article enjoined.

COMPASS And how long is it since you lost your honest husband?

URSE O the memory is too fresh, and your sight
Makes my sorrow double.

COMPASS   My sight? Why, was he like me?   35

URSE Your left hand to your right is not more like.

COMPASS Nay, then I cannot blame thee to weep. An honest man,
I warrant him, and thou hadst a great loss of him. Such a
proportion, so limbed, so coloured, so fed?

RAYMOND [*aside*] Yes faith, and so taught° too.   40

EUSTACE [*aside*] Nay, will you break the law?°

URSE Twins were never liker.

COMPASS Well, I love him the better, whatsoever is become of him.
And how many children did he leave thee at his departure?

URSE Only one, sir.   45

COMPASS A boy or a girl?

URSE A boy, sir.

COMPASS Just mine own case still. My wife, rest her soul, left me a
boy too. A chopping boy, I warrant.

URSE Yes, if you call 'em so.   50

COMPASS Ay, mine is a chopping boy. I mean to make either a cook
or a butcher of him, for those are your chopping boys. And what
profession was your husband of?

URSE He went to sea, sir, and there got his living.

COMPASS Mine own faculty too. And you can like a man of that   55
profession well?

347

URSE For his sweet sake whom I so dearly loved,
     More dearly lost, I must think well of it.

COMPASS Must you? I do think then thou must venture to sea once
     again, if thou'lt be ruled by me.   60

URSE O sir, but there's one thing more burdensome
     To us than most of others' wives, which moves me
     A little to distaste it. Long time we endure
     The absence of our husbands; sometimes many years;
     And then, if any slip in woman be,°   65
     As long vacations may make lawyers hungry,
     And tradesmen cheaper pennyworths afford
     Than otherwise they would, for ready coin,°
     Scandals fly out, and we poor souls branded
     With wanton living and incontinency,   70
     When, alas, consider, can we do withal?

COMPASS They are fools and not sailors that do not consider that;
     I'm sure your husband was not of that mind, if he were like me.

URSE No, indeed, he would bear kind and honestly.°

COMPASS He was the wiser. Alack, your land and freshwater men   75
     never understand what wonders are done at sea. Yet they may
     observe ashore that, a hen having tasted the cock, kill him, and she
     shall lay eggs afterwards.°

URSE That's very true indeed.

COMPASS And so may women. Why not? May not a man get two or   80
     three children at once? One must be born before another, you
     know.

URSE Even this discretion my sweet husband had.
     You more and more resemble him.

COMPASS Then if they knew what things are done at sea, where the   85
     winds themselves do copulate and bring forth issue, as thus: in the
     old world° there were but four in all, as Nor, East, Sou, and West.
     These dwelt far from one another, yet by meeting they have
     engendered Nor-East, Sou-East, Sou-West, Nor-West; then they
     were eight. Of them were begotten Nor-Nor-East, Nor-Nor-West,   90
     Sou-Sou-East, Sou-Sou-West, and those two sous were Sou-East
     and Sou-West's daughters; and indeed there is a family now of
     thirty-two of 'em, that they have filled every corner of the world.
     And yet, for all this, you see these bawdy bellows-menders,° when
     they come ashore, will be offering to take up women's coats° in the   95
     street.

URSE Still my husband's discretion!

348

COMPASS So I say, if your landmen did understand that we send winds from sea to do our commendations to our wives, they would not blame you as they do.   100

URSE We cannot help it.

COMPASS But you shall help it. Can you love me, widow?

URSE If I durst confess what I do think, sir,
I know what I would say.

COMPASS Durst confess? Why, whom do you fear? Here's none but   105
honest gentlemen, my friends. Let them hear, and never blush
for't.

URSE I shall be thought too weak to yield at first.
     [*Raymond and Eustace come forward*]

RAYMOND Tush, that's niceness. Come, we heard all the rest.
The first true stroke of love sinks thee deepest.   110
If you love him, say so.

COMPASS I have a boy of mine own, I tell you that aforehand; you
shall not need to fear me that way.

URSE Then I do love him.

COMPASS So here will be man and wife tomorrow then. What though 115
we meet strangers, we may love one another ne'er the worse for
that. Gentlemen, I invite you all to my wedding.

ALL We'll all attend it.

COMPASS Did not I tell you I would fetch it off fair? Let any man
lay a cuckold to my charge, if he dares now.   120

RAYMOND 'Tis slander, whoever does it.

COMPASS Nay, it will come to petty larceny at least, and without
compass° of the general pardon° too; or I'll bring him to a foul
sheet, if he has ne'er a clean one; or let me hear him that will say
I am not father to the child I begot!   125

EUSTACE None will adventure any of those.

COMPASS Or that my wife that shall be is not as honest a woman as
some other men's wives are.

RAYMOND No question of that.

COMPASS How fine and sleek my brows are now!   130

EUSTACE Ay, when you are married they'll come to themselves again.

COMPASS You may call me bridegroom, if you please now, for the
guests are bidden.

ALL Good master bridegroom!

COMPASS Come, widow, then, ere the next ebb and tide,   135
If I be bridegroom, thou shalt be the bride.
     Exeunt

5.1

Enter Rochfield and Annabel

ROCHFIELD Believe me, I was never more ambitious,
　　Or covetous, if I may call it so,
　　Of any fortune greater than this one,
　　But to behold his face.

ANNABEL　　　　　　　And now's the time,
　　For from a much feared danger as I heard,　　　　　　5
　　He's late come over.

ROCHFIELD　　　　　And not seen you yet?
　　'Tis some unkindness.

ANNABEL　　　　　　You may think it so;
　　But for my part, sir, I account it none.
　　What know I but some business of import
　　And weighty consequence, more near to him　　　　　10
　　Than any formal compliment to me,
　　May for a time detain him? I presume
　　No jealousy can be aspersed on him
　　For which he cannot well apology.

ROCHFIELD You are a creature every way complete,　　15
　　As good a wife as woman; for whose sake,
　　As I in duty and endeared to you,
　　So shall I owe him service.

　　　　Enter Lessingham

LESSINGHAM [*aside*] The ways to love and crowns lie both through blood,
　　For in 'em both all lets must be removed.　　　　　20
　　It could be styled no true ambition else.
　　I am grown big with project. 'Project', said I?
　　Rather with sudden mischief, which without
　　A speedy birth fills me with painful throes,
　　And I am now in labour. Thanks, occasion,　　　　25
　　That giv'st me a fit ground to work upon!
　　It should be Rochfield, one since our departure,
　　It seems, engrafted in this family—
　　Indeed the house's minion, since from the lord
　　To the lowest groom all with unite consent　　　30
　　Speak him so largely. Nor, as it appears°

By this their private conference, is he grown
Least in the bride's opinion, a foundation
On which I will erect a brave revenge.

ANNABEL [*to Rochfield*] Sir, what kind offices lies in your way   35
To do for him, I shall be thankful for,
And reckon them mine own.

ROCHFIELD   In acknowledgement
I kiss your hand; so, with a gratitude
Never to be forgot, I take my leave.

ANNABEL I mine of you, with hourly expectation   40
Of a long-looked-for husband.

ROCHFIELD   May it thrive
According to your wishes.
          Exit [*Annabel*]

LESSINGHAM [*aside*]   Now's my turn.
          [*Comes forward*]
Without offence, sir, may I beg your name?

ROCHFIELD 'Tis that I never yet denied to any,
Nor will to you that seem a gentleman: 45
'Tis Rochfield.

LESSINGHAM   Rochfield? You are then the man
Whose nobleness, virtue, valour, and good parts
Have voiced you loud. Dover and Sandwich, Margate
And all the coast is full of you.
But more, as an eye-witness of all these,   50
And with most truth, the master of this house
Hath given them large expressions.

ROCHFIELD   Therein his love
Exceeded much my merit.

LESSINGHAM   That's your modesty;
Now I as one that goodness love in all men,
And honouring that which is but found in few,   55
Desire to know you better.

ROCHFIELD   Pray your name?

LESSINGHAM Lessingham.

ROCHFIELD   A friend to master Bonvile?

LESSINGHAM   In the number
Of those which he esteems most dear to him,
He reckons me not last.

ROCHFIELD   So I have heard.

LESSINGHAM Sir, you have cause to bless the lucky planet   60

Beneath which you were born. 'Twas a bright star,
And then shined clear upon you, for as you
Are every way well parted, so I hold you°
In all designs marked to be fortunate.
ROCHFIELD Pray do not stretch your love to flattery,   65
'T may call it then in question; grow, I pray you,
To some particulars.
LESSINGHAM   I have observed°
But late your parting with the virgin bride,
And therein some affection.
ROCHFIELD   How?
LESSINGHAM   With pardon,
In this I still applaud your happiness,   70
And praise the blessèd influence of your stars;
For how can it be possible that she,
Unkindly left upon the bridal-day,
And disappointed of those nuptial sweets
That night expected, but should take the occasion   75
So fairly offered? Nay, and stand excused
As well in detestation of a scorn,
Scarce in a husband heard of, as selecting°
A gentleman in all things so complete,
To do her those neglected offices   80
Her youth and beauty justly challengeth?
ROCHFIELD [aside] Some plot to wrong the bride, and I now
Will marry craft with cunning: if he'll bite,
I'll give him line to play on. [Aloud] Wert your case,
You being young as I am, would you intermit   85
So fair and sweet occasion?
Yet misconceive me not, I do entreat you,
To think I can be of that easy wit,
Or of that malice to defame a lady,
Were she so kind so to expose herself;   90
Nor is she such a creature.
LESSINGHAM [aside]   On this foundation
I can build higher still. [Aloud] Sir, I believe't.
I hear you two call cousins: comes your kindred
By the Woodroffs, or the Bonviles?
ROCHFIELD From neither. 'Tis a word of courtesy   95
Late interchanged betwixt us; otherwise
We are foreign as two strangers.

LESSINGHAM [*aside*]   Better still.

ROCHFIELD I would not have you grow too inward with me
  Upon so small a knowledge. Yet to satisfy you,
  And in some kind too to delight myself: 100
  Those bracelets and the carcanet she wears
  She gave me once.

LESSINGHAM   They were the first and special tokens passed
  Betwixt her and her husband.

ROCHFIELD   'Tis confessed.
  What I have said I have said. Sir, you have power
  Perhaps to wrong me, or to injure her.   105
  This you may do, but as you are a gentleman,
  I hope you will do neither.

LESSINGHAM   Trust upon't.
        Exit Rochfield
  If I drown, I'll sink some along with me,
  For of all miseries I hold that chief,
  Wretched to be, when none co-parts our grief.   110
        Enter Woodroff
  Here's another anvil to work on: I must now
  Make this my masterpiece, for your old foxes
  Are seldom ta'en in springes.

WOODROFF [*greeting him*]   What, my friend!
  You are happily returned; and yet I want
  Somewhat to make it perfect. Where's your friend,   115
  My son-in-law?

LESSINGHAM   O sir!

WOODROFF   I pray, sir, resolve me,
  For I do suffer strangely till I know
  If he be in safety.

LESSINGHAM   Fare you well; 'tis not fit
  I should relate his danger.

WOODROFF   I must know't.
  I have a quarrel to you already, for enticing   120
  My son-in-law to go over. Tell me quickly,
  Or I shall make it greater.

LESSINGHAM   Then truth is,
  He's dangerously wounded.

WOODROFF But he's not dead, I hope?

LESSINGHAM   No, sir, not dead;
  Yet sure your daughter may take liberty   125

To choose another.

WOODROFF   Why, that gives him dead.°

LESSINGHAM Upon my life, sir, no; your son's in health
As well as I am.

WOODROFF   Strange! you deliver riddles.

LESSINGHAM I told you he was wounded, and 'tis true:
He is wounded in his reputation.   130
I told you likewise, which I am loath to repeat,
That your fair daughter might take liberty
To embrace another. That's the consequence
That makes my best friend wounded in his fame;
This is all I can deliver.

WOODROFF   I must have more of 't,   135
For I do sweat already, and I'll sweat more;
'Tis good, they say, to cure aches, and o'th' sudden
I am sore from head to foot. Let me taste the worst.

LESSINGHAM Know, sir, if ever there were truth in falsehood,
Then 'tis most true your daughter plays most false   140
With Bonvile, and hath chose for her favourite
The man that now passed by me, Rochfield.

WOODROFF   Say?
I would thou hadst spoke this on Calais sands,
And I within my sword and poniard's length
Of that false throat of thine. I pray, sir, tell me   145
Of what kin or alliance do you take me
To the gentlewoman you late mentioned?

LESSINGHAM You are her father.

WOODROFF Why then of all men living do you address
This report to me, that ought of all men breathing   150
To have been the last o'th' roll, except the husband,
That should have heard of 't?

LESSINGHAM   For her honour, sir,
And yours, that your good counsel may reclaim her.

WOODROFF I thank you.

LESSINGHAM She has departed, sir, upon my knowledge,   155
With jewels and with bracelets, the first pledges
And confirmation of th' unhappy contract
Between her self and husband.

WOODROFF   To whom?

LESSINGHAM   To Rochfield.

WOODROFF Be not abused: but now,

Even now I saw her wear 'em.
LESSINGHAM   Very likely.   160
'Tis fit, hearing her husband is returned,
That she should redeliver 'em.
WOODROFF   But pray, sir, tell me,
How is it likely she could part with 'em,
When they are locked about her neck and wrists,
And the key with her husband?
LESSINGHAM   O sir, that's but practise.   165
She has got a trick to use another key
Besides her husband's.
WOODROFF   Sirrah, you do lie;°
And were I to pay down a hundred pounds
For every lie given, as men pay twelve pence,
And worthily, for swearing, I would give thee°   170
The lie, nay though it were in the court of honour,
So oft, till of the thousands I am worth
I had not left a hundred. For is't likely
So brave a gentleman as Rochfield is,
That did so much at sea to save my life,   175
Should now on land shorten my wretched days
In ruining my daughter? A rank lie!
Have you spread this to any but myself?
LESSINGHAM I am no intelligencer.
WOODROFF   Why then, 'tis yet a secret?
        [*Draws his sword*]
And that it may rest so, draw; I'll take order   180
You shall prate of it no further.
LESSINGHAM   O, my sword
Is enchanted, sir, and will not out o'th' scabbard.
I will leave you, sir. Yet say not I give ground,
For 'tis your own you stand on.
        Enter Bonvile and Clare
[*Aside*] Clare here with Bonvile? Excellent! On this   185
I have more to work. This goes to Annabel,
And it may increase the whirlwind.
        Exit Lessingham
BONVILE   How now, sir?
Come, I know this choler bred in you
For the voyage which I took at his entreaty;
But I must reconcile you.

355

WOODROFF   On my credit,   190
  There's no such matter. I will tell you, sir,
  And I will tell it in laughter: the cause of it
  Is so poor, so ridiculous, so impossible
  To be believed! Ha, ha, he came even now
  And told me that one Rochfield, now a guest   195
  (And most worthy, sir, to be so) in my house,
  Is grown exceedingly familiar with
  My daughter.
BONVILE Ha?
WOODROFF Your wife, and that he has had favours from her.   200
BONVILE Favours?
WOODROFF Love-tokens I did call 'em in my youth,
  Lures to which gallants spread their wings and stoop°
  In ladies' bosoms. Nay, he was so false
  To truth and all good manners, that those jewels   205
  You locked about her neck he did protest
  She had given to Rochfield. Ha, methinks o'th' sudden
  You do change colour. Sir, I would not have you
  Believe this in least part. My daughter's honest,
  And my guest is a noble fellow; and for this   210
  Slander delivered me by Lessingham,
  I would have cut his throat.
BONVILE   As I your daughter's,
  If I find not the jewels 'bout her.
CLARE   Are you returned
  With the Italian plague upon you, jealousy?°
WOODROFF Suppose that Lessingham should love my daughter,   215
  And thereupon fashion your going over,
  As now your jealousy, the stronger way
  So to divide you: there were a fine crotchet!
  Do you stagger still? If you continue thus,
  I vow you are not worth a welcome home,   220
  Neither from her, nor me.
          Enter Rochfield and Annabel
                    See, here she comes.
CLARE I have brought you home a jewel.
ANNABEL   Wear it yourself,
  For these I wear are fetters, not favours.
CLARE I looked for better welcome.
ROCHFIELD   Noble sir,

356

I must woo your better knowledge.

BONVILE   O dear sir,   225
My wife will bespeak it for you.

ROCHFIELD   Ha, your wife?

WOODROFF Bear with him, sir, he's strangely off o'th' hinges.

BONVILE [*aside*] The jewels are i'th' right place, but the jewel°
Of her heart sticks yonder. [*To Annabel*] You are angry with me
For my going over.

ANNABEL   Happily more angry   230
For your coming over.

BONVILE   I sent you my will from Dover?

ANNABEL Yes, sir.

BONVILE Fetch it.

ANNABEL I shall, sir, but leave your self-will with you.
        Exit Annabel

WOODROFF This is fine: the woman will be mad too.   235

BONVILE Sir, I would speak with you.

ROCHFIELD   And I with you,
Of all men living.

BONVILE [*whispers*] I must have satisfaction from you.

ROCHFIELD [*whispers*] Sir, it grows upon the time of payment.

WOODROFF What's that? What's that? I'll have no whispering.   240
        Enter Annabel with a will

ANNABEL Look you, there's the patent
Of your deadly affection to me.

BONVILE   'Tis welcome.°
When I gave myself for dead, I then made over
My land unto you; now I find your love
Dead to me, I will alter't.

ANNABEL   Use your pleasure;   245
A man may make a garment for the moon°
Rather than fit your constancy.

WOODROFF   How's this?
Alter your will?

BONVILE   'Tis in mine own disposing;
Certainly I will alter't.

WOODROFF   Will you so, my friend?
Why then I will alter mine too.   250
I had estated thee, thou peevish fellow,
In forty thousand pounds after my death;
I can find another executor.

BONVILE   Pray, sir, do.
  Mine I'll alter without question.
WOODROFF   Dost hear me?
  And if I change not mine within this two hours,   255
  May my executors cozen all my kindred
  To whom I bequeath legacies!
BONVILE   I am for a lawyer, sir.
     [*Exit Bonvile*]
WOODROFF And I will be with one as soon as thyself,
  Though thou ridest post to th'devil.
ROCHFIELD Stay, let me follow and cool him.
WOODROFF   O by no means.   260
  You'll put a quarrel upon him for the wrong
  He's done my daughter.
ROCHFIELD   No, believe it, sir,
  He's my wished friend.
WOODROFF   O come, I know the way of't;
  Carry it like a French quarrel, privately whisper,
  Appoint to meet, and cut each other's throats   265
  With cringes and embraces. I protest
  I will not suffer you exchange a word
  Without I overhear't.
ROCHFIELD   Use your pleasure.
    Exeunt Woodroff and Rochfield
CLARE You are like to make fine work now.
ANNABEL   Nay, you are like
  To make a finer business of't.
CLARE   Come, come,   270
  I must solder you together.
ANNABEL   You? Why, I heard
  A bird sing lately you are the only cause
  Works the division.
CLARE   Who? As thou ever lovedst me,
  For I long, though I am a maid, for't.
ANNABEL   Lessingham.
CLARE Why then I do protest myself first cause   275
  Of the wrong which he has put upon you both,
  Which, please you to walk in, I shall make good
  In a short relation. Come, I'll be the clew
  To lead you forth this labyrinth, this toil°
  Of a supposed and causeless jealously.   280

Cankers touch choicest fruit with their infection,
And fevers seize those of the best complexion.°
    Exeunt Annabel and Clare. Enter Woodroff and Rochfield

WOODROFF Sir, have I not said I love you? If I have,
  You may believe't before an oracle,
  For there's no trick in't, but the honest sense.   285

ROCHFIELD Believe it, that I do, sir.

WOODROFF   Your love must then
  Be as plain with mine, that they may suit together.
  I say you must not fight with my son Bonvile.

ROCHFIELD Not fight with him, sir?

WOODROFF   No, not fight with him, sir.
  I grant you may be wronged, and I dare swear   290
  So is my child; but he is the husband, you know,
  The woman's lord, and must not always be told
  Of his faults neither. I say you must not fight.

ROCHFIELD I'll swear it, if you please, sir.

WOODROFF   And forswear, I know't,
  Ere you lay ope the secrets of your valour;   295
  'Tis enough for me I saw you whisper,
  And I know what belongs to't.

ROCHFIELD   To no such end, assure you.
    Enter Lessingham

WOODROFF I say you cannot fight with him,
  If you be my friend, for I must use you.
  Yonder's my foe, and you must be my second.   300
  [*To Lessingham*] Prepare thee, slanderer, and get another
  Better than thyself too; for here's my second,
  One that will fetch him up and firk him too.°
  Get your tools. I know the way to Calais sands,
  If that be your fence school. He'll show you tricks, 'faith,   305
  He'll let blood your calumny; your best guard
  Will come to a *peccavi*, I believe.

LESSINGHAM Sir, if that be your quarrel,
  He's a party in it, and must maintain
  The side with me. From him I collected   310
  All those circumstances concern your daughter—
  His own tongue's confession.

WOODROFF   Who? From him?
  He will belie to do thee a pleasure then,
  If he speak any ill upon himself.

I know he ne'er could do an injury.   315
ROCHFIELD So please you, I'll relate it, sir.
    Enter Bonvile, Annabel, and Clare
WOODROFF Before her husband then, and here he is
  In friendly posture with my daughter too;
  I like that well. Son bridegroom, and lady bride,
  If you will hear a man defame himself—   320
  For so he must if he say any ill—
  Then listen.
BONVILE   Sir, I have heard this story,
  And meet with your opinion in his goodness;
  The repetition will be needless.
ROCHFIELD Your father has not, sir. I'll be brief   325
  In the delivery.
WOODROFF Do, do then, I long to hear it.
ROCHFIELD The first acquaintance I had with your daughter
  Was on the wedding-eve.
WOODROFF   So? 'Tis not ended
  Yet, methinks.
ROCHFIELD   I would have robbed her.
WOODROFF   Ah, thief!   330
ROCHFIELD That chain and bracelet which she wears upon her,
  She ransomed with the full esteem in gold,
  Which was with you my venture.
WOODROFF   Ah, thief again!
ROCHFIELD For any attempt against her honour, I vow
  I had no thought on.
WOODROFF   An honest thief, 'faith yet.   335
ROCHFIELD Which she as nobly recompensed: brought me home,
  And in her own discretion thought it meet,
  For cover of my shame to call me cousin.
WOODROFF Call a thief cousin? Why, and so she might,
  For the gold she gave thee she stole from her husband;   340
  'Twas all his now; yet 'twas a good girl too.
ROCHFIELD The rest you know, sir.
WOODROFF   Which was worth all the rest—
  Thy valour, lad; but I'll have that in print,
  Because I can no better utter it.
ROCHFIELD   Thus, jade unto my wants°
  And spurred by my necessities, I was going,   345
  But by that lady's counsel I was stayed,

For that discourse was our familiarity.°
And this you may take for my recantation;
I am no more a thief.
WOODROFF   A blessing on thy heart,
And this was the first time, I warrant thee, too.   350
ROCHFIELD Your charitable censure is not wronged in that.
WOODROFF No, I knew't could be but the first time at most.
But for thee, brave valour, I have in store
That thou shalt need to be a thief no more.
          Soft music [heard near by]
Ha? What's this music?   355
BONVILE It chimes an *Io paean!* to your wedding, sir,
If this be your bride.
LESSINGHAM Can you forgive me? Some wild distractions
Had overturned my own condition,
And spilt the goodness you once knew in me.   360
But I have carefully recovered it
And overthrown the fury on't.
CLARE   It was my cause
That you were so possessed, and all these troubles
Have from my peevish will original.
I do repent, though you forgive me not.   365
LESSINGHAM You have no need for your repentance then,
Which is due to it. All's now as at first
It was wished to be.
WOODROFF   Why, that's well said of all sides.°
But soft, this music has some other meaning:
Another wedding towards! Good speed, good speed.   370
          Enter Compass and the four Gallants [Raymond, Eustace,
          Lionel, Grover], [followed by the] bride [Urse] between
          Franckford and another; Luce, Nurse, and child
COMPASS We thank you, sir.
WOODROFF Stay, stay! Our neighbour Compass, is't not?
COMPASS That was, and may be again tomorrow; this day, master
bridegroom.
WOODROFF O, give you joy. But sir, if I be not mistaken, you were   375
married before now. How long is't since your wife died?
COMPASS Ever since yesterday, sir.
WOODROFF Why, she's scarce buried yet then.
COMPASS No indeed, I mean to dig her grave soon; I had no leisure
yet.   380

WOODROFF And was not your fair bride married before?

URSE Yes indeed, sir.

WOODROFF And how long since your husband departed?

URSE Just when my husband's wife died.

WOODROFF Bless us, Hymen, are not these both the same parties?   385

BONVILE Most certain, sir.

WOODROFF What marriage call you this?

COMPASS This is called *Shedding of Horns*, sir.

WOODROFF How?

LESSINGHAM Like enough, but they may grow again next year.   390

WOODROFF This is a new trick.

COMPASS Yes, sir, because we did not like the old trick.

WOODROFF Brother, you are a helper in this design too?

FRANCKFORD The father to give the bride, sir.

COMPASS And I am his son, sir, and all the sons he has; and this is   395
his grandchild, and my elder brother; you'll think this strange now.

WOODROFF Then it seems he begat this before you?

COMPASS Before me? Not so, sir. I was far enough off, when 'twas
done; yet let me see him dares say this is not my child, and this
my father.   400

BONVILE You cannot see him here, I think, sir.

WOODROFF Twice married! Can it hold?

COMPASS Hold? It should hold the better, a wise man would think,
when 'tis tied of two knots.

WOODROFF Methinks it should rather unloose the first,   405
And between 'em both make up one negative.

EUSTACE No, sir, for though it hold on the contrary,°
Yet two affirmatives make no negative.

WOODROFF Cry you mercy, sir

COMPASS Make what you will, this little negative was my wife's   410
laying, and I affirm it to be mine own.

WOODROFF This proves the marriage before substantial,
Having this issue.

COMPASS 'Tis mended now, sir; for being double-married, I may
now have two children at a birth, if I can get 'em. D'ye think I'll   415
be five years about one, as I was before?

EUSTACE The like has been done for the loss of the wedding ring,
And to settle a new peace before disjointed.

LIONEL But this indeed, sir, was especially done
To avoid the word of scandal, that foul word   420
Which the fatal monologist cannot alter.°

WOODROFF Cuckoo!

COMPASS What's that, the nightingale?

WOODROFF A night-bird: much good may do you, sir.

COMPASS I'll thank you when I'm at supper. Come, father,   425
    Child, and bride. And for your part, father,
    Whatsoever he, or he, or t'other says,
    You shall be as welcome as in my t'other wife's days.

FRANCKFORD I thank you, sir.

WOODROFF Nay, take us with you, gentlemen.   430
    One wedding we have yet to solemnize,
    The first is still imperfect. Such troubles
    Have drowned our music; but now I hope all's friends.
    Get you to bed, and there the wedding ends.

COMPASS And so good night. My bride and I'll to bed: 435
    He that has horns, thus let him learn to shed.
      Exeunt

EXPLANATORY NOTES

Abbreviations

Brennan   *The White Devil* (1966), *The Duchess of Malfi* (1964), *The Devil's Law-Case* (1975), ed. E. M. Brennan (The New Mermaids)

Brown   *The White Devil* (1960), *The Duchess of Malfi* (1964), ed. J. R. Brown (The Revels Plays)

CC   *A Cure for a Cuckold*

DLC   *The Devil's Law-Case*

DM   *The Duchess of Malfi*

Lucas   *The Complete Works of John Webster*, ed. F. L. Lucas, vol. i: *The White Devil*, vol. ii: *The Duchess of Malfi*, *The Devil's Law-Case*; vol. iii: *A Cure for a Cuckold* (1927)

Mulryne   *The White Devil*, ed. J. R. Mulryne (Regents Renaissance Drama Series, 1970)

S.D.   Stage direction

s.p.   speech prefix

Tilley   M. P. Tilley, *A Dictionary of the Proverbs in England in the Sixteenth and Seventeenth Centuries* (1950)

WD   *The White Devil*

The White Devil

The persons of the play

Jaques, Christophero, Ferneze, Guid-Antonio: ghost characters.

To the Reader

1   *challenge*: arrogate

3   *nos . . . nihil*: 'we know these efforts of ours to be worth nothing' (Martial, xiii. 2).

4   *open . . . theatre*: the play was first performed at the Red Bull in Clerkenwell, probably early in 1612 (i.e. in the middle of winter). Elizabethan theatres were open spaces and fully exposed their audiences to the rigour of the elements.

9   *it*: the poet's work.

11–12   *nec . . . molestas*: 'you [the poet's book] will not fear the sneers of the malicious, nor will be execution garments for mackerels' (Martial, iv. 86). A '*tunica molesta*' denotes the pitch-smeared garments worn by human torches in the imperial gardens of Rome.

13–18 *no true dramatic poem . . . Nuntius*: this defiance of the neo-classical 'laws' of tragedy (i.e. the observing in drama of the unities of time, place and action as set out by Aristotle in the *Poetics* and more stringently later by Renaissance aesthetic theorists) derives from the preface to Jonson's *Sejanus' Fall*. The 'Chorus' and 'Nuntius' form intrinsic parts of classical and neo-classical drama. Their roles in Elizabethan drama are, however, generally curtailed, because the drama of this period largely ignores neo-classical restraints and prefers to act out its plot on the stage rather than report it, or interpret it for us through an authorial *persona*.

13 *non . . . dixi*: 'you cannot say more against these trifles of mine than I have said myself' (Martial, xiii. 2).

18–19 *lifen death*: make death a living reality.

20 *O dura messorum ilia*: 'O strong stomachs of harvesters' (Horace, *Epodes*, iii. 4).

23 *Haec . . . relinques*: 'what you leave will today become food for pigs' (Horace, *Epistles*, i. vii. 19). Webster slightly misquotes Horace who has 'Haec porcis hodie . . .'.

27 *Alcestides*: a version of this story, which originates in Valerius Maximus (*Facta et dicta memorabilia*), is related in Ben Jonson's *Discoveries*, where 'Alcestis' claims to be able to write 100 (not 300) verses in the same time it took Euripides to produce a mere three. Webster's use of 'Alcestides' for 'Alcestis' reflects an error in his source (Lodowick Lloyd's *Linceus' Spectacles*, 1607). No classical playwright or poet of that name can be identified, and the allusion remains, historically, obscure.

34–5 *Master Chapman*: George Chapman (*c*.1559–1634), translator of Homer, whose complete English translation of the *Iliad* and *Odyssey* were published in 1616, as well as the author of several comedies, tragedies, and poems distinguished by their erudition.

35 *Master Jonson*: Ben Jonson (1572–1637), Shakespeare's most prominent contemporary dramatist, renowned for his wide learning and application of rigorous neo-classical standards in his drama.

36–7 *Master Beaumont*: Francis Beaumont (1584–1616), poet and playwright, who as well as writing alone (e.g. *The Knight of the Burning Pestle*, *c*.1607) above all collaborated in a famous partnership with John Fletcher; their plays are classic exemplars of the Stuart taste for tragicomedy.

37 *Master Fletcher*: John Fletcher (1579–1625), the leading playwright of the King's Men after Shakespeare's retirement, with whom he collaborated on *The Two Noble Kinsmen*.

39 *Master Dekker*: Thomas Dekker (*c*.1570–1632), playwright and author of pageants and pamphlets, who collaborated *inter alia* with Webster, Middleton, and Jonson.

Master Heywood: Thomas Heywood (*c*.1574–1641), dramatist and theatrical apologist.

43 *Martial*: (*c*.AD 40–104), Roman writer of epigrams, reputed for his wit, and Webster's favourite classical poet.

44 *non . . . mori*: 'These monuments know not death' (Martial, x. 2).

1.1.2 *Democritus*: a fifth-century BC Greek philosopher and scientist, who originated an atomistic theory of the creation of the universe. He was known popularly as the 'laughing philosopher', but did not hold the views on reward and punishment attributed to him here; these derive instead from Webster's source, Antonio de Guevara's *The Dial of Princes* (tr. North, 1557).

8–9 *wolf . . . hungry*: the great, like wolves, disguise their true natures when their predatory appetites are satisfied.

18 *kennel*: gutter.

19 *one citizen is*: i.e. one citizen who is.

21 *only for caviare*: caviare was a rare delicacy in Jacobean England.

23 *phoenix*: the mythic androgynous and self-propagating phoenix was the rarest of all birds; eating roast phoenix was a byword in the period for excess in banqueting.

26 *An . . . i'th' air*: the word 'meteor' is used here to denote a falling star (as in modern English), but, by taking the form of noxious vapourssucked from the earth by the sun (rather than a hurtling towards it), the meteoric 'fall' of Lodovico reflects the wider application of the term 'meteor' in Webster's time to other atmospheric phenomena.

37 *in th'example*: by virtue of its example.

41 *close*: secret.

44 *Have . . . you*: be the fully resolved and self-reliant man.

47 *chafed*: rubbed: anticipating 'Expresseth' (l. 49), i.e. 'squeezes out', 'brings to the fore'.

59 S.D. *A sennet sounds*: Q has *Enter/Senate*. I follow Dyce and Brown in emending the stage direction in anticipation of the imminent entry of the court. Sennets were sounded to mark a ceremonial entrance.

60 *This . . . alms*: this maxim which follows is the charity which the way of the world has taught me.

make use of it: profit by the knowledge derived from it.

1.2.1 *Your best of rest*: good night.

10 *can't*: i.e. can it.

26 *gilder*: repeated exposure to the vapours of mercury used in gilding could cause tremors and insanity when inhaled. The liver was thought to be the seat of passion. The burden of the sentence is that Camillo is as impotent as a gilder suffering from dementia.

27–8 *great barriers . . . feathers*: refers to a royal tournament (played out at literal barriers) which caused the plumes to fall off, or be lopped off.

28 *shed hairs*: lost hair, with an allusion to the effects of venereal disease.

30 *wage all downward*: after gambling away everything else, he is prepared even to stake his genitals to continue gambling; if he then loses them, he will be less than a man (which is what Camillo is like, according to Flamineo).

31 *like a Dutch doublet*: the Dutch wore close-fitting doublets and wide breeches.

32 *back*: to have a weak back was interpreted as a sign of impotence.

39 *under-age protestation*: immature and adolescent wooing.

49 *travelling*: with a pun on 'travailing'; the implication is that Camillo journeys laboriously and will have no inclination to sex when he arrives.

53 *count*: a bawdy quibble on 'cunt', its near homophone (cf. 'flaw' below).

56 *flaw*: disagreement, but also (cf. l. 60) 'crack, vagina'.

62 *bowl booty?*: this is to cheat at bowls by combining with confederates in order to 'spoil' or victimize another player. 'Cheek', 'bias', 'jump with', and 'mistress' are bowling terms.

65 *Aristotle*: i.e. learning in logic.

71 *God boy you*: goodbye.

73 *horn-shavings*: shavings from the horns of a cuckold; the latter are also played on in l. 89 (below).

84 *large ears*: these are ass's ears (cf. 'an ass in foot-cloth' above).

89 *Jacob's staff*: an instrument for measuring.

90 *mutton*: slang for loose woman. The passage glances at the contemporary enclosures of common land for sheep farming, which caused hardship for the peasants who rebelled against it.

91–2 *provocative electuaries*: electuaries (medicines mixed with honey, jam, or syrup) used as aphrodisiacs.

92 *uttered since last Jubilee*: a jubilee is a year of remission during which plenary indulgences could be obtained by a pilgrimage to Rome and certain pious works. Jubilees happened every twenty-five years.

95–6 *spectacles . . . perspective art*: glasses which are cut into a number of facets where each gives a separate image; the result is a multiple image.

110 *Ida*: a high mountain in Crete, or in Phrygia near Troy.

ivory of Corinth: the city of Corinth was famous for its luxuriousness, but 'Corinth' was also a slang term for a bawdy-house, and ivory could denote sexually alluring flesh.

111 *the blackbird's . . . feather*: blonde hair was a mark of beauty in the period, whereas black was thought ugly.

118 *carved*: i.e. served him at supper; but also castrated (l. 120), since 'capon' (l. 121) means a castrated cock, i.e. a eunuch.

124 *blackguard*: the scullions and kitchen knaves of a noble household.

128 *calf's brains*: i.e. folly.

sage: a quibble on the herbs used in cooking and on sagacity (wisdom), the opposite of calf's brains.

130 *fire at the glass-house*: there was a glass factory near the Blackfriars theatre whose furnace was never extinguished.

134 *foil*: a thin leaf of some metal placed under a precious stone to increase its brilliance.

134–5 *covered . . . stone*: matched with a cheap ornament, with a pun on stone meaning 'testicle' (cf. also l. 141: 'opening your case hard').

145 *turtles'*: turtle-doves were proverbially faithful mates.

152 *breeze*: gadflies.

159 *'quae negata grata'*: 'whatever is denied is desired' (cf. Tilley, F585).

164 *progress*: i.e. Bracciano's visit to Camillo's, with a quibble on the meaning of progress as a journey by a high personage.

191 *Give credit*: believe me.

196 *Loose*: puns on 'lose' (cf. l. 196: 'lost'), but primarily means that she should not loosen him from his vows.

206 *house*: here meaning 'family' rather than 'dwelling place'.

217 *jewel . . . jewel lower*: this whole passage revolves around the *double-entendres* provided by 'jewel', meaning (*inter altera*) virtue, virginity, or married chastity.

224 *sat . . . grave*: perhaps 'sitting on the edge of a grave'.

225 *cross-sticks*: a complex phrase for which three possible readings can be advanced, none of them wholly satisfactory. The cross-sticks may be (*a*) criss-crossed osiers covering the grave and binding it together; (*b*) the patterning of lunar light and shadow on the grave from the branches of the overhanging yew tree; (*c*) 'crostics', i.e. the elided form of 'acrostics', as these were used in this period on memorial stones (cf. *Satiromastix*, 4.3.86–7). I am indebted for this last suggestion to Martin Wiggins.

229 *yew*: a pun on 'you' is intended. In Vittoria's dream Isabella and Camillo tell Vittoria that her liaison with the yew/Duke will disgrace him and transform him into a poor shrub.

266 *Thessaly*: a district of northern Greece, ominously associated with Medea of Colchis, who married Jason of the Argonauts and later murdered her children in an act of revenge. She was reported to have lost her box of drugs among the Thessalians, who were as famous for their wonder-working plants as for their witches: cf. Ovid, *Metamorphoses*, vii. 162 ff. and Apuleius, *The Golden Ass*.

284 *blood*: sensual passion; life-blood; bloodshed.

289 *great men's*: grief over great men's funerals is short-lived.

305–6 *bear . . . stirrup*: he would prefer to ride the horse rather than walk alongside it, on a level with his lord's stirrup.

311 *You . . . up*: i.e. you educated me.

315 *Conspiring with a beard*: a difficult phrase which could mean that he got the degree not through learning but by growing older and thus fulfilling the residence requirements; or, by wheedling himself parasitically into the favour of a senior man who advanced him. The latter seems the more satisfactory explanation: and the snide metonymy of 'beard' fits Flamineo's aggrieved tone, and is consonant with his rhetorical strategies elsewhere in the play. His parasitical behaviour starts at university.

334 *Lycurgus*: legendary Spartan law-giver, the subject of one of Plutarch's *Lives* from which Webster draws this detail.

344 *winter's snake*: a snake coiled up while hibernating.

2.1 S.D. *with little Jaques the Moor*: he is one of the play's four non-speaking ('ghost') characters (cf. 'The Persons of the Play'), who occurs only here, is not referred to elsewhere, and seems to have no function in the play. The other 'ghost-characters' are Christophero and Guid-Antonio (2.2: First Dumbshow) and Ferneze (5.1.41 ff.). But although these characters seem only token characters, it is worth noting that the casting list of one version of *DM* includes a 'ghost-character' (Forobosco) who may, in an earlier version of that play, have had an acting part (cf. *DM*, 'The Actors' Names'). Marcello, Flamineo's brother, serves in the household of Francisco de Medici. He enters naturally therefore in Francisco's train, but there is no acknowledgement between the two brothers of their shared parentage here, or of Marcello's relationship with his sister. This only happens in 3.1.

5 *polecats*: ferret-like animals with a fetid smell; also applied figuratively to prostitutes.

13–16 *As men . . . poison*: Isabella refers to the alleged protection against poison (spiders were thought to be poisonous) provided by the magical properties of unicorn's horns.

28–9 *have to . . . gifts of learning*: have turned high intellectual achievements to the advantage of your natural dispositions.

41 *All . . . name*: all the rights and honours of princes founder with the loss of their honour.

45 *fetch a course about*: turn tail.

48 *Some eagles . . . sun*: the eagle was perceived to be an aristocrat among birds, and its ability to gaze at the sun without blinking was taken to be one of its distinctive characteristics.

50 *dunghill birds*: scavenging birds.

52 *Happily*: haply, i.e. perhaps; the use of the longer form puns on 'happy', and intimates defiance.

60 *Switzers*: Swiss mercenaries, hired as security men by many of the courts of Europe.

75 *change . . . for plasters*: i.e. catch venereal disease from lustful indulgence.

82 *triumph . . . thus?*: animal fights were a common feature accompanying Roman triumphs, the procession through the streets of Rome by the victorious commander, dragging his prisoners behind his chariot. Bracciano compares Francisco's line of discourse to the high-risk strategy of baiting a lion (i.e. himself) as if he were already defeated, when in fact nothing could be further from the truth.

88 *wild ducks*: slang for prostitutes.

89 *moulting time*: loss of hair due to venereal disease.

91 *tale of a tub*: a cock-and-bull story; but also alluding to a sweating-tub, used to treat venereal disease.

92 *But . . . by natural reason*: but to express my verse ('sonnet') in plain words.

93 *grow melancholic*: stags become tame towards the end of the rutting season.

109 *practising your pike*: a probable *double-entendre*.

110 *Homer's frogs*: in the *Battle of Frogs and Mice*, a burlesque epic attributed to Homer, the frogs are armed with bulrushes for pikes and spears.

112 *discretion*: mature judgement, but also prudence, as at l. 114.

117 *So that*: provided that.

125 *He . . . head*: i.e. he is precocious.

136 *habit*: i.e. both custom and attire (the boy's armour).

150 *Devotion*: Isabella means married devotion but the Duke pretends to mistake it for piety.

153 *cast our reckonings up*: confront our ill deeds.

154 *Take your chamber*: go to your room.

157 *do not use to*: am not in the habit of.

161 *am to learn*: am as yet ignorant of.

   Italian: jealousy was supposed to be a characteristic Italian trait.

172 *bandy*: gather together.

179 *ancient*: (here) former.

180 *corpulent*: sneering reference to Francisco's title as the 'Great Duke' (rather than alluding to his girth).

184 *like a shaved Polack*: usually interpreted 'as of no account', i.e. Bracciano claims to despise Francisco as he would a barbarian. That Poles

shaved their heads close was reported by Fynes Moryson in his *Itinerary* (1617).

193 *latest*: last.

195 *lie with thee*: perhaps Bracciano should remove his wedding-ring at this point.

201–3 *this . . . repentance*: I will never repent (i.e. change my mind about) this vow.

204 *horrid*: fearful.

229 *modest*: well-ordered, or, perhaps, moderate.

230 *naught*: bad.

243 *apprehended wishes*: the desires of which I am fully conscious.

244 *scorpions*: from 1 Kings 12: 11, and 2 Chronicles 10: 11, where chastising with whips and scorpions are related forms of punishment.

249 *to*: compared to.

262 *'manet . . . repostum'*: 'It lies stored deep in my heart' (Virgil, *Aeneid*, i. 26). The line refers to Juno's anger at Paris's judgement when on Mount Ida he preferred Venus to Juno and Minerva, and thereby unwittingly ensured that the two spurned goddesses sided against Troy during the Trojan war.

272 *bring . . . stomach*: calm her down, scotch her determination.

273 *turn in post*: i.e. return post-haste.

276 *Unkindness*: denatured behaviour.

277 *Those . . . speak*: a proverbial idea (cf. Tilley, G449: 'Grief pent up will break the heart').

282 *stibium*: metallic antinomy, used as a poison or emetic.

cantharides: Spanish fly, used externally as a vesicant, but thought to be poisonous when applied internally.

287 *to Candy*: (lit.) to Crete; to his death.

290–1 *confessed . . . execution*: he escaped whipping for lechery by confessing to an earlier spurious charge of debt which took him into custody; but then he was forced to settle the non-existent debt by an even more cunning trickster who claimed to be his creditor.

296 *cornet*: in the seventeenth century a trumpet-like musical instrument with holes down its length.

lamprey: a fish-like creature resembling an eel, with seven spiracles on each side of the head.

300 *Saint Antony's fire*: a febrile skin disease.

303 *bloodshed*: bloodshot.

306 *by scruples*: i.e. bit by tiny bit.

311 *strain*: cunning; force; tearing (of muscles).

314 *Small . . . secure*: proverbial (cf. Tilley, C826).

316 *gallowses*: gallows-birds hanged by stepping on another's shoulders who then removes himself.

Low Countries: the Netherlands.

322 *The word . . . 'fecit'*: the motto 'Abundance has rendered me poor' (Ovid, *Metamorphoses*, iii. 466).

323 *Plenty . . . horns*: he is a cuckold many times over through others having sex with his wife and thereby depriving him of the use of his own 'horn' (i.e. penis).

333 *general world*: the world at large.

347 *fireworks*: pyrotechnics.

352 *Go change the air*: leave this place.

353 *cornucopia*: abundance, with a pun on horn as above.

379 *sister*: a courtesy title, strategically placed, as the Cardinal makes common cause with Francisco, Isabella's brother.

380 *want his absence*: miss him.

382–4 *for . . . shame*: only if Bracciano were to find himself humiliated by a resounding scandal—such as the exposure of his affair with Vittoria—will he be prompted to recover a reputation which would otherwise irretrievably be lost in adulterous dotage. It appears that Francisco may at this point be trying to save Bracciano from himself through a shock therapy (rather than trying to discredit him): i.e. Bracciano needs to be made to see and feel the shame of adultery before his reformation and hoped return to Isabella.

390 *small pity*: little cause for regret.

2.2.8 *nigromancer*: someone who practises the black art (cf. Latin 'niger').

11 *confederate*: allied.

12 *windmills*: fanciful schemes or projects.

13 *squib*: (lit.) a slight explosion; a trivial effect.

14 *curtal*: alludes to Morocco, a performing curtal (i.e. a horse with its tail docked) exhibited in London in the 1590s by a travelling showman called Banks. Morocco was trained to dance, feign death, count money, and show appropriate reactions to the names of Queen Elizabeth and the King of Spain. It was a common belief that Banks had magic powers and that Morocco was his familiar.

16 *ream*: (1) a large quantity of paper; those who produce it; (2) realm, i.e. huge numbers.

18 *lie about stol'n goods*: cast horoscopes to find stolen property.

19 *fast and loose*: shifty, inconstant.

23 S.D. That music accompanies the two dumb shows is clear from the conjuror's command (ll. 36–7). The crescendo in sound, from (presumably) muted to '*louder . . . as fits the act*', serves to contrast the martial context of Camillo's death with the mournful setting of Isabella's.

28 *dead shadow*: lifeless imitation.

37 S.D. *lays . . . horse*: thus it will appear like a fatal accident.

39 *taste*: understand, relish.

40 *charged*: laden with drink.

53–4 *This . . . hand*: this service of yours will be as valid as my signature.

3.1.11 *in by the week*: ensnared.

12 *sit upon*: sit in judgement, with a sexual *double-entendre*.

14 *tickler*: chastiser, but also provoker.

16 *tilting*: engage in armed combat (used with a sexual innuendo).

17–19 *private . . . public*: secretly . . . openly intimate.

23 *catch conies*: catch rabbits; cozen dupes.

38 *serviceable spirits*: the spirits whom they command.

44 *chamois*: chamois jerkins were worn under armour.

49 *builder*: used for building.

50 *mandrake*: the mandrake is poisonous, having emetic and narcotic properties. Its forked root was thought to resemble the human form, and was fabled to shriek when plucked up from the ground; the plucking itself reputedly caused insanity.

51–2 *Alas . . . strikes*: the slightest of their unprovoked angers destroys a person while seeming to deal out only mild punishment.

57–8 *over . . . infect*: over all considerations of policy which, the more they advance our cause, the more they corrupt.

69 *lofty tricks*: acrobatics.

70 *poulter*: poulterers went to the market very early in the morning and apparently often fell asleep over their baskets on horseback.

3.2 The conventions of this series entail the removal of the Quarto heading for this scene, 'THE ARRAIGNMENT OF VITTORIA', because it is not part of the spoken text. This is the most famous scene in the play, and Webster may have written out the heading in his manuscript to signal the scene's importance in the published version of the play (cf. Brown, pp. lxvii–lxviii).

S.D. Bracciano's entry, and his refusal as unbidden guest to sit on a chair to witness Vittoria's trial (ll. 5–7), heightens the tension, as he himself stands accused, though not in open court, of the charges levelled against Vittoria. His prolonged silence contrasts with the spontaneous protests of the ambassadors at the vehemence and unfairness of the proceedings. He only speaks at l. 155 to provide Vittoria with an alibi (which incriminates him).

10 '*Domine . . . corruptissimam*': 'My lord judge, turn your eyes on this plague, the most corrupt of women'.

22–3 *your credit . . . it*: your reputation will be rendered even more infamous by your case being heard in the vernacular.

24 *give aim*: record the score at the butts (to assess your performance).

27 *connive*: a malapropism, meaning 'tacitly pass over', when in fact he intends the opposite. The lawyer is ignorant of the proper legal terms to deploy here.

36 *pothecary's bills or proclamations*: apothecaries' wares, like the lawyer's language, were notoriously described in heavily Latinate phrases, and official notices were often in complex jargon.

40 *tropes not figures*: (generally) features of rhetoric; a 'trope' is a figurative or metaphorical use of language; a 'figure' can also be a deviation from the norm.

46 *fustian*: a quibble on the material (i.e. coarse cloth) and the lawyer's bombastic rhetoric.

58–9 *A . . . effected*: if 'effected' is Q's error for 'affected' (Brown, p. 68), then the line becomes clear and means 'a woman who cherishes the most unnatural spirit'.

64–7 *Yet . . . ashes*: the ultimate source for the story of the ashen fruit of Sodom and Gomorrah is in Deuteronomy 32: 32 and was elaborated by travellers like Sir John Mandeville.

67–8 *Your . . . do't*: she is telling the Cardinal to leave the prosecuting to his lawyer (cf. l. 36).

71 *scarlet*: the colour of the Cardinal's vestments (and also of judges' robes).

79 *character*: delineation in prose, sketch. The art of 'character' writing was popular in the period, and Webster himself contributed to Sir Thomas Overbury's *Characters* (1615).

85 *material fire*: fire formed of matter.

86 *tribute*: alludes to the exorbitant taxes on commodities imposed in the Low Countries.

88 *perdition*: through prostitution.

95–8 *worse . . . imperfect*: the dead bodies of executed felons were used for anatomy classes.

111 *Now . . . nothing*: i.e. he has repaid his debt of life.

115 *rushes*: used instead of carpets for strewing floors.

118 *Wound up*: in his shroud.

128 *Christian*: as well as contrasting Christian and pagan (or infidel) courts, Webster may allude specifically to the English Ecclesiastical courts ('Courts Christian') which dealt with adultery.

136 *To the point*: in every particular.

166 *sword*: emblem of justice.

179 *Nemo . . . lacessit*: 'No one injures me with impunity'.

200 *Casta . . . rogavit*: 'She is chaste whom no one has solicited' (Ovid, *Amores*, I. viii. 43).

211 *pistol flies*: shoot flies, but (perhaps) with an obscene *double-entendre* ('pistol' and pizzle are almost homophones).

216–17 *devil . . . picture*: Vittoria Corombona is probably the 'white devil' of the play's title, but it also fits other leading characters such as Flamineo and Bracciano who commit the blackest sins and yet can shine at times through their courage and even generosity of spirit. The title-phrase pin-points the paradox that good and evil may be inextricably linked, to the point of the one entailing the other (cf. *Henry V*: 'There is some soul of goodness in things evil, | Would men observingly distil it out . . . And make a moral of the devil himself'). Proverbially the 'white devil', i.e. the devil in disguise and a hypocrite, is worse than the black (Tilley, D310).

221 *ducats*: a gold or silver coin.

229–30 *Were . . . thoughts*: i.e. if your spies could read my very thoughts, perhaps with an insulting suggestion that the Cardinal has long ears.

235–6 *You . . . Vitelli*: the historical Vittoria was born at Gubbio in Umbria and descended of the Accoramboni.

248 *Rialto talk*: widely rumoured in Venice. The Rialto was the hub of the city's commercial life.

254 *upon your sureties*: a 'surety' is someone who makes himself liable for the default of someone else.

262–3 *blazing . . . princes*: celestial bodies were popularly held to symbolize princely rank, and their falling marked the death of great ones.

271–2 *I . . . thus*: perhaps echoing Matthew 7: 1: 'Judge not, that ye be not judged'.

283–4 *O . . . tongue*: analogical to the idea of a woman's strength being in her tongue (cf. Tilley, W675).

306 *hath . . . palsy*: wags uncontrolledly (lit., trembles with a nervous disease).

3.3.6 *list . . . Poland*: Poland was apparently thought to be a proverbially poor country with a great number of pedlars.

8 *piles*: with a play on both senses of the word.

23–4 *under the line*: at the equator.

26 *weights . . . with*: the penalty of pressing was used in England against accused persons who refused to plead either guilty or not guilty: some persons preferred to die under this torture rather than forfeit their estates upon conviction.

32 *well may*: well they should be.

35 *first . . . religion*: Cain killed Abel because his own sacrifice did not find favour with God.

46 *Wolner*: a legendary Elizabethan glutton, capable of digesting almost anything, who nevertheless died of eating a raw eel.

49 *screech-owl*: the barn owl, from its discordant cry, was supposed to be a bird of evil omen.

77 *melancholic hare*: the hare was perceived as a melancholy creature, and eating it supposedly induced melancholy (cf. Tilley, H151).

79 *grieve*: Flamineo continues his part of the 'distracted' man, and pretends to mistake laughter for grief.

85 *girn, rogue*: uncorrected Q has 'a grine rouge', while corrected Q and Q2 read 'gue', with Q3 offering 'Rogue'. It seems likely that 'girn' is a metathesis of 'grin', which is still used dialectically, and that the reading of the line proposed by Brown (p. 89), 'girn, rogue,' is the most plausible; 'girn' translates as 'snarl'.

90 *strappadoed*: tortured by hanging from a pulley with one's hands tied behind one's back.

felly: a section of the exterior rim of a wheel.

128–9 *Is . . . thus*: Lodovico trembles with rage, whereas a fencer's movements are tightly controlled.

4.1.2 *dangle . . . hair*: this was the custom for virgin brides in Jacobean England.

13–14 *undermining . . . cannon*: i.e. the knocking down walls during a siege.

16 *your back unbruised*: your back not being bruised.

33 *black book*: (with a pun on 'the black arts') a book of official records bound in black; a register of villains.

40 *reach*: grasp, understand.

49 *taking up commodities*: this describes the custom of swindlers who lent goods instead of money, and then collected money by exaggerating the value of these goods.

politic bankrupts: people using faked bankruptcy for financial gain.

51–3 *put off . . . children*: hive off at a huge profit poor merchandise to their wives' lovers when their wives started producing bastards.

56 *share . . . reportage*: they divide their spoils with scriveners who recommend them.

57 *antedate their writs*: forge the date on their writs, perhaps to block a serious charge by a minor one.

69 *tribute of wolves*: the Welsh wolves were extirpated in the tenth century by King Edgar who imposed a tribute of 300 wolves a year to rid the country of them.

70 *hang . . . hedge*: dogs who bit sheep were hung up as a penalty, as were wolves.

79 *to make prize*: capture; plunder.

89 *laundress*: supply with laundresses; washerwomen were reputedly promiscuous.

106 *melancholy*: at this time melancholy men were popularly thought to be particularly prone to hallucinatory fantasies.

129 *When . . . follow*: cf. the proverbial idea that 'When the fox has got in his head he will soon make the body follow' (Tilley, F655).

136 *Flectere . . . movebo*: 'If I cannot change the will of heaven, I shall release hell' (*Aeneid*, vii. 312).

4.2.1 *recourse*: access.

4 *The Pope*: Gregory XII died on 15 April 1585.

20 *coffined*: enclosed in a pie-dish; coffin denotes the crust of a pie.

34 *equivocation*: a speaking in quibbles which Flamineo parodies by developing 'hang' (l. 33) with 'halter', and 'mellow' (l. 36) with 'Rotten' (l. 37).

35 *willow*: a traditional emblem of unrequited love.

37 *bed-straw*: straw was used for mattresses and to ripen fruit.

38 *convinces*: with a quibble: 'all the preceding maxims this one confutes', or 'all the wrinkles of age this maxim overcomes'.

40 *atheists*: used loosely in the period, here denoting Francisco's impiety in equating princes with gods.

45–6 *Prevent . . . off*: another allusion to venereal disease and the loss of hair.

46 *changeable stuff*: i.e. fickle woman.

47–3 *O'er . . . wearing*: Flamineo suggests that Vittoria is in deep water (i.e. trouble), but he also puns on 'changeable stuff' (l. 47) with the clothes imagery of 'wearing' and 'water'; 'changeable' means 'shot', as in 'watered or shot silk'.

54 *Russia*: in Russia debt defaulters were beaten on the shins.

60 *I . . . daily*: I expect to be poisoned any moment now; 'Spanish fig' was also an expression of contempt and accompanied by an obscene gesture.

61 *ply your convoy*: perform your art (i.e. that of a pander) to bring couples together.

63 *Polyphemus to Ulysses*: the cyclops Polyphemus imprisoned Ulysses and his crew and ate two of them at each meal; as a cruel boon he offered to eat Ulysses last (Homer, *Odyssey*, ix. 369–70).

66 *face me?*: Defy me? But Bracciano also comments on the fact that Flamineo leaves backwards, all the time facing him.

70 *characters*: ciphers.

71 *receiver*: a menial appointed to receive money due (i.e. a position incompatible with Bracciano's aristocratic dignity); perhaps also here meaning 'pimp'.

79 *reclaimed*: reformed; (hawking) called back or tamed.

give you the bells: bells were attached to a hawk's legs for tracing and to scare the quarry. Bracciano threatens to abandon Vittoria by withdrawing his protection (removing her 'bells') from her, i.e. 'give you the bells' in fact means 'take the bells away from you'.

80 *Ware hawk!*: be on your guard.

85 *beheld the devil in crystal*: alludes to the play's title (cf. 3.2.216–17 n.) and to the contemporary idea that spirits could appear in crystal; the phrase means 'to be deceived'.

93–4 *furnish . . . Irish*: Irish wakes and funerals were notorious in the period for producing exaggerated expressions of grief.

98 *quicksilver*: because mercury moves very quickly.

108–9 *which . . . them*: the presence of foxes was popularly held to alleviate palsy, but their awful smell meant that the sufferer was still unfit for polite society after the cure.

108 *which, sick*: who are sick.

118 *limb*: cf. Matthew 18: 8 where Christ counsels amputation of an offending hand or foot rather than chancing damnation because of it.

129 *weep poniards*: tears which sting like needles.

130–1 *I had . . . matches*: I'd prefer to squint (rather than please you with my eyes).

136 *blown up*: i.e. exploded.

153 *mercer*: a dealer in textile fabrics, particularly silk and costly materials.

156 *stand*: resist.

157 *their*: the leverets'.

158 *full cry*: full pursuit; good weeping.

164 *Hand her*: fondle her.

165 *ferret . . . blowing*: ferrets were popularly (but wrongly) supposed to release their prey if blown at.

167 *the forgetful wine*: the wine which induces oblivion.

171 *Threaten the cannon*: threaten us with the use of force.

199 *Stay—ingrateful Rome!*: Q1, Q2, and Q3 have 'Stay ingrateful Rome',
while Q4 reads 'Stay, ingrateful Rome!' This edition follows Brown and
Brennan in reading 'ingrateful Rome!' as a separate expression of dismay
from 'Stay', which is a command to Flamineo to stop. The line which
follows, comparing Rome to Barbary, i.e. the imagined country of the
barbarians (originally the Saracen countries along the north coast of
Africa), corroborates this reading.

210 *lay her post-horse*: set relays of post-horses for her.

215 *work him*: persuade him.

230 *application*: interpretation (applying the fable to his own situation).

4.3.9–13 *Rhodes . . . Garter*: The 'Knight of Rhodes' belonged to the Order
of the Knights of St John which was founded during the First Crusade;
the Order of St Michael was founded by Louis XI in 1469, and the
Order of the 'Holy Ghost' (Saint Esprit) in 1578. The Order of the
Golden Fleece was founded by Philip the Good of Burgundy (1430) and
the Order of the Annunciation by Amadeus VI of Savoy (1362); the
Order of the Garter was founded *c*.1346–8.

35 S.D. *Conclavist*: Q has Cardinal, but the emendation to Conclavist
(Brown) recommends itself, because the character appears specifically in
response to Lodovico's demand for the Cardinal's attendants; and the
speaker's reference to the 'lord cardinals' is more apposite for a servant
than another cardinal. The 'window', like the terrace (l. 40: S.D.), gives
from the church battlements, the tiring-house façade.

38 *given . . . scrutiny*: finished the formal taking of the secret ballot.

39 *admiration*: homage (to the new pope); the more technically appropriate
term would be 'adoration'.

44–7 *Denuntio . . . Quartus*: 'I bring you tidings of great joy. The Most
Reverend Cardinal Lorenzo de Monticelso has been elected to the
Apostolic See, and has chosen for himself the title of Paul the Fourth.
ALL: Long live the Holy Father Paul The Fourth.' The real-life model
for Monticelso was Cardinal Montalto who became Sixtus the Fifth.

60–1 *Concedimus . . . peccatorum*: 'We grant you the Apostolic benediction
and remission of sins'.

65 *seat*: the throne or office of Pope.

79 *'like*: alike.

83 *resolve you*: answer you.

87 *out of measure*: excessively

95–6 *career . . . ring-galliard*: in the manage of horses, these terms respectively describe a short gallop of the horse at full speed, getting it to leap,
and (probably) putting it through motions resembling the triple-time
galliard dance performed in the riding-school ring.

97 *French rider*: the French were famous for their horsemanship.

138–9 *travel . . . intelligence*: statesmen often paid travellers to furnish them with foreign news ('intelligence').

142 *told out*: counted out; paid.

146 *puling*: (lit.) feebly wailing, i.e. protesting.

5.1.15–16 *strict . . . Capuchins*: an order which branched off from the Franciscans to return to the original austerity of St Francis.

19 *knighted*: i.e. in the Order of St John.

35 *airy*: flippant.

41 S.D. This ceremonial passage reminds the audience of the newly constituted inner core of Bracciano's household, including Cornelia who is to play a prominent part in the later stages of the action. I follow Brown in introducing Carlo and Pedro here as members of Bracciano's household who are in league with Francisco (cf. 4.3.76–7). Both are given speech-headings in Q (ll. 61 and 63) and Q has them enter at 5.2.17 and 5.6.166.

47 *incapable of*: unable to accept.

49 *monuments*: memorials.

65 *despaired*: i.e. committed suicide.

67 *pair*: not necessarily two, but a set.

68 *the pommel of his saddle*: the hands touching the pommel would convey the poison to the victim's mouth.

71–2 *struck . . . hazard!*: a hazard is one of the winning openings in the inner walls of an indoor Jacobean tennis court, but the phrase is used punningly to mean 'put his soul in jeopardy'.

91 *women . . . stick*: 'to stick like burs' is proverbial (Tilley, B724).

117 *Colossuses*: i.e. giants (like the Colossus at Rhodes, one of the Seven Wonders of the ancient world).

130–1 *under his hand*: a written (and signed) promise.

134 *miserable*: (1) miserly; (2) compassionate; (3) pitiable.

147 *constrainedly*: under duress.

148 *holds . . . ears*: a proverbial usage, explained by the next sentence (cf. Tilley, W603). The point of the expression is that it is equally dangerous to hold on to, and to let go of, the wolf's ears.

155 *gipsy*: used generally to describe someone of dark complexion

156–7 *your love . . . lover*: Zanche claims that his love has declined, whereas Flamineo deliberately mistakes her to mean that he successfully allays her lust.

163 *painting*: i.e. make-up.

381

171 *tumbling*: a sexual innuendo which concludes the series of bawdy *double-entendres* suggested by 'extremity', 'tempest', and 'vessel'.

173–4 *shoemakers . . . drawers-on*: salt bacon draws men on to drink, just as a shoemaker draws shoes on their feet.

176 *sunburnt*: because Mulinassar is a Moor.

178 *clapped . . . heels*: put in iron.

178–9 *strike i'th' court*: a serious offence which carried severe penalties in England.

181 *bedstaff*: a support for the mattress, or a stick used for making up the bed which Cornelia might use as a cudgel. The sentence contains a bawdy innuendo, where 'bedstaff' means men who keep the maids warm.

184–5 *walnut tree . . . fruit*: proverbial: cf. Tilley, W644.

192 *fan of feathers*: a taunting remark which challenges Marcello's manhood, because the fan is associated with courtiers, not soldiers; cf. also Flamineo's calling him 'boy' (l. 188).

193–4 *choleric . . . rhubarb*: the humour of choler (which induced anger) was commonly treated with rhubarb.

198 *sons of Oedipus*: Eteocles and Polynices, brothers of Antigone, remained unreconciled after death, and the flames of their funeral pyres strove to outreach one another as the brothers had done in life.

201 *gests*: stopping-places on a royal progress.

204 *fit . . . on't*: match it.

210 *Michaelmas*: i.e. 29 September; 'Mulinassar' is in the autumn of life when love, which properly belongs to spring, is rare and faint.

5.2.10 *this crucifix*: i.e. the one which hangs from Cornelia's neck.

16 *turn . . . up*: perhaps meaning 'dying', analogously with 'to turn up one's heels (or toes)'; or Flamineo may comment on Marcello's spitting blood in the throes of death.

sanctuary: a place (most often a church) where fugitives from justice were temporarily safe from prosecution.

66 *grazed*: grassed, i.e. lost in the grass and searched for by shooting a second arrow after it; but the word also puns on the 'grazing' (i.e. stabbing) of Marcello by Flamineo.

5.3.8 *bar*: probably a clasp on Bracciano's helmet rather than the barriers of the jousts.

21 *without book*: i.e. with great efficiency.

30 *rough-bearded comet*: a comet with an ominously long tail; 'comet' means 'long-haired [star]'.

36 *Franciscans*: Lodovico and Gasparo are of Francisco's faction just as the Capuchins were part of the Franciscan order.

52 *verge*: an area within twelve miles of the King's court.

55 *fed with poultry*: it was a widely held belief that ulcers (known as 'wolves') could be cured by making them feed off poultry or raw meat applied externally.

80 *O . . . abused me*. The following note to the actors occurs at this point in Quarto: *These speeches are several kinds of distractions and in the action should appear so.*

81 *conveyed . . . territories*: a serious offence in England against the state, and on the statute book since the Middle Ages.

85 *to blame*: blameworthy.

89 *quails*: (1) a delicacy, but popularly held to feed on poison, whereas dog-fish (l. 91) were cheap common fare and a term of abuse; (2) loose women.

101 *rose*: an ornamental rosette often worn upon a shoe-front.

103 *rare linguist*: good at argument.

112 *rogue*: i.e. Flamineo.

115 *Her . . . powder*: Vittoria's hair was powdered for the wedding earlier in the day.

128 *Attende Domine Bracciane*: Listen, Lord Bracciano.

133–43 *Domine . . . laevum*: Lord Bracciano, you used in war to be safe behind your shield; now you shall oppose this shield to your infernal enemy. | Once you prevailed in battle with your spear; now you shall brandish this holy spear against the enemy of souls. | Listen, Lord Bracciano, if you now also approve what has been done between us, turn your head to the right. | Rest assured, Lord Bracciano: think of the many good deeds to your credit—lastly remember that my soul is pledged for yours, if there should be any peril. | If you now also approve what has been done by us, turn your head to the left.

153 *conscience*: inmost thought.

156 *fine . . . bottles*: perhaps silver or glass embossed with jewels.

171 *avoid the chamber*: empty the room.

177 *quaintlier*: more skilfully.

182 *more . . . city*: alludes to the 'New River' project by Sir Hugh Myddleton to supply London with fresh water. Construction of the canal began in 1609 and was ongoing during the time of writing *WD*.

184 *moonish*: fickle, but also 'of no substance', as the moon takes its light from the sun.

   shades: ghosts.

188 *scores*: obtains on credit.

196 *swallowed . . . saffron*: as a cordial saffron induced merriness and was thought to be fatal if taken in large quantities.

198 *To teach . . . ice*: i.e. to instruct courtly intrigue that it is merely deluded in feeling safe.

215 *infernal*: evil spirit.

218 *passionately*: quibbles on 'passion' and 'suffering' (cf. Latin *pati*, to suffer).

232 *Irish mantle*: a blanket or plaid which, like the Irish poor, he wore over his naked body.

260–1 *sunburnt . . . white*: cf. Tilley, E186.

267 *partridge*: according to Pliny (*Naturalis Historia*) partridges and other fowl purged themselves with laurel. Francisco quibbles on the dual meaning of laurel, as medicinal herb and crowning glory; their final achievement, he implies, will obliterate the foul means they used.

5.4.24 *Anacharsis*: a sixth-century BC Scythian prince renowned for his wisdom who is confused here with Anaxarchus, a Thracian sage who, while he was tortured to death in a mortar, continued to taunt his tormentors and remained serene.

29 *decimo-sexto*: a very small book in which each leaf is one sixteenth of a full sheet; a person in miniature.

38 *Castle Angelo*: the Castle of St Angelo in Rome which, as the following line suggests, might have reminded Webster of the Tower of London.

39 *nothing about her*: no clothes on.

43–4 *flaming firebrand*: a possible word-play by Flamineo on his name.

51 *winding . . . corpse*: to wrap a corpse in a winding sheet.

62 *rosemary*: an evergreen shrub, used as an emblem of remembrance, and associated particularly with weddings and funerals.

64–6 *bays . . . lightning*: wreaths of bays were granted poets and victorious generals; bay leaves were commonly assumed to give protection from lightning.

66 *sheet*: i.e. winding-sheet.

73 *rue*: an evergreen with bitter, strong-scented leaves; a pun on 'to rue' (to be sorry) is probably intended.

74 *Heart's-ease*: pansy, but also 'ease of heart', solace; to contrast with 'rue'.

81 *strange*: eerie.

cricket . . . sings: the sound of a singing cricket coming from the oven was thought to be portentous.

82–4 *yellow . . . sure*: the imaginary spots on his hand spell his death, she claims, because he has touched the speckled belly of toads, which were believed to be poisonous.

85 *cowslip-water . . . memory*: a popular belief in the period.

91-4 *Call for . . . unburied men*: the robin and his wife the wren were thought (in popular mythology) to cover the faces or bodies of dead men.

95 *funeral dole*: funeral rites.

99-100 *wolf . . . again*: wolves were thought to dig up the bodies of murder victims.

105 *this*: the grave.

110 *without*: unless.

119 S.D. *leather cassock*: a long loose coat worn by ghosts;

a pot of lily-flowers: probably an emblem associating beauty with death, because the flowers are rooted in the skull and feed upon the dead. Quarto's *Iilly-flowers* would suggest modern 'Gillyflowers', but the phrase 'a pot of gillyflowers' does not yield a meaningful sense in this context. It is safer to assume that what happened was a substitution of italic *I* for italic *l*, either from a compositor's error, or through a shortage of type.

121 *mockery*: unreal shadow; parody.

139 *beyond melancholy*: more than just hallucination induced by melancholy.

5.5.7 *To*: down to, including.

5.6.14 *Cain . . . brother*: cf. Genesis 4:14: 'Behold, thou hast driven me out this day from the face of the earth; and from thy face shall I be hid; and I shall be a fugitive and a vagabond in the earth . . .'.

24 *dead lift*: an emergency, with a pun on 'dead'.

56-8 *body . . . house?*: what Vittoria means is that the killing of the body by suicide also murders the soul.

59-61 *sins . . . off*: whereas the taste of other sins is sweet ('candied': i.e. coated in sugar), despair is instead bitter and poisonous (stibium is metallic antimony); and yet we devour it eagerly.

64-5 *stop . . . winter plums*: meaning (perhaps) 'unnatural, cold plums', i.e. bullets (Mulryne).

71 *exclamation*: formal (rhetorical) declaration.

93 *taster*: continues the food imagery (ll. 76-7), and denotes someone who tastes the food before it is served to the King.

105 *cupping-glasses*: open-mouth glasses used to draw off blood during surgery.

108 *Lucian*: in *Menippos*, the classical Greek prose satirist describes purgatory as a place where kings and princes are reduced to doing the meanest chores.

110 *tagging points*: joining together the laces which did the work of buttons in Elizabethan dress.

111 *crying 'garlic'*: i.e. like a poor pedlar who cries out his prices.

112 *Pepin*: King of the Franks and the father of Charlemagne; also punning on 'pippin' (apple).

134–5 *fox . . . braches*: i.e. even the proverbially cunning fox often comes home dead, without his tail (because fox-hunters kept the tail as trophy).

143 *Scotch holy bread*: a sodden sheep's liver.

145–6 *drive . . . body*: the usual treatment of suicides' bodies in the period.

149 *doubled . . . reaches*: outwitted your plots.

160 *Artillery Yard*: an area in Bishopsgate (east London) used for military practice.

163 *Hypermnestra*: the youngest of the fifty daughters of Danaus, who alone saved her husband's life (Ovid, *Heroides*, 14).

166 *instruments*: pistols.

183–5 *I . . . sparrowhawk*: Vittoria claims that she would sooner trust her traditional enemies than her kindred predator, Flamineo.

190 *centre*: heart.

205 *glorious*: vainglorious.

214 *train*: (lit.) comet's tail; her retinue, i.e. Zanche.

223 *Conceit . . . me*: fear cannot kill me.

227 *red*: her blood is red, even though she is black; but 'red' also suggests courage.

234 *Toledo . . . fox*: a finely tempered Spanish sword, or an English one; 'fox' was a kind of sword with the figure of a wolf on it, which was sometimes mistaken for a fox.

245 *Only . . . them*: but their vices were not discovered.

253 *bottom*: death, continuing the image of a sinking ship.

255–9 *I . . . knowledge*: Flamineo seems to say that his knowledge is confined to his own person, that matters relating to heaven lie beyond the scope of ordinary human intelligence. The second 'knowledge' in l. 260 should perhaps start with a capital to signal that two different conceptions of knowledge apply: basic, and ultimately limited, human knowledge, and 'true' knowledge of the kind assumed by divines or theologians.

265 *lions*: there was a small zoo in the Tower of London. *Candlemas*: 2 February; according to contemporary lore, sunshine at Candlemas meant that more severe weather lay ahead.

273 *where*: whereas.

297 *limbed*: limned, i.e. painted.

night-piece: painting of a nocturnal (and evil) scene.

[*Epilogue*]

Haec . . . placui: 'These things will be our reward, if I have pleased [you]' (Martial, ii. 91).

1 *action*: acting.

3 *to . . . monster*: to distort by exaggerating.

6 *Perkins*: Richard Perkins of the Queen's Men is usually credited with playing Flamineo because of this unprecedented (in the drama of the period) tribute to him. Webster had joined Perkins in 1612 in commending Thomas Heywood's *Apology for Actors*, and here he specifically calls him his friend whose acting excelled at 'the beginning and end' of the play. Perkins is not known to have taken another lead till 1626. This is hardly conclusive evidence against his playing Flamineo. But if 'the beginning and end' is taken literally to mean the start and finish of the play, then the case against Flamineo (who is prominent throughout the play's action) or Bracciano (who dies well before its end) gains in momentum. A plausible alternative to either of these two roles would be that of Lodovico (cf. Wiggins, *Journeymen in Murder*, 172).

The Duchess of Malfi

The persons of the play

The play was a King's Men play (referred to as 'Kings Maiesties Seruants' on the title-page), and details about the actors here mentioned are provided by T. W. Baldwin, *The Organization and Personnel of the Shakespeare Company* (1927), Lucas, ii. 126–7, Brown, *DM*, pp. xviii–xxi. The use of numerals for the parts of 'Ferdinand', 'Cardinal', and 'Antonio' suggests that the casts of two separate performances are listed, a feature unique to Q1 and Q2 of *DM* among sixteenth- and seventeenth-century plays. The omission of several characters (Castruccio, Roderigo, Grisolan, Old Lady), and the attributing of a speaking part to Forobosco (N. Towley), who does not appear even as a 'ghost character' (whereas in the *WD* there are no fewer than four non-speaking parts), further suggests that the performance versions of the play differed from the printed copy (cf. *Note on the Texts, DM*). The placing of Bosola at the head of the list rather than Ferdinand or the Cardinal (whose rank and status would normally command that position) recalls Webster's special tribute to Richard Perkins (Flamineo?) at the end of the *WD*.

Forobosco: ghost character.

[*Dedication*]

1 *George Harding*: (1601–58), grandson of George, Lord Hunsdon, who had held the office of Lord Chamberlain, and had been a patron of the former Lord Chamberlain's Men, now the King's Men. He was the dedicatee of Burton's *The Anatomy of Melancholy* (1621), and both Massinger and Shirley would dedicate plays to him.

9 *conduct*: conductor.

[*Commendatory Verses*]

19–22 *In . . . Londinensis*: 'To Tragedy: As light is from darkness struck by the blow of the Thunderer, | So tragedy brings ruin to the wicked and life to famous poets.' Thomas Middleton, poet and Chronologer of London. Thomas Middleton (1580–1627), a contemporary playwright, had collaborated with Webster, and was joint author of *The Changeling* and sole author of *Women Beware Women*. He was appointed City Chronologer in 1620.

26 *bodied*: embodied.

27 *answered*: justified.

31 *Wil. Rowley*: William Rowley (d. 1626) was an actor and dramatist who collaborated extensively, including with Webster on *A Cure for a Cuckold*.

39 *John Ford*: John Ford (1586–*c*.1640) was the author of, and collaborator in, some twenty-three plays, including *The Late Murder of the Son upon the Mother* (now lost), on which he collaborated with Webster, Dekker, and Rowley. His chief claim to fame rests on *'Tis Pity She's a Whore* and *Perkin Warbeck*.

1.1.31 *only . . . reward*: the only reward.

33 *enforce*: urge.

37 *blackbirds . . . weather*: probably alludes to the habit of birds fluffing up their feathers to keep warm in winter. Bosola's restricting this to blackbirds reflects on his melancholy.

49 *crows . . . caterpillars*: i.e. scavengers (human and other).

54 *Tantalus*: as a punishment for stealing the food of the gods and imparting it to mortals, Tantalus was banished to Hades and stood up to his chin in water under an overhanging fruit-tree, both of which retreated whenever he attempted to satisfy his thirst and hunger.

55 *hawks . . . <. . .>*: a phrase seems to have dropped out from Q1 (Q2, Q3, and Q4 read 'dogs, and when'), probably as a result of censorship. Brown (p. 12) plausibly proposes 'whores' as the likely word.

57 *geometry*: 'hang by geometry' was a proverbial phrase (cf. Tilley, G82). Bosola's use of the phrase to explain the predicament of disabled soldiers is explained by the lines which follow.

68 *Gaston de Foix*: De Foix (1489–1512) was a charismatic, young military commander who won a famous victory at Ravenna, as Painter relates in *The Palace of Pleasure*. He did not, as Webster mistakenly assumes, conquer Naples.

77 S.D. Julia, Castruccio's wife and the Cardinal's mistress, is listed at this point in Q1 as one of the participants in the scene, but visually and theatrically it makes better sense to have her enter with the Cardinal at l. 141, the more so since at ll. 102 ff. she is talked about as if she were absent.

83 *ring*: i.e. the ring in jousting which the successful competitor carried off after successfully threading it with the point of his lance.

106 *children of Israel*: Quarto has 'children of Ismael', i.e. Arabs, descended from Ishmael, Abraham's son by Hagar; but Q's reading may be a misreading of 'Israel', as Brennan (pp. 106–7) points out, quoting in support of a reading of the children of Israel as tent dwellers Genesis 4: 20; Psalms 78: 55; 2 Kings 13: 5 ('and the children of Israel dwelt in their tents').

  tents: punning on surgical dressings.

110 *put up*: desist, with a sexual *double-entendre*; Ferdinand's lines from l. 105 onwards are full of sexual innuendo.

114 *Pliny*: Gaius Plinius Secundus (the Elder Pliny: AD 23/4–79), author of the encyclopedic *Naturalis Historia*, who maintained that in certain parts of Portugal mares were impregnated by the west wind and conceived foals as swift as the wind.

115 *ballasted . . . quicksilver*: quicksilver is used allusively with reference to quick motion. The jennet is faster rather than slower, because of this imaginary load.

116 *reels . . . often*: continues the imagery of 'ballast' which is meant to steady a boat from tilting; in this case because the 'ballast' enhances the horse's speed, it jibs and shies away from the ring in jousting.

132 *out of compass*: immoderately.

137 *Grecian horse*: better known as the Trojan horse, which the Greeks used as a ruse to enter Troy after the ten-year siege of the city.

142 *come about?*: i.e. returned to port.

151 *spring*: i.e. his complexion is as troubled and sinister (toads were deemed poisonous) as a pool for toads.

153 *Hercules*: the 'plots' refer to the mythical labours of Hercules (among the most famous of which are killing the Nemean Lion, cleaning the Augean Stables, taming the Horses of Diomed, procuring the Girdle of the Amazon, kidnapping Cerberus, and stealing the Golden Apples of the Hesperides).

156 *primitive decency*: i.e. the original and uncorrupted decency of the early church.

172 *shrewd*: (Q2/3) injurious, i.e. Ferdinand is vengeful. Q1 reads 'shewed', and the phrase could be read to mean 'they are debts which he settles ostentatiously, because he owns up to them in public'.

180 *in one figure*: after one original.

temper: alloy.

183–5 *and wish . . . hear her*: rather than modestly curtailing her spontaneous speech, she instead felt that it was your penance to hear her (and therefore she stopped); but of course you would prefer her to carry on.

190 *continence*: self-restraint, with a quibble on 'countenance'.

197 *play the wire-drawer*: i.e. protract or spin out excessively.

198 *case . . . up*: enclose it in a case.

216 *intelligence*: secret information.

233–4 *oft . . . root*: the more common proverb is that the weaker shrubs weather storms more easily than the stronger ones (cf. Tilley, C208: 'High cedars fall when low shrubs remain').

236 *next*: nearest.

238–9 *show'rs . . . them*: an allusion to the seduction of Danae to whom Jupiter the Thunderer appeared in a shower of gold.

274 *feed . . . dish*: eat at a lord's table.

289 *livers*: the liver was considered the seat of passion.

290 *Laban's sheep*: for the story of Jacob and Laban's sheep, and the 'parti-coloured lambs', cf. Genesis 30: 31–42.

305 *Vulcan's engine*: a net made of fine bronze thread which Vulcan used to trap his wife Venus in the act of committing adultery with Mars.

309 *eaves of night*: under cover of darkness.

319 *Wisdom . . . end:* a near-proverbial injunction to prudence (cf. Tilley, E125 and E128: 'Remember the end' and 'Think on the end before you begin').

340 *I . . . husband*: (1) I chose a husband and ignored the wrongness of the choice; (2) I closed my eyes, and chose a husband at random.

357 *husbands*: husbandmen; stewards. The Duchess's choice of words begins a series of puns on the word (continued in ll. 376, 381) which marks Antonio's passage from being her steward to being her wedded husband.

380 *In a couple*: i.e. a couple of sheets (as opposed to the winding sheet); in marriage.

381 *Saint Winifred*: an early Welsh saint beheaded for her chastity, and subsequently restored to life by St Beuno.

427 *progress through*: journey through yourself (like a prince through his territory), i.e. inspect and value yourself.

432 *woo . . . woo*: with a pun in 'woo' on 'woe'.

454 *Quietus est*: 'He is quit.' 'Quietus' means receipt, discharge from office or duty.

459 *without this circumference*: outside this embrace.

469 *Per verba de presenti*: 'through words about the present'; although a marriage thus contracted (normally in front of a witness) was legally binding, as the Duchess indicates by her emphasis on it being 'absolute marriage', it still required subsequent solemnization in church, before it could be consummated.

470 *Gordian*: the Gordian knot which could not be untied, but which Alexander the Great cut with his sword.

472 *spheres*: Antonio refers to the perfect harmony of the concentric spheres which in the Ptolemaic system of the universe were thought to revolve around the earth, and produce celestial music by doing so.

473 *Quickening*: coming to life, with a quibble on pregnancy.

475–7 *palms . . . divided*: palm trees were thought to reproduce only if in close proximity to one another; and cf. *Characters* (the collection by Sir Thomas Overbury) where 'a virtuous widow' is defined as 'the Palme-tree, that thrives not after the supplanting of her husband'.

484 *blind*: Fortune (l. 482) was commonly represented as blind.

490 *Alexander and Lodovic*: a story of two physically alike and inseparable friends, one of whom married under his friend's name and put a naked sword between himself and the bride, so as not to wrong his friend.

2.1.4 *your night-cap . . . largely*: the white coif you wear pushes your ears out widely enough (for an ass and a cuckold); 'night-caps' were worn by serjeants-at-law, and the phrase was an epithet for a lawyer: cf. below, l. 19.

30 *disembogue*: Bosola compares the Old Lady to an old boat which needs reconditioning ('careening': turning the boat over for cleaning and caulking) before it can put to sea ('disembogue': issue forth from the mouth of a river into the open sea).

34–6 *a dead pigeon . . . plague*: the rumps of live fowl were applied medicinally to human plague-sores to draw out the infection.

   I . . . fasting: given the choice between (*a*) kissing a user of cosmetics and having to fast, and (*b*) having to eat a plague-ridden pigeon, he would prefer the latter (because he would be less likely to be poisoned).

37 *sin of your youth*: youthful debauchery.

38–9 *high-prized*: i.e. valued; but 'high-priced' (i.e. expensive) is also a possible reading.

64 *loose-bodied*: in England, unwaisted gowns were normally worn by matrons, not by elegant young women like the Duchess. Webster allows English fashion to stand in for Italian here.

81 *out-of-fashion*: i.e. inappropriate to Bosola's improved circumstances.

91 *the ascendant*: the point of the ecliptic of the zodiac, which at any moment (especially at the birth of a child) is just rising above the eastern horizon. Bosola's astrological reference is particularly apt, as the Duchess is shortly to give birth to Antonio's son.

93 *King Pepin*: cf. *WD* 5.6.113 n.

110 *mother*: hysteria, which causes a feeling of swelling and suffocation.

114 *bring up*: promote.

120 *bare*: bare-headed.

124 *to-year*: this year.

138 *grafting*: Bosola overtly refers to the propagation of fruit, but the phrase carries a sexual innuendo.

139 *crab*: crab-apple tree.

143 *apparently*: manifestly.

2.2.5 *glass-house*: cf. *WD* 1.2.130 n.

17 *Danäes*: cf. above, 1.1.239–40.

18–21 *mathematics . . . centre*: Bosola hints that by deduction he will find out the truth about the mystery at court, with a sexual quibble on 'centre'.

21 *foster-daughters*: charges; the Old Lady is a midwife.

28 *Forobosco*: he is listed as a speaking part in the Q1 and Q2 cast lists (played by N. Towley), but does not appear even as a 'ghost character' in the first printed version of the play.

33 *Switzer*: a Swiss mercenary.

36 *pistol*: the word was colloquially pronounced 'pizzle', which may account for Bosola's laughter; ll. 37–43 are full of *double-entendres*.

44 *French plot*: because the plot is associated with 'ladies' chambers' and 'cod-pieces'—the French were reputedly lascivious. But the First Officer's bawdy flippancy unwittingly also speaks the truth because the person responsible for the Duchess's lying in is Antonio, who has long been in France and who is returned from there a 'very formal Frenchman' (1.1.1 ff.)

77 *whole man*: all our most masculine resolve.

79 *lay . . . breast*: heed this piece of advice closely. But if Q4's stage direction was intended originally (Q4: *Enter Cariola with a child*), the line becomes ironically literal in anticipating Cariola's entry with the baby.

80 *Old . . . best*: a variation of the proverbial saying that old friends and old wine are best (cf. Tilley, F755).

84 *set . . . nativity*: cast a horoscope.

2.3   S.D.   *dark lantern*: a lantern with a shutter which enabled the light to be shut off.

   6   *My . . . else*: my acting as a spy will otherwise cease.

20–1   *setting . . . jewels*: casting a horoscope for the recovery of the Duchess's jewels; such uses of astrology were common in the period.

31   *Spanish fig*: denotes a contemptuous and obscene gesture with the thumb thrust between two closed fingers, but it also follows naturally from poisoned 'apricots'; cf. *WD* 4.2.60.

39   *scarce warm*: just out of hibernation; recently promoted.

40   One or more of Bosola's lines may be missing here, because two consecutive speech-headings refer to Antonio in Q1, and l. 41 is obscure. Even if ll. 37–9 were attributed to Bosola, his signing the horoscope in 42/a would remain enigmatic.

48   *safe*: in custody.

55   *false friend*: i.e. the lantern.

64   The astrological details of the horoscope prognosticate a short life, but mitigatory signs may have been ignored, as the examination is incomplete: '*caetera non scrutantur*' ('other parts are not studied').

2.4.5   *devotion*: the *double-entendre* is acknowledged by the Cardinal's reply.

16   *fantastic glass*: the telescope (invented by Hans Lippershey in 1608 and perfected by Galileo in 1609).

28–30   *I have taken . . . fly at it*: Julia is compared to a falcon.

32   *tame elephant*: the hawking metaphors of the preceding lines may have suggested this analogy, as hawks (like elephants, according to popular belief) were tamed by being kept awake ('watched'). The Cardinal may suggest that Castruccio kept Julia awake all night but couldn't have sex with her (ll. 34 ff., 54). Conversely, 'watched' may mean no more than kept under surveillance (by a jealous husband).

39   *one in physic*: someone who required medical attention.

41   *to't*: compared with it.

54   *If . . . back*: if he had been stronger.

2.5.3   *loose i'th' hilts*: unreliable (because the hilts are defective); unchaste.

9–11   *She hath had . . . service*: Ferdinand's lines abound with sexual quibbles on 'cunning' (cunt), 'turn' (i.e. in bed), 'conveyances' (passages) and 'service' (sexual intercourse).

12   *rhubarb*: a common medicinal purge for bile and choleric humour.

13–14   *Here's . . . here't*: Ferdinand is probably referring to the 'paper' found by Bosola in 2.3.55 ff.; 'here't' may indicate that he places it near his heart, where he will keep it till he has exacted his revenge.

24   *balsamum*: balm.

32 *unequal*: not even-handed; unjust.

33 *left side*: (morally) wrong side.

43 *quoit the sledge*: throw the hammer.

45 *carries coals*: carrying coals commonly denotes someone who is prepared to do any dirty work.

82 *fix . . . eclipse*: set her permanently in total darkness.

3.1.14 *reversion of*: the right to succeed to.

29 *left-hand way*: illegitimately.

45 *How is't, worthy Antonio?*: Antonio does not respond to Ferdinand's address, but the Duchess picks up the unconscious irony in her brother's reflexive turning from 'husband' to Antonio (whom Bosola has identified to him as her bawd). Her intervention steers Ferdinand away from Antonio.

49 *Pasquil's paper bullets*: i.e. lampoons displayed in some public place.

57 *coulters*: the allusion is to the medieval ordeal of treading on red-hot ploughshares as a means to vindicate one's innocence. Ferdinand either means that his sister, though guilty, brazenly withstands the tortures; or that his own mind is like burning coulters.

3.2.5 *with cap and knee*: with cap in hand and on bended knee.

7 *lord of misrule*: generally someone who presides over the Christmas games and revels in a temporary world of inversion when servants supplant their masters. The application to Antonio is particularly apt as he is both the Duchess's steward and her husband (i.e. 'lord').

25–7 *Daphne . . . Syrinx . . . Anaxarete*: tales of the transformations of women who spurned their lovers (Apollo; Pan; Iphis) related in Ovid's *Metamorphoses*, i. 452 ff.; 689 ff.; xiv. 698 ff.

31 *olive . . . mulberry*: as opposed to the 'fruitless' and frigid metamorphoses of the virginal lovers.

34–40 *If . . . naked*: cf. *WD* 2.1.263.

68 *your gossips*: godparents to your children.

73 *eclipse*: cf. 2.5.79. The word 'eclipse' chimes well with Ferdinand who will shortly suffer from a lunar sickness.

87 *basilisk*: the basilisk killed everything it looked at.

89 *to thee*: compared to thee.

106 *use to sound*: the ability to articulate.

115 *hollow bullet*: cannon ball which is filled with explosives.

140 *you have*: i.e. there are.

144 *This to thee*: point this (pistol) at you.

157 *'Tis Bosola*: Cariola does not speak again till l. 314, but remains on stage throughout the mock-accusation of Antonio by the Duchess, the officers'

calumniatory reports on him, and Bosola's ingratiating trickery of the Duchess. Her silent and helpless presence dramatically foreground the Duchess's isolation.

168 *stood . . . with me*: stood security for me.

176–7 *Our . . . wheels*: cf. 'The world goes on wheels' (Tilley, W893). The expression proverbially renders life's instability and uncertainty, which here lies in the Duchess's need to use 'enginous' (cunning, crafty) stratagems.

180 *Magnanima menzogna*: a quotation (translated by the rest of the line) from the Italian romance epic *Gerusalemme liberata* (1580) by Torquato Tasso.

190 *let him*: leave him; let him go.

191 *done that*: one of several *double-entendres* in the Duchess's lines (183–93) to the officers.

225 *chippings of the buttery*: wood-chippings from the floor of the servery.

226 *gold chain*: his steward's badge of office.

244 *Pluto*: the god of riches is Plutus, who is often confused, as here by Bosola, with Pluto the god of the underworld.

248 *he . . . scuttles*: comes quickly ('rides post') and in large amounts (by scuttles).

260 *herald*: someone employed to settle questions of precedence or to record proved pedigrees: cf. below, l. 299.

267 *Bermudens*: the islands were a notoriously stormy region and hazardous to ships, as the famous shipwreck there of the *Sea Adventure* in 1609 demonstrated.

284 *unbeneficed*: unprivileged; poor; without endowment.

299 *coats*: coats of arms.

316 *Lucca . . . Spa*: Lucca near Pisa, and Spa (then in the Low Countries—'Germany'—now Belgium) were famous for their waters and springs respectively.

327 *rests*: remains.

3.3.1–5 *Emperor . . . Lannoy*: an anachronistic reference to the battle of Pavia (1525) in which the forces of the Holy Roman Emperor Charles V under the command of Fernando Francisco de Avalos, the Marquis of Pescara, defeated the French army; the French King, Francis I, was captured by Charles de Lannoy, Viceroy of Naples.

12 *voluntary*: volunteer.

21 *by the book*: according to theoretical precept.

23 *critical*: i.e. the days likely to determine the issue.

27 *from taking*: from being taken.

34 *Only . . . court*: merely to adorn the court on its progress.

35 *Bosola arrived!*: Pescara speaks for the first time in this scene, although he has been a silent party to the conversation between Delio, Ferdinand, and Silvio, perhaps because he does not wish to participate in spiteful talk, as an upright and noble soldier.

40 *goes to wrack*: is devastated.

48 *salamander*: a lizard supposed to live in, or to be able to endure, fire.

52 *porpoise . . . storm*: a proverbial idea: cf. 'The porpoise plays before a storm' (Tilley, P483).

68–9 *my young nephew . . . husband*: According to Painter (*The Palace of Pleasure*), Webster's principal source for the play, the Duchess expressed a desire to renounce her title in favour of her son by her first marriage, Alfonso Piccolomini, when she publicly announced her marriage to Antonio, desiring henceforth only to 'be honored with the title of a simple Gentlewoman'. This son does not feature anywhere else in the play, nor is he referred to by any other character.

3.4.8–23 *Arms . . . showers*: during the press-correction of the first Quarto, Webster added a note: 'The author disclaims this ditty to be his.' It is uncertain whether this refusal to appropriate the addition to his text implies disdain for the ditty or respect for its author whose identity is not known.

41 *No matter . . . to't*: it does not matter who pushes.

3.5.19 *benefit*: freely bestowed gifts.

29 *politic equivocation*: cunning double-talk.

48 *brothers*: i.e. brothers-in-law.

60 *bottom*: the hold (of a ship).

71 *eternal church*: the Duchess's marriage was contracted at first in defiance of the church. It would appear from this that she has either been married according to the rites of the church since; or else she imagines herself (in moments of chastising grief and despair as here) to be married according to the bonds of the church (cf. further 4.1.39) and feels therefore sure that she and Antonio will be reunited in the community of the Christian souls in heaven.

74 *unkindly*: against the instincts of 'kind'; unnaturally.

93 *laurel . . . withered*: the evergreen laurel was thought to wither on the death of a king. The Duchess's reference to it here suggests that she sees Antonio as her 'king' who may shortly die.

94–5 *Look, madam . . . towards us*: these are Cariola's first words in the scene. She has been standing by mute, like the Duchess's children (who never speak in the play: cf. 3.5.113) and her servants. The children's passive, mute roles underline the pathos of their parents' doomed struggle.

108 *Charon's boat*: Charon is the ferryman in Hades, who transports the souls of the dead over the Styx ('dismal lake'). Among the few who returned, Orpheus, Hercules, Theseus, and Aeneas are the most famous.

118 *counterfeit face*: i.e. the vizard.

139 Cf. *WD* 5.3.91.

144 *some great hill*: perhaps an echo of Psalm 121: 'I will lift mine eyes unto the hills, from whence cometh my help . . . ', or of the proverbial expression 'There is no hill without its valley' (Tilley, H467). The former seems more likely in view of the Duchess's increasing spiritual resignation already signalled by her reference to the 'eternal church' at l. 71.

4.1.16–17 *I . . . heart*: i.e. I will no longer attempt to understand her behaviour.

s.d. *Enter Duchess*: the Duchess is usually attended by ladies-in-waiting, or by Cariola. Here, however, she has to be alone, if Ferdinand and Bosola are to trick her successfully by delusion.

21 *elder brother*: in the play, the Duchess and Ferdinand are twins, but historically Ferdinand (named Carlo, Marquis of Gerace) was indeed, as Bosola assumes, an elder brother.

25 *gently*: i.e. please.

29 *Take hence the lights*: Bosola remains present, but hidden from view. It is he (probably) who activates the traverse which reveals the wax figures (l. 55).

42 *i'th' light*: in the public eye; but Ferdinand also intimates to her that she was 'light', i.e. sexually wanton.

44 *the ring*: the Cardinal snatched the wedding-ring from her fingers and vowed to sacrifice it to his revenge (3.4.36–9).

50 *owed*: owned.

55 s.d. *discovered*: i.e. revealed.

the figures: Q's 'the *artificial* [my italics] figures' is potentially misleading about Jacobean stage practice where motionless actors would almost certainly have played the parts of Antonio and the children. I have therefore very reluctantly elided 'artificial' from the text of an overtly theatrically minded edition. I am, however, conscious of the fact that this particular stage direction may not only derive from Webster's own first draft, but might in fact have been a last-minute addition by the dramatist himself during press-correction (Brown, pp. lxiv–lxv), in which case it would carry additional authority. It might be safest to view the problem here in terms of a clash between known theatrical practice and the author's imagined perception of the staging of the scene.

children: at 3.5.57 the Duchess tells Antonio to take 'your eldest son' to Milan, and later (4.2.193–5) she instructs Cariola to take care of the remaining two children (i.e. she knows them to be alive). The stage direction may be confusing if taken too literally, but it is effective in tricking the Duchess into believing that she has lost everyone she loves.

68 *lifeless trunk*: i.e. her husband's body.

72 *Portia*: the daughter of the famous stoic, Cato of Utica, and the wife of Brutus. She killed herself by swallowing burning coals, when she heard the news of her husband's defeat and suicide at Philippi.

81 *wheel*: breaking upon the wheel was a form of execution.

91 *vipers*: the Duchess is under tremendous strain here and 'daggers' and 'vipers' may be hallucinatory visions that torture her mind.

92 *long life*: since the servant wishes the Duchess long life, he may well be sent by Ferdinand to report on his and Bosola's success in destroying her sanity, and further to torture her. He may be the same 'Servant' who introduces the madmen at 4.2.37 ff.

105–6 *Let . . . them!*: perhaps suggesting that crowned martyrs become stars in the firmament (following the Ovidian metamorphic model) so that heaven's stopping diminishes the number of the stars.

109 *howl them this*: probably 'tell my brothers so' rather than 'tell the stars'. The usage of 'howl' would be pointedly ironic in view of Ferdinand's lycanthropia, but she could also be howling at the stars the way dogs do at the moon.

113 *curious . . . quality*: skilled . . . craft.

114 *Vincentio Lauriola*: probably a name invented by Webster.

130 *full o' th' moon!*: the full moon was popularly held to influence madness. But the line ironically also prepares the ground for Ferdinand's mental lycanthropic metamorphosis, as werewolves were thought to undergo their transformations at full moon.

135 *by my intelligence*: by my acting as a spy.

138 *Thy . . . thee*: pity does not come naturally to you; it doesn't become you.

4.2.34 *pitied*: Cariola sits still after this till l.162. Once again Webster uses her silence dramatically to set off the Duchess's isolation.

35–6 *Fortune . . . tragedy*: fortune or fate is proverbially blind: cf. 1.1.494–6.

45 *secular priest*: a priest not attached to a monastic order.

55 *in grain*: (lit.) in the corn trade; a rogue.

56 *hindered transportation*: prevented from exporting (and therefore suffering economic distress).

57 *broker*: middleman who, as a madman himself, would try to mediate between other madmen.

60 *chained*: madmen were frequently chained, but here they are let 'loose' (l. 58) on the Duchess who, though sane, is constrained like a mad person by her brothers.

61–73 *O, let us howl . . . love and rest*: on the music, score, and composer of this song, cf. Brown, pp. 210–13.

74 MAD ASTROLOGER Only four of the eight madmen speak, and Quarto identifies them by number only. I follow Brennan in identifying them tentatively by calling and profession, while accepting that the Quarto s.p.s are not entirely consistent as in the case of ll. 106–7 e.g. which should perhaps go to the Mad Doctor rather than the Mad Priest.

88 *woodcock*: because the bird is easily trapped the word is used to denote a fool or simpleton.

90–1 *Greek . . . translation*: the authorized translations of the Bible from Greek (such as the *Bishops Bible* of 1568, or the *King James Bible* of 1611) are texts for infidels (Turks, i.e. Muslims), while the Calvinist Genevan ('Helvetian') text (from 1560 onwards) is the only true one. This suggests that the Mad Priest is a Puritan: cf. also below, ll. 101–3.

92 *lay*: explain.

94 *lay*: apply.

96 *glass*: probably a magic mirror, or perhaps a telescope (if the speaker were the Mad Astrologer rather than the Mad Doctor).

104 *featherbed*: a kind of stuffed palliasse.

109 *throw . . . me*: probably 'give me up for lost'.

110 *I . . . costive*: soap-makers apparently suffered from frequent bouts of diarrhoea as a professional hazard so that to make them 'costive' (constipated) would have been an impressive feat. Also, soap was used in suppositories as a laxative. It may be the case here that the Mad Doctor has transferred the properties of the product to the producer.

119 *worm seed*: a plant considered to have anthelmintic (purging intestinal worms) properties. Bosola may also intend to quibble coarsely on seed/semen, as he tries to cheapen the Duchess's relationship with Antonio in retrospect, because only that way can he temporarily reconcile his deeds with his conscience.

120 *mummy*: a compound from dead bodies used medicinally. Bosola calls it 'green', perhaps because the Duchess is still alive, and therefore not yet 'ripe' enough to be the substance of true mummy; conversely, 'green' could denote an advanced stage of putrefaction.

164 *common bellman*: Webster's father had contributed to an endowment in 1605 which paid for the services of a clerk to ring a bell in Newgate on the night before executions, to remind prisoners of their mortality and to exhort them to repentance (cf. *Macbeth* 2.2.3–4). Bosola's reference to this custom may suggest that he eagerly wishes to view his own actions as part of a legitimate moral and legal process, rather than as those of a hired murderer: cf. above, 119 n.

168 *mortification*: the state of torpor and insensibility preceding death.

211–12 *death . . . exits*: proverbial; cf. Tilley, D140.

213–14 *strange . . . both ways*: perhaps either by suicide and therefore voluntarily; or, by being murdered.

218 *last woman's fault*: refers to the proverbial propensity of women to talk at length, with an allusion to the idea that the last thing about a woman to die is her tongue (cf. Tilley, W676).

227 *mandragora*: a narcotic.

237 *come to my answer*: be formally accused in court (and so have the opportunity to plead).

246 *When!*: Get on with it!

247 *Your credit's saved*: your reputation is saved, because no one will know once you are dead.

248 *this*: i.e. the Duchess.

253–5 *murder . . . bedews the heavens*: the biblical belief that the blood of murder victims cried out to God for vengeance (Genesis 4: 10) later developed into the idea that the blood itself would be rejected by the earth and would rise crying to heaven.

256 *mine eyes dazzle*: the effect of tears welling up.

301–3 *The wolf . . . murder*: on this superstition, cf. *WD* 5.4.100–1.

315 *take . . . blood*: run strongly in families.

328 *painted*: he now considers that the honour of his loyalty to Ferdinand is specious.

335 *sensible*: palpable.

339 *pity . . . pity*: (*a*) it would bring Ferdinand back to dispatch her; or, (*b*) Bosola, in a flush of moral awakening and sudden tenderness, wishes not to disturb the Duchess by a sudden shout, as she may be precariously poised between life and death.

346 *cords of life*: sinews, nerves; cf. heart-strings.

5.1.6 *In cheat*: in escheat, i.e. the property reverts to the crown, or to the lord of the manor, if the owner dies intestate without heirs.

8 *seise*: take possession of (a technical legal term).

19 *Benet*: Benedict.

5.2.6 *lycanthropia*: lycanthropy means literally 'wolfman'-ness, a form of dementia which manifests itself by the sufferer claiming to be a wolf.

24 *nearer*: more direct; more forceful (cf. 'buffet', i.e. 'beat' in l. 26).

25 *Paracelsus*: a Swiss-born physician (1493–1541) and pioneer of medical science, with wide-ranging speculative interests in alchemy, magic, and mythology.

47–8 *to drive . . . Moscow*: perhaps analogical with the proverbial 'You drive a snail to Rome' (Tilley, S582).

50 *sheep-biter*: a dog that bites or worries sheep; a sneaking or thievish fellow.

61 *salamander's skin*: cf. 3.3.48 n.

64 *cockatrice*: cf. 3.2.87 n.; the basilisk and cockatrice are one and the same, and its new-laid eggs presumably are the most dangerous to collect because they would be carefully guarded by the creature.

72 *fetch a frisk*: cut a caper; a 'frisk' is a quick movement in horsemanship or dancing.

76–7 *anatomies . . . Hall*: skeletons in Barber-Surgeons' Hall in Monkwell Street in Farringdon-Ward-Within.

79 *tongue and belly*: parts of the body left for the gods in ancient sacrifices, to which the court vices of flattery and lechery in the next line are syntactically in apposition. According to Ferdinand, they are all mere *disiecta membra*, offal.

80 *throughly*: thoroughly

106 *The . . . engagement*: the real initiative.

109 *oft-dyed garment*: a garment of decaying colours; ravaged.

124 *style me*: name me.

139 *brought*: Q1 (and also Q2's and Q3's) reading was subsequently emended to 'bought', which Lucas and Brown use, but 'brought' arguably makes better sense as there is little need for Antonio to buy a picture of the Duchess. He may however have taken a picture of her to the picture-makers for framing, or for copying.

147 *way to trace*: path to follow.

294–5 *lay . . . me*: either 'dress your wicked designs against me in the garb of a reassuring and seductive rhetoric'; or, 'pretend while you are talking to me that you are a decent man'.

332 *Bears up*: continues unaffected; or, maintains his courage.

334 *dead*: unrelieved, unbroken; perhaps we are meant to imagine a partition which gives a false impression of offering protection.

5.4.48–9 *That . . . myself*: what I have by your favour (of killing me) is now to be myself in death (which was not possible before because of the secrecy of his marriage). His true self, according to Antonio, resided exclusively in his marriage to the Duchess and was therefore shrouded or alienated while the marriage remained secret.

53 *We . . . tennis balls*: a familiar tag of the period.

61 *I . . . in sadness*: Antonio recognizes that in all his misfortune it is a mercy ('glad') that he is dying, when he no longer has a will to live, because he is too 'sad'.

82–3 *represent . . . bear'st*: be as silent as the body you are carrying.

5.5.2 *He*: the author of the book.

4 *lay him by*: put it aside.

31 *engines*: tools.

35 *'cause*: so that.

49 *honour of arms*: i.e. he is (at first) offering him an honourable surrender against a ransom.

53 *There . . . ransom*: because a dead man cannot be ransomed.

57–8 *Caesar's . . . disgrace*: Caesar was murdered in the senate house in Rome on the Ides of March in 44 BC shortly after becoming dictator for life, while the defeated Pompey was murdered when he landed in Egypt as a refugee in 48 BC. In Shakespeare's *Julius Caesar* Caesar lies dead at the feet of Pompey's statue (*Julius Caesar*, 3.1.116–7), an irony that Webster would have appreciated.

67 *vault credit*: overleap belief, i.e. Ferdinand will imagine that there is bliss ('high pleasures') in the afterlife about which he had been sceptical before his mortal wound.

72 *Like diamonds . . . dust*: cf. 'Diamonds cut diamonds' (Tilley, D323).

our own dust: as diamonds are cut by other diamonds, so man ('dust') is man's worst enemy. Ferdinand is a double twin (physically with his sister, and morally with the Cardinal), and kills both his kin. The Latin phrasing for man being man's worst enemy, *homo homini lupus* (man is a wolf to man), may dictate the lycanthropic nature of Ferdinand's train of thought (cf. Tilley, M245).

88 *rushes*: cf. *WD* 3.2.115.

96 *dead*: cf. 5.2.339 n.

119 *Integrity . . .* : cf. Horace, *Odes*, i. 22, '*Integer vitae scelerisque purus . . .*' ('The good man innocent of sin . . .'), and the proverbial idea that the end crowns all (Tilley, E116).

The Devil's Law-Case

[Dedication]

Sir Thomas Finch: Finch (*c*.1575–1639) had been MP for Winchilsea in the 1621–2 Parliament and lived in Drury Lane not far from the Cockpit (also known as Phoenix) theatre where *The Devil's Law-Case* was first performed. Webster's tentative tone here suggests that he and Finch had not met, but that Webster was hoping to enlist him as a patron.

3–4 *touch . . . copy*: reach out to the ultimate source, with an allusion to the Platonic ideal.

5 *Guise*: a lost play by Webster, written probably about 1615. The earliest extant play lists disagree about its genre, but it is likely to have dramatized the character and death of the mercurial Duc de Guise, who was assassinated on 23 December 1588, and who is featured in plays by Marlowe, Chapman, and (almost certainly) Henry Shirley.

8 *less*: lesser.

To the judicious reader

1-2 *Sapientia ... caruisse*: 'the beginning of wisdom is first to be free from ignorance' (Horace, *Epistles*, i. 1).

4-5 *Locus ... umbris*: 'There is room also for many shades' [i.e. the injudicious, or unbidden reader] (Horace, *Epistles*, i. 5).

8 *Auriculas ... dolentes*: 'lutes [do] ears aching from ear-wax' (Horace, *Epistles*, i. 2).

13 *in action*: i.e. in the performance of the play.

18 *Non ... venor*: 'I do not chase after the applause of the fickle multitude' (Horace, *Epistles*, i. 19).

1.1.5 *custom*: taxes (to Spain, who ruled Naples where the play is set).

9 *belvederes*: raised turrets or lanterns on the tops of houses; summer-houses commanding a fine view.

10 *musical water-works*: artificial cascades, fountains, and streams of water in the homes of the rich, often designed to make imitation birds sing.

16 *lottery*: between 1567 and 1621 lotteries were used in England to raise money for specific projects. The mention of them here hints that Romelio's financial dealings may be shady, as rumours of fraud surrounded the lotteries.

22 *To*: compared to.

23 *spring-tide*: a tide which occurs on the day shortly after the new and full moon, in which the high-water level reaches its maximum; a copious flow.

42 *portion*: pronounced here as a trisyllabic word.

46 *draw up a gudgeon*: catch [instead] a small fish used as a bait.

52-4 *in ... vices*: it may be the case that the crossing of the Alps here is incongruously viewed from an English perspective, not, as might have been expected of Neapolitan speakers, from an Italian one (Englishmen commonly viewed Italy as a den of vices and corrupt power); or, Webster may be wishing subtly to undermine the idea of national stereotyping by showing the Italians as wary of crossing the Alps from Italy as others are of entering Italy, and for the same reason.

69 *greater bonds*: with a pun on 'bond' as a legally binding deed of settlement, and the bond of marriage.

80 *scarce*: scarcely.

82 *dark*: obscure, unclear.

92–3 *ride . . . uncle's*: i.e. on a coat of arms.

99 *mainly*: extremely.

114 *gay ones*: i.e. women addicted to expensive clothes.

115 *without . . . grace*: 'into the bargain'.

117 *stands affected*: is disposed.

119 *presume*: must feel free to assume.

125 *strange*: a stranger; away from here.

127–9 *th'Exchange bell . . . abed*: refers to the bell on the Royal Exchange in London (not Naples!) which was rung when it started at 11 a.m., and when it closed at noon. Merchants dined after noon. But in the piazza, the shops—milliners, armourers, apothecaries, booksellers, goldsmiths—stayed open. The Royal Exchange and the 'New Burse' (see below) were places where gossip as well as commodities were traded.

128 *from us*: the City normally followed fashions set at court; here Leonora suggests it is the other way round.

132 *the New Burse*: the New Exchange, also known as 'Britain's Burse', opened in the Strand in 1609 and was furnished with shops of millinery and other trade. It was at first unsuccessful in its rivalry with the Royal Exchange in Cornhill.

137 *Shadows*: here meaning both 'shade' and 'pictures'. The seasonal analogy with women continues in Contarino's reply.

149 *drawing*: being drawn.

173–5 *That . . . business*: under King James noblemen were strenuously discouraged from moving to London; the depletion of the countryside and urban concentration was, *inter alia*, perceived to be a deplorable feature of Italy.

177 *into*: in.

178 *begging church-land*: Leonora piously deplores the predatory attempts by lay landowners to acquire church property, a practice ripe in Jacobean England and unsuccessfully opposed by the crown.

1.2.5 *Process*: a formal summons.

20–2 *Letters . . . university*: i.e. letters of commendation have become as worthless as the unpopular letters mandatory from the crown, which secured places at university for court protégés at the expense of free elections by the Fellows.

22 *fall*: become vacant.

23–5 *for . . . service*: a widow who wishes to secure a place at court may be more readily wooed by Ercole's royal testimonial, because it could certainly get her there.

33 *interest in*: influence over; credit with.

42 *moon-eyed*: blind; the expression derives from farriery and describes intermittent blindness that animals suffer, allegedly through the moon's influence. The use of a 'lunar' phase here intimates whimsicality, or changeability.

45 *antiquary . . . buskins*: a person of great age in old-fashioned (or worn out) half-boots, i.e. a figure of fun who, like the herald (i.e. titles and genealogy), epitomizes everything that Romelio holds to be useless or superseded.

46 *mainest*: greatest.

51 *jointure*: an estate settled upon a wife to provide for her in case of widowhood.

58 *court-mist*: delusion emanating from the court through Contarino. The phrase probably puns on 'courting', i.e. wooing and romantic love.

108 *continue . . . dumb show*: stay in your position (i.e. embraced), and proceed without speech.

111 *hearty*: from the heart; sincere.

114 *the consecration of prelates*: clerics would refuse bishoprics twice with '*Nolo episcopari*' before accepting.

116–17 *door . . . England*: you hold the latch of the door, that's legal delivery of property ('livery') and possession ('seisin') in England.

131 *Wears . . . state*: presents the more impressive show.

143–4 *time . . . degree*: the period of study for the full MA.

157 *lady of the laundry*: cf. *WD* 4.1.89 n.

168 *though . . . foot-cloth*: even if he rides on a richly caparisoned horse.

169 *hackney coachman . . . French*: Romelio means that a French-speaking coachman is more likely to be an insinuating gallant or a rogue than a plain-dealing fellow speaking vernacular.

173 *You are apprehensive?*: do you understand?

174 *travelled*: been abroad, with a sexual innuendo; travailed in childbirth.

175 *chaperoness*: (probably) an unrecorded early usage of the modern sense of chaperon.

192 *enclosing the commons*: cf. *WD* 1.2.90 n.

197 S.D. *Enter Contarino*: she summoned him in 1.1.192–4 about a matter concerning both their honours. This did clearly not relate to Ercole's suit and Romelio's plot to marry her to him. More likely it concerned her impending declaration of love for him, and the rumours about Contarino's love for her and its alleged motives, as explained by Romelio (1.1.36–46). Whatever his reasons for appearing here, they are immediately subordinated to the situation in hand, the sorrow of Jolenta.

205 *caskanet*: conflates 'casket' and 'carcanet' and used in both senses; here 'casket' is intended.

211 *forespoken*: spoken for in advance; also 'bewitched'.

230 *sweet-breathed monkey*: a term of endearment.

232–3 *He . . . kissing*: a reference to Marcus Cato ('the Elder'). As censor (184 BC), Cato was famously severe as he tried to reform Rome's morals. According to Plutarch (*Lives*), 'Cato expelled another senator who was thought to have good prospects for the consulship, namely, Mamilius, because he embraced his wife in open day before the eyes of his daughter. For his own part, he said, he never embraced his wife unless it thundered loudly . . .'.

254 *quarrel*: duel.

259 *use not*: am not accustomed to.

2.1.10–11 *other . . . consequence*: it is not clear what this refers to. It could mean the elevation of Ariosto to judge (he came to Crispiano's lodging (2.1.91–3) and Crispiano carries his patent for judge: 4.2.443–5), or the bearing of the news to Romelio of his miscarried maritime ventures; or again, his presence in Naples might primarily relate to his mission of finding out about Romelio's gold-mines, or the exorcism through the law of female abuses of domestic power (cf. 3.1). Crispiano's main part in the play, as trial judge over the suit of bastardy brought by Leonora in 4.2, is one he could not anticipate. As for his professed reason to watch over his spendthrift son, he himself invalidates it by his claim to have derived more pleasure from accumulating it than his son could get from spending it: 'If he can out-vie me, let it fly to th'devil' (l. 84).

13 *the famous corregidor*: the illustrious chief magistrate.

of Seville: born in Seville (rather than practising there), since Crispiano has been away in the East Indies for forty-two years (with a pun on 'civil'/'Seville').

14 *jubilee*: i.e. twenty-five years: cf. *WD* 1.2.92 n.

30 *collectionship*: amassing of money (at the bar).

31 *perpetual calendar*: every single day was a work day.

32 *melancholy*: gloomy.

36 *half ready*: half-dressed.

44 *out from the matter*: straying from the point.

47 *like flap-dragons*: hastily; 'flap-dragon' is a game in which bits such as raisin are snatched out of burning brandy, and extinguished by rapid swallowing.

54 *disease*: venereal infection.

60 *leer*: a seemingly uninterested side-glance.

tell: count.

61 *vailed my cap*: doffed my cap in sign of submission or respect.

63 *cry of hounds*: pack of dogs.

64 *Dogs . . . fault*: the hunting with dogs caused the ruin of many estates; a 'fault' in hunting is a check, caused by a loss of scent.

72–4 *For . . . bigger*: i.e. entertaining on a very small scale will release money for enlarging the house (cf. Tilley, K111).

74 *mock-beggars*: with a pun on 'bigger'. This word was regularly applied to fine, but inhospitable houses.

76 *tunnels*: flues.

85 s.d. *Baptista*: he is referred to by Romelio in 1.1.16 ff. He remains silent here, but is not a 'ghost-character', as he is needed to stay in conversation with Julio in 2.1.207 ff.

102 *practice*: skill.

104 *rare . . . profession*: perhaps because elevation to the bench might entail a considerable loss of income for successful barristers.

108 *in perfect memory*: of sound mind, and therefore capable of making a valid will.

133 *cantharide-mongers*: cf. *WD* 2.1.283–4 n.

136 *urinal*: an essential part of a doctor's equipment.

141 *rook*: with a pun on 'rook' meaning simpleton.

143–4 *Keep . . . longer*: Ariosto suggests that Julio should keep his hat on his head, which, he claims, is as wooden (i.e. as thick) as the block which keeps hats in shape (cf. 'block-head').

146 *put on*: i.e. put it on.

159 *breaking Venice glasses*: i.e. smashing glasses after a toast.

163–4 *overblown roses*: cf. *WD* 5.3.101.

166 *galley dung-boat for streamers*: large open row-boats used for the transport of manure which, on holidays, would be festooned with ribbons; a pun on 'gally' (breeches, hose) may be intended.

168 *arithmetic*: computation, presumably concerning a complicated bet.

171 *spangled copper fringe . . . netherlands*: with faked gold lace over her lower parts.

172 *at Padua*: i.e. at the university.

183 *selling commodities*: cf. *WD* 4.1.49 n.

185–6 *searce . . . pepper*: sift them like cayenne pepper.

187 *terriers*: they painstakingly stalk their quarry.

would: want to.

187 *in a trice*: instantaneously.

189–90 *fellows ... heads*: like the three-headed Cerberus who guarded the entrance to hell.

192 *tenterhooks*: the bent nails or spikes which hold the cloth on the 'tenter', the wooden frame on which it is stretched.

193 *intelligence upon*: secretly conveyed (and dangerous) information against you.

194 *gold ... sea*: cf. *WD* 5.3.81.

198–9 *He ... tongue*: because barbers were notorious for gossip.

208 *you ... long*: you have waited a long time for me.

209–10 *all ... about*: all the galleys have returned to port.

232 *knowing my interest*: aware, as you are, of my stake in this.

244 *Italian*: I have not arranged for you to be murdered in the devious fashion characteristic of Italians. If I had, you would now be dead and I would not have bothered to confront you.

256 *take leave*: permit myself.

263 *vary for*: are at odds over.

276 *stale ... wine*: common and drunken behaviour.

281 *We'll ... way*: we'll arrange for weapons of the same length along the way [to the field, where they fight in the next scene].

290 *privy coat*: secret armour the wearing of which contravened the code of duelling.

2.2.17 *I ... thrive*: I try hard, but do not succeed in hurting you.

22 *fair ... think*: a good thrust that hit its mark.

29 *at ... confusion*: i.e. at my mercy to spare you, or to kill you.

34 *Saint Sebastian's*: the saint recovered after being left for dead.

35 *won't*: won it.

2.3 This scene of the meeting between Ariosto and Romelio fills important gaps in the plot relating to Romelio's losses at sea, and characterizes him further as a cynical pragmatist. Romelio's twisting Ariosto's philosophical advice into an *ad hominem* attack hinged on cuckoldry sits awkwardly at this point, but in the wider structure of the play it anticipates the issue of adultery in the trial scene (4.2), when Ariosto first appears as Romelio's unfeed counsel, and subsequently as judge.

21 *scarlet*: doctors' robes (as opposed to BAs') are scarlet. Romelio sarcastically puts it to Ariosto that he has not attained the highest qualification in life because he has not seen his wife make him a cuckold; the use of 'scarlet' puns on the moral sense of the word as applied to an offence: 'heinous, deep-dyed'.

50 *looked*: i.e. imagined.

51–7 *Is there . . . superstitious*: sailors were notoriously superstitious, not least about the naming of their ships.

57 *stocks*: the framework on which a ship or boat is supported while in process of construction.

61 *handsel*: the first proof of anything, often with the notion of its being auspicious of what is to follow; (here) inauguration, with an allusion to the proverbial good luck of cuckolds.

72 *the common bellman*: the town-crier (cf. *DM* 4.2.163 n.).

77 *bead*: the bead of a rosary, i.e. a prayer; a tear of pity.

83 *canon*: decree of the church; canon law denied Christian burial to those who were killed in duels.

104 *civil wearing*: sober (i.e. grave) clothes.

105 *a good hearing*: good news.

107 *worthies die*: i.e. worthies who die.

111 *rotten . . . night*: dead trees, whose barks give off phosphorescent light in the dark.

114 *precise*: i.e. the Puritans.

115 *supersedeas*: a writ commanding the stay of legal proceedings; a check.
   sued: sought.

164 *weigh up*: counterbalance.

169 *fore-winds*: winds which move the ship forward; as opposed to head-winds.

2.4.6 *dwell in*: persevere with.

12 *compliment*: reputation.

21 *where*: whereas.

27–31 *ever . . . boat*: refers to the famous exchange of cartels (i.e. written challenges or letters of defiance) between Francis I and Charles V in 1528, when Charles V issued a challenge after accusing the French King of breaking his word regarding the Treaty of Madrid. In 1536 Charles V again claimed to have challenged the French King to a duel, this time on a boat in the middle of a river.

39 *second . . . contract*: i.e. consolidate this well-intentioned agreement.

44 *Gordian knots*: cf. *DM* 1.1.471.

3.1 It is important for the trial scene (4.2) that Ariosto and Crispiano should be seen to be united in the common purpose of doing right. But after conceding that their main object was to investigate Romelio's trading interests, the two lawyers drift into a bemused and worldly weary misogynism. Webster is preparing the ground for Leonora's plot and its repercussions.

8 *vents*: removes from the earth.

14 *silly . . . of*: ignorant . . . of.

26 *bench*: the judicial bench.

3.2 S.D. *habit of a Jew*: (probably) a gaberdine, i.e., a loose upper garment or frock worn formerly by Jews. Romelio's choice of a Jewish disguise also recognizes the fact that Jews of the period were much in demand as physicians—and therefore also had a notorious reputation as poisoners.

11 *disease natural*: seasonal illness, which imitates the rhythms of nature, and hence is not suspicious if it leads to death.

40 *attend*: listen to.

51 *extraction*: medicinal potion.

72 *toy*: sport.

91 *Bermuda pigs*: pigs proliferated in Bermuda in this period.

93 *shock*: onslaught.

101 *thee*: i.e. the dagger.

108 *absolute cure*: cure for all mortal ills (by killing him).

110 *inwards*: insides.

111 *washed . . . lead*: boiling to death in water or lead was a notorious form of execution of convicted poisoners. The First Surgeon's statement may also recall the entitlement of the College of Surgeons to the bodies of four executed criminals a year for experiments.

112 *turn Christian*: this was deemed to be the worst fate that could befall a Jew.

119 *a bloody Roman letter*: Romelio claimed to be a doctor from Rome; a play on Roman type is also intended.

139–40 *on my foot-cloth*: on a richly caparisoned horse.

145 *unicorn's horn*: superstitiously held to be an antidote against poison.

146 *Is . . . still?*: is that how the land lies? But a more literal meaning may be suggested by the context (particularly l. 152), i.e. 'Is he still breathing?'

3.3.26 *absolute will*: unconditionally by the will.

35 *Order of St Clare*: the order of the Clares was founded by St Francis of Assisi and St Clare in *c*.1212, and was famous for its austerity and seclusion.

47 *precontract*: cf. *DM* 1.1.477 n.

57 *essentially*: in reality.

62 *a plural one*: i.e. someone who holds more than one benefice simultaneously, and is therefore corruptible; with a play on 'singular'.

77 *frosty . . . youth*: the barrenness of my youth (because of Contarino's death).

95 *tendered*: held dear; acted tenderly towards.

99 *an . . . capable*: if he were fit.

117 *my quarrel*: quarrel over me.

121–2 *he had . . . coward*: he would have got the reputation of being a coward.

130 *direct falsehood*: complete faithlessness.

138 *Throw . . . it*: (lit.) return the bad egg to the one who hatched it in the first place; the irony lies in the fact that Romelio was of course hatched by his mother and that he is a distinctly worse egg than her, contrary to his glib proverbial wisdom.

144–7 *if . . . that*: alludes to contemporary science, and particularly to Galileo, whose 'fantastic glass' (the telescope) is mentioned in *DM* 2.4.16–19.

160 *for . . . flesh*: as far as blood-ties are concerned, with a possible pun on 'flesh' meaning penis.

173 *Make . . . preface*: sew on a quilted front to your petticoat (to insert a cushion to simulate pregnancy).

174 *advance*: push out.

180 *as . . . stockfish*: as amenable to it as air-dried cod (which has to be beaten before cooking).

199 *waged*: hired to go.

200 *the line*: cf. *WD* 3.3.24 n.

calenture: a tropical disease characterized by delirium, in which sailors reputedly fancied the sea to be green fields and desired to leap into it.

202 *take order for*: (lit.) 'see to'; here, ensure against.

222–3 *How . . . contract*: how much cunning it needed to contract her to Ercole.

226 *With . . . indeed*: cf. *DM* 2.1.110 n.

237 *they*: those who desire.

241 *precise curiosity*: strictly observed refinement, i.e. overly scrupulous decorum.

250 *latest harvest-home*: last chance for bringing home the harvest.

256–7 *Like . . . pap*: Amazons were warrior women who reputedly cut off their right breast to draw the bowstring more efficiently.

258 *tender*: love.

264 *fly in pieces*: explode.

269–75 *let . . . stubborn-hearted*: these lines may allude to Queen Elizabeth I's grief over the execution for treason of her favourite Essex. According to rumour (and unbeknown to the Queen), Essex sued for pardon by sending a ring as a pledge which never reached its destination, because it mistakenly ('false conveyance': l. 274) was delivered to the Countess of Nottingham who withheld it from the Queen, till she was on her death-bed. The belated discovery of Essex's suit reputedly precipitated the Queen's death by 'distraction'.

275 *Expressed . . . stubborn-hearted*: made him appear unrepentant.

290 *gave . . . o'er*: declared him lost.

299 *comfort*: 'consort' has been proposed as a reading here, because 'vowed [i.e. betrothed] comfort' is a rather odd phrase.

345 *ought*: that owned.

378 *courtly*: i.e. in a high-bred, courteous manner.

383 *minister*: administer.

387 *arpents*: an arpent is an old French measure of land and roughly equivalent to an acre.

4.1 S.D. *Sanitonella*: the character last spoke at 2.1.198. He presented himself in 2.1.30 ff. as Crispiano's servant and confidant, saw Ariosto at Crispiano's lodging (2.1.94), listened to Crispiano's description of him, and witnessed the baiting of Julio and the part played in it by Ariosto. Here, however, Ariosto seems to be a stranger to him, and Sanitonella's forensic practices are hardly consonant with his employment over the years by Crispiano—whom he furthermore, and amazingly, does not recognize (4.2.480–1), while earlier in the scene acknowledging him to be his master (l. 322). The oversight is striking enough to lead one to suspect some incoherence in the plotting here, as also at the end (cf. 5.6.85 n.)

6 *lungs of fox . . . raisins*: used, by a sort of sympathetic magic, for consumption, asthma, and other lung diseases. Raisins (whether from Malaga in Spain or elsewhere) were deemed to have similarly medicinal properties.

20 *shake hands*: i.e. encounter.

23 *presentations*: the laying before a court or person in authority a formal statement of some matter to be legally dealt with.

24 *overseers, wrong*: executors who wrong.

27 *plus quam satis*: 'more than enough'.

35 *commenced*: proceeded to a full degree.

36 *pew*: a raised seat or bench, for judges, lawyers, *et al.*

37 *dry-foundered*: lamed, i.e. unable to move from his station.

38 *non-resident*: Ariosto takes his cue for an ecclesiastical reading of the word from Sanitonella's literal usage; the term was applied to priests who held a plurality of benefices (cf. 3.3.62), and therefore were never resident.

39 *subsumner*: not even a proper summoner; summoners delivered court summonses, and were menial officers held in little regard.

40 *libel*: (here) the brief, i.e. the writing of the plaintiff containing her allegations which institute her suit.

41 *by virtue of the clergy*: out of my regard for the clergy; but possibly also 'with impunity', by analogy with 'benefit of clergy' which, if pleaded successfully, could reprieve a convicted felon from the death penalty, because it exempted him from trial by a secular court.

63 *nightcaps*: cf. *DM* 2.1.4 n.

74 *foul copy*: the draft (of the brief which Ariosto tore up).

79 *saved*: by pleading benefit of clergy (cf. above, l. 41) which by Webster's time had been modified and extended to include everyone who could read.

82 *Vivere honeste*: 'to live honestly'.

84 *Give it a dash*: cross it out.

86 *secretary*: the style of handwriting in common use at the time. Sanitonella should have done his draft in legal hand.

   takes: comes off, i.e. achieves the desired result (in the lawsuit).

88 *court hand*: a style used regularly in English lawcourts from the sixteenth to the eighteenth century.

100 *pent*: confined.

101 *rectify their issue*: set right their cause; reform their offspring: Webster puns on the double meaning of 'issue'.

115 *make account*: consider that.

4.2.9-10 *And . . . herrings*: alludes to the skirmishes between rival trading English and Dutch ships in the East Indies at this time.

15 *expect*: wait to see.

19 *Duke of Austria*: kinsman to the King of Spain who rules Naples.

21 *Palavafini*: probably refers to the Pallavicini, an Italian aristocratic family some of whose members had financial dealings with the English crown in the sixteenth century. This was the case particularly with Horatio Pallavicino who lent vast sums of money to Queen Elizabeth I and who was knighted in 1587. He died in England in 1600. Webster would have come across Pallavicini either through Horatio Pallavicino or through his sources for the *WD*, because the real-life Bracciano died on Lake Garda in a palace belonging to this family.

36 *pellitory of Spain*: a plant whose root has a pungent taste and is used both as a salivant and a cure for toothache.

44 *after-game at Irish*: 'Irish' was a form of backgammon in which the 'after-game' consists of the loser trying to win back the first game by the second. Such games may have been lengthy and tedious.

49 *more dark*: Jacobean lunatics were confined in the dark.

58 *unequal*: inequitable.

63–4 *to . . . in question*: to jeopardize my life by a capital charge.

70 *runs in a blood*: is congenital.

72 *An angry fellow . . .*: Ariosto and Romelio continue their verbal fencing, in spite of the fact that Ariosto has come to Romelio's rescue, because of his righteous outrage over the nature of the suit.

86 *prodigies in heaven*: comets and other unusual phenomena which were commonly taken to be portents of disaster.

88 *as fear*: as to fear.

104 *beams*: rays of light; but also supports, stays.

109 *Aesop's crow*: at a beauty contest organized by Zeus, the jackdaw arrived decked in feathers moulted by others, but was exposed and had his borrowed plumes plucked off by them. Aesop concludes that 'Men in debt are like this bird. They cut a dash on other people's money. Make them pay up, and you can recognize them for the nobodies they always were.'

112 *dream*: delusion.

119 *Fieschi, the Grimaldi, Doria*: three illustrious Genoese families whom Webster seems to mistake for Neapolitan aristocracy, probably mentioned here because their pedigree had been questioned in the sixteenth century.

130 *a . . . May-game*: the allusion appears to conflate the oversized figure of Jack-in-the-Green of May-games with the stuffed giants of London midsummer pageants.

135 *by th'hand*: by the bargain.

138 *at poor John*: dried hake, hence worthless fellow.

194 *housewife*: with a quibble on 'hussy', i.e. a loose woman.

196 *study*: private room.

215 *changeling*: a child swapped by the fairies, and who, as 'three-quarters of a face' implies, is often deformed.

217 *Without . . . for*: its salvation.

218 *gossips*: godparents.

219–20 *godfathers . . . arch-puritans neither*: refers to the fact that by a canon of the Church of England applicable at the time, parents could not stand as godparents to their own children, whereas the Puritans maintained that children's religious upbringing was above all the duty of the parents.

223 *cases*: lawsuits; with an obvious incestuous innuendo.

244 *makes difference*: draws a distinction.

263 *hearty*: genuine, sincere.

268 *satisfaction*: repentance was traditionally broken down into the three stages of contrition, confession, and satisfaction.

276–7 *she has proved . . . her dower*: under English law, Leonora would have incurred this penalty only if she had gone off to live with her lover.

279 *old house*: rotten edifice.

288 *powder-treason*: Webster may be alluding to Thomas Percy, one of the Gunpowder conspirators, who nursed a private grudge against James I.

295 *natural example*: examples (or similes) taken from nature.

301 *bones*: small bones were used as bobbins.

328 *Don John of Austria*: an illegitimate son of Charles V whom his father acknowledged in his will, and who was officially recognized by Philip II in 1559.

335 *Lepanto*: the navy of the Christian League under Don John of Austria defeated the Turks at Lepanto on 7 October 1571.

336 *remarkable*: easily remembered.

339 *corporal*: bodily.

342 *bag and baggage*: a common phrase, here alluding to buckram bag (i.e. lawyer) and strumpet (i.e. Winifred).

343 *ore tenus*: (lit.) 'by word of mouth', a phrase used in legal proceedings, and here meaning perhaps that Winifred will give her evidence verbally, without a previously written deposition.

350 *running*: smooth.

351 *fiddling*: i.e. cheating, with a sexual *double-entendre* (cf. similarly l. 348–9: 'lodged in her house').

369 *Latin*: puns on latten, i.e. brass; Winifred is called 'brazen'; cf. Tilley, S771.

370 *ignorant that way*: ignorant of Latin.

378 *Small drink*: light drink.

388 *stinger*: a biting, sharp speech.

397 *betimes*: early.

from the bias: off the set course. The expression derives from bowling, and the bias is the curved course in which the bowl runs.

399–401 *two great frosts . . . cod-piece*: all these are English and London references of course (and not Neapolitan ones) and intended to be understood by London theatre audiences. The two great frosts were those of 1564 and 1607–8; the three plagues probably those of 1563, 1592–3, and 1603; Calais fell to the Duke of Guise in 1558, and the large breeches with the great cod-piece came in under Henry VIII. Winifred is gradually working her way back in time to establish her alleged longevity, but overreaches herself when she refers back over a century to her last 'reminiscence'.

403 *doubles*: the hare's characteristic sharp turns in running.

427 *down with him*: i.e. speed him along on his way down.

431 *supreme law*: i.e. of God.

440 *cross tricks*: tricks which cut across the progress of the main issue; hence, red herring.

461 *this*: i.e. the picture. It may have been covered with a curtain which Crispiano now draws: cf. *WD* 3.2.243.

463 *bleared*: Q has 'bleated', but 'bleared' has been proposed and glossed by Lucas as 'thrown dust in his eyes, deceived him [Contilupo]'; 'bleared' appropriately connects with Crispiano's changed appearance over forty years.

484 *dance . . . tail*: to be whipped through the public street at the tail of a cart for being a bawd (*lachrymae* = tears).

485 *slips*: slippers (cf. l. 361).

486 *liver*: the liver was considered to be the seat of passion.

490 *arsy-varsy*: willy-nilly; (lit.) 'backside foremost'.

510 *away with*: put up with.

     after-reckonings: final accounts.

575 *Malta*: the Turks were repulsed at Malta in 1565. Webster may, however, be thinking of later skirmishes between the Turks and the Knights of Malta who were sometimes joined by young adventurers like Contarino, because a date of 1565 would render Contarino and Ercole too old.

576 *of your nation*: Contarino is disguised as a Dane (cf. 5.4.5).

584 *deeper . . . throat*: lying in one's throat means lying foully and was thought to be worse than ordinary lying.

586 *From . . . Calais sands*: from one end of France to the other; Calais Sands was a regular venue for English duellists, because duels were proscribed in England: cf. *CC* 1.2.89.

590 *Knight Marshal*: an officer of the English royal household, whose jurisdiction covered the 'king's house and verge', i.e. extended within a radius of twelve miles from the king's court.

5.1.10–11 *How . . . quickened?*: how did you know you were pregnant, since this is your first child?

20 *thing*: virginity.

23 *venture*: hazard.

26 *I . . . question*: I do not doubt.

36 *tumbled*: tossed, with a *double-entendre* on copulation.

37 *trick*: (lit.) hand of cards, i.e. a stage of the escape.

41 *shade*: shadow.

5.2.1–2 *law-flesh*: legal material, i.e. made of the stuff of lawyers.

7–10 *There's . . . forenoon*: Sanitonella seems to be saying that it is a scandal that proctors (i.e. attorneys) must not go to the tavern more than six times in the morning during term, because their clients (who accompany them) become friends with other proctors' clients there while getting drunk; in other words, the prohibition which stops the proctors from extensively conducting business in the tavern leads to the undesirable result of more law-cases than would otherwise be necessary.

12 *overtaken*: drunk.

13 S.D. *Bathanites*: perhaps a corruption of Bethamites (after St Mary or Lazarus of Bethany) or of 'Bethlemites'; one of these orders was similar to the Knights of St John of Jerusalem to which Ercole belongs.

5.3.8 *suborning*: aiding and abetting.

27 *procure*: cause.

5.4.5 *Dane*: i.e. Contarino.

6 *reverse*: turn your coat of arms upside down.

15 *upon return*: this may refer to the Elizabethan custom of taking out insurance by depositing a sum of money before the journey. In the case of failure to return, the money would be forfeited; but if the traveller returned, he would be paid out several times the amount.

19–26 *The Welshman . . . braveliest*: the Welsh were traditionally supposed to be excessively fond of toasted cheese and were frequently the butt of jokes because of this predilection.

20 *Hung . . . arse*: held back.

25 *makes . . . cheese*: uses a piece of toasted cheese for the disc on the end of his foil.

28 *put in for't*: made his thrusts.

29 *usher*: ushers at a feast who, without partaking, have to watch the guests as they dine.

32 *chaps*: jaws.

33 *breathe*: pause to catch our breath.

36 *'tis . . . dry*: proverbial (Tilley, S656); the angry humour of choler was considered to be hot and dry.

48 *sir, you may stay*: Julio stays as Romelio's second in the impending duel, but does not participate in the conversation between Romelio and the Capuchin. He only speaks again at l. 142. His silent stage presence contrasts with Romelio's buoyancy, particularly as he already repents of his decision to act as a second (5.4.1 ff.).

56 *took out*: learned.

64 *Turn you*: consider it from another point of view.

80 *give . . . foil*: defeat.

83 *commence doctor*: embark on a doctor's degree.

84 *word*: order.

86 *stomach*: appetite.

93 *to speak*: i.e. say his last words before dying.

94 *to do*: i.e. to fight.

97 *wait upon*: attend.

116 *These . . . growing prime*: these have only a time of growth.

119 *set*: planted.

124 *consequently*: in sequence.

129 *nets . . . wind*: proverbial (Tilley, W416).

136 *yonder*: in the afterlife.

143 *bandoleer*: a broad belt, worn over the shoulder and across the breast, by which a wallet might be suspended. We are meant to imagine Julio's wrapping himself in one of the winding sheets and comparing himself to a felon bound for the gallows with a halter around his neck.

144 *to hang . . . scarf*: the visual context here may have produced a figurative use of 'coffin' for the body. The 'scarf', which comes from the coffin presented to him by Leonora, is now wrapped around Julio whose body may shortly be a corpse (while his soul is immortal): cf. ll. 136–8.

153 *certify*: reassure.

169 *living*: estate.

180 *close committing*: imprisonment; secret adultery.

5.6.2 S.D. *tuckets*: flourishes on a trumpet.

8 *'Soit . . . droit'*: 'Let the battle proceed, and may victory go to those who are in the right'.

17 ALL THE CHAMP: everyone gathered on the field (of combat).

31 *sprung*: caused to rise from their cover.

42 *crimson blood*: i.e. blushing cheeks.

45 *credit . . . lighter*: double-entendre on 'lighter' meaning (1) white hue; (2) sexually more promiscuous.

65–7 *all . . . principal*: Romelio is ordered to write off all Julio's debts, except the original sum lent.

72 *Orlando*: after Ariosto's romance epic *Orlando furioso* which tells the story of Orlando's madness and rage over the love of Angelica and Medoro.

74 *They'll . . . watermen*: almost quotes from Webster's character 'A water-man': 'nothing but a *great Presse*, makes him flye from the River'. Thames watermen were particularly afraid of being impressed, perhaps because their boat-handling skills made them obvious targets for press-ing into the navy.

85 *vows' breach*: Jolenta has broken no vows to the monastic order of the Clares, and would therefore seem to be wrongly yoked together here with Leonora and Angiolella, unless one assumes that 'vows' should be taken in a more general sense rather than the specific one of monastic vows. Technically, all three women have broken vows: Leonora by getting married after declaring her intention of entering into religion (4.2.512–13), Jolenta by not marrying Contarino as she 'vowed' (1.1.83–4), and Angiolella by breaking her vows of chastity (3.3.41–2; 5.1). In that case the punctuation of ll. 85–6 would have to be '. . . vows' breach, unto the monastery | Shall build a monastery', where the first 'monas-tery' would mean the monastic Order of the Clares, and the second a physical building. If the punctuation of Quarto is retained as here, then the dealing out of punishments at the end might be viewed as a satire on judicial whimsicality, with Webster showing Ariosto as ultimately an undiscriminating (if not particularly fierce) judge.

A Cure for a Cuckold

The Stationer to the Judicious Reader

16–17 *The Thracian Wonder . . . Gammer Gurton's Needle*: the first of these plays, which is subtitled 'A Comical History', is attributed on the title-page to John Webster and William Rowley, although this attribu-tion is now rejected. *Gammer Gurton's Needle* is an early English farce in rhyming verse about the losing and finding of a needle. It is commonly attributed to William Stevenson and was produced at Cam-bridge in *c.*1553. It was printed in 1575.

20 *Rowley*: cf. *DM*, [Commendatory Verses] note to l. 31.

25 *hath been tried*: a glancing allusion perhaps to *Anything for a Quiet Life* 2.1.120–2 (*c.*1621, and a probable Webster–Middleton collaboration), in which the idea of a homecoming sailor and a temporary divorce is mentioned; or, Kirkman may claim that this cure for cuckoldry has been tested in real life and been found to work.

25–6 *probatum est*: it has been tried.

34 *Francis Kirkman* (1632–*c.*1680): after serving his apprenticeship to a scrivener, he became a bookseller in 1652 and also operated a circulating library. He was an assiduous collector of plays, and produced two long catalogues of plays (1661; 1671). He enjoyed a dubious reputation among

his contemporaries for tampering with play texts, but his attribution of *A Cure for A Cuckold* to both Webster and Rowley is now generally accepted by most scholars. That Kirkman had 'some real familiarity' with the plays listed in his catalogue is suggested by W. W. Greg in his discussion of them in *A Bibliography of the English Printed Drama to the Restoration*, vol. ii (1951), 915–16.

1.1.27 *observance*: dutiful service, i.e. he has ever served her according to the rituals of courtly love.

48 *receivèd*: acquired.

50 *imply*: attribute.

53 *windings and indents*: the twists and recesses (of the road to Clare's heart).

56 *to my fruition*: to the possession of me.

65 *period*: conclusion.

76 *She . . . without taxation*: subject to no criticism.

91 *peculiar*: special.

92 *that not respects her*: who does not esteem her.

97 *prove*: try.

108 *sent by women*: the letter was delivered by Clare's waiting-woman, and the gallants clearly suspect a 'difference' between Clare and Lessingham. Their idle talk at 1.2.31 ff. suggests that they view this as a legitimate sport.

119 *miss her*: notice her absence.

122 *Sick of the maid*: i.e. fed up with being a maid, with a pun on green-sickness (also known as 'chlorosis'), an anaemic illness which sometimes affects young women during puberty.

156 *by-blow*: (lit.) one who comes into being by a side-stroke; a bastard.

158 *within compass*: within bounds, but also puns on 'Compass' to whom Urse, the mother of Franckford's baby, is married. A further *double-entendre* on compass and 'circle' (i.e. vagina) may be intended.

159–61 *But . . . both*: The first clause ('but if . . . had') suggests that Woodroff continues the train of thought from ll. 151–3, i.e. 'I wish he were seeking an heir elsewhere'. The 'hurt' from the adultery to both Franckford and Luce is ultimately desirable, as it may mean offspring.

162 *chopping*: strapping.

166–7 *I fear . . . coral*: toys of polished coral were given to teething infants.

175 *gravity*: the presence of staid, old men.

1.2.1 *Amicitia . . . nec rarius*: 'Nature has given nothing greater or rarer than friendship'. This may be a conflated paraphrase of Cicero, *De Amicitia*, 6: '*Est enim amicitia nihil aliud nisi omnium divinarum humanarumque rerum cum benevolentia et caritate summa consensio*' ('For friendship is nothing other than the accord of all things divine and human with benevolence and love').

2 *author*: probably Cicero.

6 *to . . . he*: to become that particular person who.

24 *justice . . . th'earth*: in classical mythology, Astraea, the goddess of justice, abandoned the earth after the golden age; here it is a banishment rather than a tactical withdrawal, adding a hint of tyranny to the original idea.

40 *make . . . benefit*: take advantage of it while it lasts.

69 *open-breasted*: frank.

77 *bring off*: carry away (in case the duellist is wounded).

79 *either . . . dangerous*: both the duellist and his second will endanger their lives.

85 *late . . . discontents*: recent falling out (of Raymond and his father), but it could also imply that Raymond's father's grievances against him are imaginary.

86 *To atone . . . to*: to reconcile myself to my father.

89 *Calais sands*: Calais became the preferred venue for duels as the closest place beyond English jurisdiction, which proscribed duelling.

94 *Single sword*: a sword with only one cutting edge.

102 *I . . . that*: I was never any good at that.

107 *unseasoned*: inappropriate to the occasion (of his wedding day).

120 *burden*: principal theme.

121 *protest*: affirm, promise.

126–7 *Not to imagine . . . you*: not to suppose that I am considering to ask for your help in my venture.

128 *fortune*: i.e. misfortune.

135 *temperature*: (lit.) freedom from excess or violence; calm.

139 *Still printed in*: forever attached to.

159–60 *but . . . employment*: but (temporarily) deferred for the sake of more serious (and adult) pursuits.

176–7 *the key . . . carcanet and bracelets*: the key, carcanet, and bracelets are introduced here as a *leitmotif* (signalling faith and bonding), which resurfaces prominently in the encounter between Annabel and Rochfield (2.2.21 ff.), and in the play's final testing of the relationship of Bonvile and Annabel (5.1).

179 *at random*: untended.

182–3 *my neck . . . prisoners*: because she cannot remove the jewels he gave her.

2.1.9 *want to give*: lack the means to pass on parts of their estate.

13 *t'other's*: the other (i.e. the gallows) is.

19 *Laverna*: the Roman patron goddess of gain, hence (especially) of rogues and thieves.

30–1 *I talk . . . recovered*: I should recover through acting rather than lose by talking.

32 *forepath*: short cut.

46 *movables*: personal property that can be moved.

2.2.5–6 *hot . . . poison*: Rochfield is telling her that he is a man of enough passion to preserve him from the dangerous tendencies of someone who is cold, i.e., he claims to be a basically moderate man.

7 *'dressed*: i.e. addressed, but with a pun on 'dressed for cooking'.

19 *double state*: i.e. of 'wife' and 'virgin'.

20 *Hymen*: (consummation of) marriage.

26–7 *If . . . mine*: if these jewels (necklace and bracelet) should turn out to be symbolic of the tied knot of the hangman's rope.

30 *I . . . forget*: I will admit having a useless necklace and chain, but will forget about you being a thief.

41 *picking laws*: the technique of picking locks (such as fasten Annabel's trinkets), in contrast with the unskilled brute force needed to secure money with menaces.

55 *St Nicholas*: the patron saint of thieves (cf. Laverna, 2.1.19).

65–7 *forbear . . . now*: do not force me to yield these now, because they can only be surrendered in a way which will damage them and be dangerous to my person.

67 *assure*: feel certain.

74 *cradle purity*: virginity; innocence.

75 *tax me*: call me to account.

   articles of my belief: punning on the twelve articles of the Apostle's Creed.

88 *I . . . bribe*: I once knew someone who in all of fifteen years as a courtier never took a bribe and, unusually, went to his grave without ever doing so. I may similarly end up dead, equally innocent of monetary wrongdoing.

102 *thief's handling*: in the hands of a thief.

2.3 S.D. *two boys*: the First and Second Boy who appear in this scene (attributed to Rowley) also appear in 4.1, jointly written by Rowley and Webster. The Second Boy is called 'Jack' at 2.3.9 and 'Hodge' at 4.1.4, while the First Boy (who appears as a musician in 4.1) is called Rafe (4.1.59 and 60). I believe that they are the same boys, and I have therefore throughout called the First Boy Rafe in speech headings and stage directions. The Second Boy is Jack throughout. 'Hodge' may be a nickname.

2 *snatch up stakes*: suddenly to seize the moneys wagered.

6 *prenticeship*: apprenticeship.

9 *point*: tagged lace for fastening hose to doublet, and therefore (as here) 'trifle'.

13 *hobby-horse . . . morris*: a hobby-horse is a horse made of wickerwork, and fastened about the waist of one of the performers in a morris dance. Hackney, still a borough in contemporary London, used to be horse-pasturing land.

14 *Green-goose fair*: held every year at Bow, near Hackney, after Whitsuntide.

15 *Blackwall*: a district of Poplar on the north bank of the Thames, at the mouth of the River Lea. Blackwall Reach was a convenient place for large vessels to moor, and its shipyard, begun in the late sixteenth century, was associated with the East India Company after 1614.

16–17 *tears . . . indeed*: with a quibble on 'tears', i.e. a torn part. His tears might be tied in a true-love knot, because they are an ever-fresh expression of his love and faith in spite of being salty.

25 *I am fain*: I should gladly.

26 *case*: fortune, hap.

37 *plaguy*: vexatious, but said here affectionately.

49–50 *Wapping, Radcliff, Limehouse*: locations north of the Thames which had a large seafaring population at this time.

54 *Surat*: Surat is in India and was a trading post for the East India Company.

59 *at next wall*: the connecting wall.

66 *lusty*: joyful; full of healthy vigour (and sexual desire).

70 *taken up*: bought, but also lifted, for sexual activity.

77 *one . . . livery*: a member of the company of cuckolds.

78 *horners*: i.e. the cuckolds, but also refers to the Company of Horners who were recognized as a Mystery in 1375, but did not have a charter issued till 1638. The Horners made horn articles such as windows, lanthorns, and hornbooks. Nicholas Okes, Webster's fellow parishioner and printer of his tragedies, was the son of a freeman of the Horners.

79 *changing our copy*: changing our style or behaviour, i.e. we will be cuckolds no longer.

83 *sing at first sight*: sing by sight-reading (a musical score).

84–5 *children . . . laugh*: according to Pliny, children did not laugh till the fortieth day.

98 *goes . . . go*: to 'go' here means both 'to fare' and 'to walk', anticipating the idea that there are some people at home who are so young that they haven't yet learned to walk.

Lank: (lit.) loose from being empty, i.e. not pregnant; cf. the proverbial usage 'After a lank comes a bank' applied to pregnant women.

98–9 *Wilt . . . wharf*: 'Will it never be high tide at our wharf?' 'High tide' means good fortune, but 'full sea' can also be read as 'the swell' which is suggestive of pregnancy.

107 *Hams*: i.e. East and West Ham.

119 *If . . . more*: a mild oath, meaning 'even if you were the last sexually available woman in London'.

122 *After . . . surprised*: 'after a prolonged assault (wooing) I was seized (gave way to his advances)'. She compares herself to an assailed fortress.

125 *Shadwell*: an insalubrious suburb north of the Thames with roperies, tan yards, breweries, and numerous taverns.

134 *players*: the permanent members of a Jacobean company were share-holders in it.

145–6 *Though . . . home*: he may be a merchant-venturer (trading in goods and, here, in illicit sex), but now that I am home I shall be the legitimate owner of my goods.

151 *and . . . forwards*: a nautical metaphor ('if the wind is fair, we'll hoist sails and set off') with *double-entendre* ('if the mood takes us, we'll lift the bed-sheets and make love').

2.4.34–5 *out . . . purpose*: beside the point of my intention.

45 *arrive at the proverb*: fulfil the proverb 'Early up and never the nearer'; but cf. on the other hand 'The early bird catches the worm'.

50 *gratulate*: congratulate us on.

52 *personate*: play the part of.

56 *at a stand*: unable to proceed in thought, speech, or action; *out*: the state of having forgotten one's lines.

64 *rendered*: answered.

67 *fetch a reputation*: to go in quest of, and bring back, a reputation.

74 *thus put down*: I'd rather be dancing than lose the argument to a woman.

75 *rife*: inclined that way.

76 *free*: generous.

79 *amazement*: mental stupefaction; frenzy.

80 *recovery*: rescue.

83 *better*: i.e. better comforts.

85 *supply . . . still*: continue to fill both offices, i.e. speak for both him (Rochfield) and myself.

101 *And . . . mittimus*: and if the calf only go to the udder, it'll look as if the clerk were asking the justice to sign a warrant for committal to prison ('*mittimus*').

105 *the t'other place*: hell.

114 *break my wind*: to be 'broken-winded' is a disabling condition of horses which prevents them from bearing fatigue.

120 *lay a hand*: shake hands (in welcome).

131 *stiffer*: stronger, i.e. his hand formerly would not have trembled.

133 *'Tis . . . physic*: refers to the supposedly invigorating properties of sea-air.

As low as: as far south as.

Leigh: Leigh-on-Sea in Essex.

137 *letter of mart*: a licence granted by the sovereign empowering the holder under international law to commit acts of hostility against an enemy nation. Letters of mart were first issued in England in 1625 (cf. Note on the Texts, p. xxxii).

139 *larboard*: on the left or port side of a vessel.

146–7 *above . . . above*: the first 'above' expresses a courteous preference. Annabel picks this up and invites him to top ('Make above') the others' ventures.

3.1.20 *forgetful*: inducing oblivion.

27 *fetch . . . off*: bring to a successful conclusion.

35 *pluralities of healths*: several toasts.

44 *glorious of*: eager for.

70–1 *Although . . . England*: although we no longer have serfdom (villeinage) in England; a villein was a serf in the feudal system who had tenure of the land by rendering bond-service to the lord.

87 *privy coat*: coat of mail or armour worn under his clothes.

146 *sea . . . body*: to have a corpse on board ship during a voyage was thought to bring bad luck.

3.2.9 *as dreadful . . . Shrove Tuesday*: the implication is that the Nurse's house is a brothel: on Shrove Tuesday London apprentices would riot and wreck bawdy-houses. Wet nurses and midwives had a reputation for loose morals, and were not uncommonly associated with prostitution.

18 *white*: specious.

21 *copyhold*: (lit.) by legal tenure of land or estates. Compass malapropistically continues the legal discourse initiated by the nurse's reference to 'civil law' to claim that his wife is his tenant and the baby her holding.

23 *father in law*: stepfather.

24 *Tothill Street*: the span from the unsavoury reaches of Blackwall to the aristocratic houses of Tothill Street encompasses the London rich and poor and, geographically, the entire City and, crucially, the Temple.

38 *tied your mare*: you have tethered your more on my land, i.e. she (Franckford's wife) wants to be the mother of my wife's baby.

39 *nag*: with a quibble on 'knag', a short or a stiff projection from a tree trunk; here meaning erect penis. Compass threatens Franckford with castration.

40–1 *make . . . hair-buttons*: make him so frightened that he becomes incontinent.

42 *main*: main point, punning on the 'mane' of a horse.

45–6 *Unbreech his barrel*: lower his trousers to expose his stomach.

46 *bullets*: testicles.

gird . . . stinks: beat him till he farts.

48 *maintain*: carry on.

55 *purse*: i.e. vagina.

64 *horn-mad*: stark mad, with a punning allusion to Compass's cuckold's horn.

83 *in lieu*: in view of the fact that.

87 *mutton*: with a pun on prostitutes; loose women.

95 *I . . . hands*: she takes money from both of them.

99 *declines*: turns away; but Compass elaborates the grammatical pun launched by Franckford's use of 'gender', and continues it with 'genitive' (i.e. pertaining to generation, with a pun on genitals) and *huius*, meaning lit. 'of whom', but punning on 'huge', as the subordinate clause indicates.

108 *by-betting*: if play is understood as 'main betting', then by-betting could mean the betting on somebody else's performance, i.e. Compass hopes at one remove to win a child whom somebody else produced.

3.3.15 *cry . . . mercy*: apologize to my heart.

33 *off o'th' hinges*: unhinged.

57 *Spanish men of war*: cf. Note on the Texts, p. xxxiii.

58 *English cross*: the cross of St George on the English flag.

59 *Salute . . . strike*: greet us with a gun to get us to strike our colours (i.e. capitulate).

66 *Sea-room*: space for manœuvre and free from obstruction.

80 *unite consent*: the agreement of all.

89 *wallow*: roll from side to side.

lies on the lee: i.e. heels over to leeward.

105 *of small venturers*: from being small venturers.

4.1.1 *Three Tuns*: there was a famous 'Three Tuns' tavern in Guildhall Yard; the name was common for taverns as three tuns were the arms of the Vintners' Company.

9 *jumble bastard*: (lit.), stir up sweet wine ('bastard' is a Spanish wine), but a play on 'bastard' (illegitimate) is intended.

15 *con her thank*: acknowledge my gratitude.

19 *do not . . . Welsh*: don't sweeten it (Metheglin is a Welsh drink, a spiced or medicated form of mead).

56 *Score . . . woodcock*: record the cost of a quart for the fool ('woodcock'), i.e. Compass.

59–60 *cuckoos . . . nightingale*: both birds are harbingers of spring, and were thought to arrive on 3 April. To hear the cuckoo before the nightingale was commonly thought to augur badly in amatory affairs. Here Rafe and Jack are cuckoos because they alerted Compass to the fact that he was a cuckold, whereas Urse is the mournful nightingale whose child has been taken from her. Her situation recalls Virgil's mourning nightingale from *Georgics*, iv. 511–13.

66 *Latitat*: a writ which pretended to believe that the defendant lived in hiding and which summoned him to answer in the Court of King's Bench.

67–8 *action of the case*: technically, a special writ framed on the analogy of the old writ of trespass; but 'case' may also contain a bawdy innuendo (cf. 2.3.26) which is developed further in the lines which follow.

75 *lie . . . ward*: are in a stronger position; 'ward' is a technical term from fencing and means 'defensive position'.

75–6 *partus . . . ventrem*: (lit.) 'the birth follows the womb', i.e. the child belongs to the mother.

85 *ordinary*: Pettifog ignores Compass's jibe and instead replies to Lionel by glossing his line with legal jargon; 'ordinary' means that a judge has *ex officio* regular jurisdiction.

85–6 *Nisi prius*: a trial or hearing of civil causes by judges of assize.

96 *Sound of Denmark*: vessels passing through the straits between Zealand and Sweden had to pay toll at Elsinore. The Danes were thought to be great drinkers, so that the First Client's tribute would be especially welcome.

100 *pottle*: i.e. half a gallon.

108 *counsellor*: advocate.

116 *shall . . . speech?*: will you recover any sort of damages from this libel?

119 *ballad of Flood*: Griffin Flood was an informer, blackmailer, and murderer who was pressed to death in Newgate in January 1623 or 1624, because he refused to plead. The ballad referred to here does not seem to be extant.

124 *A tweak, or bronstrops*: a whore or a bawd; 'bronstrops' (a corruption of 'bawstrop' which in turn corrupts 'bawdstrot') is a phrase frequently used by Middleton with whom both Webster and Rowley had collaborated.

126 *goose*: swelling in the groin from venereal disease, known as Winchester goose. The brothels, like the theatres, were located in the Liberty of the Clink, which also contained the palace of the Bishop of Winchester, who in fact owned the freehold of the stews.

129–31 *cans . . . measure*: the bawd's victim reported her for serving drinks in cans which contravened the officially approved measure, known as 'Winchester measure', but in her deposition she claims that she gave him a true Winchester measure, i.e. clap.

140 *sought the cases*: gone through the precedents.

172 *that law durst*: that law which dare.

175 *common law*: the traditional law of England based on precedent (cf. l. 140: 'cases') as opposed to Roman ('civil') law, which Compass uses as an analogue for statute law.

178 *foaming*: covered with the sweat of lust.

198–9 *leg . . . venison sauce*: 'opened' means carved, or filleted, while 'venison sauce', through punning on venusian and venery, means semen.

208 *onion . . . green wound*: onions were supposed to have fantastic medicinal properties.

219 *Pease-field by Bishop's Hall*: the field of peas (with a pun on 'peace', i.e. reconciliation) near Bishop's Hall in Hackney.

220 *swads and the cods*: pods (of peas) and husks of peascods. Peascods were a popular love-token used to divine whether a wooing would be successful.

4.2.30 *rue . . . violets*: 'rue' is a common symbol of repentance and puns on 'to rue', i.e. to regret, while 'violets' symbolize modesty and requited love.

31 *wedding strewings*: flowers strewn in the bride's path to church on her wedding day.

77 *Lapland witches*: Lapland was fabled to be the home of witches and magicians with power to send winds and tempests.

112 *cross and pile*: cross and pile are the obverse and reverse of coins (cf. head and tail).

164 *bore his steerage*: conducted himself; the nautical metaphor picks up the thread of the sub-plot.

4.3.5 *come off*: come away.

10 *let it be*: even though it is.

28–30 *If . . . new*: even if I thought of a whole parish, I could be speaking truly, for street tradesmen can cry 'fresh fish' when it's old.

40 *taught*: so little educated, i.e. just such a fool.

41 *law*: the law of silence.

65 *slip*: trifling error, punning on a counterfeit coin (i.e. the bastard in the woman's womb).

68 *As . . . coin*: no court business was conducted in the vacations between the legal terms, and during a similar slackness in trade, shopkeepers drop their prices in order to get ready money.

74 *bear . . . honestly*: uphold an understanding and generous course of action.

77–8 *hen . . . afterwards*: once a hen has been inseminated by the cock, she goes on laying eggs after he has been slaughtered.

86–7 *in the old world*: in the distant past.

94 *these bawdy bellows-menders*: these ever-promiscuous winds.

95 *take . . . coats*: blow their skirts up.

122–3 *without compass*: outside the scope of, with an obvious pun on 'Compass'.

123 *general pardon*: refers to the general pardon of 1624 which applied retrospectively and did not—as Compass seems to think—exclude petty larceny.

5.1.31 *Speak . . . largely*: sing his praises so fulsomely.

63 *well parted*: endowed with good parts.

66–7 *grow . . . particulars*: i.e. come to the point.

78 *as selecting*: as in selecting (to connect with 'As well in . . .').

126 *gives him dead*: reports him to be dead.

166–7 *a trick . . . husband's*: a *double-entendre* on 'key' is intended.

169–70 *men . . . swearing*: alludes to the act against swearing which was introduced in 1624 and stipulated a penalty of twelve pence an oath.

203 *Lures . . . stoop*: hawking language: 'Lures' means 'baits' as well as an apparatus used by falconers to recall their hawks, and 'stoop' denotes the descending of the falcon to the lure.

214 *Italian plague*: because Italians were widely perceived to be of a jealous disposition.

228 *jewel*: i.e. Bonvile.

241 *deadly*: fatal; the patent is a will and therefore only applies after her death.

245 *moon*: the moon is proverbially changeable, waxing and waning, so that no garment can be made to its measure.

278 *toil*: net, snare.

280–1 *Cankers . . . complexion*: cf. 'The canker soonest eats the fairest rose' (Tilley, C56).

302 *One . . . too*: in a duel, the seconds also fight.

343 *jade unto my wants*: being like a recalcitrant horse driven by my needs.

346 *For . . . familiarity*: our intimacy (which produced this unwarranted suspicion) consisted of only this.

365–7 *You . . . be*: the need for repentance is removed, because now everything is the way we desired it to be.

406 *though . . . contrary*: although two negatives make an affirmative.

420 *monologist*: (lit.) soliloquizer, but as the cuckoo is referred to in the following line, it may mean someone who only utters one word repeatedly. A pun on 'cuckoo' and 'cuckold' may also be intended, as the cuckoo, a migratory bird, does not hatch its own offspring, but deposits its eggs in other birds' nests, as Franckford did with Compass's wife.

GLOSSARY

abroad out of doors

absolute accomplished (*DLC* 1.1.51)

abuse deceive

adamant impregnable hardness; magnet, loadstone

advance promote

adventure quarry (*DM* 3.5.98)

affect cherish

aim guess (*DM* 1.1.423)

alicant wine from Alicante

allowance approbation (*DLC*, Dedication, 7)

aloof at a distance

amain at full speed; without delay

angel gold coin originally called 'Angel Noble'

apparent obvious; manifest

apprehend anticipate (*CC* 1.2.126)

approved experienced; commended; demonstrated

arm (*v.*) embrace (*DM* 5.2.126)

arrant downright, itinerant (*DM* 1.1.43)

arras screen or rich tapestry behind which a person could hide

article clause of an agreement (*CC* 4.3.32)

aspire reach up to

atomy tiny particle

atone appease (*WD* 3.2.297)

atonement reconciliation

attainted (morally) corrupted; infected (with a disease)

auditory assembly of hearers

awful awe-inspiring; commanding profound respect

awl small tool for piercing holes

back-gall to make (a horse's) back sore

band collar; ruff

bandy knock the ball about

bat-fowling catching birds at night by dazzling them with lights; swindling

beaver the lower portion of a helmet; face-guard

bed nest (*WD* 5.3.248)

belie to calumniate

bias (bowling) the weight in the side of a bowl

biters leeches, predators

blackguard the scullions and kitchen knaves of a noble household

blanch whiten

blast wither; curse

blood passions; family

blowze beggar's trollop; a fat wench

boon (*adj.*) prosperous

brabbling squabbling

braches bitches

brachygraphy stenography; short hand

brave (*adj.*) splendid, finely apparelled; (*v.*) defy

bravery fine clothes

breeze gadflies

brief (legal) concise summary of facts and points of law

brine salt water; tears

broom-men street-sweepers

buckram bag lawyer's bag made of coarse linen

buntings percher birds (related to the larks)

buzz spread rumours

by-slips minor slips; bastards

cabinet secret receptacle or casket; private boudoir (*DM* 2.2.54); treasure-chamber (*DM* 3.2.295)

calling (*n.*) station in life

canary light sweet wine from the Canaries

Candy Crete

canvas (*v.*) to knock about, beat, batter; (*n.*) a shaking up

carcanet jewelled or golden necklace

careening scraping clean (used of boats)

career charge at full speed

carefully with much anxiety

caroche large coach

carracks galleons

case pair (*WD* 5.6.20)

casque helmet

cassia fragrant shrub or plant; kind of cinnamon; expensive perfume

catarrh cerebral effusion or haemorrhage; apoplexy

caudle warm spiced drink of mixed wine and ale

caveat notice in court to stop proceedings till the opposition has been heard

censure (*n.*) opinion; judgement; (*v.*) to form an opinion

challenge claim (*WD* 3.2.173); arrogate

chaperons hoods

character writing (*CC* 1.1.99)

charge (*v.*) cost

chargeable costly

charnel mortuary

chary frugally

cheek (bowls) the round surface of the bowl

chequeens Italian gold coins

chirurgeon surgeon

choice select; excellent

choke-pear a harsh and unpalatable pear

chopping bouncing, strapping; someone who chops (*CC* 4.3.51)

chuffs boors (*DLC* 2.1.179)

cithern sort of guitar played with a quill plectrum

civil sober, grave, polite

clearest most absolute (*DM*, Dedication 12)

clew ball of thread or yarn

close (*v.*) shut away; embrace; (*adj.*) secret, intimate

close-pent very confined

cloth of tissue rich and embroidered cloth

clouded obscure; disguised

cochineal an exotic scarlet die

cock-boat a small ship's boat

cod-piece a conspicuous bagged appendage to the front of the breeches

colour excuse

colourable plausible (*WD* 2.1.298)

come about returned to port

comical happy in their conclusion

coming forward (*WD* 1.2.164)

commeddled mixed together

commencement beginning of the law terms

commendations testimonials (*WD* 5.6.198; *DLC* 1.2.20)

compelled strained (*DLC* 1.1.148)

competent sufficient

complete without defect

compounds settles

compromiser arbiter

conceit fancy, idea

conceited witty

conceive imagine; understand

confluence a flocking together

confound confuse

conies rabbits

conjure affect by incantation; bewitch

conjuror sorcerer

constantly resolutely; with fortitude (*DM* 4.2.29)

consumption a wasting illness

content (*v.*) remunerate (*CC* 4.1.210)

contrive consume, spend (*CC* 2.2.22)

control reservation (*DLC* 5.6.48)

convert turn round (and away) (*CC* 4.2.196)

conveyance contrivance; means of communication (*WD* 4.2.24); document which transfers property (*WD* 5.6.12)

copartiments compartments in a design

co-parts shares (*CC* 5.1.110)

copperas sulphates of copper, iron, and zinc which are poisonous

cordial invigorating

corrosived corroded (*DM* 4.2.68)

count account (*WD* 5.3.187)

courses charges (*DM* 3.4.20)

court-gall scourge of the court

cousin relative; term of address between sovereigns and noblemen

cousin-german first cousin

coxcombs fools (*DM* 2.1.184)

coz abbreviated form of cousin

cozen cheat

crabbed of a hard or sour disposition

crackers fireworks

crack-rope rogue, gallows-bird (sometimes used jocularly) credit reputation; credibility (*DLC* 4.2.52)

cross coin (*CC* 2.2.59)

crotchet perverse conceit; fancy

crudded curdled

crusadoes valuable Portuguese gold or silver coins

Cry mercy I beg your pardon (exclamatory)

cucking-stool chair for the use of ducking scolds and disorderly women

cullis strong broth

cunning skill, particularly in black magic (*WD* 5.1.88)

curious solicitous; exquisite (*DM* 3.2.293)

curling-iron heated hair curlers

curry (*v.*) comb; thrash (*DLC* 2.1.199)

cut-works openwork embroidery or lace

cypress light transparent material resembling cobweb lawn or crape (*WD* 3.1.76)

Dansk Danish

dark'ning obscuring

declarations official proclamations

demesnes land immediately attached to a mansion

descant comment on; carp at

desolate deserted

determine come to a judicial decision

Deuce-ace throw that turns up two with one die and ace with the other; poor throw

dials sundials; clocks

directly plainly; immediately; unmistakably

discharge shoot

discontinuance absence

discover uncover

disembogue leave an estuary for the open sea

dishonesty unchastity

dispend squander (*WD* 5.3.181)

distraction mental disturbance

diversivolent desiring strife or differences

doctrine the act of teaching; collection of information; philosophy of life

dog-days the days of the rising of the Dog star; the hottest and most calamitous time of the year

dog-fish small shark; predatory person

dog-killer someone employed to kill mad or stray dogs

doomed sentenced

dottrels plovers; foolish persons

drapers clothiers

drench spiced medicinal drink; large draft (*DLC* 2.3.45)

durance imprisonment

earnest first instalment; pledge of what is to come

effect purpose

effects outward manifestation

emblem picture accompanied by moral allegory

emulation ambitious rivalry

enforce urge

engine contrivance, plot

entertained hired

entirely unreservedly

envious malicious

envy malice

ephemerides almanac

equal impartial (*DM* 5.5.40)

essential true; intrinsic

esteem (*v.*) estimate; (*n.*) valuation (*CC* 2.2.79)

evidence title-deeds

execution judgement

exhibition maintenance

exorbitant excessive

expense spending

extirp root out

extraction medicinal potion

extremity extreme intensity

factious given to strife

factors salesmen

fain gladly

fame reputation

familiars intimate friends; members of the same household; familiar spirits

farrier shoeing smith who also treats horses

farthingales hooped petticoats (*DM* 2.1.153)

fashion appearance (*DM* 2.2.10; *DLC* 1.1.155)

fast secure

feck vigour, energy

fell cruel (*WD* 1.2.245)

ferret (*v.*) hunt with ferrets; search out and bring to light

fetch it off bring it off (*CC* 4.3.119)

fig-dotes an inferior kind of fig

figure-flingers (contemptuous) casters of horoscopes

fins the extremity of the eyelids

firk trounce (*CC* 5.1.303)

flashes ostentatious trappings (*DM* 1.1.156)

flaw quarrel

fly-boat light, fast vessel

fogging pettifogging, i.e. practising legal chicanery

fold wrapping

folded included in the fold of the divines (*WD* 4.1.61)

fond foolish

footsteps step on which to put one's foot

force enforce, urge

forced artificial (*WD* 1.2.349)

foredeeming judging beforehand

form outward appearance

formal precise

forms manners

forswear abjure

foutre fuck

fowler bird-hunter

fowling-piece gun for shooting wild fowl

fraughted laden

freeze be sluggish

fresh-coloured flushed (*CC* 3.1.4)

frowardness perversity

fumed perfumed

fundaments anuses (*DLC* 2.1.77)

fustian bombastic; ranting

galliard lively dance in triple time

gargarism a disease of the throat which attacks swine

gay richly ornamented; lavish

gender (malopropism for 'genitor') parent (*CC* 3.2.97)

generally widely

ghostly spiritual

gilded pills (poisoned) pills wrapped attractively (*WD* 3.2.191)

gilt-head fish with heads marked with golden spots or lines

gleek game of cards for three persons; coquettish glance

glorious famous

God boy you God be with you

God's precious i.e. God's precious blood

graduatically nonce-word (*WD* 3.2.49)

grammatical according to a textbook; rhetorical

grandam grandmother

guarded ornamented

gudgeon small fresh-water fish; gullible person

guise custom

gull (*v.*) trick

gullery deception; trickery

habit attire

haggard wild hawk; intractable woman

hair-buttons buttons made of horse-hair

halts (*v.*) limps

hams thighs

happed chanced

happy lucky (*DLC* 5.1.18)

haunt resort to (*WD* 2.1.5)

haycocks conical heaps of hay

heartless without a heart

heart-whole having your affections free; undismayed

hellebore poisonous plant

hog-rubber general term of abuse

honest chaste, virtuous

horn-mad stark mad

horse-leech bloodsucking worm; parasite (of a person)

horse-tricks improprieties

huddle confusion, disorderly bustle

humorous ill-humoured; capricious

humour mood; inclination

idle vain; foolish; worthless

idleness folly; light-headedness

idly inadequately (*WD* 5.3.214)

illustrissimi best society

importunity troublesome soliciting

impostume festering sore; abscess

imprecation curse

incontinent riotous

Indian pox syphilis

inly deeply

inquisition investigation (*CC* 2.4.16)

insensible imperceptible

intelligence conveying of information, news; knowledge (*DLC* 3.3.366)

intelligencer spy

intelligencing gathering information through spies

inward intimate, familiar (*CC* 5.1.98)

Io paean an exclamation of joy or triumph (*CC* 5.1.356)

jealous watchful, suspicious

jennet small Spanish horse

juggle conjure; to play tricks to deceive

julep sweet drink of syrup and sugar to assuage the heat of passion

julio silver coin of small value

jumble copulate (*CC* 4.1.178)

Jupiter the father of the gods

keeping careful guarding

kickshaws (French '*quelque chose*'), i.e. something dainty but insubstantial, hence 'frivolous people'

kindness natural affection

kissing-comfits sweet meats used to freshen the breath

laid plotted (*DLC* 3.3.32)

lamprey eel-like fish

leaguer military camp

leash (sporting term) set of three

leech physician (*DLC* 2.3.13)

lees sediments; dregs

lenitive tending to allay

lets hindrances

leveret young hare

lieger resident

light unchaste

lights lungs (*WD* 2.1.311)

linstocks forked staves (on board ship) for holding matches to fire cannons (*CC* 3.3.83)

lists (1) strips of cloth or other fabric; (2) the place appointed for duels or tournaments

literated learned

long-boat the largest boat of a sailing vessel (*CC* 2.3.55)

lops loppings; faggot wood (*CC* 4.1.167)

lordship estate

luxurious lascivious

lyam leash

main purpose (*DM* 2.1.2)

make up complete (*WD* 5.3.215)

mantoon (probably) large mantle

melocotons fruit of peaches grafted on quinces

Marry! often used as a mild profanity (Marry = by the Virgin Mary) in an answer

matachin sword-dance performed in a fantastic dress

mathematical scientific accuracy; precise

maze bewilderment

meat food

mediate adopt a moderate course

mellow running (of make-up)

Mercury the messenger of the gods

metheglin Welsh spiced form of mead

misprision mistake

mistress (bowling) smaller bowl (or 'jack') placed as mark for the players to aim at

molest try

monomachy single combat (*CC* 1.2.70)

morphewed scurfy

motion proposition; offer; inclination (*DM* 1.1.303); show (*DM* 3.2.40)

motive prime mover; instigator

move mention (*DLC* 2.1.25)

mushroom common metaphor for an upstart

musk melons melons smelling of musk

mutton illicit sex (*CC* 4.1.196)

naught wicked

neat well-spoken

night-caps lawyers

noddle beat on the head

numerous large

o'erta'en got the better of (*WD* 4.3.110)

observance courteous attention

orris powder powdered iris root which smells of violets

overgone outstripped (*CC* 2.4.90)

overseer executor

overtaken drunk

painted artificial; adorned

painting cosmetics, make-up

palsy tremor (disease of the nervous system)

parcel piece

pashed smashed

passages proceedings (*DLC* 4.2.16)

passes events (*DM* 5.3.33)

pastry the place full of flour where pastry is made

peach inform against

peccavi acknowledgement of guilt; lit. 'I have sinned' (*CC* 5.1.307)

peevish perverse, obstinate

perfect (*v.*) instruct, inform (*CC* 1.1.44)

Perseus Greek mythic hero who slew the Medusa and rescued Andromeda

personate play the part of

perspective magnifying glass; telescope

perspicuous lucid and perceptive

phlegmatic cold, sluggish, apathetic; cool, self-possessed

physic (*v.*) relieve, cure; (*n.*) medicine

physical medicinal

pie magpie

pills rinds, peel (*DM* 2.1.115)

pitch height

placket slit in a woman's skirt or petticoat

plastic moulding

play wager

policy bond (*DLC* 3.2.140)

politician cunning schemer

possets drinks composed of hot milk curdled with ale, wine, or other liquor

postern private or back entrance

postilion swift messenger

postures carriage, bearing (*CC* 2.4.3)

pot-gun short piece of ordnance; mortar; braggart

practise treachery; cunning

precedent prior example

precious egregious (*DLC* 2.1.138)

preferment advancement in social status, promotion

pregnant inventive, capable

preparatives formal preliminaries leading up to a duel

presence presence-chamber in which a sovereign or great personage gives audience

present immediate

president chief magistrate

process formal summons (*DLC* 1.2.5)

proctor attorney

procure cause (*DM* 4.1.111)

prodigious ominous

progress state or ducal journey

projections plans

proper handsome

property tool, means to an end (*WD* 2.1.291)

prosecute pursue; execute (*WD* 4.2.72)

provisorship office of manager

public widely known; not hidden

pudding-pie a dough pudding containing meat

pumps light indoor slippers

purchase gain

purchased procured (*WD* 3.3.60)

purl thread of gold or silver wire used for embroidering

purse-nets a bag-shaped net; snare

quaint cunning; ingenious

qualified mitigated in strength, 'watered down' (*CC* 3.1.68)

quality profession

qualms sudden fits of sickness

quat (*n.*) pustule; (contemptuous) a young person; (*v.*) squat (said of a hare)

quick living

quicken refresh; restore to life

quit clear or settle an account (*WD* 5.3.269)

quite requite; reward

radical fit to be judged (*DM* 2.3.22)

radically thoroughly (from the roots up)

ranger gamekeeper

rapt carried away

rare outstanding (*WD* 4.3.96)

rate berate, scold

reclaim reform (*CC* 5.1.153)

recover have a legal judgement given in one's favour (*CC* 4.1.116)

relation account

rent revenue (*DM* 4.2.182)

reportage recommendation, reference

requite repay

resolve explain (*DM* 4.2.153); stand assured

rests remains
resty refractory
reversion inheritance (*DM* 4.2.202)
reward award part of a prey to a dog or hawk as a reward (*WD* 4.2.188)
ride post hasten
riot dissipation
roaring boys riotous louts
roundly smoothly; promptly
ruddocks money
ruffin friend; (slang) devil
rupture outburst
salary reward
salvatory box of ointments
sans without (*CC* 4.1.73)
saw-pit small pit covered by a framework for the sawing of timber by two men
school (*v.*) chastise; talk sense to (*WD* 5.2.8)
scruple doubt; small particle
scurvily sourly (*WD* 1.2.191)
'sdeath by God's death
seaming lace lace for covering seams
searce sift
searing (*n.*) cauterizing iron
secretary confidant (*DM* 5.2.232)
seed progeny
seminary seed-plot; place of education
sensible palpable
sensibly with good sense; intensely
sentence aphorism; apophthegm
sere dry, withered
service supplies, sexual indulgence (*DM* 2.5.11); military operations (*DM* 3.3.18)
settles sinks deeply, settles down (*DM* 5.2.271)
several diverse (*WD* 4.3.6, 15)
shift change (*WD* 2.1.52)
shoat piglet (*CC* 2.3.30)
shock onslaught
shoot (of a boat) pass under the arches of a bridge (*WD* 4.2.180)
shrift confession
sifted examined closely
silly deserving of pity; simple, ignorant
singular particularly
sinking flagging (*CC* 3.1.34)

sirrah term of address expressing contempt, particularly if applied to someone of the gentry or higher rank
skein reel of thread
slop wide breeches
smelt small fish related to the salmon
smoor suffocate
snuff candle-end
solicit transact, conduct (*CC* 1.1.23)
sooth truth
sophistic specious
sorrow (*adj.*) sorry (*WD* 5.1.47)
sort (*n.*) set (*DM* 3.2.237)
sovereign (*adj.*) supremely efficacious
speculative intellectually searching
speeding effective
spoil corrupt
springal stripling ,
springe (*n.*) snare
spur-gall make sore with the spurs
stains (*v.*) eclipses
stand insist (*WD* 1.2.122); withstand (*WD* 4.2.51); (hunting term) hold out (*WD* 4.2.158)
standing stagnant (*DM* 1.1.150)
standings standing places
state splendour, estate, power
stay stop (*DLC* 2.1.237)
stay for wait for
stigmatic branded by nature, deformed
still always
stockfish cod
stomach eager inclination, relish (*WD* 3.2.109; *DLC* 5.4.86)
straight immediately
strict-combined closely allied
Styx river in the infernal regions by which the gods of classical mythology swore their most solemn oaths
suborned procured
suborning aiding and abetting (*DLC* 5.3.8)
subscribed written below; signed
substantial having a real existence
sufferance sanction; consent (*CC* 3.2.82)
suffrage support
suit petition (*DM* 5.4.47)
suit together agree
sumpter-cloth saddle cloth

sumpter-horse baggage horse; beast of burden

superficies outward form or aspect

surbated footsore

suspected expected (*CC* 1.2.128)

swabber low-ranking sailor (also a general term of contempt)

switching up galloping up

table-board backgammon-board

taffeta plain-woven glossy silk; cambric

taking (*n.*) plight (*DLC* 5.1.13)

tapers candles

taxation blame

tedious dilatory, troublesome (*DM* 2.1.114; 5.5.4)

teeming pregnant

temper hardness and resiliency imparted to steel by tempering (*WD* 3.2.166)

tender care for

tenements houses, or holdings of land

tent (*v.*) probe

tester canopy

tetter pustular skin disease

touch-hole vent; small tubular hole in the breach of a firearm for igniting the charge

touchwood tinder

toused rumpled; dishevelled

toy (*n.*) sport

trade (*n.*) habitual practice, employment (*WD* 5.6.273)

traded practised, experienced

traverse curtain or screen placed crosswise, or drawn across a room, hall or stage; partition

triumphs public festivals; pageants

tumultuary disorderly; confused, with a play on 'plebeian' and 'vulgar' (*WD* 1.2.169)

turns acts

Ud's foot God's foot common trivial oath

uncivil barbarous

unction ointment (used ironically at *WD* 5.3.27)

unjust faithless; dishonest (*DM* 3.2.158)

unvalued invaluable

urge press (a case)

use usury; interest (*WD* 3.2.223)

usquebaugh whisky

valance border of drapery hanging round the canopy of a bed

variance discord

viands foods

victualling-house place where food is served; brothel

void out empty, clear

votary nun

want miss

wanton (*n.*) playful child (used affectionately)

warrantable legitimate; sanctioned

weal welfare

wheal pustule

when! expression of impatience

whipped trimmed (*WD* 5.3.113)

whispering-rooms private closets

whistler nocturnal bird with a whistling note (thought to be of ill omen)

wind (*v.*) get wind or scent of (*WD* 3.3.58); shroud

winding-sheet sheet in which a corpse is wrapped for burial

wink turn a blind eye (*WD* 4.1.86)

without unless; outside (*WD* 1.2.46)

wolf 'lupus', a malignant ulcerous disease (*WD* 5.3.55; *DM* 2.1.34)

woman-keeper female nurse

wormwood bitter-tasting plant; bitterness

wot know

wrings pinches